D0869463

Being a
Brain-Wise
Therapist

The Norton Series on Interpersonal Neurobiology
Allan N. Schore, PhD, Series Editor
Daniel J. Siegel, MD, Founding Editor

The field of mental health is in a tremendously exciting period of growth and conceptual reorganization. Independent findings from a variety of scientific endeavors are converging in an interdisciplinary view of the mind and mental well-being. An interpersonal neurobiology of human development enables us to understand that the structure and function of the mind and brain are shaped by experiences, especially those involving emotional relationships.

The Norton Series on Interpersonal Neurobiology will provide cutting-edge, multidisciplinary views that further our understanding of the complex neurobiology of the human mind. By drawing on a wide range of traditionally independent fields of research—such as neurobiology, genetics, memory, attachment, complex systems, anthropology, and evolutionary psychology—these texts will offer mental health professionals a review and synthesis of scientific findings often inaccessible to clinicians. These books aim to advance our understanding of human experience by finding the unity of knowledge, or consilience, that emerges with the translation of findings from numerous domains of study into a common language and conceptual framework. The series will integrate the best of modern science with the healing art of psychotherapy.

A Norton Professional Book

Being a Brain-Wise Therapist

A Practical Guide to Interpersonal Neurobiology

Bonnie Badenoch

W. W. Norton & Company

New York · London

For information about permission to reproduce
selections from this book, write to Permissions,
W. W. Norton & Company, Inc.,
500 Fifth Avenue, New York, NY 10110

For information about special discounts for bulk purchases,
please contact W. W. Norton Special Sales at specialsales@wwnorton.com
or 800-233-4830

Manufacturing by Quebecor, Fairfield Graphics
Book design by Charlotte Staub
Production manager: Leeann Graham

Library of Congress Cataloging-in-Publication Data

Badenoch, Bonnie.
  Being a brain-wise therapist : a practical guide to interpersonal
neurobiology / Bonnie Badenoch ; foreword by Daniel J. Siegel. — 1st ed.
       p.   ; cm. — (Norton series on interpersonal neurobiology)
  "A Norton professional book."
Includes bibliographical references and index.
ISBN 978-0-393-70554-6 (pbk.)
  1. Psychotherapy. 2. Neurobiology. 3. Interpersonal relations. I. Title.
  [DNLM: 1. Psychotherapy—methods. 2. Brain—physiology.
  3. Interpersonal Relations.   4. Professional-Patient Relations.
  5. Psychological Theory.
  WM 420 B134b 2008]
RC480.5.B224 2008
616.89'14—dc22   2008001374

*For my
daughter
Kate*

The Brain—is wider than the Sky—
For—put them side by side—
The one the other will contain
With ease—and You— beside—

Emily Dickinson
"The Brain is Wider Than the Sky"[1]

Ultimately, I find consciousness a
fascinating predicament for matter
to get into.

Diane Ackerman
An Alchemy of Mind[2]

Contents

Foreword: Daniel J. Siegel xi

Acknowledgments xv

Introduction xxi

Part I: Theoretical Foundations

1. Preliminary Thoughts 3
2. The Brain's Building Blocks 7
3. The Brain's Flow 23
4. The Relationship between Brain and Mind 42
5. Attaching 52
6. Picturing the Inner Community 76
7. The Mutuality of the Therapeutic Relationship 90
8. An Application: Embracing Shame 105

Part II: Practical Matters

9. Preliminary Thoughts 113
10. Through the Lens of Diagnosis: Depression, Anxiety, Dissociation, and Addiction 119
11. Grounding Therapy in the Right Brain 153
12. Listening to Family Histories 163
13. The Three Faces of Mindfulness 174
14. Getting Comfortable with the Brain 191
15. Patterning the Internal Work 205
16. The Integrating Power of Sandplay 220
17. Doing Art 244

Part III. Working with Couples, Teens, and Children

    18. Preliminary Thoughts 269

    19. Keeping Our Balance with Couples 271

    20. Meeting Teens with Their Brains in Mind 286

    21. Playing with Children, Supporting Their Parents 299

      References 321

      Index 335

Foreword

Being a Brain-Wise Therapist is filled with the wisdom of a seasoned front-line therapist who writes like a poet and understands science as if she were a full-time academician. What a rewarding combination! Journeying through these pages offers us an opportunity to explore the fundamental ideas of interpersonal neurobiology (IPNB), an interdisciplinary view of the mind and human development built upon a wide range of sciences and therapeutic arts. Through theory and practice, the stories ahead enable us to see the direct applications of this approach in various clinical situations.

An astute learner and deep thinker, Bonnie Badenoch has been a student and colleague with whom I have been fortunate to dive deeply into this exciting new field. When she first presented the idea of a workbook that revealed the depth of her understanding and her passion for integrating these ideas into clinical practice, the notion of this book was born. It is an honor to write this foreword for what has blossomed into a wonderful guide to this emerging field. IPNB is an approach that seeks the consilience across distinct disciplines so that we can find the parallel principles that emerge from different efforts to understand the world and ourselves. This integrative approach reveals a larger picture, the "whole elephant" view of human experience and mental health.

Applying scientific ideas to the field of psychotherapy is no easy task. Without rigor, it is easy to slip into overly simplistic views of complex conditions. This risk is always present when we draw on objective research findings and attempt to create clear conclusions that then can be applied to the subjective world of clinical interventions. In this book you will find an artist's hand that paints a clear and useful picture as it reaches a beautiful balance between what we know from science and what may possibly be occurring in the subjective inner and interpersonal worlds of our therapeutic efforts.

Beginning with theory and moving deeply into practical applications, this wise author takes us on an enjoyable educational journey into the lives of individuals and families. The pathways toward healing are illuminated by her inviting narratives as she seamlessly weaves scientific theory with humanistic interventions. These ventures into the clinical art of healing continually weave the threads of interpersonal neurobiology into the tapestry of a coherent framework of the mind, the brain, and human relationships. This text serves as a powerful starting place for those new to this interdisciplinary approach and as a deepening review for clinicians already practicing with this view of the brain in mind.

For some, science has no place in the therapist's mind. "Since science doesn't even know how the 'brain creates the mind,' why bother knowing anything about science?" some cautious critics question. Yet with careful analysis of the research findings, conservative attempts to illuminate a larger and integrated picture of the whole can be both possible and quite fruitful. When we stay close to the science, as Bonnie Badenoch does in her writing, we then build a solid foundation for all that follows.

Interpersonal neurobiology embraces the perspective of a triangle of well-being. The three points of this figure are made up of relationships, the mind, and the brain. Though some scientists would cry out "dualism" if we even see mind as more than the "mere activity of the brain," modern research actually suggests that the causal arrows of brain causing mind are actually bidirectional. The mind can also be seen to use the brain to create itself. The focus of our energy and information flow, one aspect of mind, can actually change the activity and the structure of the brain itself. In the IPNB model, we are being even more "politically incorrect" by stating that there are not just two but actually three irreducible elements of human experience. The mind in this perspective is the process that regulates the flow of energy and information. Relationships are how we share energy and information. The nervous system of our bodies embeds mechanisms by which energy and information can flow. This sharing, regulation, and mechanism cannot be reduced into each other. In this way, we examine energy and information flow as being fundamental to human experience.

As the mind is both embodied and relational, we see a healthy mind emerging from an integrated state: When elements of the system being examined—an individual, couple, family, group, or perhaps society—are integrated, that system is said to be the most flexible, adaptive, coherent, energized, and stable. This FACES flow is a description of well-being. The defining feature of this state of health is integration, which consists of the linkage between differentiated elements of a system. Using FACES, clinicians can approach evaluation from a new perspective: the assessment of states of integration. The hallmark of a nonintegrated system are its tendency to move toward chaos or rigidity or both. The quality of an integrated system is that of coherence: connected, open, harmonious, engaged, receptive, emergent, noetic, compassionate, and empathic. This FACES flow—this harmonious, coherent state—is the characteristic of a healthy condition in mind, brain, and relationships.

In the pages that follow, you will be given the opportunity to learn about these basic principles of interpersonal neurobiology and see how they can be applied in clinical work. As a part of our Norton Series, *Being a Brain-Wise Therapist* adds an important educational opportunity for us all to see the power of this approach to help others heal and develop toward well-being. Enjoy!

Daniel J. Siegel, M.D.
Director, Mindsight Institute
Co-Director, UCLA Mindful Awareness Research Center

Acknowledgments

In 2003 two of us from our small agency in Irvine, California, attended the Annual Attachment Conference at UCLA where Dan Siegel, Allan Schore, Ed Tronick, and others spoke about how science now confirms that relationships shape our brains at the beginning of life, and that certain relationships can continue to repair wounded minds throughout the lifespan. We felt as though scientific ground had been placed beneath our feet. For the 12 preceding years, building on the inner community paradigm I had learned experientially in my own therapy with Dr. Timothy Maas, we had had the experience of individuals healing profound psychological wounds in the company of a compassionate therapist. We sensed the importance of this person being a calm, comforting presence when these courageous people needed to reenter the part of their inner world where the roots of their pain lay. Now, with the discoveries of the last two decades, synthesized by expansive, scientifically grounded minds, we had the beginning of a blueprint about what was happening in the brain during this process.

We began a project of pulling these two paradigms—interpersonal neurobiology and inner community—into the pot together, stirring vigorously, and seeing wonderful results for the families who came to our clinic for care. Before sharing what we learned in that endeavor, I do want to acknowledge the depth of inspiration and support I have received from many sources. To begin, 20 years ago, Tim Maas guided my recovery from a fragmenting childhood, instilling at the same time my felt awareness of the diverse aspects of each person's inner world. Because I had the opportunity to learn about this inner community with both hemispheres of my brain, it became the support for all the clinical work that has followed in my 18 years as a therapist.

Foundational is the burgeoning research of neuroscientists across the globe. Their work is the first generation, the ground in which new theories of mental suffering and healing are able to flourish. Daily, my Mac is flooded with discoveries that constantly challenge me to keep moving, to take into account this new information as I sit with patients and colleagues. We are at the beginning of this unfolding process, with no end in sight.

Now, the second generation is synthesizing these bits of new knowledge into theories that support an expanding vision of how we can foster healing from even the most severe wounds. In recent years, my primary guide in this inner integration of science with the art of therapy has been Daniel J. Siegel, in whose study groups, trainings, consultations, and talks my mind has been reshaped to hold the broad vision of interpersonal neurobiology as it illumines our healing work with ourselves and our patients. He has challenged me to think carefully about language, so whatever precision is found in these pages bears his imprint. In my experience, it is rare to find a person with this kind of integrative imagination and original thought who is also humble and accessible—and extremely funny. I think he has added at least 10 years to my active life because my brain has not been lit up with such a flow of ideas and experiences since I was in my 20s. As a result, the feeling of gratitude is many-layered.

Dan's study group is also a place where I have found new friends, fellow travelers on the Inner-Galactic Express. I always walk away feeling connected, even with those I have not yet gotten to know well, by some magic of integrating minds. Two dear friends and colleagues from this group, Donna Emmanuel and Carol Landsberg, have been kind enough to carefully read the manuscript, contributing innumerable helpful suggestions about content and style. Whatever clarity of expression you may find here has been sharpened by them. My heartfelt thanks to both.

Out of our contact with Dan, a new group sprouted—GAINS (Global Association for Interpersonal Neurobiology Studies). Our Board of Directors—Lauren Culp, Carol Landsberg, Raven Lee, Judith Miller, Kirke Olson, Joan Rosenberg, Debra Pearce-McCall, Sue Marriott, and Kathy Scherer—continues to set my inner landscape alight with the feeling of being part of a community dedicated to fostering principles that might actually contribute in a practical way to a more awake and compassionate world. GAINS's main endeavor so far is *Connections & Reflections*, a quarterly publication about applying interpersonal neurobiology in various fields. Our staff of writers and editors—Lorraine Granit, Bea Armstrong, Jeff Anderson, Joan Rosenberg, Lauren Culp, Alex Onno, Lisa Firestone, Kirke Olson, Raven Lee, Carol Landsberg, Debra Pearce-McCall, Ron Levine, Jane Wheatley-Crosbie, Noah Hass-Cohen, Paul Cox, Donna Emmanuel, Richard Hill, and Tina Bryson—together with our advisory board contributors—Dan Siegel, Pat Ogden (with Janina Fisher), Tom Burton, Carl Marci (with Helen Reiss), Diana Fosha, Marco Iacoboni, Diane Ackerman, and the late John O'Donohue—contribute a wonderful diversity of viewpoints from their emerging understanding of how to embody these principles. Our mutual wrestlings with form and content have pushed me to sharpen my awareness of neurobiology, and deepen my appreciation for the fundamental humanity of this endeavor. At times, our creative process feels as though it is emerging from one mind with many hands.

Most of my other guides have come to me through the pages of their books and articles, with the occasional seasoning of conference appearances. Allan Schore's understanding of regulation as the primary creator of an emerging sense of self has shaped the way we therapists think about our relationships with the patients who come to us. He has inspired us to focus on the unfolding right-brain to right-brain interactions between us and our patients, a dance that often proceeds below our conscious awareness, providing an essential foundation for healing. Thinking about therapy this way, we are led to the inevitable conclusion that our own mental health is the cornerstone of our capacity to be agents of neural integration. In addition, during the preparation of this manuscript, he was so generous with his time, encouraging me to deepen my knowledge of neurobiology.

Stephen Porges has taught us about fostering healing experiences by creating environments that are dense with the feeling of safety. Ed Tronick brought conscious awareness of the processes of rupture and repair into the center of how we do therapy. Pat Ogden has encouraged us to integrate the body into the way we understand the impact of trauma and developmental injuries on the whole person. Marco Iacoboni has illuminated the wondrous way mirror neurons connect us, body to body and heart to heart. Jeffrey Schwartz pushed me to wrestle with the issue of free will, because without that, what do we imagine we are doing? Building on John Bowlby's seminal work, Mary Ainsworth, Mary Main, and Eric Hesse have provided the essential framework for understanding the crucial importance of our earliest relationships. Although the list is longer, these people's unique insights are bedrock for our integrative endeavor.

Now, we come to the third generation—those of us in the trenches, seeking ways to make these theories live in the midst of our work. The staff of Center for Hope and Healing, where I have the privilege of mentoring and supervising the next generation of therapists, is a constant source of goodness for me. Our felt preference for empathic relationships has drawn us together and continues to support each of us as we make our way through the underbrush of our patients' painful worlds. The staff also has had a large share in shaping this book through the spirited interactions that blossom in supervision. I particularly want to acknowledge Cindy Cook and Emily Gombos for their depth of experience, which has enriched the chapters on children, parents, and teens. As we have shared these materials with other therapists in the community, the lively debate and conversation we have about these concepts, along with the uniqueness of my colleagues' thoughts, has further broadened my awareness of the power of these ideas.

In addition to this intellectual and empathic support, I am so grateful for the community and corporate foundations who have long supported the work of our small nonprofit. This writing project would not have been possible without the tangible gifts of The California Endowment, The Fieldstone Foundation, The PIMCO Foundation, the Irvine Health Foundation, the Boeing Employees Community Fund, and an anonymous donor whom I hope will recognize herself here. All of these organizations and people do enormous good in our community.

It goes without saying that profound inspiration comes from the people we serve, as they willingly take us into the dark night of their pain, in order to become better human beings for themselves and their families. When events in the wider world give me cause to question the courage and intrinsic goodness of human beings, these determined people restore my faith. They continually expand my awareness of the heart's willingness to face monsters, and the mind's capacity for restoration. My admiration and respect know no bounds. I want to particularly thank those who have been willing to share their stories for this book, all of them in the hope that their suffering and recovery might become stones cast in the pond of healing, with ripples radiating to touch and inspire others.

From the first day this project reached Norton, Deborah Malmud guided it through the maze toward publication with wisdom and focus.

She also drew me into the sort of collaborative partnership I like best—a potent mixture of kindness and honesty. Kristen Holt-Browning, Sue Carlson, Margaret Ryan, and Vani Kannan answered my numerous questions, humored me in my ignorance of the process, gently helped mold the manuscript, and, with Deborah, gave me room to feel at home with many beneficial changes, while honoring my sense of the flow of the overall project. Closer to home, artist Ron Estrine worked with me to create brain images that are clear and beautiful.

A number of people whose ideas don't directly appear in these pages formed my own inner first generation. They have shaped my vision of the human capacity for transformation and the expression of truth, beauty, and compassion. Graham Ledgerwood (Ramakrishnanandaji) set my feet on the spiritual path, and remains my constant inner guide. Dave Brokaw gently directed my fledgling steps as a therapist and left such a mark by embodying profound respect for all people. Tom Burton, life-friend and provocateur of my becoming a writer, has been the kind of encouraging support everyone deserves. My sister, Patti Lampman, asks a lot of deep questions, and out of those discussions arise greater awareness and more love.

I have felt such strong support for my inner life from three people I met only once, but whose own well-cultivated lives have permeated mine to a remarkable extent. Diane Ackerman and the late John O'Donohue offered words and visions that draw my inner spaces into deeper contact with the world of grasshoppers and communion—at the same time. Their attention to detail, accompanied by a profound sense of the sacred, fills me. Spending 2 days at a conference in the presence of Jack Kornfield's compassionate heart and wise mind transformed something I can't quite grasp in words, adding significantly to my lifelong spiritual journey.

At the core of it all, my dear family—Tom, Andy, Kate, Jocelyn, and Cindy—provides the epitome of inner and outer support. They have been kind and patient as my energies have been quite internal during this work of remaking my own mind to hold all this healing goodness. When I need to apply the principles to every daily event, they tease and laugh and tolerate my obsessive ways. Most of all, they have cradled this endeavor with the gentleness and humor that are typical of them. On the practical side, they have made sure I have food, sleep, laughter—and the occasional movie night. I am so grateful for how all these lives are woven with mine, creating the ground and foundation for everything else I do.

In an entirely different vein, I thank flowing water—rain, streams, oceans, showers—as a sweet and reliable source for birthing the integration of emerging ideas. I can count on words to bubble up, mesh, and find a happy arrangement just by being in the presence of water. We never really know where or when we may find such precious companions. Or perhaps they choose us.

And, of course, any interesting mistakes are entirely of my own crafting.

Introduction

A young woman, shivering with fear and sorrow, sits across from me, talking about yelling repeatedly at her two young children. She had promised herself she would never do that because she had suffered so much from the rage that ricocheted around her home as a child. The sight of her eyes rooted to the floor and her chest collapsing in on itself in this embodiment of shame touches me. After a few words of understanding, I begin to talk to her about how her brain had wired in this angry response to frustration from the time she was a baby. I speak softly of neural nets and triggers; of the speed of her limbic circuits compared with the slow deliberation of the prefrontal cortex; of neural integration being blocked by the emotional trauma of her childhood; of how working to integrate her brain would change her responses. I say, "It's not your fault." I tell her this isn't meant to make an excuse but is simply the truth about how our brains work. As I talk, she gradually lifts out of her shame and is able to meet my eyes.

In this newly achieved state of connection, we had room between us to make a plan to work on the painful internal disruption, so that she could develop the freedom to choose her response to her children's natural misbehavior. Instead of taking months or years to relieve the guilt and shame that often slow healing, we had been able to get a good start on it in less than 5 minutes. As we developed a mutually held vocabulary about the brain and mind, she quickly used it to establish herself in the stance of caring observer of her own young self, bringing comfort to that hypervigilant part of her being, and, we knew, increasing neural integration in the process. As I watched her move with grace and speed toward being the calm, caring mother she wished to be, I was struck by the efficacy of empathy supported by brain wisdom.

At that time, I was also working with quite a few people who had suffered severe abuse from infancy onward, leaving them with all kinds of dissociative difficulties, deeply rooted perceptual biases, and hyperreactive nervous systems that repeatedly pushed personal well-being and fulfilling relationships out of reach. One man's nightmares and flashbacks had held him hostage for two decades, depriving him of an intimate relationship and satisfying work. We were making slow, systematic inroads into facing and comforting the fragmenting memories, but when his terrifying father would arise in his mind, this presence still felt like a monster living inside. The intensity of what was released in his mind and body in those moments always threatened to pull us into a vortex of out-of-control terror, so our mutual concern about retraumatizing him significantly slowed our work.

I began to wonder how we could reduce the size and power of his inner father and create a climate more conducive to regulation. We tentatively began to talk about how his father got into his brain. We envisioned synapses firing in response to years of continual terror, encoding his emotional and physical response, as well as establishing his father's frightening inner presence. We saw these synapses woven into neural nets that became isolated baskets holding terror, pain, and shame. We talked about how, with repetition, these neural nets became states of mind vulnerable to any passing trigger in his environment. Very quickly, his father was reduced from monster to synaptic firing, and the intensity of the memories went from boil to simmer. We also noticed that as he was better able "to hold his brain in his mind," so to speak, he developed a much stronger caring observer who could stay engaged even in the midst of intense memories. Therapy gained speed, depth, and ease.

As these experiences accumulated, we realized the power of weaving the concepts of interpersonal neurobiology (IPNB), particularly as articulated by Daniel J. Siegel, into the unfolding flow of therapy, sparking my wish to foster this integration in a more systematic way at our agency. At the center of IPNB lives the awareness that *mental health, defined as individual well-being and fulfilling relationships, emerges from brains that are becoming more integrated.* As we began to ask how we therapists could use this developing body of knowledge for the benefit of our patients, Allan N. Schore's meticulous work on the power of *right-hemisphere to right-hemisphere interactions between therapist and patient* came to the fore. Since many of these interactions happen through nonconscious, microsecond connections, it followed that *therapist self-awareness and mental health* are indispensable ingredients in the healing relationship. In keeping with the relational epicenter of the other principles, the following question resides at the heart of inner community work: *"What is the most empathic way I can be with this person right now?"* These four principles—neural integration, right-brain to right-brain connection, therapist health, and empathic awareness—became the focal points that provided organization for what follows. The centrality of our own mental–emotional health prompted the inclusion of many suggestions to foster awareness of, and possibly begin to heal, any right-hemisphere implicit fear and pain that might block our ability to hold our patients well. These suggestions can be found in shaded boxes for easy identification. For me, returning repeatedly to these themes for continued self-exploration opens the inner doors for deepening my capacity. I truly believe there is no end to what we can accomplish internally if we dedicate ourselves to the pursuit of neural integration.

As therapists at our agency learned concepts and tried applications, we saw several immediate benefits, in addition to our patients' long strides toward health. Confidence among our newest marriage and family therapist interns blossomed as they had a solid, left-brained, making-sense way to understand the efficacy of their focused and kind attention with patients. All of us became more conscious of our bodies, as well as the subtle waves of feeling and fleeting images populating our minds, as we consciously aligned with our right-hemisphere response to our patients. In addition, we began to conceptualize therapist mental health in ways that augmented our steady focus on countertransference experiences. We also now had a handful of practical tools (from mindfulness to brain talk) to use, as empathy guided us in the moment, when we spotted where neural integration needed certain kinds of encouragement. Over time, we became aware that this increased clarity about brain, mind, and relationships expanded our resources of hope and confidence, allowing us to mirror these health-provoking states of mind to our patients.

We were also heartened to find a fairly dramatic increase in the intensity of supervision for a period of time. Our minds were energized, lit up with new neural patterns forming, and then simmering in new juices as we began to integrate this fresh knowledge with the core paradigms of our daily practice. This seemed like the most important part—to "bake in" the new knowledge, rather than leave it as a set of potential ingredients, existing side by side with our way of working. This crucial distinction has formed the pathway for these chapters. I had learned this lesson well because my own therapy had formed the secure foundation for working with my patients. I had digested the inner community paradigm, a way of conceptualizing people's subjective experience of their internal world, in the crucible of my own years of healing. This meant that my brain had been shaped to sense the multiple aspects of my inner world, while my body learned to feel the shifts from one part to another, and my heart experienced the integrative power of being empathically embraced in the midst of pain and sorrow. When I began to see my own patients, these ways of doing therapeutic work were as natural as breathing. Now, we wanted to embody our awareness of the brain and mind in that same way. We are about 2 years into this endeavor, and over the last 6 months, a new incorporation of this way of thinking about the healing endeavor has emerged. It first showed up as the natural inclusion of the brain and mind as we talked about our patients in supervision. But then a different form of integration began to emerge. In addition to our patients' brain and minds becoming easily visible, our capacity to *hold and understand what we are holding* became the centerpiece of our discussions, and far more important than any technique. In addition, a palpable sense of energy and awareness emerged in the room, flowing in individual body–minds and between our minds. In some way, we were beginning to live these principles in our personal as well as professional lives. At this point, the integrative path seems to have developed its own wonderful momentum, carrying us along the stream of ever-evolving mental health.

The primary purpose of this book is to foster exactly this ability to fully integrate the beauty and clarity of interpersonal neurobiology with the way healing experiences flow in the counseling room. This guiding purpose means that explanations of neurobiology and other topics are not exhaustive, but are intended to capture enough detail for clarity and enough romance to encourage integration and whole-brain retention. Whether you are looking for a paradigm shift to a way of practicing that is rooted in IPNB, or seeking ways to integrate these concepts into what you are already doing, these pages may be helpful.

As with all writing, I clearly have a bias. Without intending any disrespect to short-term therapies that focus primarily on symptom relief, that is not the path taken here. Prompt alleviation of suffering is a humane endeavor; however, in addition to that worthy goal, we believe there is much benefit in a thorough restructuring of the mind–brain–body that leads to sustained well-being, the lifetime relational goodness of earned secure attachment, and the permanent amelioration of intergenerational cycles of abuse and chaos. Although this can be a lengthy process with people whose early years were shaped by all manner of relational suffering, we are finding that the process is immensely enhanced, both in speed and depth, through the integration of IPNB.

Part I, "*Theoretical Foundations,*" moves from a sufficient but not exhaustive understanding of the brain's building blocks to the richness of the therapeutic relationship. The intention is to move from the *simple* to the *complex,* in the scientific sense of that word, beginning with discrete pieces of knowledge, which are then linked. As we focus our attention, the outcome can be a harmonious whole that is greater than the sum of the parts. We incorporate both objective and subjective ways of thinking about the movement toward wholeness, as we explore both the brain's circuitry and the inner community that lives within each of us.

Part II, "*Practical Matters,*" begins by reviewing what we know so far about the neurobiological correlates of some familiar diagnostic categories, and how this knowledge can illuminate our way of working with these states of mind. Then we explore some particular ways of entering our patients' worlds with the brain in mind—establishing and maintaining the essential right-brain to right-brain connection, listening to histories, practicing mindfulness, getting comfortable with brain talk, and supporting our patients' ability to resolve the deep emotional wounds that distort relationships.

In the last part of this section, we present sandplay and art as two ways to provide a direct means of expression for the right brain. Over the years, many of our patients have been startled by the power of their first experiences with sand and miniatures, or paper and paint, as long-buried attachment struggles reach consciousness for the first time. Once these implicit wounds have surfaced, these two processes themselves provide resources for neural integration.

Then, in Part III, we turn our attention to applying the principles we've developed above when "*Working with Couples, Teens, and Children.*" These latter chapters are intended to suggest some very basic ways of thinking about these endeavors from interpersonal neurobiology and inner community perspectives, and are in no way exhaustive. We hope that these small insights may provide enriching soil in which your own methods can find some nourishment. Throughout this practical section, we have sought to season the mix with stories of how this process has unfolded in very tangible ways for us, endeavoring to further promote the essential right brain–left brain–body integration that can support the metamorphosis from concept to lived reality.

A word about vocabulary. Most of this book is conceived from the "you plus I" perspective of "we," as a way to embody the collaborative essence of *interpersonal* neurobiology. I have also struggled with the right word for the people who volunteer for the hard work of healing profound wounds. My preference would be "courageous people," but that quickly becomes unwieldy. After long thought, I have settled on *patient,* not in the medical/hierarchical sense of doctor–patient, but because of its etymological meaning of "one who bears suffering," with echoes of its use as an adjective, "to persevere calmly when faced with difficulties, without complaint or loss of temper." At times, the word *brain* is used without overtly acknowledging that this entity does not reside in our skulls alone, but extends throughout the body, so it is helpful to hold a picture of body– brain in our minds. Finally, *mother* or *father* stands deliberately in the place of the more detached *caregiver* to retain the intimacy of the relationship.

We know so much more about brain, mind, and relationships than we did even 10 years ago, yet we are barely at the tip of the tip of the iceberg. Everything is in flux as today's discoveries amend and expand yesterday's. I am finding that a humble stance is essential. However, while knowledge continues to increase, we do need methods to fully digest the information, and the processes described in this book may be helpful for that, even as scientific breakthroughs move beyond what can be contained in these pages.

In the midst of this integrative effort, we hold the belief that application of the insights of IPNB can offer one pathway toward a more awake and compassionate world. Doing therapy is no small matter, not only because of the depth and intimacy of the work, but because of the lasting impact this interpersonal exchange makes on each participant. We now know that resonance circuits in our bodies–brains–minds embed each of us within the inner world of all the others with whom we share any close contact. When we seek to foster neural integration in ourselves and our patients, we have found that, based on this interpersonal goodness, compassion for self and others sprouts like wildflowers in spring. As a result of healing together, ripples of such increasingly harmonious states of mind radiate outward, providing a small nudge toward a society founded on self-reflection, self-responsibility, mutual care, and intentional acts of kindness.

Part I

Theoretical Foundations

Chapter 1

Preliminary Thoughts

Each school of psychotherapy presents a paradigm—a vision or myth (in the sense of a living, explanatory story) of the inner world of human beings. By seeing the mind in a certain way and asking certain questions, therapists from each school energize different aspects of their patients toward healing. Psychodynamic therapists point their patients toward the deeper mind, whereas cognitive–behavioral clinicians focus on the way changes in thinking and behavior can modify the mind. Both emphasize certain aspects of the psyche while minimizing others. As clinicians, we also seem to be drawn toward certain paradigms (or toward creating them) out of our own life experiences, with both temperament and our engrained perceptual biases leading us to sense the architecture and dance of the inner world in a certain way. Studying the life histories of Freud, Jung, and B. F. Skinner, side by side with their myths of the human mind, is an instructive experience.

However, in the last two decades, our ability to peer into the brain's processes has begun to put scientific "legs" beneath our theories. At the same time, the integrative and imaginative synthesizers of the gigabytes of hard scientific data flooding our world daily are pointing toward broader theories of how minds are injured and can heal. One next step involves bringing these theories into manifestation in the daily experiences unfolding in counseling rooms. To this end, we are going to weave a tapestry with the warp of science-based discoveries and the woof of subjective experience and intuitive art, reaching toward a coherent paradigm that will encourage neural integration through the power of knowledgeable and compassionate relationship. We call the warp *interpersonal neurobiology* (a scientifically grounded paradigm of neural integration developed by Daniel J. Siegel [1999]) and the woof, integrating the *inner community* (a story of internal life born of subjective experience in the counseling room). We are finding that such a blended path, facilitated by right-hemisphere to right-hemisphere connection between therapist and patient (Schore, 2007), naturally leads people toward resilience and fulfilling relationships.

The primary intention in this book is to foster the full digestion of the four core principles voiced in the introduction: an understanding of neural integration, an appreciation of the power of right-brain to right-brain connection, a visceral sense of the centrality of therapist health, and immersion in the beauty of empathic awareness as a guide for moment-to-moment interactions. Just as my mind is changing as I write this, your mind will no doubt develop new neural pathways as you read, giving birth to changes in the way you perceive and understand yourself and your fellow humans. This expansion of awareness can be encouraged not only to occur in your logical left hemisphere, but also to take root in the right brain and body. Whole-brain knowing is more apt to make permanent changes in the way any of us do therapy and live life. You may find that sitting with the ideas and trying them out in regard to your own inner world helps deepen that integration.

Since for most of us, reflection helps cement learning, we include exercises throughout the book that appear in shaded boxes to make them easy to locate as you proceed. I continue to find that taking time for such introspection about the workings of body, brain, mind, and relationships always reveals new aspects that my gradually integrating brain can hold with increasing ease. There is no end to such self-discovery.

One particular principle of brain development guides this book. We know that brains are *complex systems*, according to the strict mathematical definition of that term (Siegel, 1999). Although the concept of complexity has many facets, one aspect has particular meaning for our endeavor: The theory says that there is an intrinsic push toward integration, or the subjective experience of wholeness, in our neural circuitry. It makes sense that the principles underlying this push might also apply to the process of taking in, and baking in, a new body of knowledge.

One way of talking about this push toward integration is that complex systems have an innate *self-organizing capacity* (Cicchetti & Rogosch, 1997), and the pattern of that self-organization involves a balance between processes of differentiation and linkage (Siegel, 1999). In terms of our brains, this means that circuits develop their specialized functions in relative isolation, then join together to create (ideally) an increasingly encompassing, harmonious system. This twofold process is called *integration*. If we apply this concept to the learning process, we can see that by thoroughly developing differentiated core understandings (intellectual and experiential) about the brain, the mind, and the inner community, linkages will emerge, helping us gain a richer sense of what it is to be human. Consequently, we're going to start with "The *Brain's Building Blocks*" and "The Brain's Flow," gradually make our way toward "The *Relationship between Brain and Mind*," linger on the neural correlates and subjective experience of "Attaching," spend some time "*Picturing the Inner Community*," and arrive at a deep sense of the "*Mutuality of the Therapeutic Relationship*." The whole will be greater than the sum of the parts, much as individual words gather into the experience of a beloved poem.

If we can be in the moment of learning each step of the way, with some tolerance for not seeing how all the parts fit together at once, we may be able to savor and digest each area, trusting our attending minds to make the connections as we proceed. When we have immersed ourselves in this new knowledge sufficiently, we will be better able to bring an embodied awareness to our patients in an organic way as part of the natural flow of therapy.

Being with this new body of knowledge in such personal ways may also foreshadow changes we wish to make in how we do therapy. Instead of leaning solely into language and interpretation with our patients, brain wisdom encourages us to first immerse ourselves in the wordless experience of being together. Many years of research tell us that the single most important ingredient in effective therapy, regardless of paradigm, is the empathic capacity of the therapist (Hutterer & Liss, 2006). Preparing our minds to hold the fullness of another's experience may then be the most important aspect of our ongoing training as therapists. From the beginning of our relationship with our patients, we can establish the interpersonal ground of healing that will guide us toward offering the most empathic ways of working together from moment to moment, if we can nurture the unfolding right-hemisphere to right-hemisphere connection. Words then become the manifestation of attunement, rather than the primary bid for relationship.

Let's begin with the 100 billion neurons (more or less) populating the adult human brain.

Chapter 2

The Brain's Building Blocks

As we start to build our knowledge of the brain, we'll be talking about the brain as a more or less static thing—something it never is in life. In fact, neural firing patterns change from 4 to 100 times per second, and axons extend through the brain and body, connecting distinct and sometimes distant regions. It turns out that even in the brain and body, relationship is everything—what parts are connected with each other, and what messages delivered. However, if we are going to understand the flow of brain, mind, body, and relationship, it will be helpful to first picture something about the building blocks and architecture of the individual domains in the brain and nervous system.

Building Blocks of the Brain and Nervous System

The brains of adult human beings have about 100 billion *neurons* that, on average, have 7,000–10,000 synaptic connections to other neurons, creating 2 million miles of neural highways in our brains (Siegel, 1999). The connecting *synapse* is actually a very small space between sending and receiving neurons, called the *synaptic cleft*. Communication between neurons is facilitated by a large number of neurotransmitters produced in the presynaptic neuron, carrying messages that increase (excite) or decrease (inhibit) electrical activity in the postsynaptic neuron. Increases and decreases in these neurotransmitters can have a dramatic impact on thought, mood, behavior, and relational style. An army of *glia* (Greek for *glue*), tiny cells outnumbering neurons at least 10 to 1, have long been known to wrap axons in *myelin* to provide stability and speed connection between neurons, act as the cleanup crew for neural debris, and provide nutrition.

The traditional picture of the neural communication network says that neurons are composed of a cell body, with a forest of hefty *dendrites* at one end and one long, willowy *axon* (often with branches) at the other. We used to believe that the electrical impulse moved down the axon, releasing neurotransmitters into the synaptic cleft, where they made the short trip to a receiving dendrite on another neuron. Now we know that the electricity occasionally flows the other way, with dendrites sometimes sending and axons receiving, that a whole class of neurons communicates very rapidly without neurotransmitters, and that the ubiquitous glial cells are not limited to a maintenance role, but are also implicated in the communication network by influencing the way neurons fire (Fields, 2006). In addition, collections of neural and glial cells in the heart and gut function as little brains, sending information that influences regulation of the autonomic nervous system, as well as our higher cognitive and emotional processes (Armour & Ardell, 2004). The brain is not so neat, orderly, or head-centered as our former pictures suggested. Varied as these processes are, they may still sound mechanistic and remote from our daily lives. However, becoming aware that this tango of rapidly firing, ever-changing electrical impulses produces the rich subjective experience of our lives can instead bring on a sense of awe.

Pruning

Researchers estimate that the brain of a 3-year-old child has about 1,000 trillion synapses (Chang et al., 2004). This number declines with age (a good thing—simplification leads to efficiency) through a process of cell death called *pruning*. Some of those cells that have not been incorporated into the developing structure of the brain are eliminated. As we will see, chronic stress may lead to excess pruning in certain brain regions as well—and this is not a good thing. At the beginning of adolescence, there is another developmental burst of overproduction, followed by dramatic pruning (particularly in certain parts of the brain), reaching stability by the mid-20s (Giedd et al., 1999). By then, we have "only" 100 to 500 trillion synapses, creating web-like networks that integrate experience throughout the brain (Chang et al., 2004). If we consider all the *potential* activation patterns among neurons, we arrive at the figure of *10 to the millionth power*, yielding a number larger than the quantity of known particles in the universe (Siegel, 1999, 2007).

Sometimes it can be good to just sit with numbers this large and processes this complex to see if we can intuitively grasp the wonder of what is happening in our skulls, along the channels of our nervous systems, and in the heart and the gut. Through such reflection, it may seem miraculous that all this activity produces a coherent experience of conscious life.

Neural Nets

Genes and *experience* guide this symphony of interconnection. Our genetic inheritance directs overall brain organization, while experience influences how and when which genes become expressed (Siegel, 1999). Throughout life, as we have inner and outer experiences, neurons form synaptic connections with one another, carrying *energy* (the actual electrical firing) and *information* (the mental representations that emerge with the firing) throughout the brain. As we will see later, the *mind directs, emerges from, and rides on* these firing patterns (Siegel, 1999, 2006). Hebb's axiom (Hebb, 1949) roughly says that *what fires together, wires together*, and now we might add, *survives together* (Post et al., 1998). This concept means that all aspects of an experience tend to gather into a *neural net* that encodes a representation of that event. When one strand of that net is touched by current experience, there is some probability that the whole net will be activated. This is called *remembering*. As we sit with patients, we watch this process unfold during every session. Recalling the image of her mother's face, a young woman feels warmth fill her body with the memory of loving connection, or her eyes turn down and away when seeing the inner face of her shaming grandfather. Thoughts, images, feelings, body sensations, and the relational valence of any experience tend to flow together.

It is very important for us to understand that *every act of recall is also potentially an act of modification* (Siegel, 1999). The very process of directing attention toward a particular memory adds, at a minimum, the energy and information of the present moment to that memory. This process is one way that our comforting presence actually may alter our patients' painful past experiences. If we are able to stay in connection with one another, the feeling of comfort—often communicated through the sound of our voice, the position of our body, the look on our face as it reflects our inner experience of compassion—will initiate new neural firings that will now become associated with, and ameliorate, the suffering contained in the neural nets of frightening and repeated childhood events. This is an immensely hopeful bit of knowledge for patient and therapist alike.

We might ask why some memories carry such power to disrupt us in the present, whereas others seem quite manageable. One factor is that *the stronger the linkages within the net, the greater the probability of it being reactivated at a later date* (Siegel, 1999). *Repetition, the emotional intensity of the encoding experience,* and *myelination* all strengthen the synaptic connections making up these neural nets. We can imagine how both repetition and intensity of an experience would cause strengthened firing of neural nets, creating greater likelihood of being accessed at a later date. If someone we don't know well hurts our feelings one time, the pinprick of pain may be barely encoded. On the other hand, if someone close to us regularly misreads our intentions, both repetition and emotional significance can create a "super highway" to painful and powerful reexperiencing. The story of myelin is about speed and stability of connection and is largely under the direction of our genes. However, research (Bartzokis, 2005) reveals that certain experiences (e.g., teen drinking and drug use) that occur during the brain's vulnerable developmental stages can disrupt the ongoing myelination process and thereby worsen any underlying difficulties, such as hyperactivity or addictive tendencies, and perhaps create new challenges. Under normal circumstances, this process begins in infancy as axons are wrapped in many layers by sheets of myelin, extending from our ubiquitous glial cells in a spectacular display of cell-to-cell coordination (ffrench-Constant, Colognato, & Franklin, 2004). Whereas myelination is complete in certain brain areas within the first 3 years, other areas continue to be wrapped throughout life, peaking in our 40s and declining thereafter (Bartzokis, 2005; Paus et al., 1999). This sheath serves to speed the electrical impulse along the axonal fiber 100 times faster than without this wrapping, leading to immensely more efficient coordination between parts of the brain. The sheath also adds strength to the axon, stabilizing connections, while reducing flexibility. As we build a more complete picture of the complexity and speed of neural firing, we may also begin to appreciate how much is going on in our brains beneath the level of conscious awareness.

Neuroplasticity

After we reach maturity, how much does brain structure change? The answer lies in the process of *neuroplasticity*, which is the brain's capacity

Being a Brain-Wise Therapist

to change the patterns of energy and information (neural connectivity) in response to new experience (Siegel, 2006). As therapists, we will pay particular attention to how the power of the relationship between us and our patients resides in the capacity for ongoing neuroplasticity. The foundation for the hope of healing lies in the brain's ability to modify wired-in painful or frightening experiences by activity both *within* the mind and *between* minds. One way of thinking about psychotherapy is as a process of mutual engagement that will change both structure and function in the brain and nervous system in the direction of *neural integration*, as discussed in detail below. Such increases in neural integration are the basis for personal and interpersonal well-being.

It is helpful to become acquainted with two of the processes that mediate neural change: synaptogenesis and neurogenesis. *Synaptogenesis*, as one would guess, refers to the formation of new synaptic connections, but also includes modification of previously established circuits. This process is continual; each moment brings internal and external experiences that change the connections within the brain. Research has shown that *structure* changes in response to the increased density of synapses that fire repeatedly (Lazar et al., 2005). These synapses often represent new associations within established circuits. For changes in structure to be detectable on a scanner, a great many new connections would have to be made (Siegel, 2007). *Function* can also change as the result of certain kinds of experience. Recently developed functional magnetic resonance imaging (fMRI) technology lets us see where blood is flowing in the brain, so we can detect changes in the way brain areas are working together as a system. In one study, people's brains were scanned while they looked at pictures of angry and frightened faces. Both left and right amygdalae (the brain's primary fear centers) showed increased blood flow. That is, exposure to the pictures altered functioning. When asked to state the sex of the person in each picture, no change was detected in blood flow. However, when asked to name the emotion on the face, the amygdalae calmed down (i.e., less blood flowing there) if the emotion was named accurately. At the same time, blood flow increased in the right prefrontal cortex, a part of the brain that contributes to emotion regulation (Hariri, Bookheimer, & Mazziotta, 2000).

We can imagine that if the change of flow were repeated, an accumulating modification of brain structure would occur as synaptic connections strengthened with repetition. In this way, a new state of mind can gradually become an enduring trait. This kind of evidence for the brain's capacity to change can give us a healthy respect for how much impact therapeutic experiences may have on minds struggling with the fear and sadness of painful histories. When the recall of such experiences is met with empathy and kindness, new synapses carry that particular information throughout the brain, and blood flow changes course to more soothing paths. Over time, our patients may engrain an expectation of kind treatment, enabling them to develop much more fulfilling relationships.

Turning to the relatively new discovery of *neurogenesis*, in 2002 Fred H. Gage (Song, Stevens, & Gage, 2002) of the Salk Institute for Biological Studies and his team reported their ability to observe the results of "daughter cells" differentiating from their stem cell "parents" in the brain. They could see that by 1 month, newborn neural cells in the hippocampus (a crucial part of our memory system) had developed "long axons for transmitting electrical messages," and by 4 months had "thick forests of complex dendrites" for receiving signals from the environment ("Neural stem cells," 2002, p. 1). At that point, they were fully integrated with the hippocampus (in the limbic region) and cortex, possibly carrying the energy and information that initiated new cell birth. Gage and his colleagues had previously discovered that exercise and new experience (among other stimuli) induce stem cells to split, creating a new cell while leaving the stem cell in place to split again, providing a possibly endless supply of new neurons (Song et al.). Therapy certainly falls into the category of "new experience" for most people, and so may turn out to be an excellent source of stimulating the growth of new neurons.

This research is in its infancy, so we don't know how many parts of the brain contain stem cells, or if these cells, once generated, can migrate to other regions of the brain. If you want to look into the latest research, putting "neural stem cells" into your search engine will give you access to the unfolding story. We have found that sharing the idea of neuroplasticity with our patients gives hope. Creating your own simple way of helping your patients feel their brain's ongoing capacity for change may be a valuable resource.

Structures and Regions of the Brain

Now let's consider the collections of neurons that form various structures and regions. The brain is sometimes described as triune—brainstem, limbic, and cortex—or as two hemispheres, right and left, that are so distinct that some researchers think of us as having two brains. Since therapy is a process that helps remove blockages to the natural flow of linkage between differentiated regions, it will be helpful to have at least a working knowledge of these basic areas, always keeping in mind the pathways that connect the parts.

To understand the triune brain, we're going to borrow the hand model, the "brain in the palm of your hand," imagined by Daniel Siegel (see Figure 2.1; Siegel, 1999, 2007; Siegel & Hartzell, 2003). Open both hands with the thumbs extended, palms toward you. Now, place your thumbs against your palms and fold your fingers over the thumbs. Turn your folded hands with knuckles facing away from you, and bring your hands together, side by side, thumbs and forefingers meeting. If you

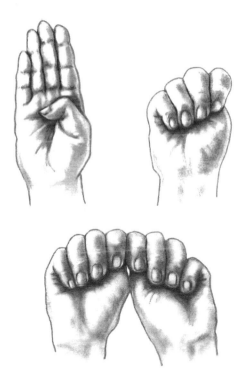

Figure 2.1 The brain in the palms of our hands: This portable representation of the brain is useful for making the brain visible and tangible. Roughly, the wrist is the spinal cord, the lower palm is the brainstem, the thumb is the limbic region, and the back of the hand from wrist to fingertips is the cortex. If we picture an eye in front of the middle two fingernails of each hand, our brains would be gazing at us. Art by Ron Estrine.

visualize an eye in front of the middle two fingernails of each hand, the two hemispheres of your brain would be looking out on the world. We have found this visual and tactile image to be extremely useful in helping patients understand what's going on inside their skulls.

Since a great deal of brain conversation in therapy revolves around what is happening in the right hemipshere, we can switch to the single-hand version at this point. Roughly, your wrist and forearm represent your *spinal cord*, the lower part of your palm contains your *brainstem* (including the medulla oblongata, the pons, and the midbrain), and, at the back near your wrist, your *cerebellum*. The brainstem is the only area of the brain that is fully wired up and ready for action before birth in full-term babies. It is genetically primed to control many aspects of body functioning that happen without our having to attend to them: respiration, vessel constriction, sleep cycles, and some aspects of the fight–flight–freeze responses, for example. Being closest to the spinal cord, the brainstem is also a major relay station for information coming from the body to the brain. With signals passed continually back and forth between body and brain, we may usefully picture body–brain as a single entity spread throughout the body.

In contrast to how much we understand about the brainstem, research is just beginning to reveal the complex functions of the cerebellum. Once thought to be responsible only for coordinating movements in time and space, studies are beginning to find that the massive streams of information pouring into the cerebellum from the cortex are processed and then redirected to many areas of the brain, appearing to coordinate complex mental as well as motor processes, including the allocation of attention and problem-solving functions (Allen, Buxton, Wong, & Courchesne, 1997). Largely undeveloped at birth, the cerebellum may accumulate information throughout childhood and adolescence, building its capacity for continual prediction and preparation in response to changing internal and external conditions (Courchesne & Allen, 1997).

Tucked away in the center of your brain (the thumb in your hand model) is the *limbic region* (including the amygdala, hippocampus, hypothalamus, and interfacing with the middle prefrontal structures; see Figure 2.2). Because the medial (middle), ventral (front/belly), and orbitofrontal (behind the eyes) portions of the prefrontal cortex, together with the anterior cingulate, work in such close association, it makes sense to gather these into a single term, the *middle prefrontal region*

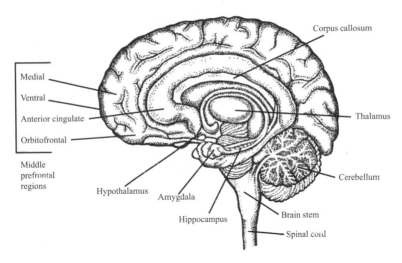

Figure 2.2 Right-hemisphere limbic and middle prefrontal regions: Fostering neural integration of these two regions is the foundation for effective psychotherapy. The corpus callosum (bands of fibers carrying information between the two hemispheres of the brain) and the thalamus (a central relay station for incoming sensory information) are also shown, together with the spinal cord, brainstem, and cerebellum. Art by Ron Estrine.

(Siegel, 2007). Taken together, we could call these regions the *social brain* (Cozolino, 2006; Siegel, 2007).

These regions, working with the brainstem, are dedicated to our motivational, emotional, and relational life, as well as the processes of memory. When we are born, this part of the brain is largely comprised of neurons that are not yet connected to each other (although it is likely that some connecting has happened in utero, based on the mother's physiological and emotional state; Field, Diego, & Hernandez-Reif, 2006). However, these neurons are genetically primed to *form connections through the relational experiences* we have with those closest to us. The patterns of energy and information laid down in these early moments of meeting develop the actual *structure* of these limbic regions. This means that the very foundation of perception, particularly in regard to relationships, relies on the quality of these earliest interactions with our parents. These three sentences are essential for understanding the crucial importance of early attachment experiences.

Limbic Region

In very brief outline, emphasizing only those functions that are most important for therapy, let's look at the components of the limbic area.

The *amygdala* is the home of initial *meaning-making processes* in the brain (Siegel, 1999). This almond-shaped structure tells us when to pay attention and makes a preliminary evaluation of whether experience coming from the environment or within us is "good" or "bad"—not in the moral sense, but in the sense of whether it is safe and warm or not. It is also the seat of *implicit memory*, the only form of remembering available to us during approximately the first 12–18 months of life (much more about this kind of memory below). The next structure, in the order of eventual linkage, is the *hippocampus*, extending back from the amygdala and lying just inside the temporal lobe of the cortex. Researchers call it the cognitive mapper because it assembles bits of information into *explicit memories*, and also plays a key role in retrieving information encoded in the past—in other words, in the process of remembering. Bundles of axonal fibers, called the *fornix*, begin at the hippocampus and arch around below the anterior cingulate, ending in the region of the *hypothalamus*. Together with the pituitary, the hypothalamus controls the neuroendocrine system, releasing neurotransmitters and hormones throughout the body–brain in the service of maintaining homeostasis. Clearly, these three components form a team that interact strongly with one another.

Above the corpus callosum lies the *cingulate gyrus*, with the part toward the front (to the left in Figure 2.2) being the *anterior cingulate*. This large region has many functions, but for our purposes, two of the most important are its involvement in the attentional processes that are central to regulation, and its capacity to assemble cognitive and affective information to make decisions that will be positive for our future. Because focused attention is a crucial component of encouraging the mind to reshape the brain, this circuitry becomes central in the therapeutic endeavor. Because streams of information, containing rational and emotional cognitions, converge here, it is one of the primary areas supporting neural integration. Finally, the *medial, ventral, and orbitofrontal parts of the prefrontal cortex* are near the end of the frontal lobe, where your fingertips contact both the brainstem and the limbic regions in the hand model. These regions are part of the cortex. However, the orbitofrontal region lies so close to the limbic proper that some researchers say it is neither fully cortex nor fully limbic. Taking these four regions together, we will follow Siegel (2007) in collectively calling them the *middle prefrontal region*. The neurons here are *specialized for integration*, and, as we will see below, play a key role in facilitating recovery from all kinds of attachment and traumatic difficulties.

Being a Brain-Wise Therapist

Deep within the brain lies one area that is not technically part of the limbic region but that acts as a relay station for communication between body (via the spinal cord and brainstem), limbic region, and cortex: the *insular cortex* (or *insula*). Researchers believe that the streams of information converging here provide an emotionally relevant context for sensory information. Working with the middle prefrontal regions, the insula is thought to serve as one vital conduit for the flow of information that allows us to form pictures of the state of our own bodies and of one another's minds (Siegel, 2007). Taking a moment to mentally review the locations and functions of these structures may help us begin to visualize how they work together.

Cerebral Cortex

Returning to the hand model, the third group of regions is represented by the back of your hand from above the wrist down to the fingertips, wrapping around the limbic regions—the *cerebral cortex* (also called the *neocortex*), which is comprised of four lobes (see Figure 2.3). These regions, particularly those toward the front of the brain that are devoted to reasoning and relationship, are most extensively developed in human beings.

Moving from back to front (and roughly in order of increasingly integrative processing), the *occipital lobe* at the back of the head integrates bits of visual information into whole images. The *parietal lobes* process information about touch, pressure, temperature, pain, where we are in

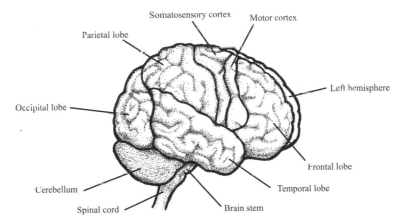

Figure 2.3 The cerebral cortex: We are looking at the right hemisphere, with the back of the brain at the left. This cortex, particularly the frontal lobe, is most extensively developed in human beings. Art by Ron Estrine.

space, sensory comprehension, understanding speech, reading, and visual functions; the somatosensory strip at the front of this lobe receives information from the spinal cord about touch, position of the body, and other matters. You can begin to sense the streams of energy and information gathering.

The *temporal lobes* at the side of the head process complex information about smells and sounds, and have many integrative functions relating to memory. Just inside the temporal lobes, in the medial temporal cortex, we find the hippocampus, the limbic structure most involved in explicit memory creation and retrieval. As an example of the temporal lobe's integrative power, the functions of the left lobe are not limited to simple perception but extend to comprehension, naming, verbal memory, and other language functions. The ventral (front/belly) part of the temporal cortices appear to be involved in integrative visual processing of complex stimuli such as faces (fusiform gyrus) and scenes (parahippocampal gyrus).

Finally, the *frontal cortex*, moving from back to front, contains regions for motor control of voluntary muscles and motor planning (motor and premotor strips), as well as for concentration, organization, reasoning, judgment, decision-making, creativity, personality, abstract thinking, emotion, and relational abilities (to name a few). If we move to the bottommost area of the frontal cortex, we have returned again to the highly integrative prefrontal region, a crucial area for healthy functioning in our relational universe. Again, you can notice how your fingertips touch both the thumb (limbic) and palm (brainstem), drawing many inputs together in a symphony of integration.

One other area of the prefrontal region is central to the therapeutic endeavor: the *dorsolateral prefrontal cortex*. Located at the sides of the prefrontal lobe (the topmost knuckle of your little finger), it is considered the home of working memory, the "chalkboard of the mind." When we attend to something, the information is brought into conscious awareness where we can play with it, adding new energy and information to reshape the memory before it is re-stored. This process is of particular relevance for us because when our patients bring painful memories into consciousness, we can add the interpersonal energy and information of comfort and understanding, creating new representations of a caring other and providing the impetus for increased integration. Then, when these memories are sent again to long-term or permanent storage, they will be both more integrated and more filled with soothing messages.

Differing Functions of the Two Hemispheres

Now let's turn briefly to the *differing functions of the two hemispheres*. In many pictures of the brain, if you look down from the top, it appears that it could be peeled into two halves like a ripe apricot. Were it not for the *corpus callosum* (the part right beneath the cingulate gyrus in Figure 2.2), a band of tissue that is the major highway for communication between the two halves, along with a few other smaller bands of fibers (all called *commissures*), this would be largely true in the anatomical and functional sense. Even though there are similar structures in both halves of the brain (e.g., two amygdalae, two hippocampi, two temporal lobes), the way they perceive experience as well as the information they process and their means of processing that information are quite different (Schore, 2007; Siegel, 1999).

The functions mostly mediated by the left, what we could call *left-mode processing* (LMP), conveniently begin with l's: logic, linearity, language, and literalness (Siegel & Hartzell, 2003). The left likes things to make sense in an "a, then b, then c" sort of way. It captures experience in words that give it a definable shape. LMP creates explanations of events and feelings, based on input from the right, producing the experience of things falling into predictable cause-and-effect patterns. Even the neocortex on the left side is wired in a way that supports such a sense of order, having more of a tendency to isolate information into neat packets that give the sensation of a yes/no and right/wrong binary system (Hawkins & Blakeslee, 2004).

Right-mode processing (RMP), happening for the most part in the right hemisphere, is more holistic and nonlinear, taking everything in at once in a receptive way (Siegel & Hartzell, 2003). It is specialized for perceiving and processing visual and spatial information—such as sending and receiving nonverbal signals, the centerpiece of social understanding. Mental models of the self, the world, and relationships are generated and experienced via the right mode. An integrated map of the body is assembled here, as well as the felt reality of our own story—our wordless autobiography as felt in and by our bodies. In short, the information necessary for understanding ourselves and others comes as direct experience through RMP. Interestingly, researchers have also discovered that there is some language on the right—the ambiguous, emotion- and image-laden words of poetry (Siegel, 1999). Even the neocortex on the right supports these ways of knowing; its neuronal columns have many more interconnections with each other than on the left (Hawkins & Blakeslee, 2004). All of this leads us to the inevitable conclusion that RMP is the indispensable bedrock of healing in therapy (Schore, 2007), and much of what follows offers ways to facilitate integrated RMP in ourselves so that we can provide regulating right-to-right connections with our patients.

What do we know about emotional processing in the two hemispheres? While there have been several hypotheses, the one with greatest research support at this point states that avoidance/withdrawal emotions (including turning inward to prepare to counteract a threat) are experienced, perceived, and expressed via RMP, whereas approach emotions are handled by LMP (Davidson, Jackson, & Kalin, 2000; Urry, Nitschke, Dolski, Jackson, Dalton, & Mueller, et al., 2004). This allocation makes sense given that researchers have discovered two motivational streams, tying the limbic regions to the cortex. In the right hemisphere, the stream that mediates avoidance/withdrawal is dominant, whereas in the left, the approach stream is stronger (Siegel, 1999). It is important to notice that both streams operate in both hemispheres, so the distinction is one of degree rather than indicating a complete separation.

When the two halves are integrated, meaning that information flows smoothly between the differentiated hemispheres via the *commissures* (principally the *corpus callosum*), RMP provides the felt context for the making-sense activities in the left mode, and LMP provides what we might best describe as the calming reassurance of logic and predictability for the right mode. Later in these chapters, we will explore more about why this integration might be blocked, how partial integration can "cement in" hurtful stories about ourselves that impact relational patterns, as well as ways to help the highway reopen and become a conduit for the more complete and balanced narrative of a person's trajectory through life.

Autonomic Nervous System

The last piece of anatomical awareness involves the two branches of the *autonomic nervous system* (ANS)—the *sympathetic* (which acts like the accelerator in a car), and the *parasympathetic* (which acts like the brakes). With this, we move into the body proper. When we think of self-regulation, the ANS is one of the systems involved. The ANS certainly doesn't operate alone, and, in fact, the amygdala, regions of the prefrontal cortex, and hypothalamus play a large role in the regulation process. When there is balance between the sympathetic and parasympathetic functions, we stay within our *window of tolerance* (Siegel, 1999), being neither too excited nor too dampened. When the sympathetic branch is in ascendance, we may experience being overly stimulated (including fight–flight responses), and when the parasympathetic branch takes over, we may feel withdrawn. Interestingly, the word we use for this latter experience is *shame* (Schore, 2003a). If both systems are overly activated, a fairly intolerable, disorganizing sensation is created, akin to jamming accelerator and brakes to the floor at the same time. As therapists, we can often feel the ANS at work in our own bodies as well as observe its fluctuations in our patients. Later in these writings, we will talk about the interpersonal and internal influences that carry a person along the continuum from ANS dysregulation to balance.

To make the picture sufficiently complete, we need to consider one other brain structure: the body–brain–mind of every person with whom we interact. We are constantly shaping each others' brains through our interactions. Let's say that someone frowns at me for no reason I can discern. Circuits in my brain containing the experience of my father being critical flare into activity, affecting my body–brain–mind in a powerful way (momentary brain change), further strengthening those circuits containing the old memory (long-lasting brain change). A caring friend puts her hand gently on my arm when I am upset. My body–brain–mind resonates with the warmth and calmness she brings to me (momentary brain change), while my middle prefrontal region is empowered to establish new soothing connections to my amygdala (long-lasting change). At every moment, we are engaged in this brain-to-brain creative dance.

How much detail about brain structure do we need to feel comfortable enough to convey this information in ways that our patients can understand and absorb? That probably varies from person to person. This chapter certainly presents a bare-bones version of brain structure, but we have found that ease with this much information, well-internalized so that it is flexibly available depending on the need of the particular patient, provides a good foundation for conversation, even with patients who are curious about the details of brain function. Also, as you make your way through the book, much more detail about brain processes will be added to this basic structure.

When I first learned about the brain, I developed a fuzzy sense of the major sections—and that was somewhat helpful. However, when I discovered that I really wanted to be able to use this knowledge with patients,

I reread my two sources with pen and paper in hand, taking notes and poring over the diagrams as though I were in school—because I was. Much like adjusting the focus on a camera, the brain swam into view with clarity, and my ability to be helpful with patients made a substantial leap as well. Getting this material somewhat engrained will make everything that follows easier, like putting a foundation under the house.

The main sense I hope you have gained from this very brief overview of the regions of the brain and components of the nervous system is how our neural equipment takes tiny bits of experience (information) and continuously weaves them together throughout the brain and body into our moment-to-moment subjective experience of life. Even though we're looking mainly at structures, a feeling of flow inevitably begins to emerge.

Chapter 3

The Brain's Flow

Although we will expand our vision to look at larger issues of flow later in Part I, it may be most helpful to focus first on connections between two right-hemisphere regions of particular interest to therapists: the *limbic* and the *middle prefrontal regions*. For the sake of review, this latter area is comprised of the *anterior cingulate* (attentional and emotional/affective integrative processes), the *orbitofrontal cortex* (integrative relational, calming, and flexibility functions), and the *ventral* (emotion regulation) and *medial* (possibly the capacity for awareness of self) *prefrontal cortices* (Siegel, 2007). It may be misleading to think of any of these areas as being in sole charge of any function because of the constant flow of energy and information between them. We may do better to focus on these as a *group* of functions that guides our relationship with ourselves and others.

I emphasize these processes in the right hemisphere rather than the left for two reasons: (1) During the crucial first 18 months of life, when foundational attachment styles and mental models are wired in, the brain favors RMP development over LMP (Cozolino, 2006); and (2) much of what unfolds in the counseling room is RMP-centered, as the social circuits in the therapist's and patient's brains dance together to rewire the attachment experience in a pattern of security (Schore, 2007). At this stage in the research, we know that much (but certainly not all) of what happens to the brain in insecure attachments and traumatic experiences can directly harm the development of the middle prefrontal circuits. These experiences can also block the flow of integration both between the various processes of the limbic area, and between the limbic and middle prefrontal regions. We might aptly use the word "dissociated" to describe limbic-based neural nets that are operating without benefit of connection to the integrating flow of the brain. As we will see, such dissociation leaves people continuously vulnerable to internal and external triggers. On the other hand, it is also true that that the limbic and cortical regions are constantly interacting with many other circuits in the body, brain, and environment, even when they aren't well connected to each other, so no process occurs in isolation. Nonetheless, there is value in focusing on what it looks like when these regions are working well together, how to mend those blockages/dissociations, as well as what it looks like when integration is occurring.

The Flow between the Limbic Region and the Middle Prefrontal Cortex

Let's backtrack just a bit and revisit the *pathway from amygdala to hippocampus to middle prefrontal cortex*, this time in terms of the flow rather than the individual structures. From this perspective, we can begin to understand the brain of both a newborn and the adult whose brain contains the neural nets of that newborn's experiences. As was noted above, the amygdala is the initial meaning-making center in the brain and a crucial part of *implicit memory*. For the first 12–18 months of life, implicit memory is the only form of memory available to us. However, at this young age, the amygdala is working with some other circuits (the movement centers in the basal ganglia, and with the sympathetic nervous system, e.g.), so we might better say *amygdala and friends* to keep a clearer perspective about the multitude of processes taking place even at this stage.

Implicit Memories

The implicit memories of our first year or so of life are encoded without us needing to be consciously aware. These memories contain elements of *behavioral impulses, affective experience, perceptions, sensations, and images* and, with repeated experience, cluster into *mental models* (Siegel, 1999). Under the impact of these continuing experiences, whether empathic or hurtful, processes in the amygdala develop generalized, nonverbal conclusions about the way life works—the essence of mental models. These conclusions create *anticipations* of how life will unfold and remain largely below the level of conscious awareness,

Being a Brain-Wise Therapist

guiding our ongoing *perceptions and actions* in ways that tend to reinforce the foregone conclusions. We often experience these as The Truth or The Way Things Are, and when we do find words for them, they are often stated as axiomatic realities. The other day, one of our patients came out mid-session to get a drink of water while I was working nearby at the computer. While she was filling her cup, she turned and said back into the counseling room, "You have to be strong and completely self-sufficient to survive." Imagine the power this mental model (likely based on early attachment experiences) has in her relational life today. In this way, our earliest experiences become the basis for our foundational themes, the very "water" in which our lives exist.

One other fact about implicit memory is of great importance in understanding how all of us experience life: When implicit memories are activated in our day-to-day experience, they have no time stamp, so we interpret the emotional/visceral/perceptual/behavioral surge as being entirely *caused by something occurring in the present moment.* A longer example may help us get more of a feel for how implicit memories make their presence known. Let's say a tall, dark stranger is walking toward you while your mind is consciously thinking about what you'd like to have for dinner. Let's also say that your highly critical father was tall and dark. If you were being aware, you might notice that your eyes turn down and away (*behavioral impulse* related to shame), that there is a groundswell of feeling (*affective experience*) leaving the *sensation* of a pit of fear in your stomach, and a fleeting picture of your father's face (*image*) might dart through your mind. All of this might happen well below the level of awareness, showing up only as a faint, possibly unnoticed, unease that quickly evaporates. However, if you then needed to interact with this man, your unconscious perception of him as dangerous to your positive sense of self, coupled with the generalized but nonconscious *mental model*—"Tall, dark men hurt me"—will bias the interaction in ways that might leave you uncomfortable, but for reasons you can't understand. Then left-mode processing (LMP) will go to work to create a present-day explanation for why you want to get away from this man as quickly as possible. Because your response doesn't make sense to him, he, in turn, might react to your pulling away from him by sending nonverbal signals (more powerful) or saying something (less powerful) that you could perceive as critical. You can see how in more longstanding relationships, these *perceptual biases* can recreate the original past experience in the present over and over again. Fully incorporating an understanding of the depth and extent of perceptual bias operating in the life of every human being is liberating for patient and therapist alike. Rather than being swept away by our reactions, such awareness encourages the ability to stand back from the tight grip of current experience to notice how our minds pull in one direction or another. Sadly, one axiom that proves true most of the time is that the greater the early wounding, the more power these implicit memories exert in the present, until there is some kind of integrative healing experience.

> You might find it helpful to pause and viscerally sense how your implicit world comes to you in daily experience. I find it useful to get in touch with consistent perceptual tendencies and behavioral impulses cropping up in my relationships. For example, given the opportunity to go toward some new experience, particularly when strangers are involved, I now notice how my body subtly pulls away. This tug of fear is rooted in early childhood trauma, and for many years it kept me from entering into potentially nourishing relationships. Once noticed, I can manage the tug differently. Implicit mental models can also support healthy relating, so it can be heartening to notice those tendencies as well. Becoming well acquainted with our implicit world is good insurance against hurtful countertransference entanglements.

Integrating Implicit Memories in Therapy

Part of the process of therapy is bringing implicit memories/mental models to consciousness, where they can receive understanding and comfort for the painful or fearful feelings they carry. This step paves the way for integrating them into explicit memory (where the past is experienced as past) via the hippocampus, and from there, into the coherent narrative of our lives. Implicit memories are lodged in the body as well as the feelings, and beginning to work with either body or feelings can lead to changes not only in the emotional tone of our perceptions, but in our behavior as well. At that point, these implicit mental models cease to exert so much covert influence over our relational choices and behaviors because they are no longer nonconscious determinants, but rather just other elements in a flexible decision-making process.

A loving, kind, and usually balanced woman persisted in calling her 40-year-old daughter every day, even though she was often aware that this caused her child irritation. When the relationship finally came to

Being a Brain-Wise Therapist

a breaking point, she sought help to see what could be salvaged. As we talked about her history, she remembered the family story of her mother being hospitalized for suicidal depression at least four times before my patient was 2. Her mother recovered, and the family simply archived the difficult time without sensing a need to address how the experience may have impacted this baby. Within the quiet of the connection between us, great sadness flowered as she got a visceral sense of how frightened and achingly lonely she had been.

From this deep place of truth, we began to ask what she would feel if she didn't call her daughter each day—a question she had not been able to answer at the outset of therapy. She felt a painful clutching in her chest and immediately made the connection between her own infant grief at her mother's absence and a fear that if she were not continually present for her child, this precious person would feel the same devastating sense of loss. She realized that every time she decided not to call, she would feel the rise of intense anxiety that now seemed to be a combination of fear for her daughter and her own inner baby's panic at the initial loss of connection. *The implicit was becoming explicit, allowing her to form a representation of the experience as past.* From this position of recognizing the origin of the anxiety, she began to be able to sit with these strong feelings, allowing our developing attachment bond to provide increased regulation. As we will see, this kind of right-brain to right-brain synchrony encourages neural integration that can permanently change our mental models in ways that support very different relational experiences. In a natural way, this woman internalized me as the calming, available, maternal person who had been so tragically missing. As this new state of mind settled in, Mother called Daughter to talk with her about the reason for the persistent calls, only to find that part of her daughter's irritation came from her own rise in anxiety as she resonated with her mother's internal state. With this new ability to mutually hold their experience, they easily worked out communication patterns that honored their care for each other and their developmental stages.

It is so important to get familiar with the feeling of the implicit at work, because patients can look quite irrational when they are in the grip of a powerful implicit mental model. For most of us, the natural impulse is to do a "reality check" with them, to help them reorient to what is "really happening" in the moment. The problem is that the only reality any of us has is the one created by the neural firings inside our skulls and bodies. So the issue is less about transferring our perception of reality to the other person, and more about helping that person integrate his or her body–brain within the interpersonal system, so that he or she can subjectively experience a more present-based reality.

Working with the Middle Prefrontal Cortex

As a toddler reaches 12–18 months, the circuits of the amygdala are sufficiently differentiated to make the next linkage. At this point, the *hippocampus* and the *middle prefrontal region* come online, and *explicit memory* becomes available (Siegel & Hartzell, 2003). We could think of the hippocampus as the puzzle master, integrating the components of implicit memory and time-stamping them as past. The first form of explicit recall to appear is *factual memory*: that is, the ability to remember sequences of events and locate them in space. Somewhat thereafter but still within the second year, *autobiographical memory* begins to take shape as the middle prefrontal region becomes more available for this integrative task (Siegel, 1999). This second kind of remembering allows us to begin to tell the story of our lives, to make sense of what is happening to us, particularly if we have parents who will collaborate with us in this endeavor. *Empathic attunement is the key factor that fosters this all-important integrative step in children*, and it is also part of the reason that solid therapy can rewire the brain so efficiently.

Linking with the middle prefrontal cortex brings other possibilities as well, including an emerging sense of self and others. Felix Warneken and Michael Tomasello (2006), anthropological researchers in Germany, found that by 18 months, many toddlers can read intention in the face of another. When Warneken repeatedly dropped an object on the floor, if his face showed need or distress, the toddler sensed his inability to reach his goal and responded helpfully by picking up the object, offering it to him with a smile. When he dropped it intentionally, the child, still studying his face, went right back to playing, sensing that this adult did not need assistance. With the dawning of middle prefrontal integration, these young ones can focus on the face, read the intention, and respond with care all at once. When this sequence transpires, a child is on the way to becoming an empathic, moral human being.

Integrative Functions of the Middle Prefrontal Region

Pausing to talk some more about the intra- and interpersonal wonders that become available as the middle prefrontal region becomes integrated with the limbic proper can allow us to savor some of the dimensions of mental health. Just to review, in the hand model, the middle prefrontal region is located where your middle two fingertips touch both your palm (brainstem) and your thumb (limbic regions). The genetic gift of these neurons is their ability to further integrate strands of energy and information flowing from all parts of the brain. Seeking to find help for a particular patient, Siegel (2007) combed through the research on the functions of the middle prefrontal region and gathered a list of nine outcomes of integrative fibers from this region extending into the rest of the brain, particularly the limbic areas. The first seven are also outcomes of secure attachment (with the last two not yet the subject of research), and all nine emerge through the sustained practice of mindfulness (Siegel, 2007). It may be helpful to notice how one capacity often flows into, and depends on, the next.

1. *Regulation of the body.* We feel at ease in our bodies when the sympathetic (accelerator) and parasympathetic (brakes) branches of the autonomic nervous system stay in balance with each other, flowing in waves of activity and relaxation. We feel safe in our bodies when we know that as stress (internal or external) pushes us out of the comfort zone, we can find our way back through a variety of personally reliable techniques for regaining balance. Picturing the yin–yang symbol in which states of receptivity and activity never take over completely, but work in a complementary fashion, might give us this feeling. Integration with the middle prefrontal region provides increasingly trustworthy access to these resources for resilience. When this region is linked with the limbic circuits, the path from perceived fear to a defensive stance (fight–flight) or extreme withdrawal (freeze) goes through a process of evaluation, giving the nervous system time to recover its balance. This longer path slows processing, allowing for a range of options to emerge in the mind, modulating the sympathetic response, rather than rushing directly from limbic evaluation to reaction. On the parasympathetic side, we are less inclined to plunge into shame and frozen terror (signs of parasympathetic overactivation). This more balanced nervous system gives us the opportunity to evaluate the situation based on present-day parameters rather than the patterns of a fearful, painful past.

2. *Attuned communication.* The ability for attuned communication, indispensable for establishing secure attachment between parent and child (or therapist and patient), rests on our capacity to accurately sense someone else's state and communicate, nonverbally (most important)

and verbally (less important), our felt understanding of their emotional experience. In order to provide this kind of contingent communication, enough implicit, amygdala-based perceptual bias needs to be modulated to be able to sense others somewhat as they are. The integrative social circuits of the middle prefrontal region are the culminating location for numerous streams of information that allow us to receive and send attuned signals to another person, many of which occur in microsecond intervals, well below the level of conscious awareness. Even if we know the right things to say to feign attunement, listeners will sense whether we are really in synchrony with them.

3. *Regulation of emotion.* When our limbic circuits do not have strong integration with the middle prefrontal region, we are vulnerable to wide and sudden swings of emotion as limbic-based perceptual biases, rooted in implicit memory, repeatedly respond to internal and external triggers. In a self-reinforcing loop, the hypothalamus and pituitary release neurotransmitters and hormones that match the emotional tone flowing from the limbic circuits. In turn, such changes in the body provide cues about our emotional state, often further intensifying the limbic alarm. When we mindfully attend to our state, we can sense the movement of emotion through both our subjective state and the flow of energy in our body. In this way, regulation of the body and of emotion go hand in hand. As middle prefrontal integration increases, the pathway between limbic activation and emotional response lengthens and becomes more complex, conferring a greater ability to keep our feelings from going to extremes. As this capacity strengthens, emotional responses will more quickly and easily return to balance even in the face of stress.

4. *Response flexibility.* The ability to pause before taking action, bring a range of possible responses to mind, evaluate them, and make a decision based on what is most appropriate for the situation often marks the difference between a person being perceived as mature or childishly impulsive. With integration, incoming stimuli take a longer path allowing the mind to craft a response to the situation. As a consequence, there is less of a knee-jerk quality to our decisions that reflects modulation of quick-trigger limbic processes, principally located in the region of the amygdala and friends.

5. *Empathy.* Empathy rests on our ability to resonate internally (and accurately) with another person's state of mind. Recent research suggests that this ability begins with specialized neural cells named *mirror neurons* (Iacoboni, 2007; Rizzolatti, Fogassi, & Gallese, 2001), which are

part of what we now know is a broad network of *resonance circuits* (Siegel, 2007). We will explore these cells and circuits in detail below. Via this resonating capacity of the brain and nervous system, a representation of the intention and feelings of the other arises within us. At the same time, we need to be able to manage our implicit perceptual biases so that we can sense the other somewhat accurately, and middle prefrontal integration provides this ability. The process of empathy involves inner awareness of our bodily states (*interoception*), followed by an understanding of what we are feeling (*interpretation*), followed by awareness that it may also be happening in the other (*attribution*; Carr, Iacoboni, Dubeau, Mazzlotta, & Lenzi, 2003).

6. *Insight (self-knowing awareness/autobiographical narrative).* Insight involves our ability to shape and tell our story in a way that is both coherent and that maintains emotional contact with its meaning. We are neither overwhelmed by, nor disconnected from, what happened to us, and we have a developing sense of meaning about our pathway through life. Only through integration of limbic-based memory with the capacities of the middle prefrontal region in both hemispheres does this capacity emerge. In therapy, one of the processes that indicates progress is a gradually expanding narrative that is able to hold more and more of the intergenerational experience of one's family with compassion and wisdom.

7. *Fear extinction.* The process of the middle prefrontal region linking with the amygdala involves axonal fibers that carry the soothing neurotransmitter gamma-aminobutyric acid (GABA), which extends from the middle prefrontal cortex to the fear-encoding neurons of the amygdala. Unless something physically destroys these axons, the influence of this neurotransmitter will continue to modulate these implicit-based fears, even if the patterns remain in place, significantly changing the subjective quality of experiences that trigger these fears. This is an excellent example of neuroplasticity through synaptogenesis.

8. *Intuition.* This sometimes-mysterious capacity may actually be our ability to pay attention to the messages of our viscera (i.e., stomach, intestines, heart, and lungs). Our bodies' signals are intimately involved in affective experience, and often the first awareness we have of our emotions comes from a bodily response. When we suddenly "know" something without a path of logic, it often comes directly from the body into the right hemisphere, where the integrated map of the body is assembled, and only then flows into the left hemisphere for understanding and expression in words.

9. *Morality.* It is not surprising that morality is rooted here since moral *action* (as opposed to *ideas* about morality) must surely be a by-product of our empathic connection with others. If we yell at someone and fear arises in his or her face, we are more likely to be able to accurately read that emotion if we are in a somewhat integrated state. As we resonate with this person's distress, we can calm ourselves and stop yelling. The profound sense of interconnectedness that gradually arises as a result of increasing neural integration creates a strong foundation for decisions that consistently take into account the needs of others.

Looking at patterns emerging from these nine functions, we can notice that one key ingredient is the *modulation of implicit-based perceptual biases* that are always present. In sum, limbic processes operate at lightning speed, whereas cortical processes take longer and also take many streams of information into account, gathering them into an increasingly comprehensive, complex system. When there is integration with the middle prefrontal region, the decision pathway lengthens to include these slower, moderating processes that have the flavor of wisdom because of their more panoramic view of the possibilities.

We will return to these nine functions many times because they are such strong indicators of therapeutic progress and increasing mental health. One of our roles as therapists is to help our patients unlock dissociated neural nets that block integration of the middle prefrontal region with the limbic areas, as well as impeding connections between the body–brain and the relational world. The brain is a system that seeks increasing complexity, so when the accumulated debris of a painful past is transformed into "food" for the integrative flow, the brain knows what to do. We are also in an especially favorable position to facilitate this natural process because empathy is such a potent promoter of neural integration.

It may be very helpful to pause here to take a humble look at our own middle prefrontal resources. We are certainly all in the process of integration, so there is no shame in deficits. Posing a kind question to ourselves about why a particular middle prefrontal quality is less developed may reveal neural nets in need of attention. We might find that our intuition is strong but that we are less able to modulate fear in stressful situations. If we then patiently bring awareness and comfort to inner experiences that leave us vulnerable in this area, we will find that fear gradually has less of a grip.

Being a Brain-Wise Therapist

The more deeply rooted we are in middle prefrontal integration, the more our capacity to steadily hold our patients' disintegrative upsets will expand, because our implicit perceptual biases will have the opportunity to be held themselves by the wisdom of our integrative circuits. One principle that underlines the importance of pursuing such wholeness of body, brain, and mind is that, in therapy, microsecond, nonconscious interactions, through an unfolding conversation of nonverbal exchange, provide the rich "soil" in which our patients can root their recovery. There is no way to control these interactions consciously, so we must rely on our own integrating brains to keep up our part of the dialogue. We hope to often hear our patients say, "I felt like you were so with me today," even when we have said only a few words. On those days, we may recognize that we have felt a harmonious flow within ourselves and within the relationship, even in the midst of working with painful and frightening experiences.

Although the right-hemisphere process of limbic–prefrontal linkage is central to personal well-being and relational goodness, it is also just one small part of the brain's overall movement toward linking its circuits into a symphony of unfolding complexity. As we widen the scope of our exploration of the brain's flow, we find another group of nine processes, also described by Siegel (2006, 2007), that illuminate the pathways the brain uses to expand interconnection within its circuits and with other brains in the social world. Much like a braided stream, these pathways are interwoven, with emphasis sometimes on one, sometimes on another. However, we have found that both by being aware ourselves and by sharing these ideas with patients, the depth of therapy increases, allowing suffering to resolve more rapidly.

Nine Pathways of Integration

In this section, we are going to briefly sketch these connecting paths, which we will revisit frequently throughout the book as we explore ways to facilitate these linkages. As always, bringing your internal awareness to how you experience each of them will help ground the concepts in your body.

Vertical Integration

A good place to begin is with *vertical integration,* meaning that the *body, limbic region, and cortex in one hemisphere are linked.* The middle prefrontal area is the linchpin because this region sits at the intersection of the brainstem, limbic region, and cortex. People established in vertical integration can listen to their feelings through awareness of their bodies, and can often tolerate a broad range of emotions without becoming dysregulated. Those with blockages may often be at a loss to locate the emotional or physical correlates of an upsetting story they are relating. As therapists, vertical integration grounds our ability to use the wisdom of our bodies and feelings to stay in attunement with our patients (Schore, 2003b; Schore, 2007), even when the interactions are happening very rapidly at a nonconscious level. Lest this responsibility for accurate empathy be too intimidating, it is good to remember that mothers attune with their children only about 33% of the time (Tronick, 2003). Most important, the difference between securely and insecurely attaching mothers is that the former are able to read their children's distress signals and make quick repair (Tronick, 2003). As Tronick (2003) stresses, all relationships are "sloppy" (p. 5). However, if vertical integration fails in ways that cause us to be trapped in implicit-based relational patterns with our patients, therapy can become a tragic replication of their earlier wounds.

One of my patients came to therapy because the intense shame she felt when anyone was critical of her was undermining the quality of her marriage. She was cognitively aware that her husband wasn't even particularly judgmental, knew the problem was hers, but couldn't stop her overreaction to even mildly negative feedback. Exploring her previous therapy, we discovered that whenever she wanted to address a difficulty in the relationship with her therapist, his face would change from open to closed, and he would direct her away from these feelings in a way that felt denigrating to her. Because they were generally doing wonderful work together, she quickly erected a barrier around expressing feelings that would cause him to react in this way, taking the shame and guilt of criticizing this good man onto herself. As a result, her feelings of shame were never processed, and, in fact, became more intense. We can guard against this happening with our own patients by developing a strong awareness of our bodies, because they are often the "canary in the coal mine" when it comes to breakdowns in vertical integration. My patient's therapist probably felt some strong, body-based sensations that accompanied his facial expression of displeasure, but he may have been unaware of them or missed their significance for the therapeutic relationship. We will revisit the topic of therapist–patient entanglement from different angles as we progress.

Being a Brain-Wise Therapist

Bilateral Integration

Often, as our patients settle into greater capacity for vertical integration, the path for other kinds of integrative processes opens. As words begin to contain the unfolding healing experience, we witness a progression to what Siegel (2006, 2007) calls *bilateral* or *horizontal integration* of left and right hemispheres. As mentioned earlier, the left hemisphere seeks to make logical meaning from the information it receives from the right hemisphere. When vertical integration is not yet established, our patients may have little ability to sense their bodies, so the left hemisphere may receive such little input that the stories it creates are hollow and not reflective of the complexity of their inner worlds. It is also possible that the left will receive a flood of partial information from an activated dissociated neural net, and make up stories that match these experiences, giving the conscious mind the impression that this story is the complete truth about the person. One of my patients had been hated from conception, creating an implicit conviction that there was something terribly wrong with her. Her left hemisphere followed this compelling lead, creating a string of stories about her ugly, hateful nature, weaving a prison of self-rejection that followed her into adulthood. While both of these situations represent some integration between right and left hemispheres, they aren't what we will call bilateral or horizontal integration. Instead, we will reserve those terms for the kind of linkage between hemispheres that unfolds as vertical integration becomes more established. Then, the left hemisphere receives a rich flow of information from the body, limbic, and cortex on that right, which contains an increasingly complete picture of our patient's inner world.

Narrative, Memory, and State Integration

Once left and right are working together, *narrative, memory, and state integration* begin to develop naturally. As we come to terms with our history, our emotionally engaged narrative becomes more coherent, and within that narrative, our memories flow from past to present in a meaningful way.

Both narrative and memory integration usually occur in tandem with state integration. Understanding *states of mind* is central to working within the inner community paradigm, so we'll spend some time here. We can begin by saying that there is no single self in the objective sense, although increasing integration may bring us a subjective sense of wholeness and unity as our states of mind work in greater harmony.

From the beginning of life, all of us develop a variety of internal states as we relate to different people. We might have an angry state of mind in relation to the critical aspect of our mother, or a frightened state of mind in relation to our older brother's rage. At the same time, we might also have a peaceful state of mind in relation to the warm and caring aspect of Mom. We can think of these states as neural nets that have developed and been reinforced by repeated experience. Because of how they are formed, they almost always occur as pairs of states—an internalized angry father may be paired internally with a frightened child, or a cold mother with a lost, shamed child. If you look inside yourself right now, you may be able to see your own linked pairs.

When these states are shaped around relational pain, they can become dissociated from the overall integrating flow of our mind, leaving us vulnerable to being taken over by them without the modulating help of other parts of our brains. We might subjectively experience this as having an inner community whose members aren't at peace with one another. For example, we might frequently be aware of the critical voice of an internal parent and feel shame well up in our bodies. Not only is there no resolution between the pairs, but the neural nets holding these relational states may also be dissociated from one another. When these states are not integrated, abrupt and bewildering shifts from state to state can become obstacles to well-being. There can be a disconcerting sense of discontinuity and lack of control, as though the mind is jumping from island to island without warning. Relationships can also be severely impacted because of the intensity of perceptual bias released when these states are touched by current experience, as well as their tendency to operate in the extreme range. When that critical parental voice is pushing at us internally, any small question from another person about why we have acted in a certain way may trigger shame and sharp anger.

In therapy, we can move consciously toward these states of mind with our patients. As these painful or frightening states are reactivated and brought into working memory, they become available for input; the energy and information of comfort and understanding can now be added to the formerly isolated neural nets. Subjectively, the therapeutic relationship will embrace these inner community members. This act of awareness brings contact with the formerly isolated pain and fear. Embracing this emerging experience with interpersonal warmth and understanding fosters linkage of these dissociated states with right middle prefrontal regions. Then, as storytelling around the experience emerges, the left middle prefrontal regions will become integrated as well. We could say that state integration is progressing in tandem with horizontal, narrative, and memory integration. We could also say that inner community healing is unfolding.

Integration of Consciousness

Supporting all these forms of neural integration is what Siegel (2006, 2007) calls the *integration of consciousness*, which involves cultivating the capacity to flexibly direct our attention to the internal and external worlds in ways that promote well-being and interpersonal harmony. *Exogenous attention* occurs when events in the outside world capture our focus. As you are reading this, an ambulance goes by, and the wail of its siren pulls your mind outward. When we *choose* a single focus, we are engaging in *endogenous or executive attention*. Having acknowledged the siren, you choose to return to your contemplation of these ideas. One way to promote this capacity for flexible attention is *mindful aware-ness*, which can be defined as paying attention, in the present moment, on purpose, without grasping onto judgments (Kabat-Zinn, 2005). We invite our patients to do this when they focus on the sensations in their bodies or a state of mind with the calm curiosity of a *caring observer*. From this state, they can experience the subjective richness of a state of mind while also being aware that this state is only a portion of their being. Even very painful memories become more modulated from this per-spective, and most patients quickly notice substantial increases in self-regulation. Practicing this kind of mindful attention for a few minutes every day is like doing push-ups for our attentional and relational capac-ities. In Chapter 13, we address the many benefits of such mindfulness practices, as well as ways to introduce them to patients. As one would imagine, doing these practices ourselves may make us more effective guides for our patients.

Interpersonal Integration

If integration of consciousness is the main support for therapy, *inter-personal integration* is the soil in which healing grows. With the discov-ery and exploration of *mirror neurons* (and the other circuits that work with them) in the last decade, we are becoming aware of how we con-stantly embed within ourselves the intentional and feeling states of those with whom we are engaged (Iacoboni, 2007; Rizzolatti et al., 2001). We increasingly believe that the capacity for empathy is rooted here.

It may be fruitful to take some time to absorb how this process of inter-personal oneness unfolds within the brain and between brains. It is important to remember that our understanding of all these processes is at a beginning stage. Even though we can start to describe the pathways through which this energy and information flow, we need to be careful not to make these separate, sequential processes, but instead imagine each part reverberating with all the other circuits until there is a sense of sharing the inner world of the other person (Siegel, personal communication, October, 2006). The sensation of hearing successive strings added to a guitar chord, until all are vibrating richly together, may come close to capturing this unfolding experience.

With this image in mind, let us take a look at how researchers are starting to describe the circuits involved in this resonating process. Neurons with *mirroring properties* are found in the *inferior frontal* and *posterior parietal* areas (Carr et al., 2003). They are activated during both the *execution* and *observation* of action, as a representation of the action is sent *from the superior temporal cortex to these mirror neurons.* If I watch you lick an ice cream cone, the same neurons will fire in both our brains, even though I only get to lick the ice cream internally. This mirroring occurs only with actions that we perceive as *intentional,* and, in fact, these two areas of mirror neurons specifically *create a bridge between motor action and the perception of intention.* We would be lost to each other, as autistic people often **are**, without this crucial ability. These convergent streams of information are sent to the *superior temporal cortex,* which now can make a representation of the other's next move (Carr et al.). This process is called *priming,* and it can be the precursor of moving in tandem with the other person (as in dancing). At the same time, we also begin to move internally with the other person, sensing what is going on through the perception of intention. We can already get a sense of accumulating streams connecting us to the other person's inner world.

At the same time, the *insula* (whose circuits form a highway between the brain and the body, processing convergent information to produce an emotionally relevant context for sensory experience) carries the flow of information from the mirror neurons and superior temporal cortex to the *limbic regions and body* (Carr et al., 2003), where appraisal of the meaning of the information occurs. At this point, perceptual bias can enter the picture, potentially interfering with accurate empathy by coloring the information with the sometimes discordant information of our own historical connotations. As therapists, we can certainly sense the

Being a Brain-Wise Therapist

importance of being mindful of these limbic–body evaluations. With the addition of awareness, we have a better chance of holding them with one part of our mind, while resonating with as much true empathy as possible with our patient.

Next, the accumulating flow of energy and information about the inner state of the other flows back through the insula, which then sends the gathering streams to the *middle prefrontal cortex* (Carr et al., 2003), that strongly integrative part of the brain. At this point, the chord is almost complete, allowing us to experience the internal state of the other more fully as it reverberates through all these circuits. If we imagine focusing our attention on a person who is standing across the room, we may have some experience of his or her state of mind via these circuits without him or her even being aware of the connection. However, such inward experiences rarely stand on their own, but are most often the precursor of rich interpersonal interactions. When we are feeling empathy for another, a strong resonance develops between the two of us, beginning with mirror neurons and echoing throughout all these pathways, completing the chord. We often experience this as a softening and relaxation in the body, accompanied by a feeling of warmth and reassurance.

To capture the full flow of this process and not confuse it with the mirror neuron system (which plays a crucial part, but is not the whole), we can use Siegel's (2007) term, *resonance circuits*, to think about the way energy and information coming to us from another's actions continually link us. While we have used the tangible example of a friend licking an ice cream cone, it is important to realize that these circuits constantly process the most subtle and minute visual cues coming from the faces and bodies of those around us. We even make representations based on familiar sounds, like someone tearing a piece of paper or sighing deeply (Iacoboni, 2007).

It is worthwhile to spend sufficient time understanding this process of resonance because it is central to the therapeutic relationship. Through this flow, we enter the inner world of our patients, at the same time they are taking in our warm and caring self. This shared resonance appears to create greater coherence in both minds (Siegel, 2006), suggesting that interpersonal integration leads to forms of personal neural integration in both patient and therapist. Such warmth and security also pave the way for self-discovery by creating the conditions for dissociated neural nets to join the mainstream of the integrating mind, where they can be bathed in comfort. In this way, what begins as dyadic regulation gradually flowers internally into the capacity for self-regulation.

Temporal Integration

On the foundation of increasing neural integration, two other experiences sometimes emerge. Both appear to be grounded in the human need for purpose, meaning, and connection. *Temporal integration* invites us to gaze on the reality of death—our own and others—and make our lives meaningful in light of their finitude (Siegel, 2006, 2007). Contemporary American society encourages us to look away from death, but our inner life eventually requires us to look at it straight on, and hopefully, we do that sooner rather than later, because coming to peace with the flow of our life is foundational to developing a sense of unfolding meaning. Patients who have consciously carried this task to completion, often by confronting the death of a loved one or even their own death, share in common certain words: They often say that their lives become more "vivid," and their relationships are "sweeter." It is as though they become more alive to their sensory experience, while savoring the individual moments of relationship in light of their impermanence.

Transpirational Integration

This deepening awareness and acceptance of our finitude seems somehow linked with the last domain, *transpirational integration*, a term coined by Daniel Siegel (2006, 2007), meaning "to breathe across." As our attunement with others increases—as we become viscerally aware of how our resonance circuits draw us deep within each other—we may become open to a felt awareness of how inextricably interwoven we are with one another. It is possible that this all-embracing state is a natural consequence of pursuing neural integration even after our suffering is relieved. As Einstein (1957) said:

> A human being is part of the whole called by us universe, a part limited in time and space. We experience ourselves, our thoughts and feelings as something separate from the rest. A kind of optical delusion of consciousness. This delusion is a kind of prison for us, restricting us to our personal desires and to affection for a few persons nearest to us. Our task must be to free ourselves from the prison by widening our circle of compassion to embrace all living creatures and the whole of nature in its beauty. . . . We shall require a substantially new manner of thinking if humanity is to survive.

It is such a privilege to accompany people on a journey that has the possibility of leading to this state of consciousness.

We will return to these principles and experiences of neural integration as we make our way through suggestions for the practice of therapy. As our integrative abilities develop, we can increasingly embody the nine outcomes of middle prefrontal engagement that signal our own increasing complexity. Most of us have found that just learning about the brain is a boost in that direction. However, studying these new understandings through encountering them in the subjective realm of personal inner experience can help us develop greater self-awareness, mindfulness, and self-compassion, increasing our ability to be a healing presence for our patients.

This may be a good time to assess our own neural integration. Are we aware of the flow of information coming from our bodies? Do we easily translate ongoing experience into words? Can we flexibly direct our attention to thoughts, feelings, and actions of our own choosing? Do we frequently have experiences of empathy and connection with others? Can we look steadily at our own death? Are there moments when we feel our oneness with others? These states of integration come and go, and the beauty of being aware is that focused attention increases these capacities.

Chapter 4

The Relationship between Brain and Mind

Now that we have come some distance in being able to picture the brain's structures and gain some sense of its flow, we can begin to ask how our minds emerge from these neural processes. As therapists, why do we care? Our work is to participate in the healing of minds, yet most of us have never had the opportunity to form a comprehensive picture of the mind or its health, apart from the particular minds we treat (Siegel, 2001, 2007). This seems rather like asking the pharmacist about how two drugs will interact when he or she has never studied chemistry.

Is the Mind More Than the Brain?

The central question is this: Is mind anything more than the result of neural firing patterns in the brain? At first glance, the answer might appear to be "no." Even my ability to think this thought or write this sentence is apparently dependent on a light show unfolding all over my brain. A number, perhaps the majority, of eminent students of brain, mind, and consciousness believe it must be so. However, if this were the whole story, our minds would be puppets of the brain, and neural change would be at the mercy of whatever experiences came our way. It would mean that free will is an illusion emerging from unseen brain processes. Morality and responsibility would be meaningless concepts without the existence of personal choice. Apart from the wish to alleviate the unpleasantness of thinking about a bound and predetermined life, is there any solid evidence that mind is more than a product of the brain's activity? We would see this evidence if the brain's structure and/or function changed in response to the volitional activity of the mind, or what Jeffrey Schwartz calls "mental force" (Schwartz & Begley, 2002).

Attention and OCD

In the late 1980s, seeking to relieve the suffering of people imprisoned by obsessive–compulsive disorder (OCD), Schwartz (1997; Schwartz & Begley, 2002) gathered the research of many neuroscientists to understand the underlying brain mechanisms. It turns out that the orbitofrontal cortex and the anterior cingulate function as an error-detection circuit, allowing us to adjust our behavior when there is a perceived threat. For people with OCD, "stuck" gating in the caudate nucleus makes the orbitofrontal cortex strongly overfire, leading to a constant sense that something is wrong. Because the anterior cingulate is also connected to the heart and gut, a visceral sense of dread accompanies any attempt to stop the frantic actions (e.g., wash hands over and over, count steps) designed to stave off the perceived disaster. A long-time meditator in the Buddhist tradition, Schwartz wondered if focused attention could actually change the gating in the caudate nucleus, so that firing in the orbitofrontal cortex could return to normal. The short answer is   yes. In 10 weeks of intensive training in a four-step method, using a particular kind of focused attention to "feed" a new set of neural nets at the expense of the those driving his patients' OCD experience, energy use in the caudate significantly decreased, and the subjective urge to wash e.g., was drastically reduced, *without* medication (Schwartz & Begley). Apparently, the mind, through focused awareness, had changed the brain.

Since that time, many researchers have found that such mindful attention correlates with changes in brain structure and function. Although correlation is not causation, the accumulating evidence from these studies is hard to ignore. Working with a group of long-time meditators, Sara Lazar and her colleagues (Lazar, et al., 2005) found increased thickness in the middle prefrontal region (interaction of emotion and cognition, moral decision-making, and other functions) and the anterior insula (awareness and control of visceral experience, facial recognition) in the right hemisphere. The degree of increase correlated with the time spent in mindfulness practices. Such increases suggest that new neural connections had been made—possibly an example of structural change through synaptogenesis—initiated by mental focus. In another study, Richard Davidson and his colleagues (Davidson et al., 2003) worked with a group of new meditators and a control group, taking measurements of electrical activity before and after an 8-week training. They measured both baseline activity and changes in electrical firing just after both groups wrote about the positive and negative events of their lives. At the end of 8 weeks, the researchers found a shift from right to left frontal dominance in the emotion-regulating circuits when the participants who had meditated engaged in this task again. There was no change for the nonmeditators. This shift in activity suggests a greater ability to approach (left-side function) rather than withdraw (right-side function) in the face of emotional difficulty, and is associated with greater resilience (as well as increased immune function). However, more important for our purposes here, this outcome seems to indicate that the focused mind had indeed changed the way the brain functioned.

All of this research is in its earliest stages, so we have only a small, seminal idea about how much transformation of brain by mind may be possible. However, the key to such change does appear to reside in the cultivation of *conscious awareness* and *focused attention*. It may be helpful to first acknowledge that most of what goes on in our brains remains out of conscious awareness, on automatic, with certain memories continually swept into consciousness through a decision-making process based on internal and external events. While our brains are constantly available for rewiring, for better or worse, conscious attention is usually not the agent of change. If I grew up in an angry household and now live with an irritable spouse, the childhood neural nets will continue to build up synaptic strength from frequent stimulation. If, on the other hand, I spend considerable time with a nurturing friend, new wiring containing soothing messages will make a home in my brain. In neither case, however, has my own mind changed my brain.

Attention and Quantum Physics

If, however, we add *attention* to the mix, a different story unfolds. This tale draws us briefly into the improbable landscape of quantum physics, so please bear with me. We can now ask our original question in a more refined form: Can the nonmaterial mind act on the material brain? The answer matters because such interaction would be the necessary condition for us to assert that our minds can alter our brains (Schwartz & Begley, 2002), that free will and moral choice exist. Even today, many respected scientists and philosophers (Damasio, 1999; Dennett, 1993) assert that mind cannot act on brain, that only physical forces create change in physical matter, returning us to the unpalatable conclusion that all mental activity is a product of the brain, no matter how much our subjectivity leads us to believe otherwise. Quantum physics comes to the rescue, first directing our attention toward the two-slit experiment. As you may remember, a single photon (packet of light) leaves the generator as a particle, passes through two parallel slits as a wave (a single particle going through two holes at once), and is again perceived as a particle when it makes its mark on a receiving plate, but landing in a pattern typical of a wave. This hard-to-conceive outcome has been replicated for decades. Between the two observations/measurements, the photon appears to live an indeterminate existence as a wave of probability that contains the information for a number of possible outcomes, with some probabilities being greater than others. Depending on how we direct our attention, what question we ask, the wave collapses into a single value. As Schwartz and Begley (2002) note: "Quantum physics makes the seemingly preposterous claim (actually, more than a claim, since it has been upheld by countless experiments) that there is no 'is' until an observer makes an observation. Quantum phenomena seem to be called into existence by the very questions we ask nature, existing until then in an undefined fuzzy state" (p. 262).

What does this experimental outcome have to do with the brain and free will? Subsequent to the original experiment with photons, electrons and ions (small bits of matter) have demonstrated this same property — one particle passing through two openings at once, behaving as a wave until noticed/measured, then settling into some fixity. In our brains, the decision to release or not release neurotransmitters (to excite or inhibit activity in the brain) rests with calcium ions, presumably existing in a fuzzy, wavy state until collapsed into a decision to either release or not release (Schwartz & Begley, 2002). The weight of prior experience most often causes these collapses below the threshold of awareness. However, just the notion that these ions are ever in a fuzzy state gives scientific weight to the idea that our brains are hotbeds of quantum activity, and that our acts of attention might influence how the wave of probability settles into a specific outcome. Since this is proving to be true, we are telling our patients the truth when we bill *acts of attention* as *agents of change*.

Attention and Clinical Practice

How does this idea apply in clinical practice? As Schwartz (Schwartz & Begley, 2002) worked with his OCD sufferers, initially the probability that the wave would collapse in the familiar way (toward compulsive activity) was great because the old pattern was heavy with repetition. However, as these determined people began applying focused mindful awareness via the four steps developed by J. M. Schwartz (1997), the odds began to change. First, they worked to *relabel* their compulsions as symptoms of OCD, and then *reattribute* them to a malfunction in particular circuits in the brain. As they shifted away from their old conviction, the odds of new circuits firing were increasing, while energy was taken out of the old ones through lack of attention. With their capacity for mindfulness expanding, the focusers became better able to direct attention toward the chosen thought, even while sitting with the discomfort of the old proclivity. Their new ability was particularly tested with the third step: *refocusing* on an alternate activity. This is where the rubber meets the road, as their attentive minds stayed with their intention to make the decision to go for a run, for example, rather than check the locks. From the quantum perspective, we might say that because of the participants' directed attention, mental force began causing the probability waves to collapse in different neural circuits, gradually shifting the balance. The fourth step, *revaluing*, loops back to a deeper awareness of *relabeling*, as the person more fully experienced the OCD symptoms for what they were: nothing but aberrant neural impulses without meaning. By the end of the 10 weeks, both subjective experience and objective scans confirmed that the circuits had significantly changed, with a very high likelihood that mindful attention was a significant causal agent (Schwartz & Begley).

In the case of OCD, there is a fairly clear view of which circuits need attention. However, many of our patients struggle with well-established pockets of neural disintegration that affect relationships between brain regions to such an extent that mindful awareness may not initially be the centerpiece of therapy. Dramatic and far-reaching attachment difficulties and trauma, fueling right-hemisphere upset, invite an additional approach to fostering neuroplasticity—one in which our patients initially borrow our minds as a resource for focused and compassionate attention to their suffering. We enter their quantum world with our own intention to attend and comfort, perhaps encouraging waves to collapse differently, or for the first time, into patterns of warm attachment. Our own mindfulness gradually mirrors its way into their neural landscape, until they find that paying attention to body, feelings, or thoughts brings renewable resources of regulation.

The Relationship between Brain and Mind

Through all this scientific and philosophical wrestling, we have perhaps come to some peace with the idea that free will exists, at least to some significant extent, and that we can be conscious agents of neural change. In this light, how can we succinctly define the relationship between brain, mind, and mental health? A good deal of the work has been done for us by a group of thoughtful people from a variety of disciplines (sociology, cognitive neuroscience, medicine, attachment research, and developmental psychology, among others). In the interest of exploring the experience of mind from many viewpoints, in the mid-1990s Daniel Siegel embarked on a series of discussions based on the principle of *consilience*, a word coined by E. O. Wilson (1998) to indicate the convergence of streams of knowledge. After much energized discussion, the group initially molded three principles upon which all participants could agree:

1. The human mind emerges from patterns in the flow of energy and information within the brain and between brains.
2. The mind is created within the interaction of internal neurophysiological processes and interpersonal experiences.
3. The structure and function of the developing brain are determined by how experiences, especially within interpersonal relationships, shape the genetically programmed maturation of the nervous system. (Siegel, 1999, p. 2)

What is immediately striking about these principles is the view that the mind is no longer contained within the individual brain; instead, its emergence is intimately linked to processes in other brains. Next, we notice that mind is an experience, more a verb than a noun. In a constant, ever-changing flow, mind emerges from the flickering firing patterns in the brain. Somehow, neural bursts, in on–off patterns, give rise to the richness of our subjective experience. This part is still a mystery. Genes and experience become co-creators, rather than antagonists, in the battle of nature versus nurture. Our genetic inheritance guides basic development and certain sequences, which are then shaped by our experiences with one another, even to the point of guiding which genes will be expressed (Siegel, 1999).

Given the dynamic nature of mind and the principle that our brains are seeking increasing complexity, it is not surprising that over time, these definitions and principles concerning the mind have been somewhat reshaped, particularly as science has illuminated the mind's active role in the ongoing rewiring of structure and function within the brain. In the last 5 years, adding to the evidence cited above, the mindfulness community has offered itself as subject of study, revealing that the focused mind can indeed change the brain in the direction of integration (Begley, 2007). Out of this research arose a new first principle and a clearer view of the goal of therapy (and life) in the new fourth principle.

The first principle is this: "The mind can be *defined* as a *process* that regulates the flow of energy and information" (Siegel, 2006, p. 248). Let's start at the end of the definition. *Energy* means the firing of synapses (which ones, how strong) in the brain, and *information* means the mental representations (from simple objects to sophisticated concepts to emotional experience) that are the content of those firings. The mind, which could also be called our attentional processes, directs/regulates the flow of this energy and information, constantly altering the firing patterns. Quantum physics would agree. Sitting quietly, we can watch this process at work, as our mind continually shifts focus, shaping the structure and function of the brain as it flows. Sometimes, these focal shifts are directed by internal cues and outer experiences. Other times, we sense that our attending minds are sorting through options before making a decision, leaning into one possibility while inhibiting another. If you pause to focus deliberately for a few minutes each day, you may first feel and observe the rhythm of the inner dance and then gradually strengthen your capacity to direct it. In this definition, regulation does not necessarily imply balance, but instead suggests that where attention goes, so goes neural firing—whether that is toward chaos, rigidity, or coherence.

The second principle is similar to Siegel's (1999) earlier second principle: "The mind *emerges* in the transaction of at least neurobiological and interpersonal processes" (Siegel, 2006, p. 248). Mind is constantly emerging in every moment, never still, riding on the neural firing patterns it is actively shaping in the brain. The term *neurobiological processes* refers to the way energy and information flow within our brains, and the term *interpersonal processes* signifies the way in which energy and information flow between brains. Again, it is easy to experience both. Just close your eyes and direct your attention toward something unpleasant to feel how your mind emerges around that thought. Then change your attention to something quite pleasant to experience a different emergence. All this activity is happening within your own neural firing patterns, your neurobiological processes. Then, the next time you encounter a person, notice how the interaction between the two of you changes the way your mind is emerging moment by moment. Part of this latter process occurs because of the rich resonance circuits that continually embed us within each other.

Moving from the moment-to-moment experience of the mind to the mind's path over the years, the third principle states: "The mind develops across the lifespan as the genetically programmed maturation of the nervous system is shaped by ongoing experience" (Siegel, 2006, p. 249). Research has shown that about one-third of our genome is dedicated to shaping the connections within our brains (Huttenlocher, 2002). For example, our genetic makeup tells the stem cells in the fetus to become hippocampal or cortical cells, as well as when to start the pruning process to remove excess neurons. Genes also determine when a region is sufficiently differentiated to begin linking with other regions, and they guide basic life-sustaining connections, such as those in the brainstem. However, the limbic and cortical regions are largely undifferentiated at birth, meaning that the neurons and other cells that make up the brain are in place but not connected to one another. Experience, which is strongly interpersonal in the first 2–3 years, guides the structuring of the brain through the development of firing patterns whose content is the relational information in this gradually expanding interpersonal system. In short, nature and nurture work hand in hand as early attachment experiences structure the brain. The third principle also means that later relational experiences can reshape the brain/mind at any point in the lifespan. Such neuroplasticity provides the hope for healing, which is why sharing these concepts with patients can be of significant benefit to them.

This principle is certainly also an invitation for us to think about how our own minds have developed over the course of our lives. What early experiences shaped us? Which people have been powerful instigators of neural change for us as our lives have unfolded? If we are clear that our minds have become more whole through our own mental effort and the empathic care of others, it is easier to deliver this hopeful message to our patients.

The fourth principle concerns the experience of mental health: "An interpersonal neurobiology view of well-being holds that the complex, non-linear system of the mind achieves states of self-organization by balancing the two opposing processes of differentiation and linkage" (Siegel, 2006, p. 249). We will take a deeper look at complexity theory in

Part II. However, here we can begin to see how the path of integration proceeds. Our limbic areas are packed with largely undifferentiated neurons at birth. Immediately, experience begins to link them into nets that carry the implicit experience of relationship. This linkage sets the stage for the next process. Limbic circuits that have been developing in relative isolation join at about 12 months as the hippocampus and orbitofrontal cortex come online, forming a partnership with the amygdala to give us the capacity for explicit memory. Our brains embody this intrinsic tendency for ongoing integration, and we are now increasingly sure we can consciously cooperate with this process. The research cited above suggests that focused attention builds the middle prefrontal regions. Because of the inherently integrative capacity of these neurons, greater complexity ensues, leading to more flexible choice, or, we might say, greater ability to utilize the quantum properties within every neuron. With a more robust middle prefrontal region comes a stronger ability to attend (if we choose), so we are potentially in a self-enriching cycle of expanding well-being and interpersonal goodness.

As therapists, we see the results of blockages to the natural path of integration, often developed within the interpersonal world of attachment relationships. With our patients, we can see that when integration is not going well, the mind moves toward *rigidity* (a state that may result from too much differentiation of neural circuits without the balance of integration) or *chaos* (an experience that may reflect insufficient neural organization) rather than playing in the middle ground of *coherence* (Siegel, 1999). As rigidity softens or chaos calms, the experience of greater well-being emerges around states of mind that are *flexible, adaptable, coherent, energized, and stable*—Siegel's (2006) FACES of mental health. In our earlier example, we saw balance emerge as the rigidly frozen gates of OCD gave way to the relief and joy of flexible decision-making. As integration proceeds, patients become able to move toward spontaneity or structure without going to extremes.

I imagine all of us can feel when we go outside the boundaries of coherence, and rigidity or chaos sets in. It would be useful to reflect on some of those times now, noticing the difference in our body–mind states, as well as the consequences for our interpersonal world. In the presence of older men who defend against shame with denigration, I can feel my body tense and my heart become guarded, both of which are internal moves toward rigidity. Gaining visceral familiarity with such states can help us spot and manage our vulnerabilities in the moment, as well as attune with similar processes in our clients.

Another way to describe this integrating state is to say that it has a tendency to stay within the *window of tolerance* (Siegel, 1999), dancing between the firm and the creative, but not spilling over into dysregulated experiences at either end of the spectrum. To expand our view it is also helpful to consider how these processes operate in interpersonal systems, everything from dyads (including therapeutic alliances) to nations. Possibilities all along the spectrum from rigidity to chaos exist within every system created by minds. It is also true that every mind experiencing increased integration will share energy and information with every person who crosses his or her path, thereby multiplying the possibilities for social change.

In general, we could say that the greater the integration, the more freedom we experience and truly possess. Although most of our brain's processes will remain forever below the threshold of awareness, the microsecond, right-to-right interactions at the heart of therapy and all contingent relationships can rebuild this nonconscious realm. Dissociated neural nets holding pain and fear can be released, able now to join the streams of the brain's flow. Through this process, *what is automatic has a much greater likelihood of supporting what is conscious*. At the same time, we can use our expanded capacity for attention to exercise our quantum right to collapse neural nets in directions that support continued integration. As this proceeds, the subjective feeling increasingly becomes one of wholeness and harmony.

These principles of brain and mind contribute to an agenda for our therapeutic efforts. We can approach each person with two questions:

- Where has integration broken down?
- What can happen in the interpersonal system and in the individual mind to encourage integration to emerge?

This is one viewpoint, coming from an understanding of the principles of brain development and the role of neuroplasticity in the possibility of facilitating change throughout our lives. With this background, we are now going to look at how attachment experiences shape the brain and begin to develop the inner community.

Chapter 5

Attaching

When we are born, our whole being reaches out to continue our connection with the person who has been carrying us for 9 months. Having been present at numerous home births, I have seen how newborns, eyes not fogged by the application of silver nitrate (which often occurs in hospital births), gaze deeply at their mothers, molding to their bodies, drinking in a continuing oneness until they fall into their first sleep. If mother turns her eyes away for even a moment, her infant becomes restless, and then quiets as soon as her eyes return. It is as though this tiny human is etching the experience of the other into his or her physical–mental–emotional being in these first moments. Imagine the power lighting up this newborn brain, wiring in an initial sense of security and warmth.

Early Attachment Processes

It is such a beautiful and useful phenomenon that our brains are genetically hard-wired for attachment, seeking the interpersonal sustenance needed to structure our brains for personal well-being and healthy relationships (Cozolino, 2006; Goleman, 2006; Siegel, 1999). The brain's attachment system directs the child to *seek physical closeness* and *establish communication* with a few of his or her closest people, usually beginning with Mom. The sympathetic nervous system dominates over the parasympathetic during this early period of life, fueling the infant's efforts to reach and connect. Right-hemisphere limbic processes, especially the meaning-making amygdala, receive relational overtures from eyes, hands, touch, sound, and smell, and in the graceful dance between mother and child, begin to assemble our deepest implicit expectations about the nature of this world. Is it welcoming and warm? Is it consistent and trustworthy? In a word, is it safe for body and for heart?

Attachment research by Mary Main gives us the powerful statistic that about 85% of the time, a child's attachment experience will parallel the working model of attachment of the principal person caring for her (Hesse, 1999). The strength of this correlation makes sense, because the way our parents approach us shapes the structure of our developing brain (Schore, 2003b; Siegel, 1999). A significant contributor to this structuring is the resonating properties of the brain and nervous system. Many research studies have shown that, even in newborns, this resonance is active. If you stick your tongue out at an infant, after a few times, she will imitate that movement (Dobbs, 2006). However, this is only the visible edge of what is occurring inside. The research of Marco Iacoboni (2007) and others is revealing that the physiological, emotional, and intentional states of one person resonate (and encode) within another who is *paying attention* to the other's facial expressions. Body, limbic region, and cortex are all involved. As research reveals new aspects of resonance circuits, the sense of an overarching interpersonal oneness process grows more compelling.

This resonance is likely implicated in two interwoven processes at the heart of interpersonal integration. First, what is alight in the parental brain lights up in the newborn brain. It is as though the parent is passing on the family's emotional legacy in regard to relationships through these initial firings and wirings. For example, if the parent adapted and survived by not paying attention to emotional life, the baby's brain will begin to wire up in the same dis-integrated pattern (Siegel, 1999). In this way, a parallel structure is wired into the baby's developing brain, passing the *structure of attachment* from parent to child. We could also say that this is the beginning of the child's *sense of self*—is he lovable, is she alone, is he safe enough to be calm? This role in shaping the child's emergent sense of self will become more tangible when we talk about the different styles of attachment later in this chapter. Second, the child's brain begins to encode the internal state of the mother and father within herself. This is likely the beginning of the *inner community*—that gathering of people inside who continue to speak to us of our value, while teaching us how the world of relationships works. We have probably all seen how babies intently focus on parental faces; we begin to imagine the emerging internal representations of the parents' moods in the presence of this infant. When we also remember that the only form of memory available to this little one is implicit, we may be able to imagine the power of these initial encounters in shaping a child's deepest subjective knowings, that is, her mental models, about the world of relationships she has just entered.

Adult Attachment Processes

One of the unfolding processes in therapy is the reactivation of the attachment system, often accompanied by anxiety and vigilance, since for most of our patients, the initial process did not go well. However, as the longing for attachment dawns, we have the precious opportunity to help our patients mend/rewire even the earliest relational fears, adding the new energy and information of compassion, care, safety, stability, and warmth that is our contribution to the interpersonal system. This experience is both tender and intense. As implicit neural nets holding these early fears reveal themselves, they become available for incorporating warmth and goodness. Then, when they are returned to long-term memory, they are changed. Our care is encoded within the memory (synaptogenesis), and perhaps some stem cells have split, sending the daughter cells off to develop in the light of this new energy as well (neurogenesis). Neuroplasticity in the service of integration is in full flower as layers and layers of such healing experiences accumulate.

Imagine again the power of the resonance circuits within and between therapist and patient, as well as their role in attachment repair. At least two vital processes are woven together: *receiving our patients' inner world into our being (wellsprings of empathy), and giving these dear people our internal state in regard to them (overflowing empathy)*. Clearly, this is a dance with both processes happening at once, even though we have to talk about them sequentially. To begin, we enter our patient's subjective experience by minding our own bodies, feelings, and thoughts as we are in the presence of the other with the *intention to attend*. In this receptive state, we can be aware of how these resonance circuits allow us to create a representation in our own mind of *the internal state of the other (ISO)* (Siegel, 2007). As we discussed above, three steps unfold in this joining process. First, listening to our bodies' response to the other is called *interoception*. Then, if we are mindful of our bodies in a way that activates our own caring observer (a middle prefrontal ability), we will begin to understand what we are feeling through a process of *interpretation*.

Last, we will *attribute* that experience to the other person by creating a *narrative of the other* (NOTO) in our mind (Siegel, 2007). Through this inner narrative, each person then becomes a permanent part of our inner community. When patients begin to sense that they live inside us even when we are not together, continually held in our warm regard, they are often startled because it is such an unfamiliar experience. However, they also begin to enjoy a greater sense of *continuity of being* that expands and solidifies secure attachment. Whereas it takes many sentences to describe this process, it continually unfolds in a responsive dance, part conscious, part nonconscious. We can know it is going well by the sense of interpersonal synchrony and harmony, felt within our own being and observed in the bodies and faces of our patients as they relax into being known.

In this empathic process, caution and humility are always necessary. All information we receive from our patient passes through our limbic region, beginning with the meaning-making amygdala, which is home to our deepest perceptual biases. So as we resonate with our patients, our own pre-encoded perceptual system will also be activated, and the interpretation and attribution may be skewed by the colored lens of our own past. If we are in a less self-aware state of mind, perhaps because some unhealed painful experiences have been activated, or we are simply tired or out of sorts, we can be swept away by our implicit limbic processes, and substantially miss our patient's world—the inevitable failures of empathy that are part of every therapeutic relationship. When we are in a more mindful state (with middle prefrontal activation slowing down and integrating more streams of information during the interpretative and attributive processes), we have a better chance of sensing what belongs to us and what belongs to the other. This clarity paves the way for more accurate nonverbal and verbal empathy. Interpersonal respect requires us to always be inwardly and outwardly tentative in offering our thoughts, allowing lots of room for our patients to correct and guide us. We have found that the people we see feel valued by such humility, and it becomes powerful glue for the interpersonal system.

An example of how we can become entangled implicitly might help. Let's say I experienced parental rejection fairly regularly as a child, although I am not yet sufficiently aware of this history to even tell myself that story. The experiences are locked in implicit neural nets. Sometimes when people aren't warm with me, I feel heaviness in my chest, accompanied by hardly conscious images of my mother's back turned toward me, the impulse to turn away myself, and stinging eyes. I feel confused about why I have this powerful reaction to little slights. Now, I am with a patient who has fallen into implicit feelings of being rejected that are leading him to turn away from me in despair. Because these experiences are so early, he has no words for them either. Instead, sometimes he is just distant and cold. I might begin to feel heaviness, stinging eyes, and the strong impulse to turn away from him as my own unhealed implicit memories are touched. If I had come to emotional peace and insight concerning my own abandonment, creating a coherent narrative about it, I would be able to use this strong resonance to bring the two of us together in a powerful empathic connection, laced with deep understanding. Siegel (1999) calls this combination of insight and empathy *mindsight*, whether it is directed toward ourselves or others. However, if my own memories remain unacknowledged, then it will be very difficult for me to calm myself sufficiently to accurately create an image of the other in myself. Instead, the distraction of my own pain will be woven together with my image of my patient's upset. Fortunately, increased self-awareness can unweave this tangled web and allow empathy to flow again. When the tangling does occasionally happen, our patients will forgive moments of lost empathy if we are humble and respectful, and they will probably become more self-compassionate in the process. Some of our patients have told us that these moments of repair have been the most moving, prompting a leap forward, rather than the usual small step, in their growth process.

You have probably recognized what is usually called *subjective countertransference* in this description of implicit entanglement. The more mindful experience is often called *objective countertransference*, indicating the therapist's ability to experience his patient and himself from the caring observer state of mind. However, there seems to be additional power and poignancy in recognizing the roots of these experiences in the mutual dance of the inner worlds of patient and therapist. Viewed in this way, we may be prompted to become curious and mindful about our own inner worlds, so that we are better able to keep our minds integrated while we skillfully encourage the inner world of the other person to enter our consciousness and inform us. Through the activity of our resonance circuits, we literally begin to carry our patients with us in a kind of exchange of being. They become parts of our extended inner community.

Now, having talked about receiving our patient's being into our own and deepening the empathic connection, let's turn to the second part of the process: how our patients' resonance circuits can receive nourishment for their healing minds. The very heart of secure attachment is *contingent communication*. This involves receiving people's signals (nonverbal more than verbal) and responding in a way that lets them "feel felt" (Siegel, 2007, p. 129). Much of this nonverbal conversation takes place below the level of conscious awareness, implicit process to implicit process, in the right hemisphere (Schore, 2003b, 2007). Resonance circuits, including mirror neurons, are at the heart of this process. For us to respond accurately, we must have a good sense of the internal state of the other as well as be settled solidly in our own middle prefrontal cortex to provide such attuned communication. Our patients' resonance circuits will then draw in the feeling of our empathic state of mind as well as our intention to connect with them. Through repeated experience, they will build an internal representation of a warm, caring presence that can comfort them when we are not physically available. Patients begin to say things like, "I feel better when I think of you." "I hear your voice in my mind when I'm confused." "I get quieter inside whenever I remember our time together." The security of having a constant, supportive companion is exactly what would have been created in childhood if family circumstances had allowed. Given sufficient attunement, within the first 8–12 months, a baby will build a caring parent within. Fortunately, research confirms the lovely truth that it is never too late to take in an empathic other for lifelong warmth.

Certain moments during this interpersonal exchange have a unique power for us as well as our patients. When we have experienced this deep sense of resonance, we will always remember the palpable change in the atmosphere in the room—an unmistakable warm, flowing, calm intensity that sometimes endures for a long time. That is the feeling of flowering neural integration. Such experiences move even the most injured person in the direction of *earned secure attachment* (Schore, 2003c), which brings us to a consideration of how attachment unfolds between parents and children.

Patterns of Attachment

We will be most helpful to our patients if we can recognize how different kinds of attachment *shape the mind* as well as create a particular kind of *subjective experience*. This recognition will help point the way toward the most efficacious use of our interpersonal resources for repair.

The attachment schema that follows was created by Mary Ainsworth, a developmental psychologist, as she built on the seminal work of her colleague, John Bowlby (1969/1983, 1973/2000, 1980/1991, 1988/2005), concerning attachment. Her categories of secure, insecure/avoidant, and insecure anxious/ambivalent capture the essential outlines of the three patterns of parent–child relationships she observed while doing research studies with mothers and infants in what is called the Strange Situation (Ainsworth, Blehar, Waters, & Wall, 1978). The process begins with observing babies and their moms in their homes through the first year of life. Then they are brought into the research setting, where the child is first with Mom, then with Mom and a stranger, then with just a stranger. Ainsworth believed that this series of events would activate the attachment system and allow researchers to observe the child's pattern of interaction with Mom upon reunion. These studies have been replicated all over the world. They appear to provide solid data indicating that initial attachment patterns are forming during the first year of life and continue to influence relationships into adulthood. Of course, we know that neuroplasticity means that other interpersonal experiences can continue to shape our mental models of relationship, providing hope for repairing damaged attachments at any stage of life.

Building on Mary Ainsworth's work, Mary Main and her colleagues later added a fourth attachment category, disorganized (Main & Solomon, 1986, 1990), and developed an instrument for measuring an adult's *state of mind with respect to attachment*, the Adult Attachment Interview (AAI; Hesse, 1999) to parallel the Strange Situation for children. In very brief summary, the *way* in which people narrate the story of their early life experiences (coupled with the story itself) indicates this state of mind. As mentioned above, this state of mind in turn correlates with the attachment status of this person's child a large percentage of the time. The AAI does not measure an adult's attachment to a particular parent, but instead looks at the way the mind has created an overall mental model/anticipation of the importance and quality of attachment relationships. Erik Hesse (1996), Mary Main's colleague and husband, has begun developing a "cannot classify" category, which may apply to people who have not developed a cohesive working model of attachment because of conflicting models that remain strongly active. Even if we don't have the resources to do a full AAI, we can use the basic principles to move toward a more complete understanding of our patients' attachment. As we talk about the four kinds of attachment, we will also discuss the characteristics of narratives revealing the adult state of mind regarding attachment.

Regulation and Our Sense of Self

To further set the stage, following Allan Schore's (2003a, 2003b, 2007) lead, we will also talk about attachment in terms of how it does or does not help the child move toward the capacity for self-regulation. A baby's immature nervous system has very limited resources for regulation and so depends on his or her closest others for patterning this ability to moderate and organize bodily and emotional states in the developing brain. Different kinds of attachment provide better or worse resources for this mainstay of mental health. Schore (2003b, 2007) might say that the quality of dyadic regulation, followed by emerging self-regulation, defines the subjective experience of the self. To understand this principle, we need only think of how pervasive anxiety, for example, shapes our perception of ourselves.

The right hemisphere is dominant for the first 2 years of life. This means that one defining characteristic of all attachment patterns lies in the *right-brain to right-brain bodily based regulatory experiences* that unfold between parent and child in those first 2 years. Because attachment begins when only implicit memory is available, the regulatory patterns characteristic of different kinds of bonding become deeply etched in our bodies and brains.

Our patients often come to us when early implicit patterns have decimated their relationships. Because these regulatory patterns are rooted in the nonconscious realm, it can be very confusing for our conscious minds to try to identify the reasons for partner choices that echo childhood chaos or rigidity. However, if we can intuitively sense the sculpting power of our earliest interactions on the largely unformed brain, we may be able to sense why such choices do not fall within the realm of logic. Thanks to neuroplasticity, we know that help through dyadic regulation is always a possibility. In therapy, we have the opportunity to provide the kind, empathic care that can rewire implicit regulatory patterns through the power of calming attunement.

Providing Safety

Being able to sustain a feeling of safety for children or patients is central to providing such regulatory experiences. Stephen Porges (2001, 2007) coined the word *neuroception* to talk about how our *neurobiological* being is genetically wired to detect *safety, danger,* and *threat to life.* As information comes into the senses, the meaning-making amygdala and associated circuits make an initial assessment about safety, below the level of consciousness, immediately triggering various neurobiologically adaptive responses. If there is a neuroception of safety, the myelinated branch of the 10th cranial nerve, the *ventral vagus,* inhibits the fight/ flight response of the sympathetic nervous system and allows social engagement/secure attachment to unfold. Interestingly, this myelinated branch of the vagus runs from brainstem to heart and is involved in perception of facial expressions, the sound of the voice, and the capacity for attuned listening—cornerstones of solid attachment. If there is a neuroception of danger (but no fear for one's life), *sympathetic* fight–flight responses are automatically activated and social engagement is attenuated. If the situation worsens and the amygdala assesses threat to life, the *dorsal vagus* (the unmyelinated branch that runs from stomach to brainstem) comes into play and initiates a freeze response—similar to a terrified backyard rodent "playing possum" to avoid being eaten by the family dog. Again, secure attachment is stopped in its tracks. As these patterns of relating are repeated, mental models of trustworthiness, danger, and serious threat to life accumulate, resulting in a biased perception of many relationships. Our patients bring their perceptual substrate with them; our conscious intent to create a safe haven for them will be a key factor in their ability to engage with us sufficiently to allow the knots of implicit pain to loosen and be touched by comfort.

Just as crucial is our mindful awareness of which relational circumstances stimulate a feeling of danger or life threat for us. If we become inwardly frightened during therapy, then we will fall away from social engagement toward fight, flight, or freeze, although we probably won't act on it. Nonetheless, attachment repair will be hindered at that point because our patients will pick up something of our state through the resonance circuits, even if they are not consciously aware of it. I remember being with a patient whose terrifying mother resonated with a patch of my own unhealed fear in a way that temporarily pulled me toward a frozen internal state. I was aware of what was happening but couldn't immediately shift it. The session appeared to continue normally—I said the right empathic words with the correct facial expressions and all the rest. Then she didn't show up for her next appointment, a most unusual occurrence. When I called her, she was hesitant to speak with me openly (again, not the norm), but after some time, she said she didn't come because she thought I had given up on her. I told her that her feeling that something had shifted was accurate, but it was more a matter of me getting caught inside myself and leaving her for the moment than me being discouraged with her. This disclosure opened the way for a lovely discussion of our relationship and the nature of healing. We came away with gains, but I also knew in a more poignant and living way how much my inner state impacts my patients.

> We know from Porges's work that the leading edge of this process unfolds below the level of consciousness and makes its first appearance in the body. To assess our own vulnerabilities, we might take some time to think about each of our patients, and, attuning with our bodies, sense if any of them provoke anxiety or fear at times. With practice, we can learn to bring our caring observer state of mind into the picture to hold this upset with compassion. As it resolves, the sense of anxiety will lessen.

Security

We are now ready to look at patterns of attachment in some detail. We are spending so much time on these patterns because understanding them in a visceral way has proven so useful for entering patients' inner worlds. Let's begin with a *free, autonomous, secure adult* providing the experience of *secure attachment* for her child (Ainsworth et al., 1978; Hesse, 1999). The use of the word *free* means that this person is not dominated by her history in ways that interfere with receiving her child's signals accurately, or moving rapidly to repair when there is a misattunement. Subjectively, she will feel mostly at peace with her history and be able to talk about it in a coherent way. In brain terms, we can imagine that she has solid middle prefrontal integration with the deeper limbic regions so that strong perceptual biases do not usually interfere with accurate empathy and collaborative communication. Her AAI/family-of-origin narrative will embrace both what was reassuring and what was troubling in her childhood, and be communicated in a way that has a sense of flow and ease, with appropriate emotional tone and supportive, detailed, cognitive content.

We may notice a similar sense of ease in our own bodies as the narrative unfolds and find that the characters in the story feel alive in the room.

There is often the sense of the inner community assembling in such a tangible way that we can internalize and remember them easily. We might imagine that this happens because our patient has integrated her childhood experiences, including the painful ones, and can deliver them to our open mind in a warm, coherent way.

We can also imagine that this parent will be able to sense her children's signals accurately much of the time, responding in ways that allow them to feel met and soothed. When empathy does momentarily fail, she will be able to quickly sense the rupture and repair it, building an expectation that when things go wrong, they will be righted again—one cornerstone of resilience. We can imagine that her children have a mostly consistent neuroception of safety with their mother. We can also talk about this early interaction as a dance of co-regulation in which her children's states affect her in ways that allow them to resonate together. The balanced mother, in turn, helps her children amplify positive states and moderate negative ones. These interchanges will gradually create an ample window of tolerance, with her children being able to comfortably accommodate a broad range of emotions. In this lovely dance, her children's brains are being structured to anticipate respect, empathy, and warmth in relationship—the essence of secure attachment, and will also slowly develop the capacity for self-regulation.

In the Strange Situation, her 1-year old will gradually become upset about Mother's absence, but on her return, will be easily soothed and quickly return to play. We can talk about this child as being more resilient because he or she has stronger inner community resources to draw on under stress, with a reassuring mother subjectively experienced as living inside. We also know that the foundation of burgeoning neural integration is laid because there is little need for painful experiences to be held in dissociated implicit neural nets. Through a variety of processes, an internal structure primed for integration is wired into this child's brain. Of course, we always need to be mindful that genetics (including temperament) significantly contribute to how the child incorporates what the parent offers. However, this basic structure of integration will, of necessity, be transmitted in some detail.

Most of our adult patients will not have a fully secure attachment initially, although some will have oases of security that become an excellent resource during the often difficult process of therapy. Research shows that a longer-term relationship with a therapist whose own integration makes him a reliable attachment figure is one effective means of facilitating change in an adult's state of mind with respect to attachment. Over time, the patient moves from various patterns of insecurity to an earned secure attachment (Schore, 2003b, 2007). The research also affirms that earned secure parents have just as much capacity to transmit a secure attachment to their own children as parents who were securely attached as children (Siegel & Hartzell, 2003). It goes without saying that we can also help the children who come to us move toward secure attachment both through the warm, mindsight-based relationship they have with us, as well as by helping their parents move toward an earned security. What an opportunity we have to help end intergenerational cycles of misery generated by painful attachments! Not only can abuse and neglect be ameliorated, but also the less dramatic internal and relational suffering that can take the joy and color out of life.

According to recent research, approximately 55% of children are securely attached, a decrease of about 10% in the last 10 years (Sroufe, Egland, Carlson, & Collins, 2005). Furthermore, in October 2001, pollster Daniel Yankelovich published a survey indicating that 44% of American parents believe that picking up a crying 3-month-old infant will spoil that child (Shook, 2001). In the absence of overt abuse, such tragic misunderstanding of their baby's developmental needs by well-meaning parents often lies behind the relational struggles of our adult and child patients.

As we now explore avoidant, ambivalent, and disorganized attachments in children (and the corresponding bonding patterns of parents), it will be good to listen to our own bodies possibly speaking to us of not-yet-healed implicit and explicit memories welling up from our earliest relationships. Sitting mindfully with these sensations, images, behavioral impulses, emotions, perceptions, and mental models will assist us in developing the kind of thorough-going coherent narrative that will make us mediators of earned security for all we meet—both as therapists and as fellow human beings.

Avoidance

Moving on to the first of the insecure attachment patterns, we see that research tells us that children who develop an *avoidant attachment* often have one or more parents with a *dismissing state of mind with respect to attachment* (Ainsworth et al., 1978; Hesse 1999). This usually means that these parents were avoidantly attached themselves as children—and thus the pain continues to flow to the next generation. Marvin, Cooper, Hoffman, and Powell (2002), of the Circle of Security project, (a group in Spokane, Washington that has developed early childhood interventions to increase secure attachment between parents and children) talk about this intergenerational factor in terms of a cycle of "miscuing." The child makes a bid for closeness, triggering the parent's fear of connection. In response, the parent sends a signal telling the child to move away—in essence, "Go play, be independent." These parents can be good at sending their children out into the world, but become upset when their offspring need connection or comfort. Gradually, their children learn that expressing this need leads to pain, so they will then develop a compensating miscue about their legitimate need by *not* asking for attention. Thus a tragic, recursive pattern becomes encased in neural cement.

We can see that in this kind of attachment, children often learn early that attempting to be close costs them pain. There could be many different ways to avoid these hurtful feelings, but the path to safety most likely to be structured in these children's developing minds will echo the parental style. Dismissing parents have learned to shut off *awareness* of their limbic longing for connection (Siegel, 1999; Siegel & Hartzell, 2003), and they pattern their children's brains to similarly turn away. In a way, the parents' miscues communicate to this child, "Don't go toward snakes [feelings]—they're dangerous." The intention in the deeper mind may be to pass down the best protective strategy the parent knows by helping the child minimize his normal felt need for closeness. From this perspective, that approach could be perceived to be a successful adaptation. This doesn't mean that the longing for connection is absent (because that is a basic human drive), but merely that awareness is attenuated, that mental models are formed around expectations of separateness, and that beliefs reflect the relative unimportance of relationships. However, measurements of heart rate changes in avoidantly attached individuals reveal that under appropriate circumstances, the nervous system is activated to seek attachment, but these signals simply stay below the level of consciousness (Siegel, 1999).

How might the brain be structured to accomplish this override of the need for closeness? What kind of dis-integration would provide the necessary protection? One possible answer is that people with avoidant attachment histories, as a result of impaired interpersonal integration, may not have fully developed connections with their bodies or right middle prefrontal region (vertical integration), as well as between right and left hemispheres (horizontal integration). From the viewpoint of resonance circuits, they have developed the capacity to ignore their natural resonance with others. Interestingly, the longing for connection appears to be embedded in neural cells in the chest around the heart, making sense of the subjective experiences of heartache and having a broken heart (both of which are held away from consciousness, for the most part, in avoidant attachment). Traveling up through the insula (gatherer of sensory streams into an emotionally meaningful context), longing would be experienced in the right hemisphere because therein lies the integrated map of the body (Damasio, 1994). In order to not know about this need, a person would, at a minimum, not allow this longing to rise to the level of consciousness (dorsolateral prefrontal cortices) and certainly not give it words (horizontal integration). Without horizontal integration, narrative, memory, and state integration really don't stand a chance. It is hard to say whether the road from body to limbic region to cortex is shut down or if only awareness is attenuated. In either case, part of therapy will be helping our patients gain a mindful experience of the body, perhaps for the first time. (I will have a lot more to say about how to do this in Part II).

When a dismissing adult is sharing his story, the flow of cognitive information is often fluent but quite impoverished when it comes to detail. Generally speaking, the more dismissing/rejecting the attachment, the greater the absence or dissociation of childhood and even adolescent memories there may be, as though there were insufficient interpersonal "glue" for anything to stick. In addition, there is rarely a vivid sense of three-dimensional people in the story. Parents are "nice," teachers are "good" or "bad," but there is usually a distinct absence of real-life substance. If you ask for more detail, you will often be met with puzzlement or irritation. The narrative might sound like this: "I come from a good family. We lived in Flint, Michigan, until I was 6, then moved to Boise because my father's company sent him there. My mother was nice. She made sure we always had clean clothes and good food to eat. I went to school at. . . . "

One way to think about this degree of narrative poverty is that at least three factors have interfered with the kind of middle prefrontal integration that produces a sense of the self within one's own history. First, parental empathy is one of the most potent resources for galvanizing a child's developing brain toward increasing complexity. However, evidence suggests that empathy requires a parental brain in a reasonable state of integration when the next generation is born. With dismissing parents, this is not the case; their brain structure seeks to support emotional separation rather than closeness, leaving them quite insensitive to their children. The second factor involves the parents' inability to imagine their own narrative, making it difficult for them to engage in collaborative storytelling with their young ones. Research strongly suggests that these kinds of shared stories are also a powerful way in which the developing mind builds the capacity for coherent narratives (Siegel & Hartzell, 2003). Third, remembering that strength of encoding is related to the emotional intensity of the experience, we could hypothesize that the deadening influence of emotionless relating simply produces such weak neural nets that memories aren't easily retrieved or may even have fallen apart entirely.

Listening to these life stories, we might feel heavy in our bodies with a sense of boredom, emptiness, sleepiness, or anxiety related to the lack of connection as we join our patients in their emotional deserts. We will usually have a lot of difficulty getting a tangible sense of their inner community because they can't bring them into their own minds, much less the therapy room. These inner people may feel elusive, faded, or wooden—or all three. With family systems in mind, the word disengaged might arise in your consciousness. All of this is excellent food for empathic understanding of our patients, especially when we are able to sit in our caring observer and watch our bodies, feelings, and thoughts respond to the lack of connection.

Given that the foundation of secure attachment is a parent who is able to read her children's signals, we can certainly sense that a dismissing parent significantly lacks this ability. Because Mother can't read her own emotional state, she lacks that resource for her children as well. Most of our ability to resonate with another's nonverbal signals lies in the right hemisphere. There is little chance for that to happen with this mother. Initially, the children feel an enormous sense of loss and frustration, until they learn (from their mother) to disconnect from at least conscious awareness of the pain. Although this is an attempt at adaptive regulation, the disconnection actually cements in a rigid response to relational overtures. This lack of connection may lead to hypoaraousal, a sense of low energy and disinterest, because the infusion of emotional richness is not available. However, if a child's temperament leans toward right-hemisphere dominance, the painful anxiety at not being able to connect may sometimes break through, leading to bursts of hyper-arousal. The dismissing parent may then say, "You're just too sensitive," or "What do you want now?" Sadly, the parent is genuinely without a neural clue of what is needed. For a child of any temperament, the window of tolerance has not been widened by a parent who can follow and regulate his infant's vivid emotions, leaving the growing child vulnerable to both depression and anxiety.

The situation in regard to this child's neuroception is a bit confusing because the usual behaviors associated with a perception of lack of safety are mostly absent. We can be certain, however, that relationships are perceived as unsafe, but it is difficult to assess the intensity. For some, relational danger may be assessed but blocked from consciousness by insufficient vertical integration. On the other hand, since relationships are generally thought to be relatively unimportant, there may be little amygdala-based reaction to them one way or the other. As with so many aspects of avoidant attachment, much is hidden.

As you might expect, in the Strange Situation, 1-year-olds with avoidant attachments show little outward emotional response to either Mother's departure or return (Ainsworth et al., 1978). Since they do not usually experience her as present, little is lost when she departs, little gained when she returns. How sad that at such a young age, an implicit mental model of despair about life-giving connection is so fully established. What gives hope in this situation is that this detachment is only on the surface. The implicit longing for connection creates measurable changes in these children's autonomic responses (Siegel, 1999). (Such research can assure us that our patients bring this living need to therapy.) We can notice how easily these children redirect their abundant energy toward playing alone. Building on this ability to focus on what they are doing, many dismissing adults lead outwardly successful lives, although their partners and children will often complain that they feel insignificant compared to the focus lavished on work. We might experience them as resilient within the world of work but disconnected in their personal lives.

One of the challenges in therapy is establishing a living interpersonal connection, always the foundation for successful work. It is so important for us to be mindful of our whole-person response to this hurting individual, especially if we have had a dismissing parent, because if we fall into despair about connection, consciously or unconsciously, we will simply reinforce what our patient most deeply believes: There is no one there. Remaining in a warm, empathic state for as long as it takes is the leading edge of releasing this person from prison. Fortunately, there are lots of tools available to foster vertical and horizontal integration, as long as we remain steadfast in our hope of connection. We will explore this repertoire of help throughout Part II.

Ambivalence

Near the other end of the spectrum, *ambivalently attached children* and their *preoccupied parents* (Ainsworth et al., 1978; Hesse, 1999) have inner worlds that feel like a jungle rather than a desert. The word *ambivalence* reflects children's uncertainty about how their mother will respond to them. Will she provide safety, warmth, and empathy, or be so internally overwhelmed (and overwhelming) that she can't accurately sense their states of mind or care for their needs? Clearly, this mother will create mostly a neuroception of potential danger because of her unpredictability, stimulating the sympathetic nervous system with its attendant anxiety. Subjectively, closeness to such a mother often leaves the children vigilant and insecure, but with some hope of warm connection. As they build representations of Mother internally, contradictory pictures will emerge. We can imagine that often the upsetting one has more synaptic strength because of the emotional intensity evoked by fear. If this perceptual bias becomes strong enough, the children may even have difficulty receiving her when she is empathic. Sadly, with their mother unable to accurately read their signals and adding her own anxiety to theirs, they will likely often erupt out of their windows of tolerance into anxious hyperarousal, patterning this uncomfortable physiological and emotional state into their developing brains. In contrast to the rigidity of avoidant patterns, ambivalence tends to draw the dyad toward chaos. Over time, a mental model of expecting relationships to be ragged and unpredictable takes firm root.

In the Strange Situation, these 1-year-olds are so preoccupied with attachment concerns that they have difficulty focusing on play. Instead, for the most part, they stay engaged with their mother until she leaves, sometimes seeming fearful and upset, and then cry when she returns (Ainsworth et al., 1978). Even if she is quite comforting, they have a hard time experiencing regulation, so they will cry, stop, and cry again, rarely finding the focus and energy to return to exploring their world. From a child's perspective, this response makes sense and is both organized and adaptive, since the primary goal is to maintain the relationship with Mother—and that's hard work. However, it is easy to see how this pattern lays the foundation for a frightened and clinging adult response to overtures of attachment, sometimes in work situations as well as personal relationships. Other people may sometimes feel overwhelmed and shy away from these adults because resonance circuits may communicate the sense of chaos inside. Of course, this withdrawal only heightens their fear and leads to more behaviors that tend to drive people away.

What is Mother's part in forming the internal world of these upset and overwhelmed children? From her own childhood, she is likely struggling with contradictory internal models of attachment, leading her to fluctuate from availability to being so preoccupied with the perceptual biases streaming from her past that she is effectively attending to the projection of herself rather than to her children. For example, a mother who has not resolved her own childhood pain, but has determined that her children will not suffer the lack of attachment she experienced, may thrust herself ceaselessly upon her babies, not able to sense when they need a calm mother or solitude and quiet. It is as though she sees her own small, abandoned self there instead of them. In more severe forms, her children may be seen accurately only when their real needs happen to coincide with Mother's ongoing projections, a truly tragic situation in my experience, because Mother's response makes no sense to her children.

Some milder forms of ambivalent attachment may also arise from contradictory messages given by Mom when her children want to move outward and explore (Marvin et al., 2002). This mom is often able to sustain a warm, empathic connection as long as her children want to remain close, but when the outward surge toward the world begins, even though her inner feeling/mental model sends the message that the world is dangerous she may say, "Go play!" The resulting confusion undermines this child's sense of safety both with Mom and in the world at large.

How can we think about the brain structure that the preoccupied parent is passing to her children? There is striking emotional dysregulation with varying intensity and frequency, so we can hypothesize that integration of the right limbic system with the middle prefrontal region (vertical integration) is patchy. We can also imagine that there are some dissociated neural nets within the right limbic region that carry considerable emotional and bodily energy when activated, sweeping her away from the present moment and blinding her with strong perceptual bias. Thus, the image of an emotional jungle is apt, especially the sense of getting lost in the undergrowth and dragging her children with her. Building on dis-integrated right-mode processing, we can also be quite sure that horizontal integration is not solid. There is no coherent sense of herself within her story, because left-mode processing is having such difficulty making sense of the chaotic experiences sometimes pouring out of the right. Instead, when we listen to the narrative of her early life, we sense how she is bounced helplessly from past to present to past again, tangled in the world of implicit surges. If we remember that implicit recall does not include a sense that these things happened in the past, it is easy to understand why this person has such difficulty keeping past and present separate, even when recalling explicit events. When this breakdown of horizontal integration is in ascendance, narrative, memory, and state integration are also out of reach.

When she shares her story, the response to a question about childhood might sound something like this: "You know, when I was small, my parents argued sometimes, but it wasn't so bad, and this morning I fought with my 6-year-old for an hour like my brother and I fought— and still do. But that's ancient history and still happens now, and I wish it wouldn't, but why should I care?" Because past and present are so entangled, it is very difficult for the storyteller to stick with one or the other. Most revealing, however, is the intensity and push of the narrative as well as the sense of going in circles. The wealth of detail may be hard to follow, so often only a confused sense of the inner community emerges. We might sometimes get the image of many emotionally vivid people milling around our offices with their emotions swirling together to conceal a true sense of who they are. From a family systems perspective, the word *enmeshed* might arise in our minds.

As we listen to these narratives, our own bodies may become unexpectedly anxious, and we might feel the need to cut off the person so that we can encourage him or her to better organize the tale. We want left-mode processing to give us the comfort of making sense of the jumbled information from the right that is washing over us and threatening to drown our own limbic region. If our history includes a preoccupied parent, the urge may be particularly powerful. However, if we can sit mindfully with our discomfort, at least three powerful processes will unfold: (1) We will develop profound, viscerally based understanding of this person's daily life experience; (2) we will provide the milieu for this distraught person to gradually have an attachment-enhancing

Being a Brain-Wise Therapist

neuroception of safety; and (3) our calmness will set up the possibility of resonance circuits ameliorating the person's upset body and emotions. We can become a strong force for beginning to pattern regulation just by being calm in the monsoon. As with avoidant attachment, gaining a foothold of initial joining is the leading edge of healing.

Disorganization

Many dismissing parents love their children, but do not know how to connect with them. At one end of the spectrum, we find parents who quietly hate or reject their children. At the other end, some preoccupied parents carry so much pain that they are continually immersed in the terror of the past, rather than only visiting it occasionally. In both cases, the pain and fear surrounding connection with their children is so extreme that the tragic result is often *disorganized/disoriented attachment* in children with a parent who has, or parents who have, an *unresolved/ disorganized state of mind with respect to attachment* (Main & Solomon, 1986, 1990). The characteristic that pushes us into this category is the parents' inner state of fright/terror or outer state of frightening/terrifying their children. This is usually the result of the parent's unresolved trauma and reflects abundant dissociated neural nets that, when triggered, isolate the parent in a state of mind unmodulated by any middle prefrontal processes. "At the mercy of . . ." is the phrase that most accurately reflects how out of control a parent feels under these circumstances.

How can we imagine what determines whether a parent remains frozen in terror or acts out? If the parent developed an internal working model of victimization (through the nature of the traumatic circumstances or through temperament), she will often carry the terror within, feeling emotionally as though she were still in the midst of the abuse. If instead that working model casts her as a perpetrator, she will be more likely to repeat the terrifying scenario with her child. Our understanding of internalization lets us know that both the victimized child and terrifying perpetrator live inside as possible states of mind.

Since development of brain structure is a parallel process, it follows that children of an unresolved parent will likely have a similarly fragmented inner world. When taken to the extreme, this pattern lays the foundation for what used to be aptly called *multiple personalities*. We can imagine an inner community of isolated pairs of parents and children in repetitive dances, unmodified by information and energy flowing elsewhere in the brain. In such a structure, some of the pairs may subjectively experience great disorganization, but the overall view of the system shows a very tight structure developed to rigidly control what kind of information is encoded with each pair. In the vicissitudes of severe abuse, there is adaptive wisdom in this response; however, we already begin to sense how this structure also creates internal extremes of both chaos and rigidity.

A sense of unresolvable dilemmas lies at the heart of disorganized attachment. When infants (whose need for closeness is in full flower) encounter a terrified/terrifying parent, they have an insoluble problem, what Main and Hesse (1999) call "fright without solution." Everything in these children tells them to go toward the parent for comfort, but every approach yields new fear. The terror can be so great that they have a neuroception of life threat and freeze. A parent in the grip of a disorganized state is incapable of perceiving her children accurately, much less mustering a contingent response, and often swings wildly from state to state. Under these circumstances, her children have no possibility of developing an organized, adaptive strategy in the moment. As regulation fails utterly for all of them, her children's brains are structured around abrupt, chaotic shifts that leave them disoriented. The window of tolerance for Mother and children is narrow and unpredictable. Images of flags still tethered to their poles, being whipped to tatters by hurricane winds, might be a helpful symbol for this anguished co-destructing dance.

If we were to observe 1-year-olds with disorganized attachment in the Strange Situation with the unresolved parent, we might witness the incarnation of impossible dilemmas (Main & Solomon, 1990). Even before Mother leaves, they might reach for her while looking away, or freeze in a dissociated trance, or take two steps forward and then collapse on the floor. The overall impression would be one of utter disarray, with no ability to imagine a way to be soothed. Once the warmth of relationship has reactivated their attachment system in therapy, our patients will sometimes relate to us in the same way when they fall into pockets of disorganization.

As with all types of attachment, there are degrees of severity. Patches of disorganization can develop in the absence of abuse as children build mental models based on their parent's inner state (Hesse & Main, 1999). Sadly, the activity of resonance circuits alone between a tender child and well-intentioned parent can result in structural disorganization for this young mind if the parent is terrified. Research has also shown that

Being a Brain-Wise Therapist

neglected children are as likely to have disorganized attachments as those who were abused—approximately 82% of the time (Carlson, Cicchetti, Barnett, & Braunwald, 1989). Without warm connections to structure the infant brain, it cannot find a coherent shape.

Main and Solomon (1986) also suggest that disorganization always exists in tandem with another attachment pattern: secure, avoidant, or ambivalent. This makes sense since the neural nets holding the disorganization are kept quite isolated from the rest of brain development. This means that a secure attachment with Dad could lie side by side with some ambivalent and some disorganized patterns with Mom. The good news is that as these chaotic neural nets open in the presence of empathy, there will be an inner community as well as outer resources to meet the disorganized members of the inner world, providing support for integration.

When we listen to our patients' narratives, disorganization is most apt to reveal itself when we talk about early childhood or address issues of abuse. We might then notice the present tense used for the past, long pauses that have the feel of dissociation, or a confused sense of not being able to find words to describe an upsetting early experience. Such a narrative might sound like this: "Mom? I don't . . . Well, . . . She died. When was that? She is a strange person. Can't quite . . . I'm cold." We might feel fear and confusion tug at our own hearts and bodies as well. This way of telling the story indicates that these people do not have a formed sense of the terrifying experience, but are struggling with the upwelling of fearful implicit sensations, images, behavioral impulses, and perceptions without being able to give them a shape. Occasionally, under the influence of patients' narratives, I have observed and felt my own cognitive functions swirl into incoherence, allowing me to experience the visceral whirlpool of their disorganized world. As always, a mindful stance to these responses is the richest entry into another's world.

It is important to keep in mind that neither our patients' refusal to talk about their painful histories nor a tearful recounting of events necessarily indicates disorganized attachment. Both may instead be healthy responses to significant pain. Also, we need to be aware that for many patients, these patches of fragmentation have been successfully isolated, except when triggered, so they may not show up in therapy for some time. As empathy deepens, bringing a neuroception of safety, these painful experiences will emerge in their own good time. It is also useful to remember that pockets of disorganization are rooted in unresolved grief, so a traumatic history does not necessarily indicate current fragmentation. The joyful news is that later relationships (including the one with us) can repair earlier interpersonal disasters, and that everything from genetic factors supporting resilience to transient but intense empathic relationships can catalyze repair. The brain is always seeking integration, and any experience that removes a blockage creates new flow toward complexity.

Adults with disorganized attachments are often filled with shame at the outset of therapy because they are aware that their out-of-control behaviors have hurt the ones they love most. This makes it so important for us to develop our resources of empathy for people who have harmed others. A profound understanding of the neural roots of implicit-driven actions is a first step, but we also will need openness to any patches of unresolved trauma lingering in us. Shamed people have both inner tenderness and perceptual biases that make them acutely sensitive to nonverbal criticism and rejection, particularly in intimate relationships such as therapy. They will pull within themselves unless they sense that we know *they are not to blame for what has come before, while being clear that they are now responsible for changing the neural disintegration that lies at the heart of these actions*. This is a powerful and sometimes upsetting idea for us.

As you sit with that sentence, notice the response in your body in particular. Our parents may have often delivered powerful messages about the meaning of behavior, tying it to our worth. Choice and responsibility may have topped their list of values. We have those parents within us, still sharing their views in a visceral way that will impact how we respond to the idea that some actions are implicitly determined.

Resolving old messages and then developing our own coherent philosophy about freedom, responsibility, and blame will become an important foundation for working with clients. In my experience, coming to peace with inner messages may allow us to embody compassion for self and other that becomes the wellspring for bathing our patients' shamed and wounded hearts.

We have spent a great deal of time getting the feel of these earliest attachments because everyone has them, regardless of diagnosis. All of

     Being a Brain-Wise Therapist

us have brains shaped by our earliest relationships and modified by all emotionally significant encounters in our lives. Additionally, they are the foundation of relational difficulty for almost all our patients. Because immature but developing brains leave people with childhood amnesia for approximately the first 3–5 years of life, most of our patients will have difficulty telling us in words what is most deeply troubling them. However, they will tell us through other means: how we feel when we are with them; what we sense is dis-integrated in their brains; the way they share their stories—in words, art, or sandplay; and their mental models of relationship as displayed in past and current relationships. Listening mindfully with our whole person—body, feelings, and thoughts—we can enter these worlds with strong, integrating empathy and insight. Once there, we will wander in the unique landscape that is each person's inner community, and collaboratively develop ways to speed the journey toward neural integration/inner community resolution.

Resting on this foundation of understanding the brain, mind, and attachment, we are now going to let the vocabulary of neuroscience slip partially into the background in order to develop another way of talking about what unfolds internally. We have found that for some patients, the concepts and visions of neuroscience have been profoundly reassuring, giving a scientific base for the relational work and making sense of their painful experiences. For some, however, our overtures in that direction have felt cold, as though the humanity were being stripped from our endeavors. For them, the vocabulary of inner community has felt more life-giving. In reality, these are two mutually compatible ways of approaching the same truths about how we get hurt and how we heal, one expressed more in terms of science and one more in the language of subjective experience. Developing ease in flowing between these two vocabularies can broaden our perspective and give us the flexibility to adapt to each patient's needs.

Chapter 6

Picturing
the Inner
Community

Most of what follows is drawn from many years of subjective but mindful experience, both in my own therapy and through having the privilege of accompanying others along their dedicated healing paths. Out of those encounters with the deeper mind has come a myth (in the sense of explanatory story) of one way in which we can picture the inner world. In one sense, it is my coherent narrative about what it means to be human. It is certainly not the only healing story, but over the years, I have found that people resonate with this vision of the inner world because it helps them make sense of their daily experiences.

You may recognize similarities to Richard Schwartz's (1997, 2007) Internal Family Systems model. As his patients talked about their experience, he began to form a picture of what he calls "subpersonalities," or parts of the self. Since all paradigms are informed by the basic perceptual patterns of their creators, Schwartz's family systems background became the framework for understanding and working with these parts of the psyche. As he says, aspects of this perspective have emerged in transactional analysis, psychosynthesis, and other forms of therapy, although not fleshed out to this extent. While recognizing many commonalities, at least three significant differences between Schwartz's work and ours spring from the different foundations on which they are built. He believes that the basic structure of subpersonalities exists independent of experience, that these parts exist as individuals rather than in the relational pairs that brought them into existence, and that the role of the therapist is to inspire self-leadership, rather than become a central presence in the patient's inner world. All of these assumptions are congruent with systems thinking and have formed the backdrop to an effective healing path.

As you will see, because our work is rooted in object relations theory, attachment theory, and more recently, interpersonal neurobiology, we have formed our paradigm around the centrality of relational experience in shaping the inner world. Beginning even in utero and continuing powerfully in infancy, interactions with the mother initiate neural firings that encode and strengthen certain states of mind, while at the same time, resonance circuits embed the presence of the mother. We believe this to be the origin of the inner community's relational pairs. Because neuroplasticity is optimally supported in empathic relationships, and because internalization is a process continuing throughout life, we experience the therapist's presence as a central ingredient in the healing process. The moment-to-moment attunement between patient and therapist helps rewire the relational inner world, while resonance circuits embed the therapist as a comforting member of the inner community. From an attachment perspective, this makes sense, since both wounding and healing occur in the context of relationship.

Overview of the Inner Community

With this basic outline in mind, we can now explore the inner community perspective in more detail. This concept invites us to view ourselves as inherently multiplistic, with rich, active internal relational lives developed and shaped in childhood and modified by later life experience. The neurobiological reality of *multiple states of mind* suggests that, with repetition, certain states would develop sufficient synaptic strength to become *traits* of mind, or stable aspects of our personality (Siegel, 1999). These stable aspects of our inner world embody implicit assumptions about patterns of relationship that then extend outward to shape and influence every aspect of current relationships. As noted above, this perspective shares common ground with both object relations and attachment theories of how human selfhood forms, is wounded, and can heal. Echoes of Heinz Kohut's (1976) emphasis on empathy as the healing agent will be heard, as will Erik Erikson's (1989) belief that we always retain the seeds of possible healing within us. In addition, his eight stages are part of the backdrop, as is Murray Bowen's (1994) rich understanding of intergenerational legacies.

The Process of Internalization

However, at the heart of the inner community paradigm lies the *process of internalization*. All paradigms find their uniqueness by directing attention toward particular capacities of the psyche. Inner community focuses on the way we take in, and then live out, the relationships we internalize in both our earliest days and throughout life. Neuroscience has given us the tools to understand how this internalization process might work through the resonance circuits that link us with one another. Quantum physics is also beginning to suggest how quantum processes in the brain might also support internalization (Schwartz & Begley, 2002; Zohar, 1991).

From a mindful, curious stance, try on these questions, sitting with whatever your deeper mind might share. When you think about your past, who comes vividly, viscerally, and perhaps visually to mind? What can you sense about the aliveness of earlier versions of yourself? How many generations have taken up residence in your mind? Do you experience them as static images or living presences? How much have they changed over time? What happens if you strike up a relationship with any of your inner community members? If you ask these questions over a period of time, you might experience a powerful unfolding of your community within. In general, the more you sense about your internal world, the more you will be able to catalyze your patients' awareness of theirs.

I'm going to begin by suggesting that some powerful form of internalization process is part of the genetic inheritance of human beings. The timeline for how early this internalization begins is being pushed back into the womb, as research is revealing that a newborn's nervous system and biochemical profile are shaped by the mother's mental state during pregnancy (Field et al., 2006). In reviewing the research, Field says: "Newborns of depressed mothers then show a biochemical/physiological profile, that mimics their mothers' prenatal biochemical/physiological profile including elevated cortisol, lower levels of dopamine and serotonin, greater relative right frontal EEG activation and lower vagal tone" (p. 455). This is also the profile of an adult in a major depressive episode, as we shall discover in Part II. The good news from this team is that massage of the mother during the pregnancy and the newborn after birth can change this profile. In a different vein, Barbara Kisilevsky and her team in China have found that babies learn to distinguish between Mother's voice and the voice of another before birth (Kisilevsky et al., 2003), as indicated by changes in heart rhythm. It is significant to discover that relational experience, as well as genetics and other environmental impacts, are influencing the earliest development of brain and nervous system—in short, that we are relational beings as soon as the neural equipment becomes available. As research pushes ahead, it would not be surprising to learn that early implicit memories also form in the womb, guided by the mother's felt experience of her pregnancy, her attitude toward the baby, and her general feeling of safety or danger in her world. A tightly woven dance between fetus and mother seems to be revealing itself.

One experience in therapy provided some anecdotal but fairly persuasive evidence for this early encoding. About 6 months after the Northridge earthquake in 1994, a woman in her early 50s came in for treatment, reporting ongoing severe anxiety. She had not been near the epicenter, but had been awakened with some significant shaking. Her family lost electrical power for awhile, but nothing was broken, and no one she knew had been harmed. As a long-time Southern California resident, she had been through many other earthquakes without this kind of persistent anxiety. We did a family history that revealed a lovely coherent narrative—warm parents who were somewhat strict, close and pleasant ties between all family members as adults, delightful sense of humor about childhood foibles, realistic acceptance of parental warts, rich sorrow about losses, and a satisfying marriage with three grown children. I felt warm and energized in her presence. She was emotionally engaged with her story and with me, exhibiting many signs of secure attachment

Then we began our detective work, on the trail of her mind–body's knowledge of the roots of her current upset. We talked about whether she had experienced anxiety at any time in her life before, and found that just preceding the birth of her first child, she'd experienced about a month of anxious concern about her child's safety in the world. This might well be in the normal range with a first baby, but we made a mental note anyway. Next, we investigated any ways in which this earthquake might have been different from others, and found that her family had moved in late 1993. She got very still, then said, "My mind is trying to tell me something." Within a minute, the auditory and visual experience of transformers exploding at the power plant in her neighborhood during the earthquake came strongly into her consciousness, together with the

feeling that this was meaningful, especially since the recollection immediately increased her anxiety. Sitting mindfully with this experience, we
asked her inner world for more connections. She began to have what she
described as a "thumping feeling" in her body. Then she lit up with new
awareness and said, "I need to talk to my mother about what happened
a couple of months before I was born. We were in Hawaii during Pearl
Harbor. My mom was very pregnant, and I don't know exactly what happened that day."

Because her parents and grandparents were in the midst of a tape-
recorded family history project, we have the luxury of having her mother's
exact words (modified only for the sake of confidentiality). "Your father
was on a ship in Pearl Harbor and I was outside, just enjoying the day
and thinking about you. Then there were planes and then bombs. I was
up on a hill and I remember running back and forth, holding my belly in
all the horrible noise and smoke, with the ground shaking. I kept thinking that I probably wouldn't ever see your father again, and you would
never have a father. It was a very long time before I knew whether he was
alive, or maimed, or OK. It seems like days, but maybe not that long.
I was just frantic the whole time. Worst time of my life. It's not something
I like to even think about." This last sentence tells us why these hours
had never become part of the otherwise well-developed family narrative. When my patient came back to therapy after that conversation, she
intuitively knew that the thumping in her body and the anxiety were
rooted in this experience, and that perhaps her prebirth anxiety with her
first child sprang from there as well. While the new insight was settling
for her mind, her body and feelings were still jittery. So together we began
to "hold" that almost-born child, soothing and regulating the waves of
anxiety that would fill the room when she was "with" the pounding of the
bombs. Within about a month of working together in this way, her natural calmness reestablished itself in body and mind, and she said she felt
like she had returned to herself.

While there may be another explanation for the emergence of her
anxiety in response to the exploding transformers, this one made sense
to her intuitively and led to rapid relief. Based on my experience with
her, I began to pay attention to my patients' prebirth experiences, and we
have frequently found meaningful correlations between those emotionally charged events and upwelling implicit-based experiences in the
present. I am most convinced of the validity of these discoveries (which
emerge most clearly in the body) when working with this information

leads to changes in longstanding and often severely disruptive relational patterns.

Regardless of our opinion of how much influence prenatal experience can have on us, the rich relational world that is being established in the earliest days after birth helps us understand what happens when we move into new relationships, only to find old patterns reasserting themselves. Internal relationships tell us what we can expect in external relationships. These myths carry so much power that we respond to them like heat-seeking missiles, consistently on target in finding people who will help us replicate what we most deeply believe. However, this very same capacity for reactivation means that when we decide to change these patterns, we can access the roots of the myth, bring in new resources of relational support, and change our foundational expectations (mental models). In my experience, when the inside changes, the outside follows. Then we can be missiles in search of a different kind of target. Sharing this viewpoint early in therapy supports hope for change in patients, especially when accompanied by explanations of how these patterns are held in the brain.

The process of internalization continues throughout life, creating a rich and complex inner community. The earliest relational processes possess a unique power because of the intensity of joining with our parents and because our brains are quite undifferentiated at the time. Our minds have little (if any) capacity to filter out or organize these energized encounters, and our brains are literally being structured in these earliest days. Infancy is also the time when we are most in need of contact, both because of our physical and emotional dependency, and because of the way empathic relationships help us form a subjective sense of a continuous self. The attachment system is in full flower, so we are intensely open to new experience. However, at no time in life do interpersonal processes stop shaping our minds—not until the last neuron has fired.

If we adopt this picture of development, it is easy to see how we would gradually take on a cast of characters internally. Every time we enter a meaningful relationship, some part of the other person becomes part of us, as does the subjective experience of the relationship. For example, if a child is consistently shamed in her third-grade classroom by an insensitive teacher, then that emotionally charged encounter will leave its mark. If most others in the girl's internal world are empathic and support a positive sense of herself, then the teacher's voice will be only a whisper and may have little effect on this child's unfolding relationships.

However, if the teacher's voice is added to others inside who denigrate this child, then a chorus of negativity will bombard her internally throughout life, changing the way she sees herself and relates to others. Expanding this small example to include all the meaningful people we encounter throughout life begins to reveal the extent of each person's inner community.

In my experience, each inner community is as unique as a fingerprint, yet these communities share some common inhabitants as well. With the proviso that no structural picture can really capture the dynamic and fluid arena of the internal world, I am going to offer a structure nonetheless, as a static starting point for what I hope will become moving pictures in your mind.

An Inner Community Schema

Our patients consistently describe layers within their psyche, from most available to consciousness to most completely buried in the deeper mind—we could say, from most integrated to most dissociated. Arranged spatially and in a very simplified form, they look something like the diagram in Figure 6.1.

This is the simplest of schemas. Actual inner communities include grandparents, coaches, friends, characters from television, movies, videogames, books, sports heroes, and many others who have made an impact on the internalizing person—for good or ill. Thinking back through our relational experiences can help us begin to find those who have the strongest presence in our inner community, as well as significant minor characters. One of my patients with a profoundly abusive mother felt she gained some rudimentary maternal attitudes from internalizing the television mom played by Donna Reed. She told me she continually asked herself, while watching the show, "What's she feeling? What's she feeling?" rather than noticing what she did. Somehow, she was able to use this experience to pick up enough ability to read her children's social signals that she became a much more available parent than her own mother had been.

There is certainly some overlap between the inner community perspective and other therapeutic models. Many paradigms recognize the continuing influence of the past on the present and may speak of internalized values, memories, family scripts, and the like. The picture here is somewhat different. It is proposed that we take in the whole person as we have subjectively experienced him or her. That person then continues

Being a Brain-Wise Therapist

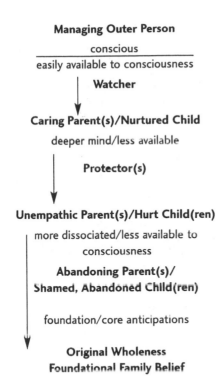

Managing Outer Person	The face we share with the world.
<u>conscious</u>	A presence within the mind designed to draw in as much empathy from the environment as possible; possibly the caring observer.
easily available to consciousness	
Watcher	
Caring Parent(s)/Nurtured Child	The part of the family experience that is most nurturing and kept closest to consciousness.
deeper mind/less available	
Protector(s)	Parts that develop to defend against incoming pain in order to protect the already-hurt children from more injury.
Unempathic Parent(s)/Hurt Child(ren)	Relational parent–child pairs who are locked in the deeper mind because of uncomforted pain.
more dissociated/less available to consciousness	
Abandoning Parent(s)/ Shamed, Abandoned Child(ren)	Relational pairs, locked away more deeply, experiencing the most profound pain.
foundation/core anticipations	
Original Wholeness Foundational Family Belief	At the bottom of all painful experience, our original hope of connection lies side by side with the core family beliefs about the nature of the world and relationships; most likely, reflect implicit mental models.

Figure 6.1 Diagram of a prototypical inner community.

to be a living presence internally, interacting with others in the community inside. This individual can change (as long as unresolved pain doesn't keep the internalized person locked in the dissociated past), converse, share feelings and experiences, as well as convey an overall impression about the value and meaning of life. We might say that through our resonance circuits we have taken in these internal ones, who now embody states of mind that continue to actively influence our internal and external life.

I would also like to propose something that may not have full scientific validation at this point, but is a common experience among the people with whom I have worked. It may be possible that when we internalize our parents, we take on their relational experience with their parents (our grandparents), whether we have ever met them or not. This makes some sense if we think in terms of our parents having had energized relationships within their families-of-origin, making those relational experiences part of their mind. When we then have emotionally salient contact with our parents, internalizing them, our grandparents and others may well be part of that internalization. My patients and I have discovered that working with these internal grandparents can sometimes be a powerful and necessary part of drawing the inner community into an empathic whole.

In the schema above, internalized children and parents are mostly self-explanatory, except possibly for the number of pairs found inside. Whenever there is repeated emotional intensity of a particular valence, a parent–child pair will form. A patient might have a shaming parent–shamed child pair, an angry parent–fearful child pair, an empathic parent–joyous child pair, and so on. Other pairs may develop around specific traumatic events. In actual practice, patients will take you to their relational pairs and teach you about their origin, meaning, and impact on current life. I experience gratitude and a deep sense of privilege in the invitation to know these inner communities this deeply.

Watchers and Protectors

A word about watchers and protectors may be helpful. Many clinicians who have worked with hypnosis or supported patients with dissociative identity disorder have discovered a kind of watching part in the mind that is subjectively experienced as a person (Putnam, 1989; J. M. Schwartz, 1997; Siegel, 1999; Watkins, 1997) and given names such as "internal self-helper," "inner guide," or "hidden observer" (Hilgard, 1977). The majority of us reveal such an inner person under conditions of hypnosis or guided imagery (Siegel, 1999). Taking a third-person perspective, as though surveying the entire territory, this state of mind/inner community member may comment on what the person is doing, or should do. For the most part (except in the case of severe depressive or bipolar disorders), the voice is benign, apparently seeking to aid integration and coherence (Siegel, 1999). This voice may be rooted in empathic exchanges we have had early in life; however, more research will be needed to better understand the neurobiological substrate of this aspect of the mind.

In our experience, the role of the watcher is somewhat expanded. Speaking in the language of subjectivity, in an environment of empathy and calmness, watchers appear to encourage the inner protectors to step out of the way so that therapist and patient can journey into the deeper mind. This emerging process involves our mind's evaluative capacity in some way and is activated in response to the neuroception of safety.

This activation, in turn, allows the interpersonal connection to flower, no doubt assisting integration. Subjectively, if the relational environment is deemed empathic enough, the children inside slowly become available. At least, this is how patient and therapist alike tend to experience it.

Some of my patients have told me about very tangible watchers, often without us having discussed the likelihood of such a presence. One watcher took on the symbolic shape of Robin Hood pacing on a high wall, seeming to be half-watcher, half-protector. Others have been a yellow bird in a sandplay tree, a mysterious fox, a quiet angel, a pair of enormous eyes, and a teenager collapsed against a wall in defeat. In this last case, the influx of traumatic events had finally defeated this watcher's capacity for hope. As therapy progressed, she recovered and became a source of increasing wisdom and support. Sometimes watchers do not have symbolic forms, but are contained more in a feeling of benevolent guidance from within. From what I can gather, the capacity for some kind of watching presence appears to be standard equipment in the psyche, but then can be impacted by relational events in the environment. Elsewhere in these writings, we have talked about a "caring observer," and the subjective experience of this state of mind seems quite similar to that of a watcher. However, a number of my patients report feeling this watching presence from very early in life, sometimes in the first year, before an age when we would expect there to be the possibility of explicit memory, much less the neural integration required to experience a caring observer state of mind. This anecdotal evidence suggests that there is more to be discovered.

Protectors are a different matter. They appear to take up their guard post in response to pain, and their job is to provide safety for the injured child within as well as the outer managing self. Some guardians direct their attention toward others whom they perceive as potentially hurtful, whereas others appear to control the amount of potentially disruptive pain coming to consciousness. Anger toward a demeaning boss, for example, puts up a protective wall, as it were, against incoming criticism, while intellect-only explanations of painful events can keep us insulated from the emotional impact so that we can function. As we might expect, these states of mind are often modeled on the defensive strategies we have internalized from our families. As with watchers, protectors often take on interesting symbolic forms internally. My patients have seen everything from fortress walls and Wild West characters to wolves.

One person who had two very injured parents, one of them psychotic, had an entire troop of internal clowns whose lives were focused around not allowing her to have any visceral/emotional connection to her strange and terrifying memories. They were enormously entertaining and creative, but, tragically, they also kept her trapped on the surface of her life, while implicit-based patterns embodying all-consuming fears disrupted her relationships. The family story told her that as an infant, she had cried every waking hour (except when she was nursing) for the first 3 months of her life, while her psychotic mother held her day and night, in a well-meaning but vain attempt to soothe her. In the arms of a calm, reassuring mother, such closeness could lead to secure attachment, but in the arms of this severely disorganized mother, her baby took in nothing but fragmenting terror. Maybe we can allow our bodies to imagine the impact of this experience on an infant wide open to her mother's world. The wail of a blues singer, echoing throughout their apartment complex, quieted her for the first time, perhaps organizing her distress through this sorrowful sound. After we had been doing therapy together for a number of years, the clowns were replaced by fog, which then gradually lifted, allowing us to begin the long work of repairing her highly disorganized and terrifying infant world. We could both sense why she had needed to spend a long time internalizing the warm resources for regulation and organization that were available in our relationship before beginning that process.

Regardless of the symbolic representation, we might think of protectors as angels with flaming swords, standing between the child or functioning adult and further harm. Their tactics include distraction, addictions, humor, anger, withdrawal, and violence, to name a few. However, no matter how ugly the defensive means, the intention is always protective. Maintaining this conviction with patients can help them develop compassion for parts they have previously feared or disliked. As with any other internal part, conversation and transformation are possible. We have also found that healing the past pain and fear reduces their need to be unrealistically vigilant in the present, gradually allowing them to become an integral and valuable part of the healthy inner community.

The drawing in Figure 6.2 illustrates a specific inner community, accompanied by a narrative (Figure 6.3) that may soften the edges of your awareness of this internal world, giving you flexibility as you approach your own and that of others. We want to avoid creating a rigid schema, but instead want to sense a highly creative internal process unfolding in each individual.

Being a Brain-Wise Therapist

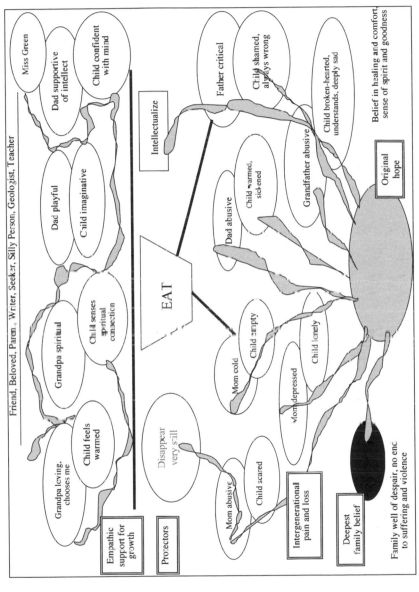

Friend, Beloved, Parent, Writer, Seeker, Silly Person, Geologist, Teacher

Miss Green

Dad supportive of intellect

Child confident with mind

Intellectualize

Father critical

Child shamed, always wrong

Child broken-hearted, understands, deeply sad

Belief in healing and comfort, sense of spirit and goodness

Dad playful

Child imaginative

Dad abusive

Child warmed, sickened

Grandfather abusive

Original hope

Grandpa spiritual

Child senses spiritual connection

EAT

Mom cold

Child empty

Child lonely

Mom depressed

Grandpa loving, chooses me

Child feels warmed

Disappear very still

Mom abusive

Child scared

Empathic support for growth

Protectors

Intergenerational pain and loss

Deepest family belief

Family well of despair, no end to suffering and violence

Figure 6.2 Diagram of Katherine's inner community.

This story and drawing emerged in response to a discussion about how inner communities might work. We had talked about the possibility of managers, watchers, helpful internal people, protectors, buried people, and deep messages. She took it from there.

When I think about myself in the world, I see that I have lots of different roles, but I also feel like there's a lot going on underneath that makes a difference to me on the surface. Still, these are ways I think people see me—and I see myself. I notice that these managers are all positive and am not sure what that means.

Since we began therapy, I had a sense of a helper inside, some little warning voice, some part that seemed to know more than I do. I think that's my watcher. I feel like she (and I know she's a she) is on my side, but can't really tell you why. It comforts me to know she's there.

When I think about the relationships that feel best to me, except for Miss Green (my very loving and smart 6th-grade teacher), it seems like they're just pieces of relationships. I had good times with both my father and grandfather, but they both also abused me. When I drew the picture, I was especially surprised to find that there's nothing of my mom in the layer of support. I think that's sad, but I really don't feel attached to her at all, so there's not much feeling about her, period. It's also interesting to me that my grandmother is nowhere to be seen. She lived with us since I was a baby, but I have no feel of her at all. She's like fog or smoke. I found myself wanting to use colors, so yellow is for what feels spiritual to me [light gray in the connecting streamers in this picture, plus watcher, spiritual grandfather, and Miss Green], fuchsia for warm feelings [grandfather in empathic layer], green for imagination [dad in empathic layer], and blue for intellect [protector layer]. I noticed that the feeling of these people came to me more vividly with the colors.

I think the most powerful way I still take care of myself in a not-healthy way is through eating when I'm lonely or anxious. I learned to do that very early in life. Even in the midst of so much abuse, there was always good food, especially fresh-

Figure 6.3 Katherine's story.

While you take in the picture and read the story in Figures 6.2 and 6.3, see what sensations and images concerning your own inner community arise in your mind. Pull out drawing materials and encourage your own internal people to appear before you. Experiencing and embracing the layers of your inner community can be a valuable way to internalize and enliven these ideas.

baked goodies. It feels like this part pops to the surface at those times and pushes my usual outer people away. I know this is a place I need a lot more work because I can't seem to consciously choose to eat well and moderately, even though I know a great deal about nutrition and am fully aware of how much better I feel when I eat well. I've noticed that the eating gets worse when I'm stressed, I'm guessing because stress feels just like childhood, so I do what I did then. The other two ways of protecting myself have gotten a lot less over the years. I used to use my mind to keep others away from me. I didn't do it consciously, but people would surprise me by saying they felt intimidated. The disappearing part doesn't come up very often anymore, but I know as a child, I would hold very still, hoping that no one would notice me. Now, that only happens when I'm really afraid. I think I could have put in a small square for anger, too, but I guess I'm not ready to make it that concrete yet. I could never be angry as a child, and now I can see that sometimes it's a good response, or at least a good feeling. Maybe if we do this again, I'll be able to draw it in.

When I started to think about the things I've buried really deep, I could feel other parts of my father and grandfather, as well as lots of Mom—but Grandma still didn't show up. And I could really begin to see how these people inside are attached to the various protective parts of me. I think these are the parts we need to work with now, and I have such a strong sense that they will each come up when they are ready. I also know that they're not always so buried as I might think; they pop out when relationships aren't going well. It's very interesting.

You asked me to think about the deepest message I got from my family as well as my own deepest belief about life—something beyond my parents. That's what the circles are at the bottom. The black part feels like a well, like something deep that could swallow me up, but the ribbons of gold [light gray] weaving through everything feel more buoyant, like they wouldn't let any of my internal world fall. The bigger circle is how much hope I feel, especially since we started doing this work.

This was helpful. I think that this world will change as we go along and I would like to do this again.

Figure 6.3 (Continued).

When inner communities are filled with conflict and pain, external relationships echo those struggles, like ripples spreading from stones thrown long ago. The rule seems to be that the more intimate the current relationship, the more likely it will draw forth helpful and hurtful relational patterns from the past. The present relationship often simply reinforces the internal picture of how all relationships work—a terribly defeating cycle when pain exceeds goodness. Often, by the time people are willing to seek therapy for their relational sorrow, they are near despair about ever having healthy relationships. This is where we come in.

Chapter 7

The Mutuality of the Therapeutic Relationship

The process of integrating brains and creating empathic inner communities rests in forming a collaboration with our patients that will foster the development of linkages between current dissociated neural nets/community members, so that they can join the flow of the integrating mind. This, in turn, supports the capacity for caring external relationships. Once the paradigm is internalized by us and shared with our patients, the methods are relatively simple, especially if we keep both inner community pictures and the principles of brain integration in mind. One vital ingredient in this therapeutic endeavor is hope, profound wellsprings of hope for healing, flowing from therapist to patient. This unbroken stream provides the milieu in which all else unfolds. Families who transmit continual messages of pain often convey an underlying feeling of despair about the goodness of life and relationships. If we are to help the inner community gain its footing, it must be on a foundation of strengthening hope. If our internal resources of hope are rich and deep, the resonance circuits that embed our being within our patients' inner worlds will become a secure foundation for them. However, if we don't have confidence in the potential goodness of life's processes, our patients will also feel that, no matter what words of hope we may speak.

As we enter the patient's inner community, we will begin to encounter parent–child as well as other relational pairs, locked in the pain that joined them in the first place. For them, it is as though no time has passed since the original wounding because they have been dissociated from the flow of the developing life—or, said another way, tethered by strands of implicit memory. Our empathic presence comes in as new energy, joining and modifying the existing relationships because our presence carries hope, attention, comfort, and delight. The absence of these energies in earlier life created the timeless jail in the first place. As the old pain is gradually released and comforted, our patients will begin to internalize us as small, sustaining Franklin stoves of warmth and goodness. Through the power of resonance circuits in both of us, we can become the empathic, hope-filled internal parents they have always sought.

Once the paradigmatic ground is established and the empathic bond between patient and therapist is firm, the journey inward is natural. Being solid in some key areas that emphasize interpersonal connectedness will allow us to be "good enough" therapists to facilitate healing. These are not techniques so much as ways of *being with* since right-hemisphere to right-hemisphere contingent contact is the golden road to neural change (Schore, 2003b, 2007). If we can begin with recognition of the mutuality of the therapeutic relationship, we will find firmer ground. This sense of partnership rests on humility about the state of our own mind. No matter how much we cognitively understand, we can be aware that just as we touch our patients' inner worlds, they touch ours as well. There is always a strong implicit-to-implicit resonance that we may feel most keenly through our bodies. It is good to remind ourselves frequently that this ongoing, often nonconscious conversation unfolds in micro second increments, weaving two people into one relationship. Clearly, we are in this together, and we will have personal healing opportunities brought to our awareness every step of the way. *Consequently, the ability to embrace and manage our continually unfolding inner awareness is our primary responsibility as a therapist.* The beauty of this task is that every stride we take toward healing will benefit our patients as much as ourselves, and that awareness can bring a profound sense of how interconnected we humans are.

Foundations of Mutuality

As we are settling into this stance of mutuality, a few inner foundations will support such ongoing connectedness. *First, we must commit deeply to going into our patient's world, no matter how painful.* The ability to make good on this commitment depends on how conscious we are of our own areas of pain. This doesn't mean we need to be completely healed, but it is essential that we be as aware as possible. If we need to block off some area of past pain, it is unlikely we will go there cleanly with our patients. Long-lost implicit triggers can make their way into the therapy in ways that damage lives. It is likely that most of the tragic violations of legal and ethical principles rest on these unacknowledged and dissociated areas of pain.

Second, we need to be comfortable providing comfort. Soothing can be conveyed in many forms—by a look, posture, breathing pace, moist eyes, tone of voice, or simply by a deep internal feeling of extending comfort. When this wish to comfort is accompanied by streams of accurate empathy, the stage is set for profound healing. This kind of connection is at the heart of helping our patients develop balance through dyadic regulation (which leads to the capacity for self-regulation; Schore, 2003b, 2007). In principle, this kind of deep work often means returning to the earliest part of patients' lives in order to provide warmth, steadiness, attention, and delight for the inner children and others. Even while this more conscious work is taking place, in our moment-to-moment interactions we are also gradually restructuring the nonconscious world. We rework mental models as we resonate in synchrony with our patient's body–mind (Schore, 2007). When these supplies of nurturance are missing in childhood, fragmented inner communities, resting on the shaky foundation of implicit-based pain and fear, prevent development of the subjective experience of a coherent sense of self. Our patients look to us to provide the rich soil and abundant sunshine that restart the natural developmental process. *It follows that we need to be comfortable passing through a period of emotional dependency with their inner children.* When this support is available, side by side with encouragement for their adult independent and interdependent states of mind, a secure internal home will gradually be built for these healing internal children. For our part, if we have an internalized sense of being soothed, if our inner children feel warmed and held, and if we understand conceptually why such a period of dependency is positive and essential, then the emergence of emotional dependency in our patients will be more easily managed. However, if we lack a sense of internal comfort, we may have one of two responses: We may feel drained and then have the impulse to move in the opposite direction—to pull away when comfort is needed; or we may cling to our patients' dependency in an effort to stave off our own abandonment, not allowing them to grow into interdependent maturity. It is so helpful to watch our visceral reactions to these overtures from our patients as the relationship deepens.

Being a Brain-Wise Therapist

Sometimes vivid images and sensations come into consciousness that can be the foundation of new waves of personal healing.

> I have found that keeping a journal of such experiences helps me be more aware of what is stirring in my deeper mind. Over time, patterns emerge that suggest new areas for personal healing. Simply being more conscious also makes it less likely that my own inner vulnerabilities will derail the therapy.

A third essential foundation is the ability to track our patients' internal movements. It is helpful to talk about this ability on two levels, conscious and nonconscious. First, let's talk about how our minds prepare an inner sanctuary for our patients by keeping us aware of the journey in the general sense, and their journey in the particular sense. When my mind is able to hold a felt sense of brain integration, mind coherence, and internal community empathy, I can invite my patient to enter this healing space with me. It is a bit like making sure the house is in hospitable shape before inviting guests. Your inner paradigmatic "house" may be different than mine. However, it is the clarity and calmness with which we hold our pictures of the healing path that matter. I have found that this capacity fosters the neuroception of safety necessary for rapid and thorough therapeutic joining.

Next, as my patients share their histories, I begin to hold images and experiences of their unique inner community, an internalized sense of their inner life. When they sense that my inner world contains their community, a fairly consistent, flowing stream of empathy connects us. At this point, therapy takes on a life of its own, as patients open their inner worlds with increasing ease and wisdom. I find that the deeper our trust in the mind's inherent push toward wholeness, the more we will be able to relax into our patients' frequently self-guided journey. Then we become like earnest detectives, drawing on all our knowledge about how inner communities get hurt and heal, to follow the trail through the underbrush. The more we can picture the inner community, the easier tracking becomes. It also seems that the more we see ourselves as companions who sometimes guide (rather than all-knowing interpreters), the more our patients are energized to find their way. In this spirit, after the first few sessions, I mostly picture myself following my patients' wise lead, while continuing to hold the bigger picture of the whole journey in mind. I feel certain that this vision continues to act as a silent map that subtly influences our passage. There are also moments when a sensation of feeling stuck wells up in the room, and it is necessary to briefly take the lead again. However, for the most part, it's just track, track, track. We will inevitably develop patience and humility in this endeavor, especially when we participate together in the joy of breakthrough moments.

A second kind of tracking is always present, and we could say that it is largely nonconscious because it emanates from the split-second, right-brain to right-brain interactions that continually animate the space between us (Schore, 2003b, 2007). We echo within one another continually, drawn together by the resonance circuits that weave us into relationship. Our intention to allow this weaving, accompanied by a sense of receptivity and attentiveness, assists our deeper mind in maintaining the responsive contact that allows us to enter fully the right-brain to right-brain dance that supports the remaking of the implicit world (Schore, 2007). We can tell that tracking is going well when we sense that we are sharing body–brain experiences with our patients, without getting lost in them. A well-integrated middle prefrontal region allows us to hold the experiences welling up in our patients and in ourselves mindfully and tenderly, even when they happen too rapidly to come into conscious awareness. A young man shared his horror at having stabbed his best friend in a fit of rage. As he talked, I felt my own chest tighten with the pain of extreme sorrow, while at the same time my strong desire to comfort him awakened, holding both our pained hearts in a sense of soft whiteness that came with an internal picture of wings. None of this was consciously driven but instead arose out of limbic-to-limbic resonance, coupled with the strong attachment bond that had developed between us. We can be certain that even beneath the sliver of experience that was drawn into consciousness, a whole world of neural firings were robustly cementing in the resources for secure attachment, changing implicit mental models. Although these mental models will remain out of sight forever, they will gradually begin to shape the way this young man experiences relationships, slipping into conscious life by the back door.

Embracing the Whole Person

A second overarching principle we can place side by side with mutuality is the need to *embrace the whole person*. We all take for granted that we will work with the feelings and thoughts of our patients, but there is more controversy about whether or how we hold their spiritual and physical being.

Spiritual Aspects

The way we are thinking about it here, *sensitivity to spiritual issues* includes exploration of not only religious beliefs and practices, but ethical and moral concerns as well as issues of the meaning and purpose of life. Many of us were trained to either avoid spiritual issues or to foster particular spiritual or ethical perspectives. However, from the viewpoint of interpersonal neurobiology and inner community work, the respect we experience for our patients guides us to enter their spiritual worlds as they bring them to us. In this sense, everyone's life has spiritual dimensions. As in many other areas, there seem to be layers to this work. Often, cognitive beliefs about the spiritual/ethical realm (in whatever form) are fairly near the surface and can be somewhat easily articulated:

> "I believe in a God of mercy."
> "I don't believe in any personal God, but there is an energy in the universe that guides everything."
> "Moral clarity is the root of everything good."
> "It's all pretty random."

Near that, but not always connected, are concepts of our relationship to the spiritual realm:

> "I am God's beloved child."
> "God wants to punish me because I am a sinner."
> "I am completely responsible for my moral integrity."
> "The energy guides my every move if I pay attention."
> "I am alone in this universe."

The question about relationship may have already encouraged us to move away from the conceptual arena and flow toward the implicit-based, emotional experience of the spiritual realm—but not always. To move more toward the roots, we could ask a person who has framed spirituality in terms of God, "What do you *feel* when you *imagine* God." A person who has said, "I believe in a God of mercy," might then say, "I feel His eyes on me every minute." Asking further might yield the response, "I feel scrutinized constantly."

As this dichotomy between concepts and feelings rises to the surface, the implicit attachment world is probably making its appearance. The intangibility of the spiritual domain makes it an easy target for implicit mental models about the nature of the world and relationship. There is probably no greater source of spiritual misery than projecting our hurtful parents onto the spiritual realm, in whatever form. This can look like a well of despair, a punitive or distant God, terror of the emptiness of space, or debilitating shame over moral lapses. Working to make the implicit explicit, comforting the wounded child, and gaining emotional clarity about the source of the broken relational feelings can create a broad highway for spiritual development. Then we have the lovely opportunity to nurture this person's individual path, watching the earned secure attachment he or she is forming with us flow into a sense of flexible compassion and goodness in the spiritual realm. This new sense may manifest as an increased feeling of hope and meaning, a congruence between moral belief and moral action (especially if both are based on empathy), a belief in a loving God who does not control every outcome, a profound sense of peace, or the loving embrace of nature. People often express something about being wrapped in a warm ocean of possibilities and experiencing a great increase in the sense of meaning, particularly through connection. This expanded awareness sometimes includes sensing the interconnection between all life forms. We might hear the whisperings of "transpirational integration" (Siegel, 2007) in these experiences and imagine them to be one outcome of a strongly integrating brain.

It goes without saying that our own issues might surface in so sensitive and personal an area. If we feel spiritually content, it may be appealing to help our patients find that feeling as well. However, we need to let our mirror neurons do the work without the cognitive content. If we struggle spiritually, we may find our own mental models resonating with those of our patient. Again, awareness is the most important aspect of modulating these inner surges. Our part in this work is simply to create a neuroception of safety in regard to bringing spiritual issues into the room, so our patients can allow their whole person to be present.

Somatic Aspects

To build on the process of whole-person awareness, acute *sensitivity to the state of our patients' bodies* can become another neural pathway into unresolved fear and pain. Pierre Janet's (1889) groundbreaking work on the physical correlates of dissociation and the work of Alexander Lowen (bioenergetic analysis; 1994), Ron Kurtz (Hakomi; 1997) and others have increased our awareness that our bodies directly carry the impact of both the positive and painful events of our lives. Given that the neural net of an experience tends to incorporate all aspects, it makes immediate sense that our muscles, nervous system, breathing rate, and other physical processes develop fixed patterns that continue to speak to our brains of old traumatic and developmental wounds.

One of the most striking experiences for me was with a patient who was "warehoused" in a wooden trunk for several hours every day from 18 months until kindergarten by a mother who had hated her daughter since conception. Her mother would come down every hour or so to give her enough air, but then quietly tell her it was "time to take a nap." After courageous work for a long time, my patient was able to allow herself to experience the utter terror of her confinement. As we worked to comfort and regulate these feelings over several days, she knew she was at last free of the trunk. If we think merely in terms of an old trauma being relieved, we will miss the real impact of her liberation. Once freed, she realized that the trunk had been her only home because she knew she had to stay there or hurt her family with her intolerable presence. In order to continue to protect everyone once she was no longer put in the trunk every day, she remained in the trunk in both her psyche and body for 44 years. In fact, one of her first statements to me when we began therapy was "I'm afraid you will be hurt or destroyed if you work with me." These words came straight from the implicit abyss, but were not fully intelligible to me at the time, particularly since she had only sketchy memories of the box. Although there is so much more to this story, the part to be shared here is the immediate transformation of her body as she stepped away from her prison. As I hugged her goodbye after the session celebrating her release, her body felt pliable and flowing, in complete contrast to the sharp stiffness of prior sessions. The change was so much more than just increased relaxation. Both of us got the image of how her body, primarily through the muscles, had *become* the trunk, so that she could carry it with her everywhere for the protection of humankind.

In the last 10 years, Peter Levine (1997, 2005), Pat Ogden (Ogden, Minton, & Pain, 2006), and others have further illuminated our understanding of the involvement of the body, gradually drawing it into the mainstream of psychotherapy. This kind of work offers elegant ways to modulate traumatic memories as well as heal subtler developmental wounds. At this point, focus on the body can stand side by side with emotional and cognitive work—and, in fact, developing our capacity to work with all three domains can increase the depth, speed, and ease of recovery.

We can begin by acknowledging that the *body has its own wisdom*. Given that all aspects of an experience tend to form a tightly woven neural net, it makes sense that pulling on the strand of the body might tug that experience into consciousness. We make use of this body–mind–brain connection when we encourage our patients to sit mindfully with their bodies in the presence of a current-day difficulty, as a way of drawing past experiences with similar somatic correlates forward. However, in addition to this kind of passive body awareness, there are additional methods that let us work more directly with the physical residue.

For example, in chronic or acute traumatic experience, and even in suboptimal attachment experiences, physical as well as emotional patterns are created in us and then become part of our relational repertoire. When my patient talks about being sexually abused as a child, I see her legs tighten as she pushes back against the couch with her upper body, her elbows nearly hyperextended in her effort to press herself into the cushions. With wide eyes and shallow breathing, she stays frozen in that position for a long time as she haltingly tells the story. The same thing happens in her body whenever she is in the presence of loud arguing. Why does the body hold on in this way? According to Levine (1997) and Ogden et al. (2006), when there is trauma, we frequently don't have the ability to complete the actions that our fight–flight system would like to initiate. Perhaps we have been physically immobilized, or we were in such fear for our lives that we froze. Now, however, with the remembered fear present in the body, and with the support of an empathic other, we may be able to complete what the body needed to do—push away, bite, yell, get up and leave. In this process, it is vital to turn to our patient's body for the answer, rather than supply our own. Small movements—a hand sliding slightly forward, fingers just starting to curl—may give both of us a clue about what the body needs. When movement begins, it is good to do it slowly to stay in the window of tolerance. In line with what we have observed, we might say, "Would your hands like to push against this pillow that I'm holding?" or "What does your tight jaw want to do next?" When we have a clear sense of what the body wants to do, we can do it together. If she puts her hands to her jaw and massages, I might do the same. If she wants to push, I could hold the pillow and then ask about how much pressure is needed. This kind of joining through resonance circuits is extremely powerful.

One young woman had been abused by her grandfather for over 10 years. We talked a bit about how the body holds memories, and then we began to notice that when she spoke about the abuse, she barely lifted the fingers of her left hand from her thigh, while pulling her torso slightly in the opposite direction. As we focused on this movement, she began to feel that she wanted to push her grandfather away. As I firmly held the pillow, she tried to push with both hands, but felt much more relief just using her left hand (possibly tied to the fearful experience in her right hemisphere or possibly to the way he would confine her). It was also important to lock her elbow so that he couldn't push back. After several repetitions, accompanied first by a loud "STOP" and then by joyous laughter, she felt complete. The next week, she reported the experience of keeping people out of her personal space for the first time. These strong movements seemed to have granted her a sense of power, a belief that she had a right to protect herself. As a result, she could request respect for her boundaries, even finding the right words to ask people politely to back off. When our patients are able to enact these "acts of triumph" (Ogden et al., 2006), delighted laughter often accompanies their gestures. Jaak Panksepp (2005), irrepressible investigator of playfulness, suggests that such socially induced laughter may promote interpersonal integration (with all its other benefits) by activating the reward–desire circuits in the brain.

Directly including the body in therapeutic work can also provide resources for regulation in several ways (Ogden et al., 2006). Often, when old pain is accessed, through the fire together–wire together principle, all aspects may try to come into consciousness at once. It is a little like pulling on the loose end of the tangled ball of string and getting the whole jumbled lump at once. However, when we help our patients mindfully direct their attention to a single aspect of the experience, we can tease out one strand so that the reactivated pain is not so overwhelming. Ogden suggests focusing the mind on a single strand at a time, using her sensorimotor techniques, to help patients stay at the edge of the window of tolerance, where there is sufficient contact with the pain to do the work but not so much that patients surge into dysregulation (Ogden et al.).

Accompanying these movements toward release are moments of what Ogden calls "resourcing"—discovering ways the body can find regulation, either in tandem with the therapist or on its own (Ogden et al., 2006). Individuality is the key here. For some, placing a hand on the heart will feel like comfort for the child within. For others, slow breathing will help sympathetic and parasympathetic systems come into balance. Changes in posture, eye gaze, or body tension may also prove settling. Always conveying a tone of respectful exploration allows our patients to make these discoveries and then develop them in a leisurely way. When patients struggle with dysregulation because of a right-hemisphere flood of memories, spending extensive time with resourcing can help stem the tide. As we expand our capacity to attend to the body, our patients will often show us that they already hold resources that can be further developed. When one patient became anxious, she began to rhythmically stroke her legs from thighs to knees. When we directed our attention to this gesture, she remembered that she had used it to soothe herself as a small child when her parents were fighting. As we sat mindfully with the rhythm and pressure of her hands, our conscious attending increased the depth of soothing, allowing the calmness to travel through more of her body.

One brief caution about the manner of paying attention to the body. Some of our patients have been scrutinized and criticized for large portions of their lives, so it is essential to cultivate an attitude of mutual curiosity about what the body is doing. Otherwise, our efforts can be felt as a shaming intrusion. A bit of education about acts of triumph, modulation of pain, and resourcing, coupled with modeling an attitude of caring curiosity, can act as an invitation to work together to understand the language of the body. Awareness of our patients' bodies will ideally go hand in hand with awareness of our own. In addition to being a rich resource of information about our patients' inner world, the body is also part of our whole-person embrace.

Rupture and Repair

Woven through all of this work are *times of rupture* and *times of repair* (Schore, 2003b; Tronick, 1989). Our empathy may go awry when our own implicit world is triggered, when we are tired or getting sick, or just because we are human. Tronick (2003) estimates that mothers are misattuned to their infants about 66% of the time. However, his research has also revealed that quick repair builds resilience in the bodies and brains of infants. Mom doesn't connect, her baby sends a signal of disruption and distress, and Mom responds, reestablishing warm contact. These experiences infuse hope and build a supportive mental model that gives us visceral assurance that things go wrong and then are set right. Furthermore, these interactions establish the cornerstone of resilience, the life-enhancing capacity to stay within the window of tolerance (Siegel, 1999) and flow easily among a rich array of emotional states (Demos, 1991). This relational pattern may be one of the most valuable we can instill in our children and our patients. Indeed the process probably goes on beneath the surface many times during any session, as the limbic-to-limbic conversation proceeds. However, our therapeutic relationships will also include some ruptures that flow up into consciousness, leading our patients to protest or perhaps dramatically dysregulate into rage or collapse. These are crucial opportunities to provide warmth and stability in the face of relational stress, and they can have a seemingly disproportionate positive impact on the healing process. One young woman burst into fury at my not calling her back as promised, but then instantly dropped into wide-eyed, frozen terror, frightened to death that she had "killed" the relationship. From some deep and wondrous place, my body just took a deep breath as I smiled at her and leaned forward. All I said was, "It's OK." Her body and emotions picked up the rhythm of connection, relaxing into a smile as she fell back against the pillows. Then there was time for my apology, but it only caused both of us to laugh. The essential moment was one of terror falling into a soothing pool, not of my conscious making. At many points in our time together, she talked about those very brief moments as pivotal to her healing. It seemed to her that years of parental dismissal and disdain had fallen away in a second, replaced by a sense of hope and trust in the larger relational world.

Integrating Interpersonal Neurobiology with Inner Community Therapy

Consideration of one last way we can move toward more synchrony with our patients circles us back toward our starting point: the integration of interpersonal neurobiology with inner community therapy. If we have been able to internalize the feeling of the process and the experience of brain integration, side by side with visions of the inner world, then these twin viewpoints can guide our next moves as we accompany our patients. We will be more sure-footed in sensing when to sustain a silence or lean forward into narrative. We will be able to inwardly support their sandplay or art with a fuller awareness of what processes are unfolding within them. Our greater awareness will likely deepen the experience for them because of the way our brains tend to move together. When they are open to it, we will be able to educate our patients about their brains and inner life in ways that nurture self-compassion and energize their own caring observer. Gradually, there can be a mutually held vision of how the integrating brain and the healing inner community are one.

With that in mind, let's see if we can cultivate the sensation of superimposing these two viewpoints, like two transparencies, now illuminated by our minds' search for integration. From my vantage point, the fit seems snug. At the most simplistic level, the people of the inner community appear to correlate with the states of mind in interpersonal neurobiology, while the process of internalization parallels the ongoing interpersonal linking created by our resonance circuitry. If we look deeper, the process of fostering an empathic inner community seems just like the outcome of brain integration, which, in turn, creates and is created by an attentive, coherent mind. Siegel (2007) captures this perspective with his triangle of well-being in Figure 7.1.

Once we are in a healing mode, integration of the brain, coherence of the mind, and empathic relationships constantly unfold together. From an inner community perspective, we could say that once new mental models of relationship have been created, we have a much easier time finding warm, attaching relationships. On the other hand, it is precisely the connection with empathic others that encourages the mental model to change. From the perspective of neural integration, we could say that coherent minds emerge from integrating brains, while it is also true that coherent, focused minds change the brain. There is the sense of "creating" and "being created by" at each corner of the triangle.

Within this overarching pattern of emerging health, we hold each unique person according to his or her need, temperament, and relational

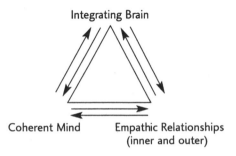

Integrating Brain

Coherent Mind   Empathic Relationships
                       (inner and outer)

Figure 7.1 Daniel J. Siegel's triangle of well-being.

style. There is a family fable from India that talks about how a good mother has one large fish and five children. Knowing each child well, she divides the fish and cooks each piece according to that child's digestion. Therapy is like that mother. Some of our patients will find sufficient safety to grant us entrance to their inner world via knowledge about their brains, others directly through the empathic connection, still others through coherent mind practices such as mindfulness. The same is true of approaches that enter through body, thoughts, or feeling first. As we gain attunement with our patients, we will find out how to cook the most easily digestible meal, so to speak, circling us back to one of our basic questions: "What is the most empathic way I can be with this person right now?" In this way, patients will feel known, and therein lies the root of the healing empathic connection. Then, around these established portals, the integrating dance will emerge.

The only significant differences in the paradigms that emerge for me occur when patients push the scientific envelope with their subjective experiences. As it should be, interpersonal neurobiology is first rigorously grounded within neurobiological research, then reaches out toward consilient findings from other fields of study. Inner community work is centered in subjectivity and acceptance of whatever flows from the patient's healing process. Surprising experiences often emerge.

One young man talked with me at length about how cruel his father could be. As part of the healing process, we began to talk with his internal father, asking him what kind of hurt was causing him to act in such deliberately wounding ways toward his son. Instantly, a strong image emerged in his mind: that of a young boy tied to the bumper of an old gray car, with a sign around his neck saying "Don't feed the dog." Sensing this boy's humiliation and rage, my patient felt profound empathy for him, but struggled to imagine that this was really his own father. This distant parent had always been taciturn in the extreme, except when he was angry, and had never talked about anything that happened to him in the present, much less as a child. His father's health was failing, and I suggested that his dad might have things he needed to get off his mind. My young patient decided to make the journey to see his father, even though he had not spoken to him in several months. During the visit, his dad talked briefly about the dirt farm where he'd grown up, and about a father who clearly didn't care if he lived or died. Then he passed on a box of old photos—one of which showed a boy tied to an old gray car with that horrible sign around his neck.

This is not an isolated case, and there may be alternate explanations for how such phenomena occur. Most people would probably say that the incident had been discussed in the boy's hearing, or he had seen the picture when he was very young. While this is possible, I have had too many experiences of such concrete recall with patients to believe the whole answer lies there. What we do know at this point is that the research can't fully explain such a complete transmission of experience from one generation to another. Such detailed and specific recall is beyond reading intention and mood from nonverbal cues through resonance circuits, although some of the newer ideas from quantum physics may bring us closer to an explanation. As noted above, we have patients who believe they experience clear memories from early childhood, despite childhood amnesia, and some whose felt recollections of their time in the womb have helped them heal. It doesn't seem useful to question them about whether what they describe is possible. I don't believe our job is to be arbiters of historical truth, but rather to act as containers of subjective experience while the pain heals. We can know for certain that science will keep coming up with new discoveries that illuminate the ways our minds create the richness of our subjective lives. We can also know that no matter how much we learn, at the end of the day, the single most important healing modality will still be our therapeutic presence, with the resources we bring to the relationship through our own emerging mental health and its lovely gift, wisdom.

Since Part I has been primarily an exercise in integration, it may be helpful to conclude with a narrative that seeks to capture the subjective experience of shame engrained as a child and healed as an adult, from the viewpoints of interpersonal neurobiology and the inner community.

Chapter 8

An Application:
Embracing Shame

The state of mind of shame and humiliation, when engrained in body, feelings, mind, and perhaps even spirit, pulls the sufferer into a cavern of longed-for invisibility such that the real person can be completely lost to us. Shame-imprisoned people say that it feels intolerable to be visible, to be known, because of the hateful core they perceive within themselves. The *anticipation* of rejection can be so powerful that all intimate connection is shunned, and the potentially healing interpersonal system breaks down. Intense shame cuts off access to all empathic others—those very people who could mirror the inherent value of the person, potentially transforming the neural nets carrying shame's message of worthlessness and becoming the internalized support for a sense of goodness. What a tightly wound recursive trap such humiliation becomes, with the body's down-turned eyes, lowered head, and collapsed chest constantly reinforcing the limbic emotional surge. When the shaming experience is early, frequent, and without repair, this person also develops a cortical invariant representation, further cementing him or her into an identity as a defective person. The circle is completed as limbic circuits and cortex converge, triggering the body to paint the portrait of shame and humiliation all over again. If we could see inside the mind, we might find a small child relentlessly pursued by an angry and condescending parent, an internalized pair implanted early and unchanged since then.

Sometimes shame clearly reveals itself, but other times it is closely bound to defensive anger or rage. Caught in the snare of perceptual bias, any *perceived* incoming slight is quickly and powerfully rerouted back to kill the messenger before the feeling of shame can painfully infect the sufferer's body. The result for the shame-bearer is the same. All empathic connectedness is blocked by the flood of dysregulated anger, the well of shame untouched and still wired to unleash defensive, hair-trigger rage again. Others may defend differently, locking themselves away from the intensity of social interaction in the left hemisphere, or physically avoiding any kind of intimate human contact. All result in a person in isolation with his or her worst enemy: the internal dyad of shaming parent–shamed child.

How can we understand what has happened to a mind drowning in the deep waters of shame and humiliation? And how can we help that mind emerge from this most painful state? Although the neural maturity required to experience shame is associated with a child's first steps toward autonomy in the early toddler years, it seems likely that infants can be primed for sensitivity to shame by initial relational experiences.

Primed for Shame

In the earliest burst of attachment in the first few months of life, we are genetically hard-wired to seek closeness and security with our caregivers. The sympathetic branch of the autonomic nervous system, which acts like an accelerator in a car, fuels this outward reaching. Whether we are met with disregard, anger, or anxiety, or have the opposite experience, our limbic regions encode the energy (arousal) and information (representations) offered by our caregivers in amygdala-centered, implicit-only memory where meaning is also initially formed. With enough consistent experience, this region encodes a mental model, a generalized anticipation, about whether relationships are trustworthy or not, already creating the inner community that embodies these expectations. These mental models stay in place below the level of consciousness as we mature, continually influencing our perceptions, kept alive by the painful interactions between parent and child that continue internally without end. We can see then how consistent anger or rejection by parents can engrain a fear of relationships in this primary meaning-making center even before the mind has enough developmental maturity to experience shame.

At just about the time a little one learns to walk, with great excitement, into his new-found freedom, his brain begins to function at a level of complexity that allows the experience of shame to emerge. The necessary ingredients include a developing parasympathetic branch of the autonomic nervous system, functioning as the arousal brakes, and a maturing orbitofrontal cortex in the prefrontal region, which allows this boy to represent himself in his mind. Both a braking system and a capacity for self-consciousness are necessary for shame. The outcome of integration is to move the mind toward greater complexity and attendant well-being, so it is not surprising that shame potentially has a positive function for this toddler.

As a child becomes mobile, with a sympathetic system capable of hurtling him toward danger, the parasympathetic can be activated by a parental "No," causing a necessary modulation of arousal. While the child experiences this *no* as a missed opportunity for synchrony, an empathic parent will immediately rejoin this toddler, bringing the sympathetic and parasympathetic into balance by acknowledging the child's wish to do the forbidden, and providing redirection toward a different joy. Over time, through this interpersonal modulating dance between outward-reaching and indrawn states, between rupture and repair, self-regulation is deeply patterned in the developing child, from nervous system to cortex. As a result, a wide window of tolerance for feelings emerges at both ends of the spectrum.

However, at the sad end of the scale, the child who is already primed for shame is probably living with the same parents who engrained a mental model of fear in relationship. So when "No" comes, it is likely more to meet the parents' needs than the child's, and it is far less likely that repair will follow immediately, if at all. So now the parasympathetic system slams into action while the parents' anger continues to accelerate the sympathetic system—a situation akin to pushing the accelerator and brakes to the floor at the same moment. Or the unmodulated parasympathetic system pulls the child into painful and isolating stillness as the parents turn away. This young one is simply left. Inwardly, the terrifying picture of an enraged and denigrating parent grows larger, while the shamed inner child cringes in the shadow.

If this dynamic is repeated often enough, the synaptic strength of the neural nets comprising the state of shame increases to the point that it becomes a trait, an accepted and expected part of this person's self-perceived identity. These neural nets are also so strong and so isolated from integration with the rest of the brain (because the empathic interpersonal relationships needed to foster further integration have not been available) that this person is a sitting duck for any perceived slight or criticism, literally at the mercy of engrained implicit mental models.

Healing the Shame

Many years later, this person is in my office or yours, his relationships in tatters for reasons he can't understand, and he is pretty much cut off from all help because inwardly he is terrified of any approach. What help can we offer? How can we draw him toward a compassionate acceptance of his shamed self so he can heal? How can we untangle the dance between humiliated child and shaming parent? We can begin by asking where neural integration may be blocked.

Since the primary breakdown in integration occurred relationally, that is where repair can begin. The first step is to embrace this person with both our kindness and our knowledge. This man will have a limited range of relational options open to him at first, and all of them will be designed to keep us at a distance. His inner protectors will hide his tender, wounded child in the belief that all contact breeds anguish. Even when this fixed perception causes him to behave in ways designed to send us away—denigrating us or staying on the very surface of the relationship—we have the capacity to *not* be drawn into a resonating dance with his wounds if we cultivate a balanced and mindful state, instead staying settled in uncompromising care.

Since fear is the limbic experience underlying engrained shame, we want to promote a neuroception of safety through awareness of what was amiss in the original relationships—providing calm in the place of rage, attentiveness in the place of a shaming face, and consistency in the place of erratic behavior. We want to become a refuge. And we want to provide that with our whole being, but in doses that this shamed person can tolerate. This delicate balance requires listening closely to both our own and the other's body for signs of overwhelm/hyperarousal.

While our middle prefrontal cortex is seeking to kindle the middle prefrontal cortex in the other through empathic presence and understanding, our left brains can also begin to join by discussing in words and concepts how shame develops in the brain. The effect is sometimes electrifying. The core experience of shame is that the person is inherently defective, and when the problem can be traced back to experiences that took place in the interpersonal world, often something connects that begins to generate a new narrative, a new bilateral connection around a change in perceived truth. At first, this is a goat path compared to the super highway of the old story about a bad child. But with repetition, the path widens and self-compassion—a feeling of care rather than rejection for the self—is born. The addition of feeling is the signal indicating that some bilateral integration is occurring.

Since this change is happening in the context of a caring relationship, that connection sometimes also becomes the crack in the protective wall that allows us to begin to approach the parent and child within more directly. He may begin to touch moments of terror, while being held in compassion and understanding. If the arousal is too great, we can modulate it by taking the experience apart, sitting first with the sensations welling in his body, then with the emotions, then with any accompanying thoughts. We can move from soothing the child to understanding the father until they both settle. In these vulnerable and tender places, the connection between us begins to take root—which inevitably brings anxiety because the attachment system is waking up, and that didn't go well the first time. We can now flow back and forth between internal work with the father–child pair and regulation in the present relationship. This stance requires gentle, patient, small moves toward full engagement. The best guide for moving forward is often our own bodies as they become more exquisitely sensitive to the harmonious flow that is developing. Some of this man's wounds are so early that they are available primarily to the micro-second, nonverbal, nonconscious interchanges that are like the sweet dance of mother and child.

Over time, we will begin to see an increasing capacity for self-regulation that indicates a number of wonderful things happening in the brain. If we could peer inside, instead of an isolated bundle of neural nets holding fear, we would now see long integrative fibers of comfort extending from the middle prefrontal cortex down to the amygdala, bringing the soothing neurotransmitter GABA to provide the ongoing reassurance that supports increasing depth of connection. A good recursive cycle is in place. In the subjective world, this man now reports seeing his father's inner child as well as his own, with compassion surrounding them both, as he surveys their similar wounds from his caring observer.

All of this signals that the middle prefrontal region is becoming wired in with the limbic regions, making a new kind of vertical integration available—and this is the heart of self-regulation. The comforted limbic areas now tell the sympathetic and parasympathetic systems that everything's OK, so the body in turn feels calm and sends this information back to the limbic regions and cortex. All of this is coordinated by the middle prefrontal region, whose job it is to maintain this new level of integration and well-being.

Side by side with these developments, we might also see the new narrative goat path widening to a highway, because the continual push of the denigrating internal father is quieted. With each repetition, the new story is amplified, taking in more of the intergenerational tragedy that is now ending with every moment this man spends healing his inner community. Neural nets on both sides of the brain have been recruited to maintain this developing tale of expansive truth. Meanwhile, the former super highway of self-hate is sprouting weeds from disuse.

At this stage, the power of integration is tangible in the room as a sense of joy filling body and mind in both of us. Everything is changing, from posture to eye contact to relationships in the outside world. There's a lot of laughter. None of this happens quickly or neatly. However, I am finding that with the guidance of an increasingly compassionate heart integrated with a developing brain-wise mind, things can go more quickly and deeply than I ever imagined.

I would like to end Part I with thoughts from this recovering shamed person. "I realize now that I lived alone in a dark cave of humiliation and terror since I was very small, but I never knew it. I thought life was just a game of manipulating people to get what I wanted—and I called that fun. I was constantly amazed at my creativity and amused by how people were wary of me. I never once let myself feel how scared I was until my wife took our two kids and moved back East. This was a situation I couldn't manipulate into shape. After they left, many nights I thought I was having a heart attack, but now I think I was just terrified.

"Then I came here, and you frustrated me completely because I couldn't control you. I thought about leaving many times because you were stupid and stubborn, so I'm not sure why I stayed. What I remember most is the first day I caught a glimpse of that little boy in my memory with his enraged father standing over him. I wanted to grab him up and take him out of the house. That was the beginning of something completely different. I don't think I ever experienced joy before, and I know I didn't miss it. I was too busy protecting myself. I still have a lot of sadness about all the people I've hurt and alienated, but I also have some new relationships that seem promising. I feel like life can go on from here."

Part II

Practical Matters

Chapter 9

Preliminary Thoughts

Now we turn to the practical matter of bringing interpersonal neurobiology into the heart of our therapeutic work. We're going to explore this endeavor in two ways: (1) through the organizational lens of diagnosis, and (2) through a series of processes that can be practiced in ways that promote neural integration. By the time we've completed this short tour, your own creative juices may be primed to take over this integrative endeavor, by bringing the brain, mind, and inner community to your own unique and cherished ways of working.

Through the Lens of Diagnosis: Depression, Anxiety, Dissociation, and Addiction

In Part I, we organized our thoughts around how brain development and inner community formation are impacted by parents' states of mind with regard to attachment. This is one valid schema for understanding the suffering of our patients, and it provides clear guidance for how to support a trajectory of healing. However, we often organize our thinking about our patients' difficulties in other ways, and one of the most familiar is diagnostic categories. Many volumes have been written on the subject of the etiology and treatment of each disorder, so with a great deal of humility, the sketches here only outline the landscape from a neurobiological perspective. This chapter is the most research-heavy in the book and is meant to provide scientific puzzle pieces that we can put in context with what we already know about brain development. By the end, we will have some idea about what we do and don't know concerning the neural substrates of these four common responses to stress, and we will explore some possible causes of these neural deficits. In this way, we may be able to craft sound treatment strategies by imagining how interpersonal warmth and wisdom might support the neural integration underlying greater well-being and relational health.

With this in mind, we will consider *depression, anxiety, dissociation, and addiction* in some depth. I have chosen these four primarily because they occur frequently, and also because each carries a distinct set of symptoms. However, we can immediately recognize that these disorders often do not occur by themselves. Depressed people are often also anxious and may seek solace and regulation through substances. Traumatized individuals often experience alternating waves of depression, anxiety, and dissociation, and may search for moments of oblivion through addictive behaviors as well. It goes without saying that we treat whole people, not diagnoses. However, being able to picture what is happening in the brain–body when our patients are caught in these different states of mind can help us mold our "being with" in ways that will encourage particular kinds of integration. Near the end of the chapter, we will spend some time considering two tragic outcomes of relational trauma and abuse: *borderline personality disorder* and *dissociative identity disorder.* Although these particular responses to overwhelming stress can challenge our limbic capacity to contain the chaos and pain, our ability to picture these torn minds can help us remain steady.

The lack of clear borders around different diagnoses makes sense when we consider that *genetic vulnerability, patterns of dysregulation internalized and engrained* from our most significant relationships, and *brain structure and function impacted by both chronic and acute stress* are common threads tying them together. When distressed parents' internal states result in significant deficits in empathy and contingency, their children's developing brains are affected, just as they are etching inner relational worlds through resonance circuits primed for connection. These are parallel, overlapping processes. For example, a shy child (possible genetic contribution) is born to a chronically anxious mother (dysregulating internalization). Without conscious intention, this mother provides dual implicit messages that the world is frightening and that the child is alone when scared, because Mom's anxiety prevents her from being present when her baby is upset. In addition to generating implicit mental models, these circumstances cause the baby's brain–body to flood with the chemistry of fear (stress response), amplifying and wiring in the painful dysregulation, often with long-term consequences for the developing brain. Over time, a child in these circumstances may become more inhibited, until this state of mind becomes an engrained trait, coloring the subjective experience of daily life and guiding relational choices that often mimic what is familiar. When we understand the origin of this common pattern, we can take possible genetic components into account, while providing regulating empathy and contingency in a relational environment that is saturated with awareness, ease, and safety. These principles can provide one internal stabilizing reference point anchoring our caring observer, as waves of dysregulation occupy the space between us and our patients.

Fostering Neural Integration and Empathic Inner Communities

In the second section of Part II, we will walk through a series of processes seen through the twin lenses of interpersonal neurobiology and inner community integration. All of us have cultivated a handful of preferred ways of working with our patients. In the best case, these are pathways toward healing that resonate with the core principles of our therapeutic paradigm and have demonstrated efficacy in easing suffering over a broad range of human struggles. In the interest of helping our patients settle into a coherent pattern of healing, we may have found it helpful to create a *nest* of processes that support one another and have been carefully tailored to help our patients move in directions that encourage integration, linking one part of internal and relational experience with another until there is a smooth flow. In the case of the model presented here, we have formed this nest out of modalities that use interpersonal connectedness to encourage members of the inner community to become more empathic with one another, or, said the other way, that support neural integration. The result is an increase in the subjective experience of wholeness and balance.

Unless we need to attend to an emergent crisis, most of us also have a *sequence* for offering these ways of working, often loosely determined by how we picture the healing process unfolding. When we do both nest and sequence creation consciously, with the healing path in mind, we have the opportunity to encourage neural coherence and a subjective sense of security for our patients simply by the clarity of our internal vision. Taking resonance circuits seriously means that how we hold the journey in our minds impacts our patients' ability to put their feet on a well-defined path.

The ground and container for nest and sequence components is the relationship. For many years, research has confirmed consistently that empathic resonance is the fuel for effective therapy, no matter how we work. Our presence is the instrument. Interestingly, when we feel secure in the way we work, we relax into relating and foster a neuroception of safety that shelters our patients' often fragile inner relational landscape. Consequently, creation of a coherent healing path may actually be most important because it supports our own inner world in the service of becoming a refuge for our patients.

In these chapters, we will think consciously about a group of processes that could form the nest and sequence for healing inner communities, employing the principles of interpersonal neurobiology. These processes include both some basic and familiar ways of working, recast in terms of interpersonal neurobiology, as well as sandplay and art as two particularly integration-friendly ways of accessing right-limbic early attachment experience. Even if you are not yet familiar with these last two ways of working, you may be intrigued by the possibilities. This section's organization, beginning with listening to history and moving to the regulation of chaos and fragmentation, may also help expand our capacity to hold dramatically distressed inner worlds. Particularly in longer-term work, our patients are gradually able to bring their deeper pain and disorganization into the room. When we are able to sit in calm compassion with the intense pain and desolation that may emerge, we can foster a sense of spacious self-acceptance in our patients as well.

Because of the centrality of the relationship in all we do, we will begin with "Grounding Therapy in the Right Brain," reminding ourselves of why right-hemisphere to right-hemisphere connection is the very root of neural change. Damaged attachments are repaired when the patient's implicit world is met and held by ours in the dance of micro-second interactions that reshape the neural landscape. Most of this chapter provides tastes of what it feels like when this kind of relational richness is unfolding. *Therapy goes best when all of our well-thought-out verbal interventions ride on, and reflect, this burgeoning attunement.* For many of us, this viewpoint requires us to rethink much of what we may have considered therapeutic, but it is undoubtedly where we must begin.

Next, we explore "Listening to Family Histories." Part of the journey toward coherence is gradually crafting a narrative that makes sense of our lives. This initial act of sharing is the first step for our patients. Just the process of feeling heard begins to spark neural integration, supporting linkages between the middle prefrontal and limbic circuits in the right hemisphere. When we listen with ears and bodies attuned to breaks in coherence, we can begin to hear and sense where the flow of integration is blocked by the accumulated debris of wounding experiences. Awareness this early in therapy can help us choose our modes of relationship with an intent to foster neural integration from the very beginning of our work together. In a beautiful way, the whole process can begin to weave two people into one relational process that becomes the fertile soil for the richness that follows.

Just as family histories are foundational for drawing both therapist and patient toward the states of mind that form the inner community, "The Three Faces of Mindfulness" provides ways for our patients to sit with themselves, even in the midst of emerging pain and fear. We will talk about mindfulness in three senses: (1) the formal practice of certain techniques that strengthen our ability to choose our focus of attention, (2) the cultivation of the caring observer state of mind from which we can hold other states of mind with compassion and equanimity, and (3) the mindful therapist as the nurturer of neural integration in our patients. Growing these capacities within ourselves will help tame even our most unruly limbic activations (also known as countertransference), while allowing us to foster mindfulness in our patients through the interpersonal power of resonance circuits.

One way to help the caring observer spring into action is educating our patients about their brains and bodies. In "Getting Comfortable with the Brain," we translate the intricacies of neuroscience discoveries into language and gestures that patients can make their own. It goes without saying that our own minds and bodies have to absorb and metabolize the science before it will flow easily to others. Even though these interventions may seem rooted in education more than attunement, when sensitively offered, they can be the most emapthic gift we can give a client floundering in shame or self-hatred, for example. Since these states of self-rejection disrupt connection, anything we can do to foster understanding so that they are less binding will speed healing. As long as these brain talks advance connection, they can be an excellent tool of bilateral integration.

Since one road out of dissociation is making contact with those neural circuits holding uncomforted pain and fear, we will explore "Patterning the Internal Work" as a way to encourage integration of past experience without overwhelming the person in the present. Working on deep, long-held misery in small bites can relieve a lifetime of bondage to destructive implicit patterns. When this kind of work rests on the foundation of empathic connection, awareness of the inner world, some capacity for mindfulness, and awareness of the brain and body, rapid progress in relieving suffering often results.

If all of this has fostered curiosity about other ways of efficiently accessing isolated right-hemisphere limbic circuits, you will find additional elegant tools in "The Integrating Power of Sandplay" and "Doing Art." Because these ways of working encourage direct relationship with the body, senses, and feelings, they can pull our patients into close contact with out-of-awareness, unsymbolized implicit attachment experiences, while modulating the intensity of recall. The figures and drawings begin to make the implicit explicit, giving form, story, and coherence to inner tales of sorrow, terror, and disorganization.

Chapter 10

Through the Lens
of Diagnosis:
Depression, Anxiety,
Dissociation, and Addiction

Most of us "cut our teeth" on diagnostic categories by getting familiar with a list of symptoms. However, here we are going to approach the issue from a more foundational vantage point, asking how the neural correlates of depression, anxiety, dissociation, and addiction develop. This inquiry will also take us into the familiar territory of damage done to the capacity for regulation/integration when people suffer early attachment trauma. Many of these wounds occur in situations that do not appear to be dramatic. Knowing what we do about the brain, we can imagine that even in stillness, as a father interminably reads his paper while mother turns her back to fidget endlessly at the sink, their young child's brain is deprived of the most basic relational nurturance. Not only can there be damage to the developing brain, but the inner communities that form under conditions such as these continue to whisper a litany of life's limitations, making it difficult for this now-grown man to imagine a future of warm, emotionally responsive relationships. We traditionally use the word *disorder* for these conditions. I struggle with this word because of its tendency to dehumanize, and because of the connotation of something messy to be avoided. However, if we can remake our inner model to let the concept of disorder include the lack of neural integration, beginning on the right with the regulatory circuits and proceeding to the left where emotionally whole narratives struggle to take shape, then perhaps it can be useful.

Neural Underpinnings of Diagnostic Disorders

First, a brief overview. I am going to keep the neural explanations some-what simple, talking only about the major regions involved. If we keep in mind that many associated circuits are part of the evolving experience, perhaps we can appreciate the complexity of the process, while we form coherent pictures that are sufficient for our clinical purposes. At this point, neuroscience has offered us enough information to know that factors maintaining the four painful adaptations to stress known as depression, anxiety, dissociation, and addiction involve a soup of *genetic vulnerability, alterations in neurotransmitters and hormones,* certain *deficits in brain structure and function, inner community disruption* based on internalized patterns of relating, and *social networks that often reinforce engrained neural circuits,* rather than changing them. As in a well-cooked broth, each ingredient influences the others, so it is often difficult to tease the components apart. It is also difficult to tell whether depression, for example, arises from certain neural deficits, or if the experience of hopelessness damages the body–brain's structure and function in predictable ways—or, quite possibly, some of both. However, in almost all cases, at some early stage in the process of attachment, regulation failed, leading to deficits in vertical integration in the right hemisphere (Siegel, 1999; Schore, 2007), along with all the changes in body, mood, and relationships that accompany such neural dis-integration.

To establish a little background, studies have found that the *dorsolateral* and *ventromedial prefrontal cortices, anterior cingulate,* and *orbitofrontal cortex* are key structures in the volitional regulation of emotions, impulses, and states of arousal (sympathetic and parasympathetic balance; Phan et al., 2005). As you may recall, the *dorsolateral prefrontal* cortex holds states of mind in consciousness, while the *ventromedial and orbitofrontal cortices* combine to regulate body and emotions (among other functions). The *anterior cingulate* provides the capacity for attention while coordinating feelings and cognition in the service of making decisions based on future well-being. If we add the insula as the conveyor of information about the state of the body, we have a good general picture of how emotional awareness arises after initial implicit appraisal in the *amygdala* and associated circuits, and how that arousal can be modulated by these middle prefrontal regions. Interestingly, research has revealed that a successful effort to voluntarily regulate negative emotions leads to an *increase* in activity in the dorsolateral and medial prefrontal regions, as well as the anterior cingulate, accompanied by a *decrease* in the amygdala and medial orbitofrontal regions (Ochsner, Bunge, Gross, & Gabrieli, 2002). This makes sense when we think about how initial arousal is mediated by the amygdala, with the orbitofrontal cortex evaluating the degree of fearfulness (Schwartz & Begley, 2002). Overactivation in the amygdala could lead to harder work for the orbitofrontal cortex, so regulation might calm them both.

Turning to the role of horizontal integration in healthy states, research has shown that focused attention on modulating negative states also *increases left prefrontal and anterior activation*, leading to an emphasis on approach rather than withdrawal states (Davidson et al., 2003). When our brains are in this activation pattern, it is possible to approach even stressful situations with relative equanimity—an excellent definition of resilience (Siegel, 2007). Before exploring disruptions to these processes that are common to many disorders, it might be helpful to take a minute to call up the mental picture of the relationship between these brain regions, developed in Part I, as a reference point for the discussion that follows.

It may also be helpful to keep in mind that regulation and integration produce greater neural synchrony and subjective well-being (Siegel, 1999). When people experience major depression, various anxiety states, dissociation, or addiction (among other painful conditions), the sufferers lack the ability to volitionally regulate their states of arousal. Because of these disturbed linkages between body, limbic, and middle prefrontal regions (particularly on the right), as well as between right and left prefrontal regions, people lose many of the nine capacities that are central to personal well-being and warm relationships: sympathetic–parasympathetic balance, flexible response patterns, emotional equilibrium, empathy, attuned communication, the ability to reflect on one's own history with equanimity and compassion, modulation of fears, access to intuition, and a sense of morality (Siegel, 2007). Without the foundation of right vertical integration, the other forms of neural wholeness have difficulty gaining momentum. As we increase our understanding of the neural correlates of these maladies, it will be helpful to see how the puzzle pieces offered by research correlate with this model of disturbed regulation and integration.

The Downward Tug of Depression

Let's begin with an overall sense of the *structure and function* of depressed brains. Later, we will consider how these painful conditions may develop. Rivers of research data on depression, some of it contradictory, pour forth continually, offering us the challenge of creating a coherent picture. Let's consider *structure* in the prefrontal–limbic interface first. Recent neuroimaging studies have revealed that the *medial orbitofrontal cortex* of people who suffer from *major depression* is 32% smaller than in nondepressed people (Bremner et al., 2002). To review, this area is thought to contribute to the integration of emotional and cognitive processes, and regulation of body and emotions, while supporting self-awareness and empathic connection (Bremner et al., 2002; Gusnard, Akbudak, Shulman, & Raichle, 2001). This area interacts closely with the amygdala to modulate emotional information, even when that information is received in the right hemisphere below the level of conscious awareness. Smaller volume means the likelihood of fewer integrative connections.

Turning to function, earlier studies demonstrated *decreased blood flow* in certain prefrontal and limbic areas in patients with depression, including the *dorsolateral prefrontal cortex* (working memory; Mann, et al., 1996), and the *medial prefrontal cortex and anterior cingulate* (awareness of self and others, regulation/integration of emotion and cognition, capacity to direct attention; Drevets et al., 1997; Mayberg et al., 1997). In what appears to be contradictory information, other studies have shown *increased* blood flow in the orbitofrontal cortex, perhaps in a compensatory attempt to modulate negative feelings. However, with the decrease in gray matter, such attempts may fall short (Drevets, 1999). Some OCD research suggests that overactivity in the orbitofrontal region can lead to an ongoing sense of dread, another characteristic of some depressions (Schwartz & Begley, 2002). Overall, we can sense the challenge presented by deficits in these primary integrative areas, particularly when the underlying structures are already compromised.

Moving to the deeper limbic structures, imaging studies have demonstrated a reduction in volume of the *hippocampus* of almost 19% (Bremner et al., 2000), with the degree of neural loss possibly correlating with the duration of the depression (Sheline, Wang, Gado, Csernansky, & Vannier, 1996). One school of thought believes that the stress of depression may inhibit neurogenesis in the hippocampus (Gould, McEwen, Tanapat, Galea, & Fuchs, 1997). Additionally, the action of stress chemicals may destroy existing neural tissue, particularly in prolonged depressive states (Sapolsky, 2000). Such loss of volume may account for some of the cognitive and memory deficits experienced in major depression (Sapolsky, 2001). Some antidepressants increase hippocampal neurogenesis (Santarelli et al., 2003), stimulating a rousing debate about the centrality of the hippocampus in major depression (Sapolsky, 2000). As we will see below, a full understanding of suffering and cure is probably more complex, involving other limbic and cortical structures.

It isn't surprising that changes in size and function of the amygdala also appear to correlate with major depression, considering its centrality to processing and experiencing emotion. Evidence suggests that both right and left amygdalae have larger volumes accompanying the first episode of major depression (Frodl et al., 2002). However, with repeated episodes, studies show decreased volume in the core nuclei of both amygdalae (Sheline, Gado, & Price, 1998), or in the left amygdala more than right (Siegle, Konecky, Thase, & Carter, 2003). The decrease in volume also suggests the possibility that the stress of repeated depressive episodes continues to destroy neurons and glia in both the amygdala and hippocampus via excessive secretion of stress hormones (Nemeroff, 1998).

Turning to studies of blood flow, decrease in left amygdalar volume is coupled with greatly increased activity when subjects are exposed to fearful faces below the level of conscious awareness, with the level of increase correlating with the severity of depression (Sheline et al., 2001). Paradoxically, this increased blood flow may actually dampen affect as the left amygdala works to create homeostasis (Drevets, 2003). This makes sense when we remember that the right limbic region may mediate intense emotions, while the left linguistic region produces regulating words for the information received from the right (Schore, 2007).

Moving toward the right hemisphere, another study demonstrated that increased baseline activity in the *right amygdala* correlates with the subjective experience of greater negative affect in depression (Abercrombie et al., 1998). Overactivity in the right amygdala, even after treatment and symptom remission, possibly creates vulnerability for relapse (Drevets, 1999). Even in sleep, depressed individuals continue to have abnormally active amygdalae, perhaps contributing to insomnia (Drevets, 1999). This finding suggests a hypothesis that the overactivity of both amygdalae may correlate with rumination on painful memories, particularly given diminished linkages with the middle prefrontal regions (Drevets, 2003), and contribute to the overall suffering of major depression (Drevets, 1999). Supporting this idea, Siegle and colleagues (Siegle et al., 2003) found that activity in the amygdala persists for an unexpectedly long time in depressed individuals who are asked to contemplate sad words or are exposed to sad faces.

Recent research has shed more light on what occurs when depressed people attempt to shift away from pervasive negativity. Nondepressed people can engage the left prefrontal region to quiet the amygdala when making a volitional effort. In contrast, those suffering with depression engage the prefrontal region on both left and right, with increased activation of the amygdala, insula, and thalamus (Johnstone, van Reekum, Urry, Kalin, & Davidson, 2007). This difficulty in shifting to the left keeps them in greater contact with the painful feelings on the right. To make matters more difficult, depression acts as a stressful condition in its own right, so many depressed people show heightened cortisol levels—the final step in the chain from amygdala to hypothalamus to pituitary to adrenals (HPA axis; Drevets, 1999). Sadly, these stress hormones can continue to chew up tissue in the very neural structures that could send soothing fibers to the amygdala. Research tells us that for those who respond to medication, increased serotonin (and sometimes norepinephrine and dopamine, depending on the medication) in the amygdalae moves activity toward normal levels (Drevets, 2003; Sheline et al., 2001), which can potentially intervene in this vicious cycle. One of the struggles for researchers is that all depressions don't manifest alike in the brain. For example, the neural signature of a more genetically based depression is different in some ways from a major depressive episode following a traumatic event. Individual differences compound the problem. However, it seems fair to say that there is a common process in which regulatory capacity and neural integration are disrupted and then maintained by changes in structure and function in the brain.

Wide-Eyed Anxiety

Expanding our inquiry to the neural correlates of anxiety, we might think that this group of disorders lies at the opposite end of the regulatory spectrum from depression. However, approximately 58% of depressed people also experience anxiety, according to the National Comorbidity Survey (Kessler, 2006). Also, even though they present differently, depression and anxiety are both correlated with an imbalance in the autonomic nervous system, tilting it toward sympathetic activity. Research shows that depressed people often have higher concentrations of norepinephrine (Veith et al., 1994), elevated heart rates (Veith et al.), and lower heart rate variability (Rechlin, 1994)—all signs of decreased parasympathetic and/or increased sympathetic activity. With this in mind, we might wonder about similarities in brain structure and function between the two kinds of disorders. The neurobiology of fear is a good place to start, since all struggles with anxiety begin there.

Said simply, the common pathway for the subjective experience of fear is activation of the amygdala by internal or external events that are *perceived* to be threatening; in turn, this activation triggers a cascade of neurochemicals that ready the body for defensive action (LeDoux, 1994). The survival value of such a capacity is obvious. However, for those who suffer with the various forms of anxiety, hypersensitivity in the *right amygdala*, coupled with disrupted function in the prefrontal region (including the anterior cingulate), push modulation out of reach, even in nonthreatening circumstances (Rauch, Shin, & Wright, 2003). Under healthy conditions, the *ventromedial prefrontal cortex, orbitofrontal cortex*, and *anterior cingulate* work with the amygdala to tie emotion and cognition together and regulate both the physiological and emotional responses to fear (Schore, 2007; Siegel, 2007). Good connections with the anterior cingulate also allow us to shift our attention from one focus to another. If we take posttraumatic stress disorder as our example, researchers find that the *right amygdala* of traumatized people is strongly activated under three conditions: when reminded of the trauma, when shown generally fearful faces, or when exposed to images of fearful faces below the level of awareness. Hypersensitivity persists, even in the absence of specific trauma reminders. The greater the activation, the more severe the symptoms (Armory, Corbo, Clement, & Brunet, 2005). At the same time, the *ventromedial prefrontal cortex* and the *anterior cingulate* show reduced activity (Rauch, Shin, & Phelps, 2006), so their potentially modulating influence is disrupted. In addition to overall reduction in activity in these areas, trauma survivors with posttraumatic stress disorder (PTSD) show more firing in the right anterior cingulate, whereas non-PTSD participants are able to recruit more circuits in the left anterior cingulate (Lanius et al., 2002). These findings are consistent with our picture of how horizontal integration advances regulation through the capacity for verbal narrative.

Another of the amygdala's near neighbors may also be implicated. Several studies reveal reductions in volume of the *hippocampus*: 8% in the right hippocampus of Vietnam veterans (Bremner et al., 1995); bilateral reduction (26% left and 22% right) in veterans in general (Gurvits et al., 1996); and a 12% reduction on the left in female survivors of chronic child abuse (Bremner et al., 1997). Deficits on the right correlate more strongly with verbal and memory difficulties than on the left, probably because of disturbed encoding at the time of the event. Even in the absence of tissue loss, the hippocampus shows decreased activation, particularly when survivors with PTSD are asked to complete narrative tasks (Shin et al., 2004). This finding may account partially for the difficulty many people experience when seeking to assemble the story of their traumatic experiences. Taking all of this evidence together, we can sense how dis-integrated the right hemisphere circuits are from each other, as well as from resources on the left.

Standing back for an overview, we can see that hypersensitivity of the amygdala, coupled with poorer connections with potential regulating and integrating circuits, can sustain and even amplify anxiety. If we take a moment to imagine the subjective experience of people who have these deficits, we may catch a glimpse of the helplessness PTSD-stricken trauma survivors experience when trying to regulate the waves of hyperarousal, without success. When we couple these deficits with the additional experiences of uncontrollable irritability and anger, guilt and shame, loss, sadness, generalized anxiety, and a disturbed relationship with physical pain embodied by many PTSD survivors (Frewen & Lanius, 2006B), we may sense the mountain these brave people have to climb as they attempt to integrate their brains.

A good deal of the subjective experience of anxiety comes from the flood of *neurochemicals* pouring through the body when the *amygdala* interprets inner or outer events as dangerous. It may be helpful to understand how the amygdala receives its information. Research suggests that there are two pathways by which stimuli enter the brain: one remains out of awareness (a subcortical pathway from sensory cortex to midbrain to thalamus to amygdala), whereas the other makes use of the prefrontal cortex to come into conscious awareness (LeDoux, 1994; Morris, Ohman, & Dolan, 1999). It is hypothesized that these are parallel tracks that can operate independently. These two tracks may account for the finding that the right amygdala of healthy people increases in activation when they are shown pictures of fearful faces so rapidly that they cannot consciously register the images. Imagine, then, how this faster processing track might affect a traumatized person who is briefly exposed to an image or pattern similar to the original trauma. That person might be hypersensitive to apparently minor external events (*sensitization*) that occur both in and out of awareness, while also being challenged by internal events that are reawakening (*kindling*; Scaer, 2001). There is also speculation that the nonconscious pathway may be responsible for initiating panic attacks that appear to be spontaneous (Rauch et al., 2003). One study captured a spontaneous panic attack and found a decrease in blood flow in the right orbitofrontal cortex and anterior cingulate (Fischer, Andersson, Furmark, & Fredrickson, 1998). This pattern of brain functioning would leave the sufferer with minimal regulatory help, particularly when the amygdala is firing so strongly. Although this is not the whole picture of panic states, it is central to understanding the runaway train feeling that accompanies this overwhelming experience.

Once the amygdala assesses danger, the cascade of stress chemicals flows along the *HPA axis* (hypothalamic–pituitary–adreno). Activation of the sympathetic nervous system is marked by faster beating hearts (to push blood to the muscles), accelerating breath, rising blood sugar (to increase energy), tensing muscles, and dilating eyes. In general, the hypothalamus produces hormones, called *releasing factors*, that control the pituitary gland. Under conditions of perceived threat, it produces *corticotropin-releasing factor* (CRF), which, in turn, tells the pituitary to release the *adrenocorticotropic hormone* (ACTH). This travels to the adrenal glands, which then release the hormone *cortisol*, raising the level of glucose in the blood to respond to the threat (Sunderland, 2006). Under ordinary threat circumstances, cortisol levels drift back to normal after the threat has passed. However, with any kind of ongoing anxiety, levels can remain high, potentially destroying tissue and/or disturbing connections in various parts of the brain. In addition, elevated levels of stress hormones depress immune function (Palacios & Sugawara, 1982) and have been implicated in cardiovascular difficulties as well (Glassman, & Shapiro, 1998). One example of function change under stress is the modification of hippocampal functioning, so that cognitive information is stored less efficiently, while emotional information is strongly encoded (Perry, 1998). This hippocampal connection may be another way station for the disconnection of emotion from cognition. Overall, we may get the sense that the amygdala is left to fend for itself within a flood of ongoing internal and external perceived stressors, amplified by the rivers of cortisol coursing through the body, sending the false message that today is as threatening as the original traumatic time.

Although we have considered only posttraumatic stress in detail, all anxiety disorders share the focal points of a hypersensitive amygdala and disruption of regulatory circuits, coupled with some unique features. For example, in *social anxiety*, abnormalities in dopamine receptors have also been noted (Stein, 1998). Given that dopamine is believed to mediate the experience of pleasure, it is hypothesized that unrewarding early interpersonal relationships may have thrown the dopamine system out of balance (Rauch et al., 2003). In *generalized anxiety disorder in children*, on the other hand, the hallmark discovery has been decreased gray matter in the left amygdala (Milham et al., 2005). Their additional finding that, thanks to childhood neuroplasticity, 8 weeks of intervention with psychotherapy or medication may not only alleviate symptoms but may also increase amygdalar size is heartening, especially given the fact that severe childhood anxiety is a precursor of adult depression. We can expect to see many more pieces of the anxiety puzzle emerge with additional research.

The Last Resort: Dissociation

When we are chronically depressed and anxious, the ascendance of the fight/flight *sympathetic* response pulls us away from the socially engaging *ventral vagal branch of the parasympathetic* system. However, as perceived danger reaches the point of life threat, the sympathetic system shuts down in favor of *dorsal vagal parasympathetic* activation, leading to a freeze response (Porges, 2001). The floating, absent feeling of *dissociation* is the result. As the word suggests, the brain dis-integrates as the situation progresses toward impossible. Having reached the far limits of tolerating terrifying helplessness, brainstem resources throw the circuit breaker, feigning death to escape death. This very primitive response suddenly reduces heart rate and blood pressure, slows digestion and loosens the bowels, while slowing metabolism. Research suggests that from the foundation of structural and functional changes in the brain attendant on hyperarousal to the point of panic, circuits in the *medial prefrontal cortex* and *anterior cingulate* dramatically increase their activity (Lanius et al., 2002) in an apparent heroic effort to suppress emotional arousal in the interest of survival. A further study by this group found that survivors who dissociate during reminders of the trauma show a strong increase in those circuits that represent the body, compared to others who experience flashbacks (Lanius, Williamson, Bluhm et al., 2005). Perhaps this finding reveals the initial pattern of encoding when the body's implicit processes registered the trauma, while consciousness went elsewhere. Since conscious awareness is required for encoding explicit memories via the *hippocampus*, only implicit triggers remain, leaving the sufferer prone to flashbacks and bodily reenactments, experienced as happening in the present. In addition, when this pattern is well engrained very early in life, due to trauma and/or abuse, this dissociative process can easily take over in times of perceived stress.

When we sit with people who adapted to trauma by dissociating, we can sense that this was once a good solution to an impossible problem, intended to split the sensation from the emotionally intolerable meaning of the event (Kalsched, 1996) as well as protect survival. However, this once-adaptive dis-integration becomes a tear in the fabric of the current subjective sense of self that can leave hollowness, bewilderment, and a strong sense of ongoing helplessness. A feeling of one's own unreality (depersonalization) or a wide gap between the self and the world (derealization) often lingers at the edge of trauma-induced dissociation. Overlapping these experiences, ongoing emotional numbing appears to represent a somewhat disorganized attempt to modulate hyperarousal, athough it takes away any capacity for positive feeling and robs sufferers of words for their emotions as well (Frewen & Lanius, 2006a). As numbing and hyperarousal oscillate in rhythm with the brain's struggle to manage the unmanageable, feelings of helplessness can increase. However, despite these structural and functional challenges, we know that uncoordinated regulatory circuits can be linked when mediated by our containing presence (Frewen & Lanius, 2006a). Our mindfulness with them during this time will also help patients develop their caring observer's capacity to hold even the most painful memories, making us full partners in the integrative effort.

Preparing the Ground for Emotional Struggles

If these are the neural pathways underlying the suffering of depression, anxiety, and dissociation, what has brought brain structure and function to this condition? Before exploring the role of early attachment experience, it will be helpful to briefly acknowledge that genetic vulnerability, brain injury, and temperament may play a role in some cases.

The Genetic Contribution

One group of studies can help us understand the complexity of the *genetic contribution*. In 1996, a study by Lesch and colleagues suggested a correlation between the three forms of a gene in the serotonin transporter region (5-HTT) and susceptibility for anxiety disorders in the general public. Individuals with two long alleles exhibited less likelihood of becoming anxious than those with one long and one short, or, especially, two short alleles. Then, in 2003, research by Caspi, Moffitt, and their colleagues suggested (but did not completely confirm) a correlation between the three 5-HTT configurations and the likelihood of major depression occurring after a stressful experience. Again, the two-long-allele version appeared to confer greater resilience than the other versions (Caspi et al., 2003). It is noteworthy that this study added an environmental factor (major stressor) to the equation. This kind of research model is called G × E because it takes into account the intricate relationship been genes and environment. By 2005, other G × E studies were confirming the correlation between gene configuration, stress, and major depression as well as alcohol dependence (Hoefgen et al., 2005; Kendler, Kuhn, Vittnum, Prescott, & Riley, 2005; Nilsson et al., 2005).

At the same time, Joan Kaufman (2006) and her group began to wonder if other genetic and environmental factors might ameliorate the impact of the short-allele genes on vulnerability to psychological difficulties after stress. Using a four-way research design that involved (1) the two-short-allele version of the 5-HTT gene, (2) an additional gene possibly implicated in prefrontal function (brain-derived neurotropic factor [BDNF]), (3) children with a history of maltreatment, and (4) varying degrees of social support, they investigated depression vulnerability after maltreatment. Happily, their study revealed that when maltreated children could establish consistent, warm relationships, the depression vulnerability conferred by the short alleles was partially or fully reversed. Of even greater interest is the fact that with no maltreatment, there was no correlation between the genetic vulnerability and increased depression (Kaufman et al., 2006). This is a great detective story. As genetic and environmental factors intertwine, environment modifies gene expression, and genes modify the impact of the environment. When we remain mindful of the complexity of these interactions, we can understand why some trauma survivors fair better than others, possibly broadening our ability to "hold" people long and well when their struggles seem unending.

We might also be able to use this information to give our patients concrete additional reasons for them to nurture as many warm connections as they can in this world, because such connections are the primary factor that insulates us all from the effects of the inevitable painful stressors of life.

Brain Injury

As clinicians, it is important to keep in mind that injuries to certain parts of the brain may contribute to disorders simply because neural connectivity can be attenuated or absent in affected regions. Although an exploration of the consequences of specific injuries is beyond the scope of our inquiry here, we need to be aware of how past physical injuries might continue to influence our patients' current functioning. One of my patients told me of running full-force into the dining room table at 3 years old when he was being chased by his much-older brother. The blow hit directly on his eyebrows and left him unconscious for half a day. As an adult, he was profoundly anxious in ways that made no sense to him, given a family history most notable for its quiet restraint. Because of the much greater sophistication of brain scans 35 years after his injury, he eventually opted for a look inside. Diminished blood flow was found in some of his regulatory circuits. This discovery gave him permission to feel much more compassion for his struggles. No longer feeling like a failure for being jittery, he was willing to take a low dose of medication, in addition to spending more time at home doing the mindfulness practices we were developing in our sessions. The story had a happy ending, as he reported large gains in self-acceptance and calmness.

The Role of Temperament

Let's turn, for a moment, to the influence of temperament on vulnerability for mental difficulties. It is helpful to acknowledge that we may never be able to sort out what part of temperament emerges from genetics and what part from experience in the womb. However, it is clear that children come into this world brimming with individuality. Jerome Kagan (1994) worked with severely shy children and their parents to see if this characteristic of temperament was fixed or could be ameliorated by the way these children were understood and encouraged. He found that when parents were attuned to the needs of their children, provided with a secure base, and supported in their exploration of new vistas, their young ones gradually became more outgoing, even while the neural patterns of fear persisted in their brains. It seems safe to say that their parents had helped them move from a stance of withdrawal to a stance of approach through the power of attachment. These parents also became an encouraging inner community that went everywhere with their children.

Set Up for Emotional Pain: Neural Patterning in the Womb and Just Beyond

The influence of parents on their children's temperament takes us back to the main theme of the book: *the impact of early attachment experiences on mental health*. Even at the level of basic science, disturbances in the processes of regulation/integration are being recognized as the core of mental suffering (Frewen & Lanius, 2006b; Johnstone et al., 2007). Whether we consider easily identifiable traumatic experiences or the subtler devastation of quiet but disturbed relationships with parents, the consequences for brain development can define the trajectory of a life. The dramatic neuroplasticity of early childhood makes baby brains fully available for and vulnerable to the supportive or destructive patterns being wired in with every interaction. Even before birth, research is now showing us that the *emotional–neurochemical environment in the womb* can cause newborns to enter this life calm, depressed, or anxious. When we remember that implicit memory is all that is available for the first year, we can sense the power of the perceptual foundation being created by these earliest interactions, before and after birth. At least through the second year, the toddler's right hemisphere remains dominant. This is a time most notable for developing connections between the middle prefrontal circuits and the limbic region on the right. When a synchronous dance between parent and child is the centerpiece, sunshine floods through this open window, nurturing the neural pathways of flowing vertical integration and secure attachment. With the advent of language, collaborative narratives of the inner life begin to emerge, nudging this young one toward horizontal integration as well. In contrast, when the inner world of the parent makes it impossible for him or her to truly hold the child, neural disruption and the various shades of insecure attachment are the tragic results. Mary Main (1996), premiere attachment researcher, suggests that all forms of insecure attachment put people at risk for later mental disorders. However, the very same neural pathways that are disturbed by these losses can be brought to the fore within the therapeutic bond, where they can be rewired into patterns of earned security.

Being a Brain-Wise Therapist

Let's begin at the very beginning. For the last three decades, Tiffany Field and her group have devoted themselves to discovering the *effects of maternal depression* on babies before and after birth. Although depression was the primary indicator of the mothers who were studied, anxiety, anger, and irritability were also part of the picture. Here is a small but representative sample of the effects of maternal depression *during pregnancy* emerging from their prolific research. Using the Brazelton Neonatal Behavioral Assessment Scale, these researchers found that newborns of mothers who had been depressed during pregnancy had lower scores on orienting to faces and voices, cuddliness, and hand-to-mouth activities (Hernandez-Reif, Field, Diego, & Ruddock, 2006). If we picture the genetically encoded surge toward attachment hard-wired into infants and fully active at birth, we can sense how tragic it is for this surge to be dampened when babies have experienced their mother's depression during pregnancy.

Several studies noted *physical and biochemical changes* with depression during pregnancy. At the physical level, these included greater fetal activity, delayed growth, more frequent prematurity, and low birth weight. In addition, the baby's biochemical/physiological profile at birth paralleled that of the mother: elevated cortisol and norepinephrine (stress indicators), lower dopamine and serotonin (chemicals of enjoyment and balance), greater relative right frontal activation, and lower vagal tone. Elevation in the mother's cortisol during pregnancy, indicating ongoing stress, was the strongest predictor of these patterns in the newborn (Field et al., 2006). When the right frontal circuits are activated at the expense of the left frontal circuits, the infant will be more withdrawn and less likely to engage socially, because right-brain resources are more devoted to withdrawal and left-brain to approach (Urry et al., 2004). We can easily imagine the negative consequences for attachment when the infant is pulled inward, away from the natural outward surge toward connecting, especially when the mother is similarly turned inward.

Lower vagal tone is another indicator that may be related to availability for attachment. If we think back to Stephen Porges's (2001, 2007) work with the two branches of the parasympathetic nervous system, we may recall that engagement of the ventral vagus makes us available for social connection. The ventral vagus regulates eye gaze, facial expression, the ability to listen, and the prosody of the voice (the use of rhythm and tone convey emotion). The ventral vagus also calms the heart. *Vagal tone* refers to an impulse sent from the vagus to the heart, inhibiting (in a good way) the frequency of the beats. Subjectively, we feel calmer and more balanced, a state that leaves us open for sociability and connecting. What happens when a depressed mother is not available? When engagement of the ventral vagus does not provide safety through connection, the fight/flight sympathetic system is engaged as our next strategy for protection. Vagal tone decreases, allowing heart rate to rise so that we will be able to take action to protect ourselves. Lower vagal tone in a newborn may be one indication that the baby is feeling unsafe, just as the mother did during pregnancy, as measured by Mother's higher cortisol levels. With ventral vagal activation declining, this little one will also be less able to reach out to establish warm interpersonal connections. The accumulating impact of poorer attachment on the newborn's already stressed system potentially creates the picture of a downward spiral into some form of insecure attachment, as well as predisposition for depression, anxiety, and other emotional ills.

To add fuel to the fire, when stress levels remain high, damage to both brain structure and function are probable consequences, as there can be loss of both tissue and connectivity in the all-important prefrontal and limbic regions. The normal infant brain experiences an early, genetically driven overproduction of synapses that are then sculpted by experience, through a pruning of unused synapses, while shaping and reinforcing certain circuits (Schore, 2003a; Siegel, 1999). However, in an elegant demonstration of how genes and environment constantly work together, even before birth, Mother's hormones guide which genes will be expressed, biasing the nervous system in the same direction as the mother's (Dowling, Martz, Leonard, & Zoeller, 2000). Later, when the neural pathways connecting the limbic system to the prefrontal cortex are overpruned by stress and the established circuits are formed around upsetting interactions, the neural landscape becomes vulnerable to ongoing emotional difficulties with social and emotional regulation. If we imagine an adult whose brain and nervous system have been patterned this way both before and immediately after birth, we can perhaps more easily understand why some of our patients feel so helpless in the face of their symptoms. They simply cannot imagine a different emotional life, and initially they lack the resources to independently modulate their mood and arousal.

As this distressed baby moves from *birth to 3 months*, what might we see? One of the crucial questions is whether distressed infants are able to respond to nondepressed adults, with a full movement toward

Being a Brain-Wise Therapist

attachment—a potentially repairing situation. Unfortunately, the research suggests that this may not be the case. As early as 3 months, many infants have generalized their relational expectations to all people and so have less active and positive responses to nondepressed adults (Field et al., 1988). It seems as though implicit mental models have already settled in to such a degree that the happy approach of a welcoming adult cannot easily overcome the perceptual bias. Because of the burgeoning neuroplasticity of a child's brain, the situation is not hopeless. However, when this child's main companion is a mother in the grip of chronic depression or anxiety, the balance is much more difficult to right through the presence of other caring adults.

The most damaging outcomes for infants appear to come from depressed mothers who are *withdrawn*, not *intrusive*. Biologically and functionally, two significant differences showed up in Field's (2001) study. Intrusive mothers have more dopamine in their brains and greater relative left frontal activation. Increased dopamine likely means a greater ability to take pleasure in the infant, and right frontal activation leads to a reaching outward. This relative strength does not mean that the mother is able to fully regulate her infant, but she is at least able to engage. In fact, sometimes intrusive mothers became so dysregulated during the study that they were aggressive enough to require intervention by social services. Henriques and Davidson (1990) suggest that in these circumstances, the left frontal region is being activated at the expense of the right, rather than the two functioning in a more or less balanced way. Field (2001) found one indication of this lack of regulation in the difficulty preschool children of both kinds of depressed mothers had in showing empathy to their schoolmates—although, predictably, children of intrusive mothers were more aggressive, while those of withdrawn mothers remained focused inward. On the brighter side, Field (2001) also found that at 1 year, intrusive depressed moms had recovered more from depression than withdrawn depressed moms. It might be that these mothers' greater engagement led to a dance of co-regulation that helped both mother and child. All of these discoveries can also help us appreciate the extent to which mothers and infants lead parallel lives at many levels.

In tandem with their research concerning how maternal depression affects infants, Field and her colleagues were always in search of ways to ameliorate the often-devastating effects on mother and infant. In a series of studies, they have empirically demonstrated the power of medium-pressure massage to ameliorate painful dysregulation in mothers during pregnancy and after birth, as measured by decreased cortisol and norepinephrine levels accompanied by increased serotonin and dopamine levels (Field et al., 2004; Field et al., 1999). This kind of research can give us resources for guiding our patients to multiple avenues of help.

The Devastation of Trauma and Neglect

If maternal depression and anxiety have this kind of deleterious effect, what can we say about the impact of *early abuse and severe neglect*? Although it is counterintuitive, there is some evidence suggesting that neglect alone is most harmful for infants and children—more harmful than abuse or even neglect coupled with abuse (reviewed in Hilyard & Wolfe, 2002). If we think about the differing impacts of withdrawn and intrusive mothers, this finding makes some sense. Integrated brains develop from a steady diet of warm, contingent interactions with parents, so if there is virtually no meaningful connection, we can imagine that the emotional equivalent of starvation ensues, both subjectively and neurally. Neglect is an invitation to not exist. Estimates say that approximately 30 out of 1,000 children suffer neglect (Sedlak & Broadhurst, 1996). On the face of it, we might expect avoidant attachment to result from such restricted contact. However, coherence develops around attentive parents, so it is not surprising that neglected children are as likely to be disorganized as are those who are abused, about 82% of the time (Carlson et al., 1989). When we sit with patients who, one way or another, let us know that they had no meaningful contact with their mothers, we can know that the quiet exterior may belie dramatic internal fragmentation.

One of my patients had been sent away by eight earlier therapists who could not make sense of his suicidal feelings since he was 6 years old. They saw him as a quiet, self-hating, self-indulgent person who simply needed to get out of himself. His mother had been a noted professor, beloved by all in her university community, and devoted to charitable work. She also inwardly rejected her children. However, all he could share with me was his conviction that he continued to be a ruinous, intolerable creature who should be isolated from the rest of the world. Not being able to identify any explicit memories that would account for his torment, he couldn't make sense of his desolation or share it with others. In addition, since this picture of himself in no way correlated with how others perceived him, including his therapists, they couldn't hold his

Being a Brain-Wise Therapist

mind any more than his mother did, creating a perfect replication of his earlier experience.

It says something about this man's resilience that he continued to look for help. With humble thanks to this body of knowledge, I could at least have some idea about what might have happened to him at the beginning of life. I am convinced that our visceral beliefs about our value arise from the esteem in which we are held, so I thought I could see the outline of a mother who had no capacity for connection or delight when it came to her children. Tentatively holding his mind in mine seemed to establish threads of connection, and his attachment system slowly began to reemerge. While I talked with him softly about attachment and other ideas, he responded to the intention embodied in the prosody of my voice rather than the words I spoke. His eyes widened in terror, words failed him, his breath became shallow and rapid. However, his eyes never left mine, and I think he felt my breath deepen and slow as I sought to ease him into regulation. Over time, our spontaneous visits to these disorganized states became less frightening and then less frequent. What were we rewiring during these many months together?

If we keep in mind the effects of maternal depression and anxiety, we can simply amplify them to understand the impact of early abuse and neglect. As fear rooted in attack or abandonment intensifies and accumulates, the *HPA axis* escalates into more dramatic dysregulation, pouring glutamate, the major activating neurotransmitter, throughout the brain (Chambers et al., 1999) and engraining limbic hypersensitivity. The *amygdala* is on fire with fear and with the expectation of more fear to come. Because these experiences of terror are generated within a relationship, the child's window of tolerance for fluctuations in the caring of another may diminish to near zero. Initiated by the continuing anticipation of frightening circumstances, streams of stress hormones continue to disrupt both brain structure and connectivity, particularly impacting those *regulatory circuits* connecting prefrontal areas to the limbic region, and right and left prefrontal regions. In this way, the brain's most basic integrative system is reduced to a fragile condition, predisposed to break apart under the slightest stress.

In tandem with negative neurochemical experiences, this child is also deprived of the consistent wash of *opioids, oxytocin*, and *proloctin*, the bonding chemistry released by a warm, attentive mother (Panksepp, 1998). Crafted in the safety of a secure relationship, these chemicals shift perception to the moment-to-moment feeling that all is well, tracing patterns of resilience on which the child can later rely. A rich flow of opioids also mitigates feelings of anxiety, anger, and hostility under stressful conditions (Sunderland, 2006). When a mother's ability to provide this loving acceptance is intermittent, with periods of complete withdrawal of contact, the sudden decrease creates pain similar to withdrawal from heroin (an artificial way to cause opioids to flow in the brain; Schore, 2005). Such separation distress also activates the same circuits in the anterior cingulate as physical pain, but without the obvious connection of a visible wound (Eisenberger, Lieberman, & Williams, 2003; Panksepp, 2003). The developing infant brain does not have right ventral prefrontal circuits available to modulate such pain, so without comfort, the anguish can seem endless. Under these relationally generated chemical conditions, negative emotions come to the forefront and positive ones recede (Panksepp, 1998), while excessive amounts of acetylcholine wash through the brain, pushing toward anger and hostility (Sunderland, 2006). If these are the borders of ambivalent attachment, imagine the continual painful longing of the neglected child. As Margot Sunderland (2006) says, instead of "loving in peace," these children will "love in torment" (p. 186), because children will attempt to bond, unless there is an organic inability to do so.

This push toward bonding means that a baby's brain will continue to form new *social circuits* even in the midst of all these losses. We now know that these pathways will develop in parallel with the mother's, so her patterns of dis-integration will become her child's (Schore, 2003b; Siegel, 1999). What is wired and reinforced will follow the mother's tragically skewed relational experience. Because prefrontal–limbic connections will be created around her inability to respond to her baby's signals, the child may be oblivious to the facial expressions of others and clueless about how to give an attuned response (Schore, 2003a; Siegel, 1999). When the baby's bodily needs go unseen or this child experiences harm, protective chemicals may provide enough numbness to reduce present suffering, but leave the pathway from insula to limbic region and prefrontal cortex without sufficient nurturance to become a reliable highway of information about the body. Since this body gives the baby the first awareness of feelings, without such connection the child may be emotionally blind (Craig, 2002). Because the baby's space was violated when the mother consistently misread cues to come closer or move away, connections between the parietal and prefrontal regions form patterns that will leave this child with little ability to read these signals in others, so he may become an intrusive or avoiding presence (Sunderland, 2006). Because Mother's timing is governed by her own needs rather than by her baby's, pathways from the cerebellum (below the brainstem) to the frontal regions will engrain a pattern that disregards the rhythm of emotional expression in conversation with others (Sunderland, 2006). Stress may cause excessive pruning of neural connections between the hemispheres and disrupt genetically prompted myelination of these pathways, making it difficult for this child to generate words for feelings or create a meaningful and containing story of inner experience, especially since Mother lacks the resources to shape her own story or give words to her child's experience (Schore, 2003b; Siegel & Hartzell, 2003). When such traumatic experiences are not repaired, the child may stay in dysregulated misery for long periods, increasing the strength of these out-of-balance circuits. As the child grows up in the same environment, ongoing emptiness or trauma continue to compound the initial brain-wide dis-integration, a tragic reverse image of the symphony of integration that flows between an attuned mother and baby.

All of this disruption may happen during sympathetic overactivation, when the baby's neuroception still believes there is a chance to survive. However, when fear flows into impossible terror, the last resort is dissociation, as the slightly older infant takes refuge in the dramatically diminished activation of the dorsal vagal branch of the parasympathetic nervous system (Porges, 2001, 2007). This response is different from the hyperalert, sympathetically mediated stillness that may precede an attack (Frewen & Lanius, 2006). Here, the safety strategy is to become unseen, unnoticed. Prior to this collapse, the sympathetic system was likely at the height of its activity, inducing a state of panic (Frewen & Lanius). Even in parasympathetic freeze, the dorsal vagal brake is accompanied by high sympathetic acceleration (Schore, 2003a). This intolerable sympathethic–parasympathetic overload is perhaps externalized in a disorganized child's frantic attempts to move toward, then withdraw, then freeze when the terrifying/terrified parent returns during the Strange Situation. Over time, the tendency to dissociate under stress can be engrained, while the window of tolerance for emotional intensity narrows to a slit.

Whether abuse or neglect is the root, implicit mental models of dangerous and damaging relational possibilities drop deep roots, while the resonating circuits embed the being of the hurtful other in the child's mind, creating an inner community that sustains the disastrous relational exchange, even when outer circumstances are more favorable. Because what wires together, fires and survives together (Hebb, 1949; Post, et al., 1998), these initially thread-like circuits gradually become thick ropes. With enough repetition, particularly at this time of heightened neuroplasticity, state can become trait, with personality disorders and other severe emotional conditions resting on this bedrock of debilitating, sustained dysregulation.

The Making of Borderline Personality

We have given the names *borderline personality disorder* and *dissociative identity disorder* to states of almost total regulatory disruption, resulting from attachment trauma and/or abuse. Although genetics may play some role in intensifying and biasing the response, research has made it clear that the defining causes are severe overt or covert trauma. Just the diagnostic labels often draw up feelings of dread for us. It may be useful to spend a few minutes with your bodily sensations, behavioral impulses, images, emotions, and (least important) thoughts in the presence of these words. Perhaps your own previous experience treating such wounded people has left a visceral response, or perhaps negative comments of professors and colleagues about these clinical populations have stirred up fear. However, now that we have spent some time understanding the neural and inner community effects of attachment trauma and abuse, we may now be able to hold these symptoms in a more stable way, in spite of the challenge offered to our limbic circuits by the intensity of the suffering. When we remain internally steady, our own regulatory/integrative resources will ground recovery. If we sit with the borderline symptoms in the *DSM-IV-TR* (American Psychiatric Association, 2000), we read "frantic efforts to avoid real or imagined abandonment" (p. 292). The imaginary part is real for them because the amygdala is sending implicit messages of imminent, terrifying loss, accompanied by the physical and psychic pain of opioid withdrawal. Believing that abandonment is the inevitable outcome of relating, these individuals suffer with a hair-trigger perceptual bias toward loss. Next, we find "a pattern of unstable and intense interpersonal relationships characterized by alternating between extremes of idealization and devaluation" and "affective instability due to a marked reactivity of mood" (p. 292). This language describes the engrained upset in the stress system, coupled with disabled connections between the hypersensitive amygdala and middle prefrontal region (Hazlett et al., 2006; Herpetz et al., 2001). Because of the early origin of loss, the search for the "perfect mother" in every relationship—paired with the inevitable disappointment at not finding her—leads to these dramatic oscillations in evaluation, accompanied by swift changes of mood.

Further evidence of the regulatory system's inability to manage the terror and rage of abandonment comes from "impulsivity in at least two areas that are potentially self-damaging," "recurrent suicidal behavior, gestures, or threats, or self-mutilating behavior," and "inappropriate, intense anger or difficulty controlling anger" (pp. 292–293). When the sympathetic nervous system is activated into a pattern of high arousal and poor regulation, defensive impulsive and rageful responses toward self and others are inevitable, particularly in the face of perceived relational disappointment. A mother's utter rejection and hatred are among the pathways to this vulnerability. Not surprisingly, "transient, stress-related paranoid ideation or severe dissociation" (p. 293) are among the symptoms. Paranoid ideation conjures the picture of unwarranted fear; however, if we give due weight to what is implicitly encoded in the amygdala during the early months after birth, we can perhaps see the reason overwhelming fears balloon into the present under stress. Not surprisingly, one study found indications of dissociation even in borderline sufferers without a history of abuse (Goodman, Mitropoulou, New, Sprung, & Siever, 2000). This finding points to the kind of infant attachment trauma that produces helpless, hopeless feelings to such an intolerable extent that, over and over again, protest falls into collapse.

The final two symptoms, "chronic feelings of emptiness," and "identity disturbance: markedly and persistently unstable self-image or sense of self" (pp. 292–293), no doubt have neural correlates in the inability of the middle prefrontal cortex to manage smooth state transitions in the midst of overwhelming limbic upset. However, from an inner community perspective, we can perhaps see an infant looking into an unresponsive, and therefore terrifying, maternal face, internalizing her commitment to this infant's nonexistence. There is certainly no fullness and no continuity to be found there.

When these people come to us, their right hemispheres in tatters, perhaps acting out in anger or fear-induced seduction, our ability to consistently hold their deeper minds can slowly rebuild lost neural structures. To date, psychodynamic psychotherapy (Bateman & Fonagy, 2001) and dialectical behavior therapy (Linehan, 1993) have produced lasting improvements. In both cases, although by somewhat different methods, the structures of regulation are gradually rebuilt within the embrace of a densely supportive therapeutic relationship.

There is little doubt that borderline personality disorder develops within overt and covert traumatic conditions, and that the resulting damaged attachment bonds are its foundation. One study found that 91% of sufferers reported childhood abuse, and 92% grew up with some form of neglect (Zanarini et al., 2000). Consequently, co-diagnoses of posttraumatic stress and borderline personality are common (Herman, Perry, & van der Kolk, 1989). Other minds handle abuse in a different manner, with *dissociative identity disorder* actually maintaining some semblance of order through packaging different responses to abusive experiences in separate personalities. Our unsettled feelings may come less from a tidal wave of relational chaos than from the parade of different people—different voices, ages, clothing, interests, diagnoses, memories, emotional styles, autonomic activation patterns, and, possibly, profiles of integration—spending time with us.

The Making of Dissociated Identities

Dissociation can mean something different than dorsal vagal collapse, although its intention to protect may be the same. In this case, the separation is between different states of mind rather than between conscious awareness and the body. Putting multiple personalities on a continuum with what we might call the normal multiplicity of the inner community can be an accurate and reassuring conceptualization. As all of us walk our healing path, one of the results is a greater sense of wholeness, a coherent sense of self. What does this mean? In terms of *neurobiology*, it appears that the right orbitofrontal cortex oversees this integration of states of mind (Schore, 2003a; Siegel, 1999), providing a felt sense of smooth transitions between states (e.g., violinist, mother, wife, photographer). At the same time, the conversation between right and left prefrontal regions generates the coherent narrative, a life story that embraces all these states (Siegel, 1999; Siegel & Hartzell, 2003). If we think in terms of *inner community* relationships, we can imagine that many of the spiky relational patterns that kept inner people at odds with one another have been resolved, so that we have the subjective experience of empathy between the members of the community, as well as confidence in the appropriate emergence of different aspects under the varying conditions of life. In other words, the highly disciplined violinist does not show up when it is time to read a bedtime story to her 2-year-old.

As we move down the continuum away from this state of health, we will find as many different self-state configurations as there are individuals, although some patterns do emerge, representing *progressive degrees of dissociation* between states of mind. When a *traumatic event* occurs after we have established a flow of energy and information between our selves, and the impact is sufficient to fully block integration from the implicit amygdala to the explicit hippocampus, we might picture a small pie slice removed from an otherwise satisfactory sense of continuity. When this event occurs in the midst of otherwise traumatic circumstances, recovering lost memories may form a small but important part of the overall recovery from the effects of trauma.

As a public service to our new group of veterans returning from Iraq, G. B. Trudeau's (2006) daily editorial strip *Doonesbury* has given us the opportunity to follow former football captain BD's recovery from an insurgent attack. In the midst of his struggle with rage, flashbacks, and alcohol, he also has partial amnesia for the attack that cost him his leg. His counselor, Elijah, is a fellow vet. As BD struggles to connect with that day, Elijah says, "Right now your memories are burned into your brain, but they're not integrated" (p. 206). The first phase takes BD into emotional connection with the part he does remember: the actual loss of his leg. However, he is still left with so much shame that he wants to give up his military benefits. Elijah talks to him about leaving his leg on the battlefield, and as BD turns to go, he says, "Yeah, well, that's not the only thing I left on the battlefield" (218). After a pause, he says, "Okay, that probably means something, doesn't it?" (p. 218). Eventually, in the safety of his relationship with Elijah, BD pushes into the split-off part of his memory. In the chaos and terror of the deadly attack—"We're in a kill box!" (p. 219)—he orders his driver to gun the Humvee through a crowd that includes children. That was the memory he couldn't bear to keep in consciousness. As he remembers, he can barely breathe, really doesn't want to, but Elijah comforts and encourages him. "BD, what you have to understand is that you can't heal without facing what happened. I know it's painful to revisit that day. And it will probably always be painful. But you can choose not to be trapped there. You're not controlled by your memories of Iraq—you can move away from them" (p. 220). Far from trivializing the war experience by making it the subject of a cartoon,

Trudeau's work may be helping raise awareness of the impact and some of the parameters of recovery.

A broader foundation for dissociated states of mind is laid when parents' inner communities are not coherent, with states of mind at odds with one another and little conscious control over which part is activated. Then, children must learn a *range of dyadic dances* to maintain connection. These dances are often not based on the child's real needs, so the integrating power of contingency is absent. As a result, the child's inner community/potential states of mind form around self–other pairs that are disconnected, in varying degrees, from other inner pairs and not well-connected to prefrontal sources of regulation and continuity of states. When we work with people who have had these backgrounds, it can be helpful to generate our own inner pictures of their communities.

As an example, let's imagine the inner world of a woman who has not healed from her father's drunken rages and all the family dynamics that accompanied them. Her inner community contains a *terrified child– angry father* pair, side by side with a *playful father–joyous child* and *studious child–proud father*, formed during the times when he was sober and available. In addition, she has an inner mother who was impotent in the presence of her husband's rage, and, in response, this child became alternately angry or protective, creating *impotent mother–angry child* and *impotent mother–protective child* pairs. When safety returned to the house, her mother was sometimes warm and sometimes critical, forming two more pairs: *attentive mother–contented child*, and *critical mother– shamed child*. Now, as her own high-spirited daughter turns 2, she can find no consistent response to her child's expected meltdowns. In her cognitive mind, this mother understands how she can use tantrums as a chance to build regulation, but she can't control her visceral/emotional response. Consequently, she alternately feels impotent, terrified, enraged, critical, or calm, depending on how the circumstances pull people up from her inner community. Since her daughter can't predict how her mother will react, she learns to mold her moment-to-moment response to her mother's triggered state. As these scenes are repeated, she develops her own group of inner pairs: *impotent mother–protective, inhibited child, terrified mother–terrified child, critical mother–shamed child*, and so on. In the absence of repair that could engage the orbitofronal cortex and restore continuity between states, synaptic strength grows over time, and these separate dyads take long-lasting shape inside.

Some patients have described this experience as living on islands in their minds. When they are helplessly thrown into one state of mind, at the very least, they have no emotional or behavioral access to others and sometimes cannot even cognitively remember that their minds contain other possible subjective experiences. Because these states have not been regulated (and, therefore, not integrated), the orbitofrontal cortex is not able to provide sufficient modulation for them, when they rise up from the limbic regions, to connect with the larger flow of self-experience. One bewildered patient reported: "I don't know why I did that. One minute I was determined to be calm, and the next minute my hands were around her neck. It felt as though boiling water welled up from my stomach to my chest and throat, and then down my arms." A fleeting mental image of their five young children pulled him away from this rage state before his wife passed out, but the outburst cost him his marriage. His mother had conceived him as the result of a rape. He spent his first 3 months in foster care and was then adopted by a family where discipline by violence was the rule. Beginning with his teenage years, any threatened abandonment pulled him onto the island of rage or despair, and from there, violence toward himself or the other person seemed the only answer. Over time, we were able to process the agony of his early days, symbolized in his mind as a Nazi concentration camp. In the warmth of our strong connection, his rage decreased as his abandonment terror diminished. As his states of mind began to flow through his better-connected orbitofrontal cortex, they could help one another even under very stressful conditions. One day, his mind gave him a sustaining image, drawn from the storehouse of his many backpacking trips. He said, "You know, I think I can swim from island to island now. I'm not helplessly trapped in one place. I can even picture less water and more land until one day there will be just ponds and then meadows with everything connected." This image became a touchstone of his progress for the rest of our time together.

As we listen to our patients, we will find that the degree of separation varies, depending largely on the intensity of the trauma/abuse, the lack of repair during initial encoding, and the lack of opportunity to process at a later date (with genetics and temperament also possibly playing roles). However, under these island circumstances, the conscious mind is able to maintain explicit awareness of events while jumping into states of rage, despair, loneliness, heartbreak, hatred, or helplessness.

We can imagine that when these disastrous impacts begin before a child's developing brain has the resources to create a flow between states, these separations might lead to the *complete structural separation of dissociated identities*. Neural nets draw similar information together, so when a parent offers only dramatic relational inconsistency, coupled with the fragmenting experiences of abuse and near-total lack of repair, it makes sense that a child's brain would create strong nets to encapsulate these differing relational pairs. Once this pattern is established, it extends to the creation of nets/selves holding positive experiences as well.

A patient of mine was a concert flautist for a major symphony orchestra. Even under the stressful conditions of performance, her mind was able to settle into the flow of the music without interference from the dissociated parts of her that held severe posttraumatic dysregulation. Paradoxically, the rigidity of the separation sometimes gave her greater flexibility of response to environmental conditions. However, the stress of interpersonal relationships frequently brought on a cascade of switches, particularly when sexual behavior, confrontation, or fear of abandonment were part of the relational mix. Even kind treatment would unsettle her, as child selves wanted to supplant the adults to share their story and be nurtured. The helplessness of switching from state to state, with the accompanying of awareness, was frightening and disabling for her.

Recent neuroimaging studies support our thought experiment about how the mind creates and sustains multiple selves. By reading a trauma-related script and a neutral script to a person who had conscious control over the ability to switch between personalities, researchers were able to see differences in brain activation between the trauma-aware person and the person with amnesia for the event or the belief that the event did not happen to him or her (Reinders et al., 2003). When the trauma script was read to the latter person, deactivated brain areas included the right medial prefrontal cortex and other associational areas in a pattern consistent with reading a trauma script to a person who had not been abused. In this self-state, the mind did not integrate the visual and somatosensory information, and so did not experience autonomic dysregulation or feelings related to the event. However, in the trauma-aware self-state, autonomic arousal as well as visceral/emotional responses revealed integration with the neural nets holding the trauma. The walls between the two selves were impermeable.

Seeking to understand brain structures that may help to maintain multiplicity when the environmental need has passed, a study reported a 19.2% reduction of right and left hippocampal volumes and a 31.6% reduction of right and left amygdalar volumes (Vermetten, Schmahl, Lindner, Lowenstein, & Bremner, 2006). Recall that the hippocampus and amygdala are central to emotional and cognitive memory, so significant losses here may impede memory processing. However, this picture is similar to brain structure in borderline personality sufferers who were also abused, so we can speculate that the loss of volume may be related to the action of stress chemicals in destroying tissue, while acknowledging that genetically determined initial smaller volumes may predispose people to both adaptations to traumatic stress. Interestingly, the parallel results do not illuminate the reason why one person will become borderline while another will develop a community of alternate selves—a question to which we will return later.

Given that our brains intrinsically push toward integration, are there other kinds of early neural patterning that might contribute to blocking that process in adults? Kelly Forrest (2001), building on the work of Putnam (1997), Fuster (1997), and Schore (1994, 1996), offers an elegant hypothesis that brings us back to the centrality of the left and right orbitofrontal cortices in creating the subjective experience of wholeness, together with the coherent narrative that shapes that wholeness in words. She pictures a continuum from mothers who provide the security of warmth, consistency, and repair; to dismissing or preoccupied mothers who do not contingently respond to their infants but do provide a *pattern* of behavior that makes sense; to disorganizing mothers whose behavior lacks pattern. Movement along this continuum is accompanied by increasing degrees of dysregulation and decreasing opportunities for repair. For some babies, the dance of disorganizing connection creates discrete emotional/arousal states, while still allowing for a continuous awareness across these disrupted states. For them, *the agony of broken attachment may be the most salient feature of their environment.* However, as abuse intensifies, *moment-to-moment survival strategies take center stage*, and the attachment dance becomes focused on the immediate interaction to the exclusion of any ability to link states—the central characteristic of dissociated identities. The dramatic lack of consistency, coupled with no nurturance (the food of prefrontal integration), no words for the experience, and continual threat make it impossible for the child's orbitofrontal cortex to generate a regulatory system independent of the immediate context (Badenoch, 1991A; Forrest, 2001). The terrified child cannot fade away into dorsal vagal dissociation because survival demands hypervigilance, but she also cannot go into sympathetic overarousal to such an extent that she becomes disorganized, because those behaviors are likely to intensify the abuse. The only solution is to narrow the lens and isolate arousal states around specific interactions (Forrest, 2001). It is precisely the ability to experience a flow of regulation across states that creates the felt sense of wholeness, so when this fails utterly, a community of discrete selves emerges.

If the inability of the oribtofrontal region to sustain integration lies at the heart of the problem, then therapy with a consistently calm, empathic companion can be central to the solution. However, several capacities will be required of us (Badenoch, 1991a, 1991b):

- An ability to hold a clear, settled picture of this person's inner world and neural processes;
- Trust in the relationship's capacity to gradually rewire the orbitofrontal region to sustain integration across states;
- An ability to contain, comfort, and regulate the pain and fear that will emerge as younger selves process the abuse and relational trauma in preparation for becoming part of a flow of self-states;
- Patience for this long-term process.

Although this is no doubt challenging work, we can ease the way by learning to flow with the regulatory/attachment needs of each person as he or she emerges. Some conceptualizations of dissociated identities suggest that integration of personalities must take place, leading to a single self. However, neurobiology suggests that no one is a single self, but rather that health lies in the harmonious flow among our many selves, so that they can wax and wane within a wide window of tolerance in response to life's stresses and delights.

We are beginning to see how PTSD, borderline personality, and dissociative identities group together as responses to intolerable relational and traumatic experiences, while major depression and many shades of anxiety may also take root in the soil of early emotional and physical maltreatment. Over time, using disturbances in attachment, regulation, and neural integration as points of understanding, we might see a rewritten *DSM* reflecting these consilient viewpoints and providing more potent guidance for scientifically grounded treatment.

Chaotic Coping: Addiction

One sad and ultimately counterproductive way in which sufferers may try to manage any of these patterns of dysregulating stress is to seek relief in distraction, numbness, or compensatory, chemically-induced feelings. This kind of chaotic coping through *addiction* (with or without substances) seeks to influence the balance of neurotransmitters in the brain, altering function in the direction of feeling better. However, the substance or activity becomes the momentary salve that never actually soothes the underlying pain and fear. Craving may begin to dominate the mind, for reasons we do not yet fully understand, and behavior often deteriorates, further isolating the person from interpersonal resources of support and healing. Research has helped us understand how stress unbalances neurotransmitters and hormones to set the stage by changing the way the brain functions. When this change is coupled with inner community models of addictive behavior, attachment losses that hamper integration of the middle prefrontal region with the limbic areas, and possible genetic factors, multiple neural pathways are contributing to the maintenance of these addictive behaviors.

Even this very brief overview may allow us to picture the addicted brain in a way that can help us hold our struggling clients with understanding and compassion, even in the midst of their often unpleasant behavior. Addiction narrows the motivational aperture; people with addictions feel compelled to pour all their resources toward getting their next infusion of imagined goodness. Neurochemical pathways form a constricting circle whose components include (but are not limited to) the *stress system* (HPA axis), the *reward system* (primarily dopamine, but also opioids, GABA, and serotonin), and the *emotional/motivational meaning system* (amygdala), whose responses impact the stress system (Koob & LeMoal, 2006; McCauley, 2003). As the person continues to engage in the addictive behavior, these systems become increasingly dysregulated, both by the activity itself and by the periods when the drug is not available.

One common pathway to addiction begins with *chronic overactivation of the HPA axis*, in response to which stress chemicals cause a decrease in dopamine levels, leading to difficulty in noticing and experiencing pleasure. This is the same pathway that ordinarily mediates our movement toward food, water, shelter, and sex (Kelley & Berridge, 2002), so it is not surprising that addicts may lose interest in all of these. Both addictive substances and behaviors change the chemical balance, with most dramatically increasing dopamine, while others also raise GABA (alcohol) and opioid (heroin) levels. All of these chemicals increase positive feelings, either by mediating sensations/feelings of pleasure, providing comfort, or soothing anxiety.

Whereas some patients take a disorganized approach to drug use, we have found that many dabble until they find the substance or activity that provides the best relief for their particular neurochemical imbalance. Unfortunately, these experiences do not change the brain in the direction of integration the way that relationships can, so as the drug leaves their system or an activity ends, dopamine and serotonin levels tend to plunge, activating the stress system and often leaving a sense of desolation that can lead to more craving and relapse (Koob & LeMoal, 2006). The intensity of these feelings has been compared to the urgency for food when we are starving; in the deeper limbic structures, the hyperactivated amygdala may define acquisition of the drug as necessary for survival (McCauley, 2003; Volkow & Fowler, 2000). This message of survival may partially account for continued addictive behavior when pleasure has diminished or vanished. When many patients shed their addictions, they sink into a grief state and speak of having lost their "best friend." This is not metaphorical. The pain suffered is visceral, such as what the non-addicted feel upon the sudden absence of a dear friend.

The pervasive sense of helplessness described by addicts might lead us to ask why the brain systems that confer flexible responses (*middle prefrontal*) and the ability to make decisions based on a cognitive/emotional sense of what such actions will mean for our future (*anterior cingulate*) seem to offer little help. Recent research shows that once the neurochemical processes outlined above play their role in initiating the addictive behavior, functioning in the orbitofrontal cortex is disrupted, possibly by the bursts of dopamine that occur during use (Volkow & Fowler). When cocaine was employed as the study drug, neuroimagining studies showed dramatically increased activity in the prefrontal region during the craving that arises shortly after the last administration of cocaine and during early withdrawal—a state reminiscent of the pattern with OCD (Schwartz & Begley, 2002). During prolonged withdrawal, the orbitofrontal area demonstrates significantly decreased activity. Both dysregulations were found to be in proportion to the levels of dopamine receptors in a connecting brain area, the striatum. Another study explored structure in the oribtofrontal region and the anterior cingulate, finding a 5–11% decrease in gray matter in both (Franklin et al., 2002). It may be that decreases in these two regions, coupled with changes in functionality, leave the addicted person with the subjective experience of being trapped between a debilitating compulsion and too few resources to make decisions based on long-term consequences.

As we learn more, we discover that addiction is very much a whole-brain process, drawing many neural circuits into destructive cooperation, particularly in the absence of empathic interpersonal connections. We may also notice that the very circuits implicated in depression, anxiety, posttraumatic stress, borderline personality, and dissociated identities are implicated here. As we increase our awareness of the many harmful effects of disturbed attachments and other forms of maltreatment on brain development, we may possibly glimpse the roots of addiction as well. Appreciating how *this compulsive process is rooted in stress and dysregulation*, treatments that take shame and punishment out of the equation and emphasize interpersonal connection and mindful awareness may engender greater success.

Concluding Thoughts

It may be helpful to conclude this chapter with a few words about medication. Sometimes our patients need this kind of pharmacological support to enter their window of tolerance. A deep depression or disruptive anxiety, for example, may so dysregulate the sympathetic nervous system that the social engagement circuits are out of reach. Since our ability to help repair the right-brain circuits and foster other forms of neural integration depends our patient's ability to experience connection, some supportive change in the brain's function through pharmacological intervention may be necessary. We have found that working with a psychiatrist who appreciates the benefits of co-treatment and will participate in ongoing dialogues for the benefit of the patient is a gift for everyone. The soothing experience of having a cooperative team can cradle recovery. Also, medication requirements may shift throughout therapy, so having a caring feedback system can allow for appropriate adjustments. Even though most of us are not licensed to prescribe medications, it can be helpful to keep abreast of new discoveries about how various medications impact the structure and function of the brain. For example, we now know that many antidepressants stimulate neurogenesis in hippocampi that may be devastated by long-term depression (Santarelli et al., 2003). Mouse studies are linking these new neurons with symptom alleviation. Our awareness of these developments can inform our conversations with both patients and psychiatrists, so that some of the fear and mystery are removed, allowing our patients to make more informed decisions.

Having spent some time becoming comfortable with the neurobiology of a few diagnoses, where might we go from here? In considering any diagnosis, it may be helpful to ask what role deficits in regulation/integration may be playing. As we saw earlier, with some cases of OCD, the problem lies mainly with improper functioning of a few brain circuits. Through mindfulness practice, it is possible to integrate these circuits in a different way (Schwartz & Begley, 2002), leading to the capacity to regulate the urge to repeat certain actions. If these malfunctioning neural pathways were solely part of this patient's genetic inheritance and had not arisen as an attempt to deal with implicit attachment anxiety, that piece of integration would be sufficient. If, instead, early losses were significant, this single piece of integration would be an important but incomplete part of relieving suffering and widening the window of tolerance. If this patient so chose, symptom relief could then perhaps open the door to internal work that would bring the limbic and middle prefrontal circuits into integration as well.

Perhaps this chapter can provide a template for inquiry into other diagnoses as you have the need. Putting the words "neurobiology of . . ." into your search engine will give you an afternoon of exploration. We have found that the ability to hold such pictures steadies our minds as we plunge into our patients' painful worlds. Sharing some of this information about the impact of their history on their brains, minds, and relationships with our patients can help take the fear and shame out of their struggle as well.

The centrality of failures in regulation and integration for people with these familiar diagnoses brings us now to an exploration of ways to participate in healing those right-hemisphere circuits that underlie mental health. When people have experienced great relational and traumatic pain, we find that vertical integration, facilitated by interpersonal joining, is the indispensable cornerstone on which coherent narratives and fulfilling relationships will eventually rest. Our ability to be with and follow our patients into their inner worlds is the foundation for that endeavor, so we will begin by exploring ways to ground therapy on the right side of the brain.

Chapter 11

Grounding Therapy in the Right Brain

A young man came to therapy because his anxiety was affecting his behavior in ways that were impacting his most important relationships. During our second session, Don talked at some length about a previous experience in therapy. "I worked with a psychologist for about 6 months, and I still don't know what went wrong. When we started out, I was really intrigued. She had lots of good ideas about why I was always getting into bickering matches at work and with my family. But then something started to bother me. Whenever I wanted to tell her about something that was making me upset, she would talk to me about how to make it different—you know, give me ideas about how to change it. You'd think that was just what I would want, but I started to feel hollow and kind of antsy inside. I tried to talk to her about that, but all I got were more ideas and more suggestions. I began to feel like she was shoving me into a box. More and more, I was reminded of my mother because she always knew the answers and never cared about how I might have wanted to do things. I finally just gave up, made an excuse, and stopped seeing her. So now I'm really scared to come here because what if it starts out well, but I just get to that miserable place again."

What might have happened in Don's therapy? Perhaps his psychologist had a wonderful set of therapeutic principles that she understood would help him with his anxiety. Perhaps these were clearly formulated in her left brain, and she was focusing her conscious awareness on how these principles could be put to work for Don. We know that where conscious attention goes, so goes neural firing, so she might have had most of her energy in the left hemisphere. Perhaps when he would discuss his anxiety, a list of possible interventions would pop up in her mind, and she would choose the one that best fit his current circumstance. This kind of left-centered thinking can cut us off from our right-hemisphere social circuits, rendering us unaware of our bodies and the subtle waves of primary emotion that whisper to us about fluctuations in the quality of connection. Without this awareness, we may not be able to flow well with our patients. If this was the case, his limbic circuits/inner community may have experienced abandonment, especially at moments of discomfort. Since this so closely paralleled interactions with his mother, it may have awakened old anxiety, possibly stirring similar feelings in his therapist, even though she may not have been aware of them. This might have led her to look for even better interventions from her list. What a sad cycle for both of these good-hearted, well-intentioned people. The despair that led him to leave therapy may have been exactly what he felt in his family every time he gave in to his mother's wishes—except that as an adult, he was free to leave the relationship.

From this example, we learn that if we hunker down in our own left hemispheres, trying to think our way to the best intervention or keenest interpretation, we are likely to initiate at least two shifts: Our patients will initially follow us to the left, then perhaps become uncomfortable when right-hemisphere attachment needs go untended; and we risk becoming disengaged from our bodies, an important source of information about our patients' inner worlds. Instead of the graceful, fluid dance of co-regulation that leads to integration and healing, we may fall into a lock-step forced march. Our interventions will no longer be as connected to the felt needs of the person, and will therefore often fall on relatively sterile ground.

We might ask where theory comes into the picture. Is it always an unhelpful left-brain force? On the contrary, solid *grounding in a felt understanding* of how body, brain, and mind are wounded and recover can actually lend us confidence, giving therapy a shape and steadying our minds. This paradigmatic clarity can be like having a road map that gives us the security to savor the scenery to the full. Rather than guiding every moment, such a theory forms the backdrop against which the ever-flowing relationship can unfold. Most of us seem to do our best work when we are grounded in theory, easily conceptualizing cases in our minds so that we feel safe and secure enough to settle into the right-brain to right-brain dance, particularly when emotions become intense. It is helpful to acknowledge that we now have enough neuroscience available to us to evaluate whether our theories embody efficacious ways to foster healing, and hopefully enough wisdom to adjust if they don't. This carries us to the next crucial question: *How* do we ground therapy in the right hemisphere?

Expanding the Therapist's Mental Health

Throughout these chapters, there has been a continual nudge toward doing everything we possibly can to expand and solidify our own mental health: getting to know our inner community, finding areas where neural integration needs encouragement, and increasing our capacity for mindful awareness. Working to establish the internal space to welcome and then contain the pain, fear, and desolation our patients bring us is the most essential work. Although therapist sensitivity is partly a function of temperament, the far larger component is our ability to maintain neural integration under emotionally trying circumstances. As we forge inward ourselves in service of this goal, we find that at least three interwoven processes have a chance to unfold: (1) We heal what we can, widening our window of tolerance; (2) we become conscious of our implicit vulnerabilities, letting go of any belief that we can or must be perfect containers; and (3) we develop sufficient mindfulness to become aware *in the moment* when we are activated by our patients' struggles. This last capacity allows us to minimize tendencies to replicate hurtful relational patterns, reinforcing the very neural nets we are seeking to change. However, when the inevitable ruptures do occur, mindful awareness allows us to repair them promptly and well.

This process begins with establishing and strengthening our *vertical integration*, especially in the right hemisphere, linking body, limbic region, and cortex. As we engage with our patients in the back-and-forth, microsecond, implicit-to-implicit interchanges that deeply connect people, vertical integration will give us a greater ability to sense the ebb and flow of empathic connection in our bodies. We will be able to make better use of our resonance circuits to enter as cleanly as possible into our patients' emotional "house," without undue perceptual bias distorting our sense of what they may be experiencing. We will more easily feel in our bodies when the doors to our hearts close, so that we can locate the limbic upset and remedy the rupture. Most of all, we need to have confidence that the process constantly unfolding within us, out of awareness, most often supports the kindness and understanding of our outer behavior.

What can happen when this nonconscious dance unfolds in all its beauty? When our middle prefrontal region is steadfast in its linkage with our limbic circuits and bodies, the flow of nonverbal information coming to us from our patients has a much greater chance of being held, with empathy as the most consistent underlying state. This linkage allows us to move in nonconscious synchrony a good part of the time. At the same time, the flow of warm regard from us can bathe our patients' body–brain in the regulating care that was attenuated or absent in childhood. This broad capacity for holding the many forms of pain and fear works behind the scenes to rewire our patients' often-tortured limbic world, linking it to the widely integrative prefrontal regions, first on the right, then flowing to the left. Such interpersonal richness encourages GABA-bearing fibers to grow from patients' orbitofrontal cortex to the amygdala, calming old fears. In all our interactions, resonance circuits can wire in a representation of our caring presence.

In this kind of safety, the patients' attachment system can reawaken, sometimes flooding the mind and body with dread, terror, or anxiety. Waves of protective anger may also course through the body. In our stability, we can now meet these surging emotions with regulating warmth and security. With this reassurance, cortisol levels in patients may gradually move into the normal range as oxytocin and opioids are released by the experience of connection (Sunderland, 2006). Over time, the autonomic nervous system can establish greater balance, not swinging to extremes, but oscillating more frequently in gentle waves between sympathetic enthusiasm and parasympathetic relaxation. Thanks to the many accumulating experiences of interpersonal regulation, when stress does push patients out of their window of tolerance, they can draw on inner resources to resiliently return to a balanced state. Many patients report feeling more whole as these increases in regulation/integration link states of mind into a continuous sense of self (Siegel, 1999). Based on the trustworthiness of the therapeutic relationship, implicit mental models gradually change for the better. When we fall away from empathy, as we inevitably will, we feel the break as unease in our bodies, and we work with our patients to restore connection. All of this healing is held and facilitated by the way our bodies–brains–minds dance together in the flow of right-brain to right-brain attunement that patiently unfolds over weeks, months, and often years, if the injury has been great.

When our deeper mind knows a good deal about the choreography of secure attachment, it supports and informs the nonverbal, right-hemisphere-based ways in which we connect with our patients. Riding on the flow of an integrating brain, our tone of voice, our gestures of care, the rhythm of our breathing, the tenderness in our eyes, and the receptivity of our posture can help open the door to our patients' implicit worlds. When powerful emotions surface—even those we might consider ugly or hurtful—we can consciously recognize the inner source, while our whole being holds this person with regulating care. These are the very ways a mother moves with her baby when the foundation for secure attachment is being formed. The mother's sensitivity to her baby's signals promotes a back-and-forth flow, a dance of responsive co-regulation. She both consciously and nonconsciously moves with changes in her baby's face, voice, body, and eyes, responding to the information being gathered by her resonating body–brain. Such sensitivity, whether in mother or therapist, heightens the capacity to respond to even very small changes within the other person, as they make their appearance in the body (Bugental, 1992).

All of these points suggest that the crucial ingredient for healing is staying in sustained, regulating contact with our patients. *One of our gifts to them is consistently seeking to remain in the sometimes ample and sometimes narrow space between the desert of cognitive empathy and the jungle of limbic overwhelm.* If our heart goes dead, we may still be able to say the right words or even put on some semblance of the right face, but our patients' resonating circuits will let them know our real condition, even if only below the level of conscious awareness. Many times, this loss of living contact will be the exact replication of their earlier attachment wounds. When this visceral move toward deadness is recognized by our caring observer, our numbness can become useful information about our patients' inner worlds, helping us to maintain the embrace of empathy. When the deadness takes over entirely, and our whole being makes comment on how boring this patient is, the healing ground becomes another graveyard of lost connection. At the other end of the spectrum, we may be able to maintain an appearance of calm, even when our hearts are racing with anxiety or withering in despair. None of this goes undetected in our patients' implicit experience of us, and may, in fact, be reinforcing neural circuits established by an overwhelmed parent. Falling into cognitive empathy or limbic overwhelm will make the relationship temporarily unsafe for our patients. Sometimes, drawing a few focusing breaths can pull us back into regulation, where we can hold the upset rather than being consumed by it. Other times, supervision, consultation, or visits with our own therapists can help us widen our window of tolerance. Reflecting on all that patients have told me over the years, the most meaningful moments have been marked by a heightened sense of connection, often noticeable in a hush and an intensity that flowers between us. These times can't be artificially manufactured. In the richness of attunement, they simply unfold in their own way.

These are ideal pictures, which can be invited with open arms. As attention goes, so goes neural firing, so there is no harm in having an ample imagination of all that can go right. However, we also need to be able to tolerate the moments when everything breaks down, and it seems as though the relationship may wash away in the flood. Sometimes it actually does, but more often, new bridges of humility and wisdom can be built.

In the Trenches

Lily and I had been working together for about 4 years, making gradual inroads into the hatred her mother bore her. Our alliance was strong and flowing most of the time—not a difficult feat since no one had ever listened to her before. She experienced my genuine interest in her as a miracle. However, she had not been able to break free of the severe isolation that locked her out of all relationships, except with me. Neither of us was clear about why this was an immovable obstacle. In the midst of this confusion, we both began to experience an increase in intensity, coupled with Lily's lower threshold for irritation. Her eyes began to blaze with hatred at times. I felt myself beginning to wrestle with every word I spoke in order to stay in what felt like an increasingly narrow band of connection as her window of tolerance shrank to almost zero. I sensed that a step to either side might shatter the bond, at least in that moment. For some weeks, I was able to hold onto images of the pain she had endured when she was enveloped in the withering energy of her mother's hatred and abuse. I could sense that in my extreme tentativeness, I was living her experience as a child, while her internal mother's rage began to consume her.

Then one day, instead of just flowing with her, I spoke about how sensitive she was to every word or gesture. In retrospect, I realize I was seeking to protect myself, to shift away from the raw emotion toward some way to decrease its impact on both of us. Perhaps I needed to pull us out of the intolerable right-brain into the manageable left-brain version of her agony. She exploded in rage. I had derailed her from the most important work of her life, and now she would never *ever ever ever ever* trust me to get back to it. "YOU HAVE RUINED EVERYTHING!" While my mind told me this was straight from her mother's lips to Lily's ears, my body rebelled and I froze. Right at the moment she needed me to contain her overwhelming pain by carrying it in my emotional and physical body, my limbic circuits surged, shutting down the shreds of integration still remaining. If this response had merely been my body reacting to a towering wave of energy, I believe I would have been able to mindfully hold on. Instead, those words of ruination echoed down the corridors of my own history, severing the last remaining strands of connection with myself, and, consequently, with her. She felt all the energy drain away between us. I might as well have left her exposed in a hurricane. Abandoned in a way that probably felt as devastating as her mother's hatred, she stormed from the room. I felt exhausted and hopeless, only able to listen to fragments of voices in my own mind, trying vainly to make up reasons for what had happened. Over the hours that followed, I slowly regathered myself, and made what I hoped would be a mending phone call. Her wound was so great that only words of rage were available to her. I realized that, above all, I needed to stay present, straddling the line between withdrawing into safety, leaving only cognitive empathy to further wound her, and being overwhelmed again by my own limbic surge. The phone call was reassuring enough to give her room to return. She was calmer, but not because much had healed. Instead, she was on guard against me abandoning her again.

After a few tentative sessions, she asked for an apology, and, still somewhat internally entangled, all I managed was some weak version of partial responsibility, blaming the magnitude of her response on what her mother had done to her. This was profoundly unsatisfying for both of us. Still, we moved deeper. Over the weeks, I mostly stayed with her. Occasionally, when the surge again threatened to breach my inner integrity, I would feel myself pulled from containing to explaining, each time leaving her alone and awash in the feelings. At times, the connection between my limbic and prefrontal would give out from the sheer weight of rage and hatred. However, she was able to handle my failures with more resilience. As part of increasing horizontal integration, on rare occasions, we could both back up briefly and survey the territory enough to get our bearings again. In this start-and-stop fashion, we managed to ease forward, both of us floundering at times in deep waters of exhaustion and despair. I can now thank the earlier strong bond we had developed and lovingly nurtured for getting us through this period. I also marvel at Lily's internal wisdom for delaying this deepest work until she knew our connection had become a thick enough rope. Looking back now, we also realize that during this trying period, everything in her was fighting against descending into the full subjective experience of an intolerable and foundational memory: her mother locking her in a box for a portion of every weekday from when she was 18 months old until she was 6 and entered first grade. At the same time, her rapidly integrating brain was pushing toward that cliff of visceral awareness.

After several weeks of this titanic struggle, the tsunami of terror did break over her. Once the full subjective truth arrived, we were easily able to lock onto each other again. A towering energy of needing to cling filled the room as she burst free of the box. As the boards fell away, she was able to attach fully for the first time. At that same moment, I was released from carrying Lily's experience as she resumed that burden, while her mother's raging energy simply evaporated. For me, the sensation was like popping to the surface of the ocean after being repeatedly pulled under, often breathing water instead of air, in the unpredictable surge of the storm. The subjective change was astonishing, rendering me able to easily support Lily with my whole being again. If I were to think theoretically about the large outlines of this difficult passage, I would say that her mother's rage against Lily was Mother's defense against her own childhood terror. Lily had internalized that mother, and during these rageful months in therapy, Lily, in essence, allowed her internal mother to protect her from the intolerable terror of her incarceration. When Lily's integrating brain finally had the momentum to manage the unmanageable, the terror poured forth and there was no longer any need for the protective rage.

For about 2 days, Lily quaked as the waves of terror rolled through her body. I responded to her clinging by keeping in very close touch by phone. She was even able to supplement this care by reaching out to a few people who came to her aid with food and company. As the acute panic became more regulated, with the waves now merely lapping at our feet, we rejoiced in her freedom. Dancing in the streets would have been appropriate. After dwelling for months in a state of utter separateness, with the words "all you people are useless" delineating her absolute aloneness, she now said over and over, "We did it! Just you and me! We did it!" It goes without saying that there is still much repair to be done. It is no light thing to have been locked in an internal box for 47 years, with her implicit assumptions defined by its borders. No wonder she felt friendless. However, Lily now looks out on the world from outside this prison, almost as though we are standing on a hill together, overlooking the carnage of a great battle and recuperating, side by side.

Not many passages are this demanding of therapist and patient. Here is another story, this time about the beginning of therapy. Two years ago, a man came to me in despair about becoming a "decent human being." He felt that his coldness froze everyone near him, and that he needed to protect others from the damage he caused. His voice was strident, his posture rigid, and his eyes intense. As he talked, my body experienced a sense of wanting to be very careful with him, feeling what I could only describe as his fragility—not like a soap bubble, but like glass blown too thin, sure to explode at the slightest touch. Noting that this feeling was very much in contrast to the strength he was presenting, I found myself leaning forward a bit, being tentative in my words, wanting to make sure he felt me seeking to slowly but thoroughly be with him. Even though his body was very tense, almost as though he needed to ward me off, I felt immediate warmth and empathic attraction flower within my body. We hadn't yet discussed family history, but it was easy to imagine the boy who had been chilled to the bone. About midway through the session, he said, "Just teach me how to behave in a way that won't hurt other people." As some wispy tendrils of connection were forming between us, his inner world allowed the desperate child to drift toward the surface, manifested in the way his voice slid from commanding to pleading as he made this request. Additional tender and gentle resources welled up unbidden in me. I don't remember much of what we talked about that day. I'm sure I introduced the brain in some way, sensitive to his visceral response to these overtures. Sometime in the first couple of sessions, we probably also talked about how inner communities form, as we made our way through his wasteland history. However, what has stayed with me is this drift from adult to child, from defensiveness to vulnerability—and the warm response it elicited in me.

A few months later, we were talking about his journey so far. He said the moment he remembered most from our first session was me leaning forward and stumbling over my words a bit as we began to talk about his "legitimate needs" as a child. In that moment, he felt I would be kind to him and was surprised by the sting of tears in his eyes—although he didn't let me see that at the time. He said that the phrase "legitimate needs" remained illuminated in his mind from that day forward, helping him be much kinder to himself. With that, I felt the sting of my own joyous tears. Sometimes, when our words are embedded in the richness of attachment, they take root in surprising and transforming ways.

With great humility, it is helpful to acknowledge that, whatever our theoretical orientation, healing gains its toehold in this right-brain to right-brain attunement dance. The next few chapters explore specific ways of being with patients, so they can better be with themselves. While we might technically call these specific ways *interventions*, we might better think of them as *languages of attunement*. When we are flowing with our patients, our use of these methods will arise out of and deepen connection. When we ask ourselves, "What is the most empathic thing to do in this moment?" we often arrive at the next helpful step.

Chapter 12

Listening to Family Histories

Listening to history can be less about learning the facts and more about thoroughly dropping into the world of the other. As a first step toward interpersonal joining, we seek to convey our interest in the depth and breadth of our patients' inner world. Our intention to be fully present to the nonverbal as well as verbal nuances of the story provides the foundation. Although we may have certain questions we want to ask, it is equally important to let the story unfold organically from the relationship in the room, with full respect for the tenderness of what may be revealed. It helps if we think about *why* we want to participate in this history right at the beginning of therapy. Part of the answer lies in our desire to inhabit our patients' worlds, to stand right by their side in order to feel/see/smell/touch/hear as much as we can. We want to experience the internalized relational worlds that guide our patients' daily choices now. We want to sense what was empathic and not empathic from the youngest ages that they can recall. At a different level, we also want to begin to hear if there are places where brain integration is not com-plete—where the body and limbic region may be disconnected, leaving people without a felt sense of their lives, or where right and left discon-nection make words difficult or boring. In the *how* as well as the content of the narrative, we can listen for signs of our patients' current expecta-tions about attachment. In the way their bodies move, their eyes shift, their breathing fluctuates, their stories rush ahead or pause, we can catch visceral glimpses of the tidal forces pulling for or against regula-tion and well-being. We may even catch sight of the mental models that lie at the foundation of relational choices. A feeling in our body, heart, and mind of gentle, caring attention can open this door.

Our minds (including our bodies) will be working at several levels at once. The body is a rich source of *right-brain to right-brain communication*, which is at least as important as the content of the story. Sometimes our patients, who are usually new to this therapeutic relationship at the time of sharing their history, make conscious and nonconscious choices about what they will and won't share. Nonetheless, they do bring their whole being into the room, and much of that can flow to us via the body. We may also notice a shift in our emotions, or images flowing through our minds, as well as emerging thoughts. If we are able to stay in our caring observer, with practice, we will see that all the levels will gradually come together to form a felt sense, visual picture, and cognitive awareness of both their inner communities and the status of their brain integration.

Intergenerational Compassion

At a more concrete level, this may be the one time in therapy when we choose to take notes during a session. These notes can be taken in the genogram format that many of us learned in our training programs, now adapted to fit individual needs and preferences. It will be helpful to ask for history about at least three generations: our patients, their parents, and grandparents. If they have children, then there will be four generations to explore. In addition to whatever useful information we may garner, this longitudinal approach can build the foundation for *intergenerational compassion*. As we listen and begin to understand the wounds and resources that have been passed down in the family, our empathy for each member will touch our patient, even if it happens initially below the level of consciousness. In recent years, we have found that many people are knowledgeable about intergenerational patterns and have at least a little top-layer compassion (often coming from cognition rather than an internal experience of the family struggles). However, when that intellectual compassion is used to cover deep wells of pain and anger or minimize our patients' childhood struggles, it is of little long-term use. The empathy we hope to build will be based on the visceral understanding of our patients' childhood and their parents' inner world. That usually flowers as deep work around our patients' early pain, fear, and anger accumulates.

We want to be conscious that the whole family lives inside, as our patients experienced them in relationship and internalized them, so siding with one generation over the other ultimately does a disservice to our patients' healing process. It may be helpful to envision the whole inner family sitting in the room, as we imagine how we would embrace each one with compassionate understanding. Kohut (1982) talks about changing our perspective from *guilt* to *tragedy*. When we sense that all members of the family may have done their best, given the status of their inner worlds and the quality of their outer support, we can hold them in a generous space in our own minds. As listening to a particular history allows us to see patterns flowing down the generational stream, understanding may replace the need to assign blame. If we are able to hold this view in our consciousness, we can assist our patients in gradually moving toward this peaceful, panoramic viewpoint. If instead we set one generation against the other in our own minds, our patients will have less chance of eventually coming to this kind of resolution.

> To support this vision for our patients, we need to first believe it for our own families. Taking some time to sit with your intergenerational history can be a first step. Bringing what you know about the power of early neural patterning and cultural pressures to your family's story may make room for compassion even in the midst of acknowledging your own sorrow. As with our patients, it is important to celebrate the positive legacies as well.

The beautiful thing about laying groundwork for visceral, multigenerational empathy is that eventually people are able to *compassionately release*—in essence, forgive—their parents and others in a way that deeply frees them from ties of anger, resentment, and hatred, all of which impede brain integration and subtract from well-being. This act of acceptance often also brings them relief from their own shame. All of this is a long process, with the fullness of it usually unfolding near the end of therapy. However, being conscious of it during the first few sessions can give us a running start.

As much as we want to experience empathy for the whole inner community, initially this is often best conveyed in a more nonverbal way, with facial expression, tone of voice, and body position revealing our understanding. At this stage, it usually is not very helpful to say things like,

"As painful as it was for you, it makes sense that your father would have difficulty knowing how to express love, given his own father's coldness," unless we are confirming what our patient has already expressed. Such directness may come later, but at this stage, our patient might only hear that his pain doesn't count as much as his father's.

Whole-Person to Whole-Person Joining

In the chapter on attaching, we talked a bit about narrative patterns and what they can tell us about current working models of attachment. You might want to review those now. We know from the research that when we ask someone to do the twin tasks of engaging with us and telling stories from childhood, their early attachment experiences are likely to be stimulated. Then, regardless of the content of their early history, the *way* the story unfolds will often reflect the degree of resolution they have achieved. We can use our bodies and emotions to sense the subjective experience of their wounds, and our insight to understand the ramifications for brain integration. This experience is very far from what is usually called "history taking." Instead, it is a *whole-person to whole-person joining experience* that quickly lays the foundation for a powerful therapeutic alliance at many levels.

Part of the process is listening for areas that are not talked about. Is there a reluctance to discuss sexual experiences? Work? Earlier relationships? It is interesting to notice which members of the inner community keep slipping through our fingers. Is there a strong sense of Dad, as though he's in the room, but great difficulty in getting the *feel* for Mom? When this kind of discrepancy happens, it can be helpful to share it with our patient to see if the two of us can understand why. Sometimes there is a need to protect a parent who has been both hurtful and helpful. Other times an avoidant attachment leaves our patient without a visceral clue about a particular parent. Sometimes the reluctance reflects the need for more trust to build before tender pain can be shared.

It is helpful to also ask our patients about people who were particularly empathic toward them, past and present. If there wasn't much care in the family, who did provide support? What kind? Being aware of body language, tone of voice, eye gaze, and other nonverbal signs when asking this question can leave us with a treasure trove of mindsight about available internal relational resources. If our patients' pain-inducing people live on inside, certainly their empathic ones do as well. When there is a definite brightening in discussing a particular relationship, support from that internal relationship may well be available to our patient as we move into the painful underbrush. One of my patients grew up with two violent, alcoholic parents who were a constant source of terror. However, she also had one brother who was 10 years older. At first, she felt as though he had little place in her inner world because he had left home for the open road when she was 5. I asked, "What do you feel in your body when you think of him?" Unexpectedly, her usually tense shoulders relaxed and her face softened into smile. "I feel warm, and I can almost feel his big hand holding my little one." Closing her eyes, she saw the two of them walking hand-in-hand down their shaded street. We lingered for quite awhile in the late afternoon glow of that memory. Then, as we began to approach the terror of her early memories, she was able to invite her inner brother to accompany us. Although he had been unable to provide much protection when she was small, the warmth of his inner presence made this current fearful passage much easier. In addition to providing this kind of inner help, when our patients have implicit and explicit memories of supportive others, these patterns usually make it easier for them to find and sustain external sources of goodness and warmth in the present. Not surprisingly, my client had two wonderful male friends who buoyed her up during her lengthy healing process.

Most people are fairly eager to share their stories. However, some of our patients may need a little coaxing. It can be helpful to have a variety of ways of talking about the importance of history, in order to tailor the one we choose to our patient's situation. For example, in working with couples, if there is reluctance to discuss history, we might say, "We all learned our patterns of communication in our families, so sharing some history can help us understand why the two of you have so much trouble reaching one another." This is often a less threatening entrance than "Tell me about your parents." Another helpful approach is to ask some fairly specific questions, especially when our patients begin with a vague sense that their families were "normal," "nice," and "just like everybody else's." Sometimes these statements reflect an avoidant attachment, but they may also signal a simple lack of familiarity with what we want. Asking questions like "Who helped with homework and what was that like for you?" and "How was discipline handled in your family?" may jump-start the narrative.

When patients are open to storytelling, it may be helpful to begin by focusing on two areas: experiences between child and parents, and feelings the child absorbed from swimming in the relationship between these parents. From there, siblings or grandparents might be the next focus. Sometimes, however, patients will give us hints that there is another place to start—an abusive uncle or a supportive teacher, for example. Following this guidance can be most fruitful. While family history is unfolding, patients may begin to move deeply into one particular experience. Again, we can generally trust our patients' inner process more than our own agenda and flexibly follow their lead. Having an overall outline of history is useful only to the extent that it allows us both to enter these tender inner worlds to heal/integrate areas of dissociated pain and fear that block well-being and healthy relationships. If the storytelling pulls our patients deeply into a memory, we can follow empathically, using our presence to comfort and regulate the upsetting experience before returning to the story.

Some Possible Questions

The questions below can be used as guidelines for multiple paths into the inner world. In general, there is no hard-and-fast rule about what to ask, with the single exception that the first set of questions just below do need to be presented in some form somewhere in the storytelling. They are particularly important because they are meant to draw our patients closer to their *implicit attachment world*. It could be quite threatening to lead off with these questions, so it might be good to save them for what feels like an appropriate moment.

Did you ever feel rejected or threatened by your parents?
Did you have other experiences that felt overwhelming or traumatizing in your life, during childhood or beyond?
Have there been losses or deaths in your family?
How did they impact you at the time?
Do any of these experiences come to your mind regularly now?
In what ways do you experience them influencing your life?

These questions will sometimes startle our patients with their directness and their power to touch very early experience. Allowing lots of time for the answers and paying particular attention to what is happening in their bodies and our bodies will ease us into the experience of how our patients cope with whatever pain there may be. This is one place that the *how* of the answer is important because attachment patterns will often be revealed in speech patterns, as we discussed above.

What comes next are groups of questions that can provide possible pathways inside. Your patients' presenting struggles can often guide the selection.

> Tell me about how your parents communicated with one another: Silence? Anger? Demeaning words? Manipulation? Honesty? Kindness?
> Who had the most power in the family? Always?
> What were arguments like? Who argued with whom? Over what?
> How did the family communicate when times were tough?
> Was it all right to say how you were feeling?
> Were people in your family good listeners? How could you tell?

As we said above, sometimes these kinds of questions open the easiest path into history when there is considerable resistance. Almost everyone coming to therapy will admit to having communication difficulties in relationships that are not working well. So merely explaining that we all learn communication patterns in our families and asking about them is relatively innocuous and often opens other areas.

> What was discipline like?
> Who did the disciplining? When? How often? How young until how old?
> Did it seem fair? Was one child more disciplined than others?
> What was actually said/done?
> How did it feel to you when you/your siblings were disciplined?

With these questions, we can listen for the degree of fairness and empathy in the stressful times that generated the need for discipline. We can see if the parents supported one another or worked in opposition. We might be wondering about perceived favoritism. If discipline was harsh and our patients just had to watch, we can be aware that the effects may actually be worse than if they had been the one being whipped or humiliated. Patients can be shamed into believing they deserved even the most horrendous punishments, completely losing sight of their own goodness. We also want to know if discipline was consistent or erratic. If punishment was experienced as senseless and random, it leaves far more anxious and damaging tracks inside than if people have a legitimate reason to believe that they "earned" the lecture or spanking.

> Was there a lot of hugging and physical affection? From whom? When?
> Did your parents show affection in front of you?
> If not, how could you tell they loved one another?
> Would you say your family felt warm toward one another?

Who do you feel closest to in your family? Why?
Were some periods of your life warmer than others?

It is not necessary to ask all of these questions. What we are listening for is a sense of how much warmth and attachment happened in this family. When there has been a great deal of emptiness, people sometimes don't even know how to talk about warmth. All they can observe is that dinner got on the table, everyone's clothes got ironed, and no one got hit. So even if our patients can't yet consciously acknowledge that something was missing in terms of affection, at least we can hold that truth for them, creating an unspoken empathic bond.

Were there times people in your family felt agitated? When?
What was happening at the time?
Did anyone seem to really feel down sometimes? For how long?
How did you feel in the midst of these experiences?

Sometimes families can get so mired in anxiety or depression, they don't even recognize the pattern. Often this is a multigenerational problem. By using the words *agitated* and *down*, we can often get a better sense of family mood, because people sometimes view these as more acceptable states than anxiety or depression. Some patients have become aware of a pattern of depression that runs through five generations just by talking in this way. The follow-up questions to these initial ones will suggest themselves once our patients latch onto the topic.

Did your family have any major disappointments when you were young?
How did these affect you?
What did it feel like around the house when these events were happening?
How did your Mom/Dad handle these experiences?

Sometimes beginning to talk in this way can help patients feel a quality of disappointment (which can be a near neighbor of despair) running through the family as a whole. Sometimes it will help pinpoint particularly stressful times. Sometimes it will open areas that are supposed to be secrets. Sadly, patients will sometimes discover that they were the disappointment, and that becomes a major area for healing work.

Who was there when you got home from school?
How was homework managed? Who helped whom? How often? With what subjects? What was the message you received from the help?

What was your experience of school?
What happened when you brought home report cards?

The school arena is an opportunity for parents to support their children's esteem and aspirations, or to shame, discourage, and otherwise harm their feelings of competence and worth. Neglectful parents don't get involved at all, nor do parents who are too preoccupied with survival or their own internal struggles. Understandably, sometimes our patients will need to be protective of parents who worked three jobs to keep everyone fed. Just earmark the pain this caused for later work.

How was spirituality brought into your life as a child?
Did spiritual life seem important to your parents? How could you tell?
How did you feel about God when you were small?
Any experience with church? How was that?
How has your experience of the divine changed over time?

With these questions, we are listening for congruence between spiritual beliefs and the way life is lived and experienced. As discussed above, many people have well-thought-out theological beliefs that don't match their *feeling* about the divine at all, much less their actual behavior. This kind of incongruence is painful, confusing, and usually harmful in relationships. Also, issues of hope/despair and meaning/meaninglessness often emerge when spiritual life is discussed.

How was your health when you were small?
What happened when you were sick?
Were your parents sick very often?
What did getting sick mean in your family?

It is of interest to find out about possible genetic vulnerabilities; attitudes toward illness and recovery; using illness as a way of not feeling emotional pain; and believing illness is the only viable way to gain needed attention. Around questions such as these, sometimes alcohol and drug use may emerge as well. If they don't, it is important to ask about that area directly under the topic of how they cope.

Outside of your family, who were the most important influences in your life?
Were there people who were particularly helpful? Hurtful?
Do these people still feel like an important part of your inner or outer world?
Who are your major resources of support now?

When there are no people available, what helps you cope with stress and difficulty?

Most of our patients had key people outside the family—coaches, teachers, neighbors, friends, enemies—that live on in the inner community or inhabit daily life. Understanding this part of the inner landscape can remind us of positive resources that can be accessed internally or visited externally as the process of therapy unfolds.

Have you ever been in therapy before?
What was it like for you? How has it helped (or not)?
What do you need/want from this experience?

This topic seems to go best toward the end of the story (unless it has already come up naturally). We know that experience shapes the brain, so previous therapy is clearly going to affect how this patient will come to the new situation with us. If there have been boundary crossings of any kind, it will be helpful to explore how our patient experienced that and affirm our intention to protect boundaries. However, if therapy was ethical but not very effective, it can be most helpful to talk about the differences in what we do, but not criticize other approaches. In actuality, every empathic connection is helpful to some degree, and every approach has a range of benefits.

> One of the most effective ways to prepare for listening to our patients' histories is by taking time to ask ourselves these questions. Many of us have already shared our stories with a therapist. Reflecting on that experience, did it help you move more deeply into your inner world, or was it a flat historical account? Since our stories deepen with each telling, and meanings change over time as our narrative becomes more coherent, you might want to take these questions to a trusted friend or colleague for another opportunity to explore your inner world.

The suggestions in this chapter are certainly not exhaustive. They focus primarily on childhood experience, so we will want to augment them with discussions of the world of work and relationships in adulthood. Taking our direction from our patients' concerns will be our best guide in these areas. The basics of history will usually unfold in a session or two and then gradually be fleshed out over weeks, months, and, in the case of longer-term work, years. Once the family tree is on paper, it can be very useful to sit with it before each session until an instantaneous, illuminated picture of our patient's inner community flowers in our mind when this person enters the room. This kind of inner attentiveness is a form of mindfulness, the topic of the next chapter.

Chapter 13

The Three Faces
of Mindfulness

For a moment, see what happens if you picture your mind as a wheel, with hub, spokes, and rim. Imagine sitting in the calm of the hub and directing your attention along the spokes to any point on the rim you choose—a feeling, a thought, a memory, the smell of the gardenia on your desk. Daniel Siegel (2007) developed this wheel metaphor to embody the subjective experience that can emerge through the practice of mindful awareness. This is a very different inner state than having your attention involuntarily pulled to the rim by some inner or outer event, such as the sudden thought of ice cream or the dog barking, just when you are focusing on completing your taxes. It is even farther from the discomfort of living only on the rim. Many of our patients, especially those with severe attachment pain or trauma, have attenuated access to a peaceful home inside, but instead jump from point to point on the rim, at the mercy of the next internal or external trigger. Under these circumstances, it is easy to develop an identity of victim (passive) or perpetrator (striking back against victimization). This kind of internal hyperreactivity can also breed helplessness and despair.

More and more, we are bringing mindfulness into the therapy room in a variety of ways, tailoring it to individual needs. We find that the changes in perspective fostered by mindful awareness strengthen the therapeutic process. These states of mind can modulate the intensity of memories, dampen reactivity in daily life, build hope that healing is possible, and establish a new identity as a mindful person with painful memories. Gradually, with some practice, all of us—patients and therapists— can experience sitting in the hub while also participating at the rim, knowing that we are more than the experience unfolding at the rim. Powerful therapeutic work happens right at this juncture—at the boundary between the window of tolerance and dysregulation. In this space, our memories retain emotional life while we also hold them with compassion. A mindful stance both expands the window of tolerance and gives us a better capacity for managing the pain and fear of emerging memories.

Even when our struggles are more day to day, mindful awareness brings many gifts. Life at the hub of the mind is filled with a sense of freshness, compassion, tranquility, gentle humor, and in some sense, mastery. The latter is paradoxical because it comes as a result of cultivating the ability to not seek control, but instead to *pay kind attention, on purpose, without grasping onto judgments, to whatever arises in the mind from moment to moment* (Kabat-Zinn, 2003). One foundation for this kind of awareness is *acceptance of whatever is arising as it arises*. The goal is not to stop the mind, but to be present in the moment with its unfolding events. When this state is well cultivated, a time may come when perspective deepens and shifts, allowing us to rest on the ground beneath the many thoughts and feelings that arise in mind and body. However, with even a little consistent practice, many benefits come.

Research on Mindfulness

Turning briefly to the research, recent studies show us that the middle prefrontal cortex and the right anterior insula thicken through the practice of insight (mindfulness) meditation (Lazar et al., 2005; Siegel, 2007). Brain activity also increases in the right anterior insula, the superior temporal gyrus, and the anterior cingulate, whereas there is a decrease in activity in the amygdala (Lazar, 2007). Increased activation of these components of the paralimbic cortex adds a layer of integrative processing, connecting the limbic region to the cortex with pronounced regulatory benefit. This research suggests that (1) *meditation may change brain function and structure* in the direction of greater integration, (2) it can be a *powerful agent of neuroplasticity*, and (3) it might even *offset some detrimental brain changes associated with aging*. This kind of intentional focus is like doing push-ups for our attentional capacity, increasing our ability to *choose* where our mind flows. Another way to think about this topic is in terms of building self-regulation, an ability that is at the center of mental health—and, as we may remember, is a gift of middle prefrontal integration. Even more delightfully (but not unexpectedly), these practices have the potential to increase our capacity to be present with others with greater clarity, attunement, and compassion. The dessert for this feast is that immune function and healing rate improve, along with cardiac health, and the subjective experience of pain lessens (Davidson et al., 2003; Kabat-Zinn, 2003). Given these discoveries, it is not surprising that all nine functions of middle prefrontal integration are one result of mindfulness.

Although originating in the Buddhist tradition, these practices began to enter the mainstream in a variety of ways about two decades ago. Marsha Linehan (1993) developed dialectical behavior therapy (DBT), which placed mindful living at the center of treatment for people suffering with severe borderline personality disorder. It is now recognized as the most efficacious method. On the medical front, Jon Kabat-Zinn (1990) developed mindfulness-based stress reduction (MBSR) to provide help for people suffering with such severe chronic pain and stress-related illnesses that the medical community had run out of options. At InnerKids, Susan Kaiser-Greenland (2006) and her colleagues teach children and the teachers of children basic reflective skills, so that they have a head start on a mindful life. In Southern California, Jeffrey Schwartz's Westwood Institute for Anxiety Disorders employs his four steps to help OCD sufferers use their mental force to reshape the circuits in their brains that bind them to their compulsions (Schwartz & Begley, 2002). At the Mindful Awareness Research Center at UCLA, in a recent 8-week pilot study using mindful awareness practices (MAPs), adults and adolescents struggling with genetically loaded attention-deficit/hyperactivity disorder (ADHD) experienced clear reduction in distractibility and impulsivity (Siegel, 2007). These gains are a small part of a long list of emerging benefits. We have found that having a good supply of evidence at our fingertips can help us present mindfulness to our patients in a way that makes it accessible and inviting. When we are comfortable with its relevance and power, our patients will take to it with much greater ease.

Mindfulness as Relationship

In *The Mindful Brain* (2007), Daniel Siegel suggests that we might think of mindfulness as a *way of relating to self and others*, rather than as something we practice each day, like the piano or violin. We can try a simple experiment to make this tangible. For example, I might say, "I am very sad," and notice how I immediately draw the pain close to me, identifying myself as a sad person. It is as though the sadness engulfs all of me, in a very close, uncomfortable relationship. If I say instead, "There is a feeling of sadness right now," the part of me that can compassionately hold the sadness is encouraged to come to the fore, standing a bit apart but in caring relationship to the feeling. The change of language facilitates and reflects a change of inner location, helping the brain function in a more integrated way.

It may be very helpful to take a few moments to experiment with this approach right now, since it is probably one of those practices we will only encourage others to do if we have developed it in ourselves. Who is most annoying to you at the moment? If this person happens to be angry, what would happen if you said—and felt—"There is a state of mind of anger in him right now" instead of "He's an angry guy?" Daily practice of this shift in perspective and language regarding ourselves and others may quickly produce a strong current of tranquillity.

We are finding that when our patients tackle this change of perspective, regulation immediately increases, together with self-compassion, followed shortly by an increased capacity to see the potential goodness in others.

We may observe similar gains when we become mindful of our inner community. Instead of feeling swamped by fear, our caring observer may be able to see and hold the child inside who is frightened. *In the process, a more integrated state of mind is drawing a dissociated, painful state of mind into the comforting mainstream of the brain's gathering flow.* Subjectively, we may feel that a child part of us, who has been trapped in the painful past since the initial fragmenting experience, is for the first time stepping into the sunshine of the present. Sometimes, when the emerging experience overwhelms our patients, they become all child and may need to reach into the interpersonal system to borrow our caring observer until their own develops through internalization and integration. As long as the caring observer is somewhere in the combined brain–mind of the two people, the resources for embracing the child are available.

The key to all these processes is our *state of mind* when we relate to our sad feeling or the child within. Daniel Siegel (2007) offers an acronym for this felicitous inner state: COAL—curiosity, openness, acceptance, and love. We might think of a warm coal radiating in the center of our chest (since this is where the neurons that tell us of our ongoing need for connection live). This is very different from simply noticing something. Many people have developed the capacity to be aware without connection to feeling, usually as a defense against pain. For example, a person may remember being scolded as a child, but feel no visceral sense of the pain it caused. *To be truly mindful of that child is to place his or her suffering in the warm embrace of our caring observer—hub and rim at once.* As therapists, we seek not to slip into merely noticing, a kind of detached, protective stance. Instead, if we nurture a COAL state toward ourselves, we have a good chance of being able to maintain such a stance with our patients as well. It is hard to imagine a more effective way to help remodel the circuits of the implicit world.

Neural Underpinnings of Mindfulness

In thinking about mindfulness so far, we have suggested at least three ways we might understand it: in terms of the practices of mindful meditation; as an ongoing state of mindful awareness in relation to ourselves and others; and, in the interpersonal system, allowing the mindful care of an empathic other help us integrate our brains. We have found that the mind of each patient has a different appetite in regard to what is most helpful. First, let's explore the neural processes that these three ways of being mindful have in common by returning to our original definition of mindfulness: *paying kind attention, on purpose, without grasping onto judgments, to whatever arises in the mind from moment to moment.* Some people hear the goal as being nonjudgmental and almost immediately feel as though they are failing. If we think about how our minds work, it is not possible to suspend judgment entirely. Everything that comes to us, internally or externally, is subject to the amygdala's initial assessment of its value and importance. The amygdala first tells us when something needs attention, pulling our consciousness in that direction. Then, from a lifetime of encoding, perceptual biases—the essence of judgment—come into play, activated by each new experience. So the key phrase in the definition is "without *grasping* onto judgments." Practicing the kind COAL state, we may merely note that a judgment has arisen and let it go. As Buddhist teacher and psychotherapist Jack Kornfield (2007a) says, "Oh, there's a judgment. Thank you for your opinion."

Returning to the definition, paying kind attention on purpose, can mean a number of things, one of which is attuning with our senses to notice what is happening right now, whether that is the *sensation* of the breath coming and going in our nostrils, our footfalls on the grass, or the whine of our neighbor's motorcycle. It can also mean attending to whatever arises in the mind from moment to moment from the various *streams of information* that can come into awareness: sensations, observations, conceptions, and a kind of nonconceptual knowing that is hard to capture in words (Siegel, 2007). If you were to try either of these processes right now, you might notice that your mind has a tendency to go on frequent side trips to the remembered past or imagined future, to get caught in thoughts or feelings that pull away from the experience in the moment. However, you may also notice when a few seconds or moments of staying present flow, there is a feeling of openness and receptivity, brimming with several flavors of well-being.

What is happening in our brains when we are able to stay centered in this new way of experiencing for even a brief bit of time? Through our intention to attend, we are actually changing the way we are processing information in our six-layered neocortex. In an extremely simplified form, here's the story the way Jeff Hawkins tells it (Hawkins & Blakeslee, 2004). Each of the six layers is about as thick as a business card, and our brain has the appearance of a rumpled gray shirt because the dinner-napkin-size neocortex has to fold to fit in the rigid confines of our skulls. Leaving aside differences in right- and left-hemisphere cortical structure for the moment, let's focus on the function of the six layers. In tandem with limbic judgments made about incoming experience, the top two layers contain what are called *invariant representations*, meaning that they *anticipate* what will happen next, based on past experience. This is called *top-down processing*, and it is enormously useful if we want to drive a car or avoid dangerous situations. These representations create expectations that are so precise that, if someone moved our front door knob a quarter of an inch to the right, for example, we would be instantly aware that something was "wrong." We have all likely had numerous such experiences.

However, our invariant representations can also bind us to old experiences in ways that are detrimental. If I have been struck as a child, every time I see someone raise a hand, I may have a flood of top-down convictions that I am about to be harmed. Sadly, this reaction can distort my inner experience as well as the way I relate to others. Generally speaking, the greater the unhealed hurt, the more power contained in the invariant representation—unless there is another source of information to balance it. Here is where the bottom two layers of the cortex can be great allies. Their job is to process new information coming in through the senses—the breeze on our face, the green of the leaves against the neighbor's yellow house, or that whining motorcycle. When we attend to them, they pull us into the freshness of the moment, as though we have never experienced just this breeze before—because we haven't. The sensation is often enlivening and soothing at the same time. Smiles and laughter may erupt. This is *bottom-up processing*. Although there is nothing we can do to stop top-down processes (nor would we want to), strengthening the strands of bottom-up information will often bring a creative balance. Mindful awareness is one such strengthening process. Some would say it is precisely when top-down crashes into bottom-up that creativity flourishes. In that moment, it could be that what we already believe will ignite in the energy of the new. From this, we know that when we focus on our senses or the arising of experience, we are cultivating the ability to be a bit free of the automatic processes that have accumulated in our invariant representations. For those who have suffered in childhood, even a brief respite from the tyranny of perceptual bias brings relief. With practice, we may live more often where the cortical layers meet.

Bringing Mindfulness Practices into Therapy

In what concrete ways might we bring these practices into therapy? Let's start with what we might call *ordinary mindfulness*. When we bring a COAL state into therapy because it is alive in us, our capacity to attend to our patients in the moment, on purpose, without judgment, is present. In our experience, even the most frightened, dysregulated, or detached patients will eventually respond to this spacious interpersonal environment, as long as we don't give in to our own implicit tugs, but continue to provide this steady warmth. Giving resonance circuits their due, we can understand how such mindful presence might make its way in, like water finding a crevice in the stone. On the foundation of this connection, which is beginning to change the nonconscious implicit expectations about relationship, we may then naturally start to encourage mindful awareness in our patients as well. Let's say that our patient comes in and tells a story about how enraged he felt when someone took his parking space at work. He recognizes, while telling the story, that he is much angrier than the situation warrants. While he recounts the details of the event, we could say he is in ordinary consciousness. Then, in order to shift to mindful awareness, we might ask him to attend to the sensations in his body (Ogden et al., 2006). He moves from his memory of the incident into this moment's experience of it, then accepts and sits with it, making it available for an infusion of compassion and regulation. We can use this same process to attend to emotions or to look for the inner children who were ignored. *From the hub of attention, we can journey to any point on the rim, embracing it with a COAL state of mind.* Even though it is rarely a steady course, we will begin to see the caring observer state of mind emerge, as ordinary mindfulness strengthens.

Jack Kornfield (2007a, 2007b) and Tara Brach (2007) offer the acronym RAIN to describe this process: recognition, acceptance, investigation, and nonidentification. First, we pay attention and recognize the presence of an experience. Then, we accept its presence, sustaining our attention, finding the courage to remain in our vulnerability. As attention deepens, we may become aware of the full dimensions of the experience as they unfold within our minds. We may come to understand the origins of the experience, hold it in kindness, and then notice that this experience is a small part of us, not our whole identity. In this way, we may gradually know that we are people who have a history, but our identity is not defined by that history. As therapists, we can develop the capacity to stand in this rain with our patients, allowing the spaciousness of our own cultivated minds to create a refuge in which this process can unfold.

When there has been great trauma, the full resources of our two brains may be required for quite some time, as one dissociated limbic experience after another percolates to the surface, sometimes drowning our patient's adult self in the ocean of the child's pain. Borrowing our caring observer, our patients can find sufficient stability and regulation to stay within their windows of tolerance even with very painful memories. As moments of calmness emerge after deep processing, we might picture that the two of us can sit together in the interpersonal hub of the mind generated by our strong connection. This image of two in the hub can be a great aid in helping our patients carry a sense of safety and companionship into the world. As we go there together again and again, we will find we can rely on the lifelong human capacity for internalization to gradually allow them to take in our living, mindful presence.

At the same time, the brain's intrinsic push toward integration will develop the circuits to hold regulation.

Side by side with the mindfulness that flowers in the right-brain to right-brain relationship, we can offer some specific ways for our patients to practice a more mindful relationship with their experience outside of session, what we might call *daily mindfulness*. Ruth Baer and colleagues (Baer, Smith, Hopkings, Krietemeyer, & Toney, 2006) synthesized data from numerous existing questionnaires about mindfulness and identified five factors common to the various studies. Understanding these five may help us create exercises that are tailored to the unique needs and challenges of our patients. They may also help us spot our own strengths and growth edges in regard to mindfulness:

1. Being able to perceive our emotions without reacting to them, without becoming dysregulated
2. Staying present with perceptions, sensations, thoughts, or feelings, even when they are unpleasant or painful; not distracting ourselves
3. Staying present with our actions, without distraction
4. Being able to describe or label in words beliefs, opinions, emotions, expectations
5. Being nonjudgmental of our own experience

Next, we consider a few practices that can develop these capacities. We have found that some have particular power for people with certain struggles. However, those you develop with your patients may have the even greater power of being a unique creation of the two of you. A few pages back, we talked about a change of language from identifying with states of mind to observing them with compassion. This practice, which fosters the ability to *perceive emotions without reacting to them*, has proved powerful for people struggling with the disruptive states of mind resulting from ambivalent or disorganized attachments. By consciously disidentifying from the overflowing emotions—saying, for example, "There is a feeling of anxiety here right now" rather than "*I'm* anxious"—perspective may change, the caring observer might make his or her appearance, and there is a strong possibility that regulation will increase.

Staying present with sensations or feelings can help avoidantly attached people, often trapped in their left hemispheres, begin to find their bodies. Such bodily connection underlies our ability to be aware of our emotions, so body focus can be the first step in right vertical integration (the integrated map of the body is in the right hemisphere; Damasio, 1994).

With many people, simply helping them sit mindfully with their bodies when they are sharing an emotionally charged story (positive or negative) will activate the necessary connections in the brain. If they have difficulty, we can offer them a "menu," as Pat Ogden suggests (Ogden et al., 2006). For example, we might ask "What are you feeling in your throat? Chest? Arms? Stomach? Legs?" After some experience in session, they can take this practice home, perhaps even writing down their experiences with it (see Baer et al.'s [2006] fourth principle). We might also provide the encouragement that repetition of the process will begin to create reliable links between their brain circuits.

Sometimes, however, their bodies are so far off the radar that something more basic becomes the starting point. We have had good success through a simple exercise of tensing and relaxing each part of the body. Focusing your mind on your right foot, try tensing and relaxing it three times, then the left foot, then the right calf, and so on. You may notice an increase in the aliveness of your body. After doing this every day for about a week, even our most locked-out patients can begin to notice their personal physical correlates of sadness or anger.

Staying present with activities is simple and challenging at the same time. For several weeks, I made teeth brushing a time of dedicated mindful awareness. Attending to each small movement can bring such an enlivening sense, almost a sweetness, to the most mundane activity. With this kind of practice, we may also become immediately aware of how *not* present we are most of the time, with the body appearing to pull the weeds, while the mind is ranging from lunch plans to worries about money. However, even a little practice tends to increase our presence in all activities. Once we have made these new links in the brain, they are more apt to be activated with just a little nudge of awareness.

Perhaps the most surprising discovery made by Baer and her colleagues (2006) is that being able to *describe inner states (sensations, feelings, thoughts) with words* correlates with mindfulness. When our patients' parents have not been able to provide these words early in life—"You look so sad right now," "You're really happy with that truck!"— it may take a good deal of practice to recognize that inner experiences can even be described in words. What does this capacity have to do with mindfulness? Clearly, we have to attend to the feeling, be conscious of it, to find words. From earlier, you may remember that when people were shown frightening pictures in an fMRI scan, they could calm their amygdalae and encourage blood flow in the prefrontal cortex by naming the emotion accurately (Hariri, Bookheimer, & Mazziotta, 2000). Recently, Creswell and colleagues (2007) have found that mindfulness practice increases the efficacy of describing emotions with words, finding that nonmeditators showed some regulatory benefit, whereas meditators showed more. Linking language to emotions is an inherently integrating activity for the brain. We can almost picture the feeling trooping across the corpus callosum to find explanatory words. Building on our collaborative and reflective process with patients in session, we have found that one way to encourage this trip is daily journaling about inner states, a process that encourages both awareness and regulation. Many patients have said, "I had no idea all that was going on inside me."

Turning to Baer et al.'s (2006) fifth principle, our consistent experience tells us that therapeutic progress accelerates when our patients are able to shift from the stab of self-blame to the embrace of self-compassion. Being the caring observer of their own young selves fosters such a change toward *nonjudgment of their experiences.* No matter how compassionate we are to people in the outside world, we often treat our inner selves with the same disdain or cruelty that our parents visited on us. This makes sense since those family members live on inside, embodying our mental models of relationship. As we are present with our patients in a COAL state of mind, they will begin to internalize some capacity to treat themselves more gently. Sometimes, especially when the injury began at a very young age, patients have implicit-only memory of being a bad child. Whenever they do something they find wrong, the full fury of that implicit-based criticism and hatred rains down on them, as though they deserve it in the present. One man, who was consistently labeled the "bad child," would rail against himself for tiny infractions—thinking a nasty thought about a careless driver, having an angry feeling. As we began to work with his young self internally, he could sense that underneath the acting out was a child in deep shame at his father's demeaning ways. He quickly developed tenderness for this boy, and the tenderness became the headwater for a trickle, then a flood, of self-compassion. Once we had accomplished this connection in session, he began to catch himself whenever he would begin the inner tirade. Reminding himself of that tender child, he developed strong resources for mindfully holding the injured part of himself with gentleness.

This state can be cultivated through a simple practice drawn from compassion meditation (Kornfield, 2007B). Asking our patients to place one hand or both over their chests, we can explore the feeling that arises there. If we have found this practice to be personally beneficial, making the same gesture allows our resonance circuits to support our patients' exploration. For many, there may be a sense of warmth and comfort, sometimes accompanied by the visceral awareness of touching their children inside. We might also invite them to say these words inwardly or aloud to their inner ones: "May you be well. May you be held in compassion" (Kornfield, 2007). Often, a tender quietness pervades this experience. Many of our patients have found they can easily say these words to others, but have difficulty granting themselves the same kind regard. When there has been great attachment trauma, just the act of putting a hand on the chest can bring enormous sorrow. One woman, whose parents had completely rejected her for being a girl, felt all the energy race from her hand to her elbow even before her fingers made contact with her chest. She became aware of the implicit terror and need to flee that accompanied the actuality of any kind of emotional connection with herself or others. Her progress with this practice became one powerful marker on the road to self-acceptance.

> The more we cultivate a COAL state toward ourselves, the more we can encourage our patients to do the same. Most of us may be able to find deep empathy for our patients, but may not often ask if we feel the same way about ourselves. You might want to experiment with putting your right, your left, and then both hands over your upper chest to see if there is a difference. With some experimentation, you may find just the right spot on your chest. Sitting in acceptance of any sensations and images that come, you may notice that there is variation from day to day. Then you may want to try out the words, "May you be well. May you be held in compassion." As with any activity, it will be more natural to ask our patients to do the same when we are willing to undertake daily practice ourselves.

If we think back to how neural nets initially form and then are strengthened by repetition, we can sense how these isolated experiences of mindfulness will eventually cohere into a more reliably accessed state of mind.

In the initial stages, effort is required to activate these neural nets. We are still aware of doing mindfulness practices of various sorts. However, with ongoing dedicated attention, we will one day notice that we just *are* mindful, without any effort. We could then say that *a state has become a trait.*

Doing Formal Mindfulness Practices with Patients

We can also encourage this state-to-trait transformation by doing *formal mindfulness practices* with patients who are open to it. We have found that enjoying a short meditation with our patients can be useful to either focus the beginning of our time or integrate the work at the end. One patient, who came because his doctor told him his intestines were being destroyed by his emotional upset, would spend the early part of his session working hard with his inner community to relieve the pain of frequent beatings. Then, we would join in a mindful breathing practice for at least 10 minutes. For the first while, he paid attention to the breath in his nostrils, but then intuitively began to move the rhythmic sensation to his intestines, as though they were actually breathing, too. After just a little practice, he noticed a feeling of "peace" in his intestines, a change that proved to have notable benefits for his health, as confirmed at his next doctor's appointment.

What follows is a simple but profound beginning practice. As always, cultivating our own mindful capacity will provide our patients with the beneficial possibility of experiencing resonance with our growing equanimity.

To begin the mindfulness practice, you can remain at ease in a chair with feet flat or you may choose to sit Indian-style on the floor. A straight spine will also help, as will allowing hands to be in their most relaxed position.

If it is comfortable, allow your eyes to close and then just pay attention to the sensation of the breath coming and going in the nostrils. This is different than thinking about breathing. Just let the mind rest in the physical sensation, the coolness in the nostrils or the rise and fall of chest or belly. There's no need to change the depth or length of breath. Just be present with the sensation of what is happening. You might also experiment with noticing the breath in the rise and fall of the chest or the belly until you find the place where your mind rests with the coming and going of your breath most easily. This place may change from day to day.

When the mind wanders, notice without criticism and gently redirect your focus to the sensation of the breath. With practice, an expansive calm will often emerge and linger—the sensation of spaciousness. You may begin to feel as though you are at the bottom of the ocean looking up at the waves of activity, or resting on a firm foundation beneath the streams of awareness, watching all the processes of the mind come and go. Gradually extend the length of practice from 5 to 20 minutes or more. This lengthening may happen naturally.

Just attending to the sensation of the breath energizes the bottom two layers of the neocortex and encourages neural integration as the prefrontal cortex and insula gradually thicken. There is a shift toward left prefrontal activation, fostering the ability to approach even difficult situations with more equanimity rather than withdraw in fear. Subjectively, this state of mind brings a profound sense of well-being that includes qualities of openness, tranquility, receptivity, and comfort. This state may appropriately be called *eudaimonia* because it is accompanied by a sense of meaning and purpose in life. It is neurally distinct from *hedonia*, a state associated with the experience of plesaure (Urry et al., 2004). During this process, a wandering mind is not a sign of failure but rather the expected event. The process of *calling the mind back without judgment and with kindness* is the heart of the practice, the point at which we are strengthening our ability to attend and relate, both to ourselves and to others. This single practice could suffice for a lifetime of mediation experience, but some will want to extend it, so two possibilities follow.

Relax the focus on the breath and begin to allow sensations to come in from all the senses—fingertips on clothing, air stirring in the room, squeaks in the air conditioner, the smell of someone's lunch—as well as thoughts and feelings in the mind and sensations within the body. Just sit in receptivity to all that is arising in the mind. If the mind wishes to judge—"That's a really loud lawnmower"—receive that judgment as well. You may begin to notice that there are different streams of information flowing within your mind— sensations, observations, conceptions, and, as the practice deepens, a kind of nonconceptual knowing that integrates and perhaps underlies the other streams (Siegel, 2007). At all times, your only job is to rest in awareness of all that is arising in the mind.

Another practice purposefully extends the sensation of the breath beyond the nostrils, the chest, and the belly to an awareness of how the breath gives rhythm to the whole body. As you sense this harmonious flow, you may gradually find that you move beyond the confines of your own body to experience the dance of the seasons, the movement of the earth around the sun, and the rhythm of the expanding universe. Often, this awareness flows into a sense of oneness with all beings.

Although many of us may have had the subjective awareness of separable streams of awareness, research is only recently identifying the neural underpinnings. A study by Farb and colleagues (in press) found that two forms of self-awareness—the self across time and the self in the moment—have distinct neural correlates in the brain. Even more important for us here, the study also found that participants who had been given 8 weeks of mindfulness training demonstrated greater ability to be aware of the two streams as separate from each other, even though they are usually automatically woven together. Why is this important? When the study shows that we have the ability to differentiate one stream from another, it might mean that there is empirical evidence of an additional stream that can observe these two (Siegel, in press). This caring observer capacity is essential for being able to direct the mind toward different streams, or, to use the wheel metaphor, different points on the rim, where, through focus, the neural firing patterns of the mind can be consciously modified. From this state of mind, new states of integration, linking one stream to the other, can be encouraged (Siegel, in press). Instead of being constantly entangled in our implicit and explicit stories, we can hold these streams in the moment with compassion, an act that encourages the emergence of states of greater well-being through neural integration.

As we introduce these formal mindfulness practices, we find that for most, the breath practice feels natural and easy, whereas for others the sound of a brass singing bowl can bring deeper focus. Still others have found the mindful movements of yoga or tai chi more helpful. Although the neural correlates for each practice may differ somewhat, research is gradually showing that the common thread of *intending to attend* leads to increased well-being. As our patients become intrigued, we point them toward the abundant resources for various forms of mindfulness— books, retreats, conferences, meditation centers. Creating such a list of your own might be an enjoyable experience.

How might patients react when we introduce these practices? Some might resist because it is unfamiliar and because it can sound scary to become that quiet if a person has been running from awareness for a long time. We are finding that the initial practice of mindfulness can increase

Being a Brain-Wise Therapist

anxiety or elicit powerful memories in a few patients. For one patient in particular, it was the first time she'd had easy access to her memories of severe abuse. Prior to this, a part of her inner community she called The Editor had not allowed us passage to these dissociated places. Now, just watching about two breaths begins a powerful integrative flow and grants us entrance. She has chosen to continue this practice, but only when we are together, and we are noticing that each time there is more regulation of the process. However, not everyone who finds that conscious breathing brings anxiety will want to continue, and it is so important to always be respectful of our patients' judgment.

Some patients do the practice with us, but not at home. Empathically exploring the reason for this choice can uncover the next therapeutic steps. One patient told me that she was too afraid of the intensity (so we only practiced together), whereas another said that it brought so many good feelings that she knew she was being way too kind to herself. In this latter situation, we immediately began to work on the ways her inner community continually whispered, "You're worth nothing." We switched our focus to compassion meditation with excellent results. Another patient simply said, "Not now. I know it's not time yet." Again, respect and trust are the keys. Many patients, however, will do very well with the practice, particularly if we do it with them, and especially if we have developed some capacity for it ourselves.

Some of the resistance we encounter, whether with patients or ourselves, comes from how our lives tend to be organized these days. For many people, life seems to push in the direction of automatic responses. Satisfaction often lies in the future, so we live in our imagining of *when* . . . and *if only*. . . . If we are rushing toward the imagined future, invariant representations are appealing because they require no conscious attention and are thus more efficient, leaving lots of energy for the unreal, but compelling, fantasized future. Cultivating ongoing newness, on the other hand, requires a lot of conscious attention, a somewhat more leisurely pace at the beginning, and possibly the emphasis on different life values. Weaving mindfulness into life often involves more than just acquiring a new discipline, because it may challenge our invariant representations of the very purpose of life.

We recently purchased Zen meditation timers for each of our offices. The lingering sound of their chimes carries us into and out of mindfulness with our patients, so we can focus on our breath without having to think about the clock. We hope our increased focus provides stronger resonance for our patients. Several of them have remarked on this small shift in the atmosphere, noticing a palpable increase in tranquility. We feel it, too, even when we aren't meditating. This chapter concludes by circling us back to the hub of the mind, that place inside ourselves where we find the capacity to be receptive, compassionate, and stable for all those who come into our care.

Chapter 14

Getting Comfortable with the Brain

When patients begin to understand how their brains were shaped in childhood and beyond, and how those same brains now influence their decisions, they can feel such relief, especially when the very good news of neuroplasticity comes into the picture. Perhaps the greatest benefit is a lessening of shame, as they understand in scientific terms that they are not to blame, that they didn't always have free choice when they made what they regard as terrible decisions, and, at the same time, that they are now fully responsible for changing those patterns. This is very empowering stuff.

There is a certain level of confidence about this material that needs to get settled in our own minds before a kind of playful inclusion of the brain's contribution to mental health flows easily with our patients. Whatever each of us can do to encourage the integration of this differentiated body of knowledge into our larger awareness of everyday life will enormously benefit our patients. When we feel confident, we are much more likely to sense when talking about the brain is the most empathic way to connect in the moment. We know that whole-brain learning produces a different kind of incorporation than left-brain knowledge. Sitting with any of the principles in this manual in a way that encourages actual experience in body and feelings, as well as thought, will foster this integration.

Benefits of Brain-Wise Therapy

Let's look at a range of benefits for our patients that might emerge as we become increasingly mindful of our brains:

• To begin, the *decrease in shame*, mentioned above, often produces a noticeable increase in self-compassion, accompanied by an almost immediate deepening and speeding up of the therapeutic process.

• Then comes awareness that these same forces shaped parents, grandparents, and everyone else. Wisdom begins to emerge in the form of *embracing the intergenerational tragedy*.

• There can also be a significant *decrease in the dysregulating intensity of memories* as our patients come to realize that their abusers don't actually live in their brains or their homes (often the subjective experience), but rather are merely neural net patterns firing in their brains in search of healing empathy. That mindful stance is such a powerful moderating influence.

• The language of *rigidity, chaos, and coherence* can help our patients spot where they are at any given moment, and just cultivating that caring observer awareness will help ease them toward coherence. (There is more about the technical aspects of this point in the section on complexity, a few bullets down.)

• Using some of Daniel Siegel's (2007) acronyms of mental health can give our patients a touchstone of progress. For example, as the *FACES of mental health* develop, patients become more *flexible, adaptable, coherent, energized, and stable*. A lot of joy emerges as we track increases in these lovely capacities. Or we can talk about *SNAGging* the mind—*stimulating neuronal activity and growth*—or SIFT[ing] the mind by attending to *sensations, images, feelings, and thoughts*. As the touchstone for the most helpful inner state, COAL—*curiosity, openness, acceptance, and love*—is a regular fixture of conversation. Sometimes patients will internalize these acronyms immediately and use them to guide the therapy. They are also a pleasant source of integrating humor. Make some up yourself, if you like.

Applicability of Complexity Theory to Therapy

Talking about the larger principle of *complexity* helps some people understand why the assertion that their brains are leaning into healing is mathematically/scientifically true (Siegel, 1999). When people have a lot of internalized despair, it sometimes takes the big guns of science to help them have hope. So now is a good moment to bring in a little information about the applicability of complexity theory to brains/minds. This material is a little dense, but if you pause to sense your resonance with it, you may begin to incorporate the subjective experience of emerging complexity, a process that fosters well-being. To begin, theoreticians tell us that complex systems have several characteristics (Siegel, 1999):

1. Brains/minds are *self-organizing*. This means that they have a driving force moving them from simplicity toward complexity, as long as excessive internal and external constraints don't block that flow. Complexity doesn't have to do with complication but rather with more components being brought into integrative harmony, yielding a more stable system. In the brain, this process moves through two stages: *differentiation of anatomically distinct parts, followed by integration of those parts into a larger system.* This is a genetically driven process that focuses on differentiation in the earliest months of life and then gradually flows into greater integration. *Internal and external constraints* can block that hard-wired movement. An example of an internal constraint would be a mental model that causes us to perceive a greater threat than really exists. This type of distorted perception is common with survivors of abuse, and makes daily life a dysregulating experience far too often. An external constraint might be involvement in a verbally abusive relationship, where the energy and information being exchanged lead to chaos rather than empathy-based coherence in the interpersonal system. One goal of therapy is to change the constraints, and that process can develop more rapidly when our patients can mindfully identify those hindrances. This step often leads to an ability to do deep emotional work in a more intentional way that widens the window of tolerance and modulates the intensity of the memories.

2. Complex systems are *nonlinear*. This means that small changes in one component of the system can lead to large changes in the whole system. On the negative side, if a memory of abuse is activated, there will be a cascade of effects in the body, feelings, and thoughts that immediately changes the way a person subjectively experiences life in a big way. On the positive side, opening such a neural net to empathy can lead to rapid increases in comfort and coherence throughout the system, enhancing well-being and relationships.

3. Because these systems have both *emergent and recursive properties*, we can have a sense of newness in every moment as well as a sense of familiarity as patterns are repeated and engrained. This complementarity might bring to mind the six-layered cortex, where recursion happens in the top two and emergence in the lower two, with creativity and balance flourishing in the middle. When balance fails in the direction of emergence, we may have the subjective experience of chaos; when it fails in the direction of recursion, we may feel rigid. When the two are in balance, the feeling of coherence and well-being flourishes as we ride gently on the waves of stability and spontaneity.

How can we use this information in therapy with someone who isn't already conversant with complexity theory (a category including most of our patients)?

• Having a real feel for this concept and process ourselves can let us say with confidence that the mind will heal as the obstacles are removed (contingent only on there being no organic reasons hindering the process—and even then, significant improvement is very likely). This assertion is no longer an article of faith but a mathematical certainty (Siegel, 1999).

• This knowledge can also help our patients understand why they can go from calm to out-of-proportion rage in an instant. As soon as they can feel how a small shift inside (usually triggered by a perceptual bias rooted in childhood) can cause huge changes in their body (fight/flight activation), feelings (terror protecting itself with rage), and thoughts (shut down of middle prefrontal empathy and reasoning), they can become more mindful in the moment of activation. Anger-activating shame is also reduced. This is proving to be a great tool for anger management.

• We can have a much better feel for the roots of rigid and chaotic behavior. What kinds of repeated patterns, developed in childhood and beyond, continue to lock our patients into a lack of flexibility and creativity? How do those patterns reinforce themselves? How can we call on in-the-moment awareness to move rigidity toward coherence? On the other side, how did the nonreflective, in-the-moment patterns of chaotic behavior get set up in childhood, only to be reinforced later? How can we marshal the forces of integration and order to ease chaos toward coherence? Employed at just the right moment, these kinds of questions lead to good co-detective work that increases access to the caring observer and enhances interpersonal integration. Having a living picture in our bodies and feelings can help us be aware of the fluctuations between rigidity, chaos, and coherence. It is also helpful to think about how these global attributes manifest in specific individual, interpersonal, cultural, and historical contexts. These three states—rigidity, chaos, and coherence—are everywhere because society is a creation of our minds, and this awareness may lead us—and our patients—toward behaviors that seek the balance of coherence as a way of life.

• Perhaps you can dream up some more creative applications.

We are finding that if we take the time to become at home with complexity theory, we can find words and ways to convey the feeling of it unfolding in the brain that actually promote neural integration just in the discussion itself. It becomes much more than left-brain knowledge when our discussion is infused with our own right-brain understanding.

Additional Benefits of Brain Talk

• Sharing the difference between *cohesive* and *coherent* narratives may help our patients begin to let go of assuming that the story they're telling themselves about their worth and about possibilities for fulfilling relationships is The Truth. It's certainly a learned truth, but not the immutable truth of their being and identity. Our minds make a *cohesive narrative* through very limited bilateral integration. It goes something like this. Based on an internal or external trigger, an implicit mental model, developed through being shamed as a child, wells up in the limbic region (without benefit of middle prefrontal intervention), bringing disquiet to our body and feelings. The job of the left hemisphere is to make sense of the emotional context being supplied by the right, to create a cause-and-effect explanation. As a result, the left hemisphere will seek words to frame the experience. We might then hear our mind say, "Those people don't like you because you don't talk to them right." Or "What do you expect? You're always so clumsy and stupid." It's interesting to listen to how often our minds speak to us in the second person—"you"—probably because these messages spring from an internalized voice. We could call this voice the uncaring observer.

Now we have a cohesive narrative about why people don't like us that has the ring of truth in the present, because the feelings on which it is based stem from implicit memory (where there is no sense of past). This narrative will also have recursive power, because as these thoughts/feelings as flow through the brain, they influence action. This kind of horizontal integration is like a rigid iron footpath connecting a very limited part of the right hemisphere to an explanation in the left. If this same trigger came to a mind developing a *coherent narrative*, it might go more like this: "I feel a lot of shame in my body, and that's very familiar. There's a lot of sorrow that I still have to deal with these feelings sometimes. Let me take a deep breath and calm down. Maybe later I'll have time to see what set this off. What a sad thing that everybody in my family has had to struggle with this." At least two processes must happen for a wounded person to be able to experience this kind of coherence. First, in moment-to-moment empathic interactions in therapy (or elsewhere), the nonconscious implicit world is reshaped in the direction of secure attachment, so the old implicit meanings have less absolute power. Second, in this process, middle prefrontal integration progresses, making the caring observer state of mind more available. Then, remnants of the old implicit meanings can become explicit and feel the caring touch of the middle prefrontal cortex. The shameful experience can now be incorporated into a larger sense of the self in history. The calmness and solidity of this perspective can also help us act in a way that does not bring on more shame. It's also lovely to note how the us/them inner community feeling of cohesive narratives transforms into an empathic, we're-all-in-it-together connection between community members within coherent narratives.

• Sometimes our patients may become quite discouraged when they fall back into some familiar form of pain and fear again after achieving a sense of peace and balance. When we help them understand that new states of mind are fragile, whereas old states continue to have momentum for a while, hope often returns, along with the determination to continue reinforcing the new states. We know that with enough practice, *states can become traits*, those more stable aspects of personality that rest on changes in brain structure. This can be particularly touching when the old state was a dramatically insecure attachment. As our tender, warm intention to connect offers an invitation to our frightened patients, they gradually feel safe enough to allow their injured attachment system to reach toward us. These delicate moments initially bring anxiety, followed by regulation and the sweetness of intimate meeting. Sometimes, this new state of connection may persist for a few hours or days initially, only to be overwhelmed by the torrent of self-blame flowing from the old neural nets of parental disregard. At these moments, we can offer pictures of little threads of connection that we will gradually weave into a tapestry of secure attachment. These images can support a mindful understanding of the overall process that in itself is reassuring and regulating.

• Many of my patients are in love with the idea of *mirror neurons* and *resonance circuits* as the leading edge in their ability to sense the internal worlds of others. Just the idea of brains/bodies resonating together helps them make sense of their lives. Before, they needed to take on faith that they had absorbed some part of their family-of-origin. Even if they could accept that idea, it was unclear how much or in what way. They could then wonder if they were making up their subjective experience. Even more hurtful to the therapeutic process, if denial was rampant in a family, the fuzziness of the idea of internalization could make it easy to deny that anything was hurtful. Now, we can describe how each of us is always taking in the state of mind of the other and making it our own.

Sometimes, sharing the story of how macaque monkeys taught us humans about mirror neurons seems to so capture the imagination that this amazing human capacity becomes part of their permanent whole-person awareness about how relationships work. As you may recall, Italian researchers Rizzolatti, Fogassi, and Gallese (Murata et al., 1997) had wired up neurons in a monkey's premotor cortex to observe neural activity in this planning area when the monkey ate raisins. Then, Fogassi walked in and picked up a raisin himself, only to be startled when the very same area lit up in the monkey, even though he (the monkey) hadn't moved. After many repetitions, they realized they had found something completely new and called them mirror neurons. On the very hopeful side, incorporating the idea of mirror neurons and resonance circuits seems to open our patients' minds to experiencing healing resonance with us as well.

• Finally, talking about the *various forms of neural integration* at just the right moment can allow our patients to understand their distress or amplify a new state of connection. One man whose abuse had left him with such profound disorganization that he couldn't speak whole sentences about his childhood was so relieved to understand both the disintegration in the right hemisphere and the left's inability to make sense of it. He sat transfixed as I talked with him, drinking in the explanation, but even more powerfully, the feeling that I understood. From that moment on, thanks to a more linked middle prefrontal region, a small observing part of him was able to hold his fragmentation with more understanding. Experiences like this show us that *brain talk can offer so much more than education, actually becoming a powerful form of contingent communication that also works to rewire nonconscious implicit processes.*

Countertransference Benefits of Brain Knowledge

Patients also benefit from our being able to better manage our side of the relationship because we are aware of how brains work. This is especially true when our patients are awash in implicit-only processes. From that trapped viewpoint, what they sometimes say makes no current-day sense. A patient of mine suddenly began experiencing intense anxiety and became convinced that her husband should never have looked at another woman before meeting her. They were both in their 30s, and she had had several meaningful prior relationships. Exploring her anxiety, we got no further than her absolute conviction that his having briefly dated several women was the cause of her misery. It would be easy to lose empathy for her and distance ourselves at that point, replicating the terror of abandonment she was already experiencing. However, knowing her history of extreme birth trauma, followed by a prolonged separation from her mother because of a her mother's battle with cancer, began to bring images of this tiny being searching, searching for her in the midst of the loss, and then falling into fragmenting anxiety. She would say to her husband, "You didn't wait for me," over and over again in an anguished voice. It took a very long time to rewire safety and security within the therapeutic relationship, but we were able to become a team to weather the ongoing storm through a good understanding of the implicit world. Being able to recognize the style of implicit processes as they twist current reality allows our caring observer to be present, overriding our need for things to make current-day sense. In this way, we can stay connected with our patients instead of falling into the confusion and separation that can result from our own experience of cognitive dissonance—a particularly unsettling form of personal incoherence.

Patient Responses to Brain Talk

Once we get to the stage of self-confidence and belief in the power of these ideas, we will be ready to weave them into therapy. Here are some responses you might get from patients.
   • After the initial exposure, some patients will immediately adopt the language of the brain to explain how they are subjectively experiencing themselves, showing continuing curiosity about all the nuances. They will want the big vocabulary words and the more technical explanations. Watch for hungry eyes and a palpable sense of excitement in the room.

One patient with a powerfully avoidant attachment had her biggest breakthrough on the heels of understanding how her left and right hemispheres weren't communicating. Once this made sense to her, the inner world of connection with her therapist opened, she became aware of her body, and visceral memories of yearning for attachment bubbled up easily.

• Others will begin to gradually absorb this new view of their inner world and become quite playful with it. They are not so interested in the technical aspects as in absorbing a visceral sense of the flow in their minds.

• Some will find that this information steadies their left brain, giving them the security to plunge into right-brain experience with confidence that touching the pain-filled subjective world will help them. When they need further intellectual bolstering, they'll ask for more.

• Others will use it as background, making only occasional references.

• So far, only a few have found it upsetting because it feels mechanical or dehumanizing. It seems as though their very early injuries can't tolerate anything that interrupts the view of the maternal face. As with everything else in therapy, it is important to take our cues from our patients and use this body of knowledge in ways that are respectful and therapeutic.

Although we have a model of the brain in every counseling room, we find that Daniel Siegel's hand model works best with patients. They can take their new awareness home with them in a very tangible way: a brain in the palm of their hand, as he says (Siegel & Hartzell, 2003). The experience of the brain becomes visual and tactile. With just a little education, many patients will begin to use their hands talk to you about what feels disconnected. One says she has "knots in her amygdala" that are keeping her triggered, as she points to her thumb. Another shows how he "blew his top" with his daughter, as he opens his fingers. Someone else lovingly tucks her fingertips against her palm and thumb, hugging her hands together and savoring the sense of comfort. We can even use our two hands to bring the world of our two brains into view. With patients who initially rely on me for regulation, I will fold my left hand together, thumb tucked tight, and tell them that this is me, caring about them. With my right hand a little higher and fingers uncurled a bit, I say that this is them when they are frightened: their middle prefrontal cortex shut off by their scared amygdala. Then I pull the two hands together, curling the fingers around my patient's brain as well, until there we are, brain to brain and eye to eye. Patients almost immediately repeat the action over and over, experiencing a strong sense of connection and relief. Many of them say that these two little fists become their constant companions. Rather than dry science, all of this can become quite a compelling tale (as long as we're true to the science as well).

Using the hand model immediately brings the body into the equation, while gently prodding our caring observer into action. We can imagine that this action encourages vertical integration on the right, while at the same time, conversation about the brain stimulates horizontal integration. Without the body's involvement, it is more likely that the information would stay locked in the lonely left where it can do less to rewire the nonconscious implicit process and thereby support integration. With what we know about mirror neurons, using our own hand to demonstrate or to mirror what our patient is showing us about his or her brain will strengthen those connections as well. I am finding it helpful to share the hand model with most patients in the first one or two sessions, as the situation presents itself. However, most of my long-time patients are taking to it with significant interest as well.

After this introduction to the brain, the art of keeping brain talk alive is finding ways to allow our budding knowledge to creep into conversation *at just the right moment to be experienced as empathic, so that patients feel not only smarter but more seen.* As with any other offering, our patients will let us know if they feel met or not. Be watchful for brain images dancing in your mind or sly sentences emerging from some deep place. These are the heralds of knowledge becoming wisdom. Once again, it is lovely to see how all our efforts on behalf of our patients lead us toward greater personal integrative possibilities as well—part of the mutuality of the therapeutic relationship. In the "Brain-Wise Narratives" that follow, you will find some concrete examples of how brain wisdom can be applied in helping our patients remake their implicit worlds and create coherent narratives of their lives.

Brain-Wise Narratives

One manifestation of the unfolding healing process is our patients' development of a coherent narrative, meaning an emotionally rich story that makes sense of one's life and does not carry the narrator out of the window of tolerance toward rigidity or chaos. This is the life story that grows out of the deep process of transforming the implicit world and the neural integration flowering in its wake. With all my patients, these stories come together one piece at a time, until near the end of therapy, there is often a moment when the panorama of the intergenerational tragedy unfolds before the inner eye. It reminds me of the scene in *Gone with the Wind* when Scarlet O'Hara goes to the train station receiving the incoming wounded from Gettysburg. The camera first focuses our field of vision on a closeup of Scarlet looking for Dr. Wilkes, then gradually widens until the sweeping vista of human suffering wrought by the war lies before us. For me, there is a feeling of hush and awe and deep sorrow in the body—but it is a quiet feeling, too.

Over the course of therapy, the brain integrates and the mind coheres to a state where it is possible to hold these inner perspectives and make full sense of what happened in this family. These moments are often permeated with a sense of compassionate release, completing the resolution of all hatred and anger at the broken people who were the unwitting architects of suffering for their children. This experience is more than the sum of the little narratives we have built along the way. It makes the story whole and deep, much in the way a symphony is more than the sum of the instrumental parts. Being able to have conversations about the brain gives us an additional narrative strand that helps modulate and contain the sometimes overwhelming experiences of terror and rage revisited. What follows are two vignettes, small narrative moments, sparked by pictures of the brain—a point of integration on the way to the compassionate embrace of these patients' histories.

Loralei's father was a daily source of disruption for her from her first days. His ongoing, uncontrollable rage, even when aimed at no one in particular, flooded her developing brain and nervous system with a torrent of disorganizing energy, wiring terror into her earliest experience of the world. Now, just thinking about him or being in the presence of someone who was mildly irritated with her could shake her body and push her breath into panting, on the way to panic. We worked on easing this suffering in several ways, one of them being to help her picture what was happening in her brain and body. We were building new neural nets of narrative about what the panic meant, because initially it felt no different than still being in her long-dead father's presence. We needed to corral this perceived monster.

First, we built inner representations of her whole brain, and talked about its insistent push toward integration. Holding this vision between us, we could now begin to see when she went into a dissociated piece of neural "real estate," trapping her on an island of terror. Dad began to be less dominant in the room when we could contain the experience within her skull and skin. Her caring observer was developing the capacity to tell her small terrified self this story, this small coherent narrative about her amygdala and sympathetic nervous system, when the panic began to blossom. This information kept the middle prefrontal cortex at least within shouting distance of the agitated amygdala, a step on the way to more thoroughgoing integration. Because all this was occurring in the warm space between us, the brain knowledge became another strand connecting us, another way that comfort could come into her implicit world. Together, we pictured axons, bearing the soothing neurotransmitter GABA, growing down from the orbitofrontal cortex, synaptic "hands" outstretched to soothe the shaking amygdala. We talked about the principle that where attention goes, synaptic firing follows, leading us to believe that we were the cheering section for these healing neural encounters when we simply held the process in our minds. By now, Dad, the monster, was completely out of the picture, replaced by a set of neural firings that we could contain. Loralei's body was growing more responsive to calming thoughts. Overall, she was feeling a sense of mastery as the panic was losing its power to sweep her away. These experiences, built on the foundation of brain awareness, were now beginning to inform her life narrative, as she followed her body–brain–mind's development in tandem with her relational history. Not too long after that experience, she said, "These same things happened in my father's brain, didn't they?" With that question, we felt the leading edge of her coherent family narrative appear in her mind.

Here's another story. When I first started working with Andy, he was struggling to contain waves of anger that boiled to the surface whenever he felt slighted. Although he was never physically violent, he felt ashamed of the words that poured from his mouth. He told me, "This yelling is completely unacceptable to me, and yet it happens at least once a week." His current narrative included his view that he was just a bad human being, incapable of self-control. I could see these angry outbursts as remnants of his implicit world pushing to the surface. Strongly centered in the care between us, we began our discussion about bodies, brains, and minds, as I focused on ways to combat both the shame and anger. When these feelings were quieter, our attachment bond could have better access to his implicit world, leading eventually to the development of a different narrative. We talked about how his developing brain wired in the anger of his parents' fights, and we discovered how lonely he felt when they were preoccupied with their own disputes. He got to know his amygdala and sympathetic nervous system and began to be able to talk to them when he felt the physical cues that warned of an outburst welling up in his body. "I'm going to breathe slowly now and help you find the brakes." With some concentrated work, he began to develop real affection for the child inside, instead of seeing him as a brat because he followed his father's angry lead. As he felt the wish to comfort this frightened child, we began to picture how his adult self/caring observer, emerging as the middle prefrontal cortex, could embrace his small self. We talked of the precious GABA elixir soothing the amygdala, making permanent synaptic connections that could provide a river of comfort. Then one day, he closed his left hand, showing me the feeling of his tense amygdala, and then lovingly wrapped his right hand around it in a gesture filled with palpable comfort. Both of us took a deep breath simultaneously as we pictured our autonomic nervous systems coming into balance. This tender gesture became part of our weekly conversation, and I began to share it with others as well. Without fail, just the sight of one hand cradling the other—supported, no doubt, by the feeling of comfort within me—brought waves of regulation. We also talked about how eventually all this new self-awareness would make its way across his corpus callosum, the bridge between hemispheres, and become the deeply felt and beautifully contained story of his life. About 2 months after that, Andy began to string his narrative together: "You know, it's not surprising that I've struggled with being angry all my life. And it's not even strange that my father was angry. His father was the meanest person I've ever met. What kind of guy doesn't even like his grandkids? But then I suppose somebody did it to him, too." We paused, allowing the truth to just sit between us. "I guess there's no point in being mad at anybody about all this."

We are finding that introducing pictures of the body, brain, and mind into the flow of the therapy is offering a speedier pathway toward inter-generational compassion. It seems as though once patients have the felt sense of how their own brains have been impacted, which often produces a fair amount of self-compassion, extending it to others soon becomes natural. Looking at that sequence from the neurobiological viewpoint, such compassion is the expected consequence of increased connections between the amygdala and the highly integrative middle prefrontal regions. The only prerequisite for us to be effective with this process seems to be gaining a great deal of comfort with the science, coupled with sensitivity about when such talk will also advance our primary objective of deepening contingent connection. When that capacity develops to the point that we are mostly seeing through at least two lenses—nurturing the relationship and spotting opportunities to foster brain integration in a way that makes sense to our patients—we will have absorbed the information in a whole-brained way that makes it easily accessible to our minds.

Chapter 15

Patterning the Internal Work

Many of our clients come to us barely treading water in an ocean of attachment pain, sometimes with a great deal of overt trauma. The ground of the healing process is the way in which we join with our clients in a right-brain to right-brain dance that rewires the implicit world in new patterns of secure attachment. Along with this rewiring comes a processing of both implicit (centered in body and feelings, but without cognitive shape) and explicit (containing cognitive awareness of the events) memories that are part of the neural debris blocking the whole array of integrative processes. We can picture an inner community with isolated (dissociated) pairs continuing to experience the same anguished and terrifying events over and over, as though they are on an island without help. When internal or external events pull us onto the island, nothing else exists.

From the perspective we are taking, working with memories is a central process because dissociated experiences make people continually vulnerable to the emergence of disruptive states of mind. We are using the word *dissociated* in a specific sense that means not fully linked with the brain's integrative processes. Feelings can be dissociated from the cognitive memory of events, bodily sensations can be split off from thoughts, or entire memories can be held away from conscious awareness. Over the years, we have found that being skillful at helping our patients touch these dissociated neural nets/memories allows them to take in warmth, comfort, and insight right at the root of painful experiences, thereby encouraging integration. This process works on two levels: (1) by coming into visceral contact with dissociated neural nets so they can move into the mainstream of neural integration; and (2) by transforming the implicit world through the warm, contingent contact that holds our patients through the pain. Being able to facilitate this two–pronged process skillfully, without being swept away by our own implicit processes, is bedrock for the establishment of earned secure attachment. The result of adding this healing energy and information to patients' experiential worlds is a change in their mental models regarding attachment and relationships. From there, other empathic relationships tend to blossom.

Reclamation of Dissociated Neural Nets

Let's first take a brief overview of the process, then explore the details of application. It goes without saying that our ability to work with memories is built on our capacity to stay with our patients, limbic process to limbic process, and repair the inevitable breaks in empathy with humility and warmth. This basic work builds the ground of trust that supports the journey within. The work begins with helping our patients shift from *outer focus to inner focus*, often using feelings currently in the body as a fulcrum. If patient and therapist have done some mindfulness practice together, this shift may feel more natural. However, even without that, most people can make this shift rather easily, following bodily sensations in the present and connecting them with other times their bodies have felt the same way. This process encourages them to move toward the subjective awareness of past events, wherein they begin to experience what we could call *empathy of identification* through connecting viscerally with their younger selves and other inner community members. We often refer to this type of experience as *internal time travel*.

Thinking neurobiologically, we can imagine inviting attention to flow first toward the body in this present moment and then toward times in the past when the current bodily feeling was present. Focusing in this way has some probability of pulling on neural nets that contain the energy and information of this bodily state, bringing the fullness of one or more experiences forward. At this point, the memory (usually in the form of feelings or images) comes to consciousness—to the chalkboard of the mind (dorsolateral prefrontal cortex)—where it is available for the addition of new experience, both from the warmth of our relationship and from resources in the patient's inner world. There is often a sense of the patient's adult self joining with the inner child, so that the adult begins to have a visceral experience of what it was like then. Patients often have a tendency to minimize the impact of past experience, but these moments of inner merging usually change this attitude, and self-compassion may blossom. Because of the mindful nature of the experience and because there is dense interpersonal integration, it is likely that middle prefrontal integration will be strongly supported in this process. Then, both during and after the experience, the emerging coherent narrative will reveal progress toward horizontal integration, as both memories and states are assimilated into our patients' developing sense of themselves within their own histories. Because of the warm linkage, implicit rewiring is a parallel process, out of conscious awareness, but revealed in the way our patients begin to think differently about themselves and relationships.

As we do this work, we want to be mindful of helping our patients stay within their *window of tolerance*, and liberal applications of empathy and presence help in that regard. This window of tolerance can be widened by the initial practice of mindfulness, as our patients begin to develop a stronger capacity to sit in the hub of their mind and look *to ward* memories without becoming completely absorbed in them. This dual focus of caring observer and empathic participant is the ideal, and our patients will fall to one side or the other frequently at the beginning, just like toddlers learning to walk. When emerging experiences become too overwhelming, we can also help patients separate the experience into layers, focusing first on the body and its regulation before moving on to integrate other parts of the experience (Ogden et al., 2006). In what follows there will be some suggestions about how to help patients keep their balance until they have developed their own inner regulatory system. We could think of them borrowing our brains as regulatory training wheels during the early part of the inner work.

Steps to Reclaiming Dissociated Neural Nets

At the beginning of therapy, we find it helpful to introduce our patients to a variety of ways of working deeply with the attachment losses and traumatic experiences of their inner community. At our agency, internal work, art, and sandplay form the nucleus. You may wish to add other modalities that are conducive to entering these deeper layers of the mind. In the first weeks, our patients usually try each modality that interests them. In subsequent sessions, we often invite each person to make an intuitive choice (listening to his or her body) regarding the kind of work that will most help him or her on days that working in the deeper mind seems the most empathic route to traverse. Once patients indicate they want to do internal work, there are some helpful steps to follow. Each of you will find your own language and style for doing this process. Each therapist–patient couple will also develop a unique dance. However, there are certain basic steps, which also serve as principles, that form a secure scaffolding for that dance.

1. *Begin with the present as the patient sees it.* For many people, once their feet are set on the healing path, their minds exhibit a marked ability to guide the therapy process. This makes sense when we remember that brains are genetically wired to move toward integration. Because of this inner wisdom, we can usually start sessions by asking patients how they're feeling or what is most on their minds. After a short discussion, what is internally relevant emerges, particularly if our minds are receptive. We want to prick up our ears and our bodies to sense emerging meaningful states of mind. After only a short time in therapy, the internal worlds of our patients may begin to prepare for the session about 12–24 hours in advance. Dreams may come, relationships may shift, moods or body aches may arise. Some of my patients say, "I knew it was my appointment day because I started feeling lousy last night." My reply: "What kind of lousy?"

2. *Start with the body.* Once the person has focused on a troubling area, we want to facilitate moving toward the roots of the issue. To invite neural nets holding dissociated energy and information to open, we have found it most helpful to encourage our patients to focus on their bodies as they think of the difficulty, and then experience any sensations that may emerge. We can think of this as putting down roots at the starting point for right-brain vertical integration of body, limbic region, and cortex. Once our patients have found the focal point of the bodily feeling, we invite them to just sit with the sensation for awhile. Shifting too quickly to words can pull toward the left hemisphere prematurely, not allowing emerging states to deepen.

Sometimes patients will tell us that they have difficulty finding sensation in their bodies. Guiding their explorations can be helpful at that point. "How does your head feel? Throat? Chest? Stomach? Limbs?" When we sense they have settled into a sensation, we encourage them to stay with it. Very occasionally, just that much exposure to experience may seem dysregulating. We may notice this shift as changes in breathing, agitation in the body, heightened emotion, physical collapse,

Being a Brain-Wise Therapist

among other signs, as well as parallel changes in our own bodies. It seems most respectful to check with our patients about their level of discomfort, because what we interpret as too upsetting, our patients may be holding mindfully. One indication that the window of tolerance has been breached is an inability to put the bodily experience into words. If it does turn out that there is too much discomfort, it can be helpful to encourage people to just sit with their feelings while we are with them to see if they can begin to calm in the light of this focused attention. If the feeling of overwhelm persists (a very infrequent occurrence), we help our patients shift attention to something else, which almost always eases the intensity. Most people begin to identify how much physical and emotional energy they can tolerate without becoming overwhelmed, and, over the course of time, the window of tolerance widens.

3. *Invite closed eyes.* Most people go into the inner world more easily with closed eyes. We could say something like, "You have as much right to walk into your inner world as your outer one, and you might find that easier to do with your eyes closed." If someone is too uncomfortable to do that, we can explore why that is the case. As an important part of trust and respect, we never insist and never convey that patients have done something wrong by not closing their eyes. Very occasionally, I have had someone who actually focuses better with eyes open, usually gazing at a single spot in the room. Whatever helps the person leave the present and go toward the deeper timeless mind is fine.

4. *Invite the internal community.* An attitude of invitation is a precious resource. I am very fond of the scene in the movie *ET* when Eliot lays out a trail of Reese's Pieces to get ET to come out of the shed. Empathy and patience are the Reese's Pieces of therapy. We might say something like, "Let's ask your deeper mind to take us to a time when your body felt just as it does now." Remain in a patient state of mindful relaxation yourself, filled with COAL. Tell your patients there's no rush. Encourage them not to dig around in their deeper minds with the shovel of their conscious minds, but just wait and allow something to arise. After a bit, we can ask if they are sensing something.

Most often, either a symbolic image or past memory will come to mind (although sometimes implicit feelings will intensify without any visual accompaniment). If an image comes, patients usually move naturally toward describing the scene, especially after a few inner travels. They may share where they are, who is there, and the angle of vision—are they watching the scene or seeing it through their young eyes? There may or may not be a lot of emotion at this point. However, patients often experience this as a process of drawing us into the scene, and when that happens, the sense of companionship often allows the experience to deepen. To encourage the empathy of identification (i.e., viscerally entering the world of a dissociated part), we can suggest that patients look into the inner person's eyes or touch that person in some way. With a simple suggestion to let down the emotional boundaries and allow this person's feelings to come into the body, a powerful joining experience often emerges. As this happens, words from us that encourage and normalize the experience may be stabilizing and comforting.

If no image comes, sitting with whatever feelings are welling up from the implicit world is also helpful. If patients feel that they are doing the process incorrectly because the experience remains mostly in the body and emotions, it is important to reassure patients that implicit-only memory often doesn't have a visual component. Encouragement to become aware that we are doing this together often allows the feelings to arise, intensify, modulate, and recede—a process that gradually builds patients' inner resources for self-regulation.

Because many of these memories were unbearably intense when originally experienced, our patients may be concerned about being carried away by memories in ways that are retraumatizing rather than healing, not only in sessions but in daily life. Two aspects of the overall process of therapy can decrease the likelihood of retraumatization. First, part of integrating the inner community is helping our patients sustain a balance between adult functioning and childhood experiencing. If that is developing well in the ongoing process of therapy, we can generally trust that the inner world is expanding its ability to manage the depth and intensity of processing, even in cases of severe abuse. Second, the power of the interpersonal connection is part of encouraging regulation in the midst of memories. When we are able to sustain a mindful COAL state, the sound of our voice and resonance with our state can bathe our patients in an awareness of the goodness of the present moment. Our calmness, confidence, and connection within the process of intense remembering becomes a potent anchor. If our patients are momentarily lost in the memory, we can focus on the body to regulate that layer of experience first, use our gentle words to help remind them that this is a past memory being tasted again now, or help them come fully back to the present. Again, this is an art, and over time, we will develop a wonderfully co-regulating dance with each of our patients.

Being a Brain-Wise Therapist

5. *Track, track, track.* If all is going well (and it usually is), once we are on the inward journey, our job is to stay with our patients and follow wherever they need to go. In the early stages of the work, they may need more guidance and more questions, but as we repeat the process, experiences will almost always unfold along an inner logic. For example, Mark followed his agitated body to the memory of trying to tell his mother he was being abused by his stepfather. We might say, "What happened then?" *"She doesn't believe me."* (Notice the shift to presence tense.) "What is that like for you?" *"I feel frozen inside."* "Can you *take me* into the frozen place?" *"I want my mommy to love me!"* As I make only the smallest sounds of comfort, the dense silence fills with truth and empathy. The invitation to *take us there* can often spark enough interpersonal warmth for the person to feel substantial security, the all-important neuroception of safety. Wrapped in that, our patients can let themselves fall into the more foundational and painful feelings underneath. When we track well, our patients will feel *felt* and *understood*, both necessary food for the implicit mending that builds secure attachment. Effective tracking is happening at both conscious and nonconscious levels, with the latter supporting the former. When we stay connected, right hemisphere to right hemisphere, the guiding words we offer our patients reflect the inner connection.

As a word of caution and an encouragement for awareness, sometimes our own dissociated wounds make us want to avoid a certain patient's pain, because it mirrors parts of our implicit world that have eluded our conscious awareness. We will notice this because we will begin to route that patient away from certain topics, or tracking will break down in the midst of deep work. As you may recall from an earlier chapter, this is what happened to me with Lily, as I moved from tracking to teaching. Under these circumstances, therapeutic work gets delayed, and to set the ship right, we need to sit mindfully with our own emerging inner experience or head for our own therapists—or both.

6. *Be aware of layers.* As we track the memory, we will begin to notice that feelings are often layered. Anger, numbness, boredom, and emptiness are usually secondary and somewhat defensive emotions, what we have called *protectors* in the inner community. It is important and respectful to work with these when they arise, to taste them and develop an appreciation of their origin and value. We can also be aware that there is more underneath. Because of the resonance circuits that join us to our patients, our inner attentiveness to these layers will help them continue

to move inward. *Pain* takes many forms—anguish, shame, jealousy, grief, to name only a few. *Fear* can also reveal itself as anxiety, terror, dread, anticipation of the worst, and even despair. With our help, our patients will experience the feelings and find the words that match these foundational inner experiences.

7. *Bring yourself into the picture.* If we think about how our minds embed other people in our inner worlds, we can sense the importance of the therapist becoming a permanent resident of the inner community. We can become a source of ongoing comfort, reassurance, and encouragement, a process that is particularly important when both internal parents have been a source of disruption and pain. Initially, we are a resource for regulation and, once internalized, become ongoing support for self-regulation. In this process, implicit mental models of relationship also have a chance to shift, patterned this time on the empathic bond between the two of us. Anything we can do to encourage internalization will be of benefit.

One way to aid this process is helping our patients picture us in the midst of the remembering process. As we head inward, I may say to my patient, "I will go with you wherever you need to go." Or in the middle of a memory, "I'm right with you." After the memory is complete, I may ask if the child can feel me there, and does he or she like me being there. Whatever the answer, track, track, track, and keep making contact. Usually the child will be welcoming, sometimes cautious, and rarely rejecting. However, if my patient says the child is uncomfortable with me in this inner space, I ask if the child can tell me what feeling my presence brings. Maybe this person can trust no adults. Maybe I remind the child of someone who has been hurtful. Then I will ask where he or she would like me to be and go there, even if it's out of the memory. This kind of contingent response to the inner community is so helpful in building an earned secure attachment.

As we complete the work for the day, I may suggest that patients can picture me with their child through the week, if they like. For most, this is a comforting thought. Occasionally, our patients may only want to comfort themselves and resist our participation both in the memories and afterward. Exploring the roots of this distrust, usually found in early attachment experiences, is the important first step. Although self-comfort is certainly better than self-rejection, patients are still not gaining a different experience of the larger relational world if they cannot invite someone into their inner community.

For the most part, our more wounded patients have not had enough empathy as children to develop what is called *object constancy*. This capacity allows us to experience an increasingly complex representation/felt sense of the whole person of the other within ourselves, both when they are not with us physically and when the relationship is disrupted in the moment. Whatever name we give it, this is one of the most important foundations for well-being and healthy relating. When children achieve this capacity, they can say, "Mom is mad at me, but I know she loves me." Relational resilience resides in this ability because we can ride out rough seas on this solid internal raft.

As empathy deepens in the therapeutic relationship, and our patients internalize us as a warm and caring presence, we become the prototype of empathic relationships elsewhere in life. Our patients will begin to tell us that they hear our voice when they are making a decision, or feel our comfort when they are hurt. At first, it will be sporadic and unreliable, but gradually it may become the background of their everyday life. I had a severely injured patient who needed me to touch base with her every day for about 2 years just to maintain any sense that I hadn't vanished. Gradually, the need for the calls became less frequent, and then one day she said, "I don't have to think about you every moment any more. And you're here whether you call or not." That was a great day. In reality, our sense of independence depends on being able to rely on internal and external others to meet our lifelong need for attachment.

8. *Stay with the feelings to completion.* As long as our patients stay within *their* window of tolerance (not ours), it is good to encourage the inner experience until it naturally rounds itself out. Sometimes patients will fall into what appears to be such intense feelings that we have the natural desire to provide comfort to pull them away from the pain. Better to provide comfort in the form of validation *within* the pain, allowing that soothing to become a regulating energy while they complete the work. Affirming their experience is at the heart of this process—"It hurts you so much;" "You need your mother here right now." When these words spring from a sense of our deep inner connection with our patients, they will echo with healing power in the depths of their being. Part of fully releasing the memories may be finishing actions that could not be completed in the moment of loss or trauma. This closure might include the ability to reach for comfort, run away to safety, or push back against an aggressor. These "acts of triumph" allow the body to sense

that the painful situation is finally over, and that new forms of movement are possible in the present (Ogden et al., 2006).

9. *Make lovely images.* The deeper relational mind, lying in the right hemisphere, contains experiences, symbols, images, and poetry-like words. Some education about the therapy process and the brain can relax the logic-seeking left brain. However, in the midst of doing deeper work, metaphors and images can sink deeply into the right hemisphere. Sometimes after months, a patient will tell me, "You know the time I was so discouraged and you said that therapy is like moving pebbles from one side of the scale to another until there's more weight on the empathic side than the painful side? Well, I see that picture in my mind all the time."

When we are deep inside with our patients, we have an opportunity to seed the mind with images and stories. We have found that these tend to work best when they are developmentally appropriate. For example, if a patient is experiencing something from infancy, images of surrounding warmth, cradling, and safety may resonate, especially when supported by rich rivers of that experience flowing in us. If a patient is in a memory about not feeling competent, images of us helping the internal child with some task may find fertile ground to take root. Sometimes, the images just come spontaneously. They are often homey and don't have a lot of resonance outside the moment. However, when they reach into the heart of the struggle, they can take up residence in patients' right hemisphere, becoming a permanent source of stability and comfort. This image emerged organically when one patient lost sight of the gains in therapy because she was in a bad patch: "It's like falling down a well. You can't see any of the surrounding land, but it's still there." This image provided a picture that the caring observer could use to help the inner world stay out of despair with the next tumble into painful memories. Another patient was passionate about his study of geology, so we dropped into a way of talking about his inner world in terms of flood tides and fossils, volcanoes and tectonic shifts. The best metaphors and images spring from some felt inner truth about the way you envision the inner world working in that particular moment. Your right brain is fertile with these images, and you may find that they soon begin wandering through your mind unbidden.

10. *Bring the child back into the room.* When the inner work has rounded itself out, it can be very helpful to bring the child out of the past, into the present. When there has been no previous comfort for a particular experience, the child has been living the old painful reality

every day since it happened (trapped, as it were, in a dissociated neural net). So this particular child aspect has no idea about how present life feels. We can invite the child to come into the warmth of the relationship in our counseling room, into the present, telling the truth that this little one is part of this adult's world, and is now safe/secure/cared for (whatever is appropriate), at least in this moment. We can help our patient picture the child coming into the room, and, when able to feel that, sit with the experience for a bit. This is a powerfully integrative process that seems to involve narrative, memory, and state integration all at once.

At the beginning of the work, our patients may not have touched enough of the pain or absorbed enough empathy to leave the memory fully and come into the present. Some aspects may remain dissociated and require more attention on another day. However, after a few visits inside, we can begin making the invitation regularly, never expressing disappointment if the child can't come yet. Let me share an example. After several months of working with memories of devastating abuse, we extended an invitation for the child to be with us in the room for perhaps the 10th time. Prior to this point, there had always been too much pain for her to believe the abuse was over. However, this day, my patient's eyes popped open as we encouraged the child to come with us. She said, "She's right there, sitting in the sand tray cart." We expressed our joy and also valued her need to be somewhat separate still. However, the very next week, when we made our suggestion, my patient felt the child slip into her arms and cling. For some clients, these visceral experiences, symbolizing what is happening internally as the neural dissociation resolves, become quite external and tangible. From that day forward, my patient spent a meditative time every day with that child, and therapy took wing.

How can we understand what happened? I picture us building a hammock of security for that little girl, and as soon as enough comfort had come into the dissociated neural net, she was free to flow into that waiting hammock. When we make our offer, we will sometimes find that our patients have a different idea, like staying in the old environment to play or rest. It is so important to respect their inner wisdom unless it will recreate a hurtful situation. One patient said, "Just leave me here because Mom is going to come back and hurt me again anyway. I might as well be ready after you leave." I said, "Mom isn't here anymore and she will never abuse you again. You might have more memories of her abusing you, but nothing new will happen, so you don't need to wait for her. You can come with me and then we'll work on the memories together."

11. *Respect and explore resistance and defenses.* We can know that any blockages to integration, in the form of resistance and defenses, developed for a reason and were often adaptive in the moment. Consequently, they deserve respect and exploration as a valuable part of the inner world. For example, when working with patients who have dissociative identity disorder, it is helpful to congratulate their inner defensive team on the brilliance of their organized protective strategy, saying that without it, they probably would have had a much worse outcome— possibly schizophrenia or death. Often, if we are open to it, these defenders take a very tangible form, being part of the inner community. When seen this way, they are no longer an impersonal defense but community resisters who believe that they are defending the community against real danger. We can have the same kinds of conversation and empathy through identification as with any other internal part.

When working internally, we will find that these resistances and defenses can take some interesting forms—as walls, fog, clowns, pictures flipping by too fast to focus on, King Arthur sitting in a tree—literally, endless possibilities. As with any other part of the process, track, track, track, and maintain continuous contact. "Can you take me into the fog?" "How does the fog help you?" "I wonder what would happen if the fog were gone." (Just as a note, *what if* statements are so helpful because patients can play with the idea without actually going all the way there emotionally.) "I want to ask your internal protector if she could lift the fog just a bit if I went toward the scary/hurtful/shameful (whatever the patient has said) experience with you." If the answer is still "no," it is essential to validate that decision. If we don't trust the inner wisdom of our patients, they will have much more difficulty learning to trust themselves. When we develop the capacity to truly back off internally, it is a sign of respect—and also turns out to be a good strategy for encouraging our patients to find the resources to open their worlds at their own pace.

It is important to believe that our patients' deeper mind has good reasons for not going "there" yet. Sometimes not enough trust has been built. Sometimes the fear of the pain is so great that more time is needed with the therapist to internalize comfort and begin to assemble some feelings of security in the attachment. Sometimes the shame is so powerful, inner children don't want to show themselves. With time and oceans of empathy, all these resisters will become part of the relationship and grant admittance to the deeper places. I had a patient with two psychotic parents, and it took us about 5 years to make our way through the defenses—wolves, then dogs, then a maze, and finally, the magical disappearing act where everything we went toward dissolved/dissociated. However, once our security with each other melted this gauntlet of distrust, therapy sped by in about a year because she had actually achieved considerable brain integration even while her defenders were blocking her from conscious awareness of the gains. Understandably, the more fragmented the inner world, the more likely there will be strong resistance to going there. However, once these defenders are integrated into the inner community, they can also become powerful allies. We all need the sense we can protect ourselves, and once the defenders are responding more to current-day events than implicit surges from the past, they are usually quite good at their jobs.

12. *Be mindful of the internal generations.* When we have visited a horrible memory with our patient, we may feel inclined to verbally thrash the perpetrator in way that affirms our patient's unfair treatment. At that moment, it will be helpful to picture that the perpetrator also lives in the internal world, and that we alienate him or her at our patient's peril. One difference between other forms of work and inner community process is the emphasis on working with the internalized others as well as the inner child. When we have interpersonal experiences as a child (and even later), the resonance circuits that tie people to one another embed a representation of the relational *pair*, not the child's experience in isolation. For example, a shamed child is always linked with the shaming parent. As a result, the healing process needs to ease the pain and fear of both partners in the relational pair. Otherwise, we may have comforted children, but they are still being abused/lectured/ignored internally by the people who originally hurt them. This situation also continues to foster hatred/fear/resentment of the parents, feelings that rob our patients of energy and joy.

At the beginning of therapy, for most patients it is wise to focus on the children when doing internal work, while being open to discussions of painful and fearful family legacies. Even if our patient can't yet consciously acknowledge it, some truths about intergenerational pain will have surfaced during the family history. This perspective gradually removes blame (but not responsibility) from parents, grandparents, and all past generations. In the last stages of therapy, our patients will often spontaneously visit this grand vista of pain in the family, grieve it in a whole-person way, complete the coherent narrative of this history, and move on to compassionate release. This process is greatly facilitated if our patient has empathically tasted the pain of parents, grandparents, and others who have had a hurtful effect.

To facilitate this visceral awareness of the inner community, at some point in therapy we begin to work with the internalized parents (and others) in exactly the same way as with the inner children. Our patients' inner children will see the parents inside and be ready (with us accompanying them) to approach these parents with the question, "What's hurting or scaring you?" Gradually, the internal parents draw us into their children's world, often with images or symbols of startling clarity. Then the work proceeds in the same way we have talked about in the preceding paragraphs. There is profound relief in having a formerly hurtful parent become quiet or even empathic. Doing this inner work with parents, one woman whose rageful father had been screaming in her mind every day for 50 years had a profound experience of his helplessness. On that foundation, she was able to reach up and touch his face in a comforting way in her mind. Over about a month's time, he responded to her compassion, falling into a gentle sleep. In terms of brain integration, we are fostering the full integration of the neural net holding the whole experience of parent and child. It also makes sense that this kind of resolution could move the transformation of implicit mental models forward, since the push of ancient attachment struggles is being reduced.

One helpful way to talk to our patients about the parents they internalized when young is to say that they are different than outer parents because they are formed from our patients' consciousness. Although they have all the tendencies, feelings, values, behaviors, and perhaps memories of the outer parents of childhood, they also participate in the basic desire to heal that the patient experiences. It is important for our patients to understand that the outer parent may never change, but the internal one always can. In our experience, after that happens, the relationship with the outer parent often changes as well.

Some outer parents do become more available and empathic as they age, and patients may find it difficult to look back at the internalized tormentor of childhood. However, once they catch glimpses of the relational pairs inside, they sense that the internal parents are as stuck as the inner children, and they see the value in forging ahead. They also usually find that understanding the roots of their parents' hurtful ways means they don't have to disrupt the current relationship.

Being a Brain-Wise Therapist

13. *Learn from each patient. Cherish internal diversity.* The ideas and images in this chapter are such a tiny percentage of the burgeoning creativity you will encounter within your patients. We are just beginning to know a bit about the infinite possibilities available in every mind. If we approach these inner journeys with COAL, accompanied by deep respect for individuality, our resonating mind will soon populate our inner universe with a most diverse community. Our awareness of the way minds generally work and the layers of inner people can serve as guideposts that then allow us to open our minds to the beautifully crafted inner world of each patient, a jewel like no other.

Chapter 16

The Integrating Power of Sandplay

Although sandplay has been considered something of a specialty, its notable ability to awaken and then regulate right-brain limbic processes can make it a powerful way to address painful, fearful, dissociated experiences. Whether these wounds are the result of trauma or difficult attachment losses, sand worlds may offer an elegant language when words fail. The work unfolds in the warm embrace of the relationship, as both people listen to the tray with their whole bodies. Working in the sand invites the implicit world, home of our earliest attachment wounds, to take symbolic form. Sometimes it provides a road around defenses; often it lets preverbal pain emerge; sometimes it makes concrete the feelings that a person has had difficulty communicating; sometimes it externalizes and contains inner anguish that has been too powerful to call to consciousness in other ways. Grounded in the body, sandplay unfolds through limbic region and cortex, and spans both hemispheres as the symbolic world unfolds into words.

After many years of working with sand and miniatures, my walls contain thousands of objects, but in the early days, when I had only plastic trays that we hauled from floor to ottoman and back, and five drawers filled with carefully chosen objects, my patients still did profound work. My best suggestion would be that if this work intrigues you, begin wherever you can, do your own trays for a number of months, and allow the process to unfold from there.

As we begin, grateful acknowledgment needs to be given to Margaret Lowenfeld (1979), whose child patients discovered this way of working, and Dora Kalff (1980), a Jungian analyst who recognized the power of sand and miniatures to draw the human mind inward, and through her writing and lectures, carved a path into the wider world for this work. She also coined the term *sandplay*, which we now borrow with appreciation. Most of the literature concerning sandplay has come from the Jungian perspective; however, with the brain in mind, we offer guidelines for practice that may be somewhat different, while honoring the basic purpose of journeying into the deeper mind.

Brain Processes Activated by Sandplay

In my experience, patients who find sandplay a natural medium immediately begin to partake of its integrative power as soon as their fingers touch the sand. How might that happen? Imagine plunging your hands into either moist or dry sand. What do you notice? There is an immediate connection between body, feeling, and (sometimes) thought. We can picture the sensation of the sand flowing up the arms to the thalamus, and then to the parietal lobe of the brain, which processes touch. In addition, the occipital lobe will also be activated for sight. This confluence of sensory streams may partially account for the immediate richness of the experience.

As this sensory information reaches the limbic structures, meaning is assigned—does this sand feel safe or unsafe? Integrating further with the hippocampus, memories of previous encounters with the sand may emerge—either in the form of beach scenes or sandbox, or in the form of experience reactivated by the texture of the sand. For example, clumpy sand may bring images of sand castles of yore or activate implicit feelings of dirtiness and disgust. The insula gathers all of this sensory data into an emotionally meaningful context, helping all this information converge in the middle prefrontal cortex, and a rich *relationship* with the sand often unfolds. People get absorbed in arranging the sand just right. This whole experience encourages vertical integration, linking body, limbic region, and cortex in the right hemisphere.

Experiental Processes Activated by Sandplay

For most, this is a rich, pleasurable experience at first, evoking days at the beach or giving some sensation of well-being as integration blossoms a bit. However, some will have chosen the kind of sand precisely for the discomfort it brings, moving quickly toward association with painful memories. In this case, wet sand may feel sticky, lumpy, gross, or frightening, and dry sand can feel out of control, unruly, resistant to form, and even frightening. When this happens, we might sense the perceptual bias in the meaning-making limbic areas coming quickly online. This may be the start of connecting to early implicit attachment experiences as well as the implicit layer of later experience.

If we attend to our own body–mind as our patients play in the sand, we may begin to notice ripples of feelings, images, shadowy thoughts, body sensations, memories, and other signs that our own deeper mind is stirring. We might imagine that this is a particularly powerful experience for our resonance circuits, since we likely won't be distracted by words. Instead, we will be directly registering the actions, feelings, and intentions of our patients. It is important to remember that this information will instantly become integrated with our own perceptual biases, so humility about drawing absolute conclusions is necessary. However, when the relationship is attuned, there is a good chance that we can remain present in the moment with our sandplayers.

Occasionally, patients choose to stay with the sand rather than choose objects from the shelves. Some will find powerful, soothing regulation in the sensory experience. Others may form linkages with painful memories. As long as we are maintaining a warm connection, the experience has a tendency to unfold organically, within the window of tolerance, until it rounds itself out. Sandplayers simply take their hands from the sand when they know they are finished. We can imagine that this is the completion of a cycle of integration, very likely involving the prefrontal regions, with their capacity for regulation of both body and emotions—mediated through the power of empathic, interpersonal connectedness.

Most sandplayers head for the shelves when they feel satisfied with the look and feel of their sand. I simply suggest that they *stay connected to their bodies* and take from the shelf those objects that *attract them and feel alive or full of energy* in that moment. I also suggest that they don't think about what the pieces mean or what they're going to do with them in the tray. For convenience, they may choose a basket for collecting. These are nudges toward remaining connected to right-hemisphere processes through paying attention to the body, listening for visceral/intuitive clues about what is important, and allowing nonverbal, nonconscious implicit memory to take the lead. The experience is so centered in symbolic/visual and tactile processes that it actually takes work to get left-brained about it. However, we are generally so conditioned to think things through that without a little guidance, people can take refuge in processes that are more cognitive than is helpful, especially if they are initially nervous or embarrassed about playing with toys in the sand. Just as when they were working the sand, it is helpful for us to stay emotionally connected throughout this process. Much is happening within this person, and we can participate by feeling the implications of body language, facial expression, breathing, ways of handling the pieces—resonance circuits again filling us with the experience of the other.

Now, with a basket full of meaning from the deeper mind, the time has come to return to the sand to place the objects. I might say something like, "You might find that each piece knows where it belongs." After considerable experience, I have abundant confidence that this is true, and it gives people the freedom to make the minute shifts of placement they need to get it "just right." What might be happening in the brain at this stage? If we think in terms of integration, the sandplayer is assembling a largely right-brained narrative, often based in implicit, previously nonconscious themes. What was only implicit is becoming explicit (but usually without internal or external words so far). The interpersonal system between us is strongly activated, both through whatever attachment has occurred so far in the relationship as well as the current resonance. Because of our strong empathic connection, I imagine that the middle prefrontal regions are active in both of us, increasing the integrative possibilities.

Then there often comes a moment when the energy in the room will suddenly "relax." That seems like the right word for the feeling of satisfaction that comes as the last piece finds its necessary place. Even in profoundly painful trays, there is often a sense of *rightness* that brings a kind of regulating joy amidst the tears. We then just sit together and hold the tray between us, allowing interpersonal warmth and resonance to continue doing their integrative work.

Bringing in the Left Hemisphere

Some theorists in the Jungian tradition suggest stopping here, trusting that the deeper mind of the patient will continue the process internally. There is no doubt truth in that, because new neural firings have occurred and will continue to influence how the emerging mind unfolds over time. However, because the kind of therapy we practice is rooted in the relationship, the process would feel incomplete without an exchange about the emerging meaning of the tray. In terms of brain integration, talking about the tray at this stage can help foster connection between the hemispheres by adding words to the rich experience that has unfolded nonverbally. Often this phase brings coherence to painful memories as they are shared and received, and creates greater understanding of different states of mind (inner community members) as they interact in the tray. In addition, having the symbols in the sand in a boundaried box often encourages a stance of mindfulness concerning the objects and their impact on body, feelings, and thoughts, allowing the caring observer to be present with, but not overwhelmed by, the inner community. As this part is able to hold the larger story that has unfolded in the tray, many states of mind may find connection.

In an effort to begin where our sandplayer is, we can ask a question about the *feeling* of the tray in both body and affect, rather than going straight for cognitive meaning. *We don't want to catalyze a leap from right- to left-hemisphere processes, but rather open the highway for the right to offer itself to the left.* Often, that initial question is enough for a narrative to begin as the person starts to notice different nuances of feeling in different parts of the tray. At that point, the most important thing we can do is remain attuned to the process, tracking his or her journey through the tray. Often, this part of the process takes the form of co-storytelling that occurs in words, body language, and continuing relationship with the objects. We may find ourselves leaning forward or away in synchrony with our patients. As their arms surround some part of the tray, we may find our eyes lingering there as well, and a gentle question about the meaning may emerge. Sometimes, if infant experience has come to the surface, we may find that we have no words at all for awhile. Instead, there may be a sense of delicate tenderness, often feeling almost sacred, that can only be honored in quiet joining. Other times, a robust story will develop around armed clashes or dinosaur wars. Always following our patients' lead, we can become collaborators in the unfolding process. It makes sense that this would be a valuable process when we remember that parents foster their children's ability to develop coherent narratives through co-creating stories.

Gradually, the storytelling will round itself out, often yielding a second sensation of completion. We take a picture to memorialize the artful experience, but usually do not give a copy to our sandplayers, in order to allow the experience to remain fluid in their minds. Under most circumstances,

Being a Brain-Wise Therapist

we take the tray apart after the sandplayers leave, even if they offer to help. Sometimes, the experience will generate powerful dreams about the themes uncovered, and sometimes whole new trays will unfold in sleep. Clearly, the pot has been stirred and things are moving internally toward greater integration.

The experiences just described probably happen about 80% of the time with adults—with a great deal of individual variation. However, it is important for each of us to be open to our patients' unique processes, especially when they diverge from the norm. For example, a person suffering with an avoidant attachment may create a tray that is almost entirely a product of left-brain processes. This sandplayer usually selects several objects that remind him or her of previous events, placing them in the tray with little sense that the objects need a special place, and then talking in a disconnected way about what each object brings to mind— a trip to Disneyland, liking to surf, a child's first birthday party, etc. The real signature is the internal sense in the therapist that this is a meaning-less process. However, what better way to truly sample the plight of a person trapped in his or her left brain? In that sense, the experience is deeply meaningful—and sad. On the lighter side, I had a patient who ini-tially felt overwhelmed by the size of the tray and so would "do Kleenex" instead. Using that small rectangle of tissue, he would choose just three or four pieces to express some deeply painful bit of disorganization within. It worked very well for him, and eventually, as he felt more organ-ized internally, he made it into the big tray.

Using Sandplay with Children, Couples, and Families

It is helpful to also consider how sandplay with children is different from the experience with adults. The actual process in the brain is no doubt similar, given that children are certainly busy with the tasks of dif-ferentiation and integration by the time they are old enough to do sand-play (about 3 years of age). Little stage setting is needed beyond the parameters of not breaking the objects. Generally, we reserve the sand-play pieces for work in the tray and do not allow them to be brought into other kinds of play. In this way, they have a specialness about them that pervades the process. To facilitate this separation, we have a separate sand tray room in our play area, so the distinction is reinforced for the children. The simple question—"Do you want to do a sand tray?"—begins a dynamic process, with or without words, with or without mixing the sand first. Our child specialist finds great benefit in allowing children's momentum to carry them either into the sand or toward the shelves. With fewer defenses, less self-consciousness, and familiarity with play-fulness, children know how to use the sand for self-regulation and emo-tional release. Often, the tray stays dynamic from start to finish, and the story emerges as the scene changes. Sometimes, the young sandplayer will request pictures at various stages of creation—and a digital camera makes this easy.

We have observed that some children begin their sandplay experi-ence in order to comply with a suggestion from the therapist, but within a few trays, the process takes on a life of its own, as the room fills with the felt experience of concentration, expression, and regulation. Our children also don't tell stories about the tray the same way as adults, but instead often make up little fictions that clearly reveal the themes. One 3-year-old boy, who was selectively mute when he came in, replayed the violence in his home with a family of gorillas and caves. When he began to speak, rich stories of terror and its resolution emerged, but always about this gorilla family and their quest for peace. Another child, filled with rage, rarely used objects, but just poured water into the sand, working it into all kinds of shapes until his body was calm, gradually building the capacity for self-regulation as his par-ents continued to battle at home. Flowing with these children's flexible processes is the key to staying attuned and supporting their emerging integration.

Sandplay certainly does not need to be confined to individuals. In fact, doing trays with couples and families can provide an opportunity for them reveal relational patterns that are not yet in their conscious awareness. Even the process of negotiating wet or dry sand may evolve into an illustration of how all decisions are made. One couple spent the entire session in a very polite discussion about why each person should have the right to decide on wet or dry. At no point did either of them say which sand they preferred. As our time ended, they looked at the empty, untouched tray and said, "This is what we do all the time at home. Noth-ing ever gets done. All we do is talk philosophy." They had come to ther-apy because of sadness over their difficulty conceiving a child, but this work created awareness of how fearful they both were of moving forward in all areas of their lives. Rich work ensued, some of it in the sand.

Another couple became fascinated with the objects on the shelves in their first session. Following their inner wisdom, even before we did

Being a Brain-Wise Therapist

family history, they did a tray. They quickly agreed on wet sand, and as soon as it was thoroughly mixed, one partner drew a vertical line down the middle to delineate his territory. Once they chose objects, his partner then spent the rest of the time trying to breach the divide with planes, trains, and automobiles—literally. By the end of the time, both men were weeping in sorrow and frustration at their ongoing difficulty in maintaining closeness. As we talked, they both realized they were afraid of abandonment, but one of them defended by staying alone, while the other frantically pursued. This tray provided a quick entrance to the extensive internal work that gradually resolved these fears, opening the door to sustained emotional intimacy.

When couples or families do trays, we have sometimes found it helpful to be a little more directive than with individuals. We often suggest that each person find about six or eight objects and then take turns placing them in the tray. Alternating seems to facilitate the emergence of relational patterns in a form that feels like a conversation. However, it might also be interesting to see what would emerge if the couple or family were given free rein. Both ways of playing would likely yield different aspects of their relational dynamics.

Even without using the trays, the images can help people talk to one another. We frequently ask families to find objects that remind them of each other, always including one for themselves. Adding visual symbols to the verbal conversation can stimulate bilateral integration, an inherently regulating experience. The images can also summarize the family situation in jarring ways. In one family of four, the parents chose nothing but angry figures—lions, panthers, a raging face, a stern policeman—to represent one another, while the children selected vulnerable baby animals for themselves. The parents were not as in touch as their children with how the arguing was impacting their offspring, but the sight of the tiny fawn and bunny was like a slap in the face that led to immediate changes. Hours of conversation may not have made their situation this clear with such forceful impact.

Simply having the objects in the room can keep our own right hemispheres more deeply engaged. Each morning, I spend a bit of time finding which symbol speaks to me that day. Sometimes, particular objects will draw my attention as patients talk with me, deepening my visceral awareness of their inner state. The creative possibilities are endless when we invite these living symbols into our space. In addition to healing implicit pain, they sometimes become a way to celebrate life's triumphs.

I saw a couple for several years, helping them with the disorganizing wounds of their childhoods. They promised each other they would do everything possible to create secure attachment for the children they hoped to have. Then, their first child was born, weighing 1 pound, 11 ounces. He spent 99 days in the neonatal ICU. In spite of every challenge, his two parents worked to maintain living emotional contact with him throughout the ordeal. As he turned 4 years old, the three of them came to my office for a visit. He immediately spotted the large lion on the bottom shelf, paused, and asked, "Where are the babies?" I retrieved the cubs from the top shelf, and he tucked them securely against the lion's legs, then moved on to find his favorite trucks. The cubs remain there to this day, a symbol of hope in extreme adversity.

Guidelines for Using Sandplay with Adults

For those not familiar with sandplay, what follows is a more fleshed-out version of the guidelines in the first part of the chapter, particularly as they apply to the more challenging situation with adults. These are not set in stone, and sometimes we will intuitively do something else (such as move pieces in the sand ourselves—always with patient permission—or help a sandplayer with the tray). However, these basics are a good place to begin, and will provide a solid environment most of the time.

1. *Invite your sandplayers to tune in to their bodies before beginning.* Usually, we will have begun the session by talking about what's going on in our patients' lives. Then, some area of concern will emerge, opening the doorway to deeper work. It is so helpful at that point to ask people to sense what their bodies are feeling as this issue emerges. Most people seem to be able to identify this sensation fairly easily. However, if it is difficult, we can either help them sit with their bodies, checking each part, or we can just let this go. It isn't essential, because just touching the sand will help increase connectedness to the body; however, when body awareness happens easily, it often provides a focus for the unfolding work.

2. *We generally give minimal directions to our sandplayers, allowing the experience to unfold in its own way from start to completion.* However, first-time sandplayers need some basic guidance. Ask if they *need* wet or dry sand. *Need* seems to elicit a more deeply connected-in-the-moment decision than *want*. Let them know they can work in the sand

with or without using the objects on the shelves. Kay Bradway, sandplay teacher extraordinaire, says something like, "Do whatever you wish with the sand" (Bradway et al., 1990). Sometimes patients get relief from intense anxiety just by leaving their hands in the sand for a lengthy period. It can be a powerful regulator, partly because vertical integration is stimulated.

If they are going to work with objects, encourage patients to dig a bit in the sand before going to the shelves, either mixing in the water or at least breaking the surface and playing a bit. This brief activity seems to help them move beneath the surface of their minds. Leaving the watering can available for adding more water is a good idea, too. We may notice that people are reluctant to put their non dominant hand in the sand, perhaps because of a conscious or nonconscious wish to not stimulate the experiential half of the brain (or perhaps because they have a pretty ring on that hand). Encouraging (but certainly not requiring) a both-hands approach has proven effective in creating a richer sandplay experience.

When they move to the shelves, ask patients to be in touch with whatever objects feels *attracting/ alive/ full of energy* and choose those. Encourage them to relate to the different objects through their experience of them in the present moment, rather than choosing objects to complete a picture they have already created in their minds. (Occasionally, people's deeper minds will have already given them a powerful completed picture, sometimes in a dream, one that now needs to be externalized and shared. What we are trying to avoid is left-brain sand trays, formed to illustrate a cognitive point, because that effort detracts from the deeper implicit processes trying to unfold.)

Encourage patients to let the objects "place themselves" in the sand and continue until the picture feels "right."

Let patients know that they can return to the shelves as few or as many times as they want, and that they don't have to include everything they choose in the tray.

When they seem finished, ask patients if their tray feels complete. If not, we find it helpful to just sit with them while they decide if they need to do something more with the sand or return to the shelves for more objects. Sometimes, although the tray isn't complete, that's as far as they can go with it right now—always a tantalizing situation because it suggests that the implicit world is stirring, but not ready to reveal some aspect of itself.

3. While they are placing the objects and sometimes during the story-telling, we find it helpful to *record patients' experience through notes of some sort, jotting down what our sandplayers say, and then recording the sequence and positioning of the objects.* Sometimes our players will move or bury certain symbols, a process that can only be captured if we take notes. We can tell our sandplayers that we write things down to be able to recreate the dynamic process of building, rather than just have the static picture at the end.

4. *It is also useful to record our own experience of their building process.* Because so much of this work happens in silence, we may find that our bodies are a particularly good guide for what is happening, since they are continually responding via resonance circuits. The challenge is then to separate what is coming from the sandplayers and what is coming, from our own implicit world. Keeping people's inner communities in mind and seeing everything in the context of where they currently are in therapy helps (along with generally being self-aware).

5. *Maintaining a respectful, intensely interested attitude during the choosing and the building makes the room feel alive and contained for patients.* Sometimes it may be tempting to think about other things, especially as patients slowly peruse the shelves. If we do this, however, a feeling of disconnectedness will enter the room and inhibit the process, signaling that the interpersonal system is disturbed. It is helpful to keep our comments to an absolute minimum. Unless we sense that something is happening with the sandplayer that would nudge us toward asking what he or she is feeling, just being quietly attentive can be the best support. Sometimes tears will come as sandplayers approach the shelves. If it seems helpful, we might sometimes stand near them for support and comfort as they stay with the unfolding experience.

6. *When patients feel that the tray is as complete as it's going to get, we may want to look at it from different angles or just sit with it for a bit.* Or, our sandplayers may begin to talk about it immediately. One frequently heard opening comment is "I have no idea what this is about." Such a statement is probably a good sign that implicit, right-hemisphere processes have been strongly involved. We might say something like, "Let's just be with it for awhile. See what you feel about the whole tray perhaps." We may find ourselves responding to movements of our sandplayers' bodies, either leaning into or away from the tray. We may begin to feel the energy deepen in the room. When it feels like the connection between the builders and their trays has happened, we might want to ask

various kinds of questions if our players haven't spontaneously begun to narrate the tray. All of these questions are intended to encourage storytelling, not so much in the sense of a well-constructed narrative with a beginning, middle, and end, but to discern the unique story revealed in the tray. With experience, questions will emerge more organically. It is also important to remember that verbal interchange is perhaps the smallest part of the unfolding story. The rest reveals itself in our mutual dance around and with the created tray. Weaving verbal and nonverbal together is the art of it.

All of these questions are intended as starting points, and what happens next depends on the direction our sandplayers take.

(Pointing to various objects or groups of objects): "Tell me about this." "How does it feel here?" We might even encourage the sandplayers to touch the object to see how it feels.

"Where is the center of energy in the tray?"

"What is happening right here?"

"Are you in the tray?" (Asking this question usually helps the players move more deeply into the tray.)

"Am I in the tray?" (This is an attachment/transference question, usually asked after several trays have been completed and after patients have been with us long enough to have us somewhat internalized. We need to exercise caution with this question so there is no implication that we *ought* to be in the tray, but rather that it would be OK to notice if we are or aren't. We want to help patients be as comfortable with a "no" as a "yes" to this question.)

"Are your internal parents (or other significant people) anywhere in this tray?"

"How do all these parts relate to one another?" (This will help patients begin to see the whole picture and feel the relationships in the tray—a crucial part of the process.)

You may notice the complete absence of "why" questions. Such questions almost always pull people into left-brained cause-and-effect responses that disrupt the process. A tangible shift in the energy in the room is often the result. It is helpful to record the unfolding story in at least a sketchy form, unless our full presence is needed for regulation.

7. *Even if our sandplayers want us to interpret the tray, it is best for us to remain in the collaborative storyteller stance rather than become the expert.* I find that any interpretation at this stage can overly influence the story that's unfolding, sometimes because there are inner compliant

parts who are eager to please, and sometimes because people struggle to trust themselves. As a result, it may be more helpful to say something like, "I want to just share this experience with you as your deeper mind begins to open to us both." There usually comes a time to look at the pictures of a series of trays together, and there may be some mutually shared interpretation of both the trays and the process at that point. As with each of these guidelines, there will be exceptions, and our intuition may prompt us to make a much-needed comment, even with the first tray. Listen to yourself and see how it goes.

8. *When our sandplayers indicate a sense of completion in the narrative, we take a digital picture.* Generally, we don't give one to patients, because we want to keep the process fluid in their minds rather than having it become concrete and fixed. We might say something like, "You will carry the picture inside you, and your deeper mind will continue to work on it during the week. I don't want to give you a frozen image." Occasionally, there will seem to be a powerful need to carry away the new experience that has emerged in the sand. This has seemed especially true when a stage of consolidating a positive new state has been reached. When we sense that, it may be appropriate to give a copy of the photo to the patient.

9. *In general, do not take sandplayers up on their offer to put the objects away*, unless there is a compelling therapeutic reason to do so. (Occasionally, a patient may need to disassemble the tray to declare that an abusive experience is over, for example). We might tell them something like, "I will do it because I want the picture to stay in your mind intact, just as if you had painted a powerful picture." When that happens, the objects can just go back in the basket rather than on the shelves, so there is enough time to absorb the sense of completion and freedom.

10. *When we clean up, we try to put things back where they came from, as much as possible.* We have discovered that patients expect to find their precious symbols in the same place next time. Be sure everything is removed from the tray and then stir up the sand as though sending the energy in the picture out into the universe. (This last part may sound strange, but I offer it because I have found that if I don't do this, the next sandplayer will sometimes be so influenced by what his or her predecessor has done that he or she chooses some of the same objects and comes up with a picture that feels confusing and somehow not his.)

The process is so highly individual and profoundly moving, it is impossible to capture it on paper. At best, this is a road map, and only doing our own trays will actually put us on the road. As with most therapeutic processes, doing some of it ourselves gives us the visceral familiarity to advocate it for others. This may be particularly true if we are going to do sandplay with adults. Any lingering feelings that it is silly, babyish, demeaning, or dangerous will pass to patients on the super highway of resonance circuits. Finding a colleague who will share the experience with you and doing several trays in a few weeks time will give a living sense of the power of sandplay.

After completing a few trays of our own when we say, "This is such a powerful way to deeply experience ourselves," patients will believe it as well. Perhaps the three stories that follow will make this process more tangible for you.

Finding Regulation in the Sand

Whether daily life pulls us briefly out of regulation or childhood experience has left us with gaping holes in our ability to maintain autonomic nervous system balance, sandplay demonstrates a remarkable ability to pull the brain together. From the first touch of the sand, there is often a palpable release of tension, and as the large muscles sift or knead the soft earth, the body usually begins to find its natural rhythm again. Even when sandplay begins as a means of externalizing emotional distress, the eventual result is almost always the calm embrace of the implicit-narrative-made-tangible that has unfolded in the sand.

Here are three stories, one that sprang from the trays we do in our sandplay classes, one from a woman whose early life left her with large patches of disorganized attachment, and a very short story about the resolution of a depression. Inviting our own bodies to follow these experiences may yield a rich awareness of how these activities with sand and miniatures can wire in increasing capacities for self-regulation.

Jeanine

When Jeanine came into class, she had just been impacted by a highly frustrating encounter with her contractor—something everyone in the room had also experienced, leading to nonverbal offers of understanding.

However, Jeanine was slightly outside her window of tolerance, her hands all over the place with a "last straw" feeling, and she couldn't make immediate use of our empathy. The class is experiential, so Jeanine had the opportunity to move these feelings into the sand. Paying attention to her body, she immediately knew she needed wet sand. The tray had dried out overnight, so the first project was to mix in water. As soon as the sand was well mixed, Jeanine began to push big handfuls strongly away from her. When we talked later, all of us had the visceral experience of her pushing the contractor across the room. Pat Ogden (Ogden et al., 2006) would call this an "act of triumph," completing an action her body couldn't take at the time of the stressful incident. Jeanine seemed to feel a big release, signaled by the deep integrating breath she took. As her state echoed within us, all three of us breathed with her, and the room relaxed. There were no words, just a feeling of growing synchrony between us.

When she was ready for the shelves, I suggested that she attend to her body and sense which pieces carried energy for her, seeking to help her stay connected to the right-mode processing she had already activated. As she chose her pieces, we heard her murmuring, "Isn't this beautiful?" several times. When she felt satisfied, she returned to the tray to place her symbols. Almost immediately, she ran into an obstacle. She needed a lake for her boat, but the sand quickly sucked up any water poured into it. With her invitation, we collaboratively found something on the shelf that would hold water. Then the boat wouldn't stay upright in its little tub, so we got stones to support it, but that didn't work either. All of us in the room were mindful of how frustrated Jeanine had been when she came in, and we experienced a little contagious tension, wondering how this new frustration would impact her. However, after several minutes of working with her boat, she simply got a different one that would do what she wanted. Then she said, "Well, it isn't my first choice, but it works fine." That delightful, flexible response regulated all of us. After that, she placed her other objects and then talked very gently about the energy of each piece. Figure 16.1 contains a photo of Jeanine's tray.

You can see the two boats, one in back of the other. Originally, she had wished for the one not in the tub to float in the middle. Instead, her second-choice boat did float, but off to the side, while a fountain has brought water to the center of her tray anyway. She said, "The fountain flows and is an endless source. That's me!" Her hands caressed each

Figure 16.1 Jeanine's tray.

piece as she talked. The boats spoke to her of adventure. The two figures peeking out from behind the boat are yogis, and they felt "whimsical, exciting, like a team, with freedom and dance." Jeanine particularly lingered with the beautiful glass tree, savoring its grace and the fruitful feeling it brings to the tray. By now, we were all smiling and there was gentle, integrating laughter. She continued, sharing that the spiral path feels like ascent, as the lighthouse watches over all. The mother angel tenderly holds her baby, and the amethyst backdrop brings in the solidity of earth. We could all see that her body had become flowing and flexible during the process. If you check your own body, you can perhaps get the visceral sense of how this artful creation moves you. For me, there is balance and harmony, beauty and hope—and perhaps most of all, the sensation of emerging coherence. I experience Jeanine in that state most of the time, so her trip back was relatively quick and easily carried all of us with her.

Caroline

We might expect this process to be somewhat different when someone has had a disastrous childhood that has left her with large patches of disorganized attachment. However, similar regulatory patterns do emerge, even under such difficult circumstances. Caroline began to see me when her much older brother suddenly died, leaving Caroline in charge of their abusive, alcoholic, suicidal mother. Caroline had been the de facto mother in the family from age 4 until she'd left home at 18, much to her detriment, so the other siblings assumed she would just take over. These events triggered every dis-integrated implicit and explicit circuit in her brain, leaving her barely able to speak at times, dramatically outside her window of tolerance. We quickly found that when she fell into these shattered places, sandplay helped her. All sandplayers have their unique ways of enacting the process, and much can be learned from simply observing their approach to the sand and miniatures. When Caroline comes to session in a highly dysregulated state, feet firmly glued to the shore of chaos, she immediately asks for the sand. She always takes off her jewelry like someone preparing for construction work. Fragmented, implicit, unintegrated terror has her sympathetic nervous system running tangibly wild, making coherent speech very difficult. She always engages fully with the sand, after asking herself whether her body wants to touch wet or dry. Her immediate joining with the texture and density almost always brings some relief, and we can imagine that vertical integration is part of the reason. As some line of continuity between body, limbic areas, and cortex begins to form, her breathing slows and her body becomes less tense.

When she calms down, I encourage her to stay connected to her body, and this somatic focus allows the early implicit attachment patterns to make their way into the process. She usually chooses fairly frightening objects. Then, as she begins to place her symbols of terror, loss, and fragmentation in the sand, one of two amazing things happens almost every time. She either leaves her left hand in the sand to maintain her emerging internal balance, or holds onto one of the pieces, telling me she feels soothing energy moving up her arms and into her chest. No one else has ever done just this before, and her ingenuity in finding ways to be soothed fills me with deep joy. I see all this activity as her ability to generate an interpersonal system with the sand and her chosen symbols. It is a way for her to talk to herself about what has changed since the horrors of childhood, creating new representations of comfort and release in a visceral rather than cognitive way. She can then carry this process inside, where it continues to transform her body–brain–mind's nonconscious processes, changing mental models that tell her relationships may explode at unpredictable intervals.

Caroline created two trays, which are emblematic of so many others, about 6 months apart. Both sprang from moments of severe disorganization, and both also resulted in her reclaiming some neural real estate for coherence, as manifested by the regulation of her nervous system in the process and her ability to organize and express another piece of her narrative. Making sense—a sign of emerging horizontal

Figure 16.2 Caroline's tray.

Figure 16.3 Close-up of family.

integration—has been an integral part of Caroline's process. It is as though the sand assembles the pieces, and the new narrative provides the cement to hold the emerging picture together.

This first tray (Figure 16.2, seen in full view, and Figure 16.3, seen in close-up) was created out of an experience of mental and emotional upset as Caroline was being forced into constant contact with her highly chaotic mother.

Day after day, Caroline felt compelled to take multiple phone calls, fearing that her mother might harm herself if she left her untended. Very soon in the process of choosing her images, she picked up a black cat and held it. She said it was a "nasty cat," but it somehow calmed her as she stroked his plastic fur with her thumb. This cat stayed in her hand throughout the process. As she placed the figures, several vignettes emerged within the boundaries of the octagonal tray, while the enormous, bright sun remained alone in the basket. She said, "It's hiding from the eyeball in the center [of the tray]." This glass sphere contains a spiral design that Caroline described as a "vortex," filled with judgment, guilt, and evil, exerting its influence over the whole tray. For her it was an "omnipotent presence," as well as all-knowing and all-seeing. She said, "It sees everything in an evil context at all times." The sun is hiding, believing in a brighter, sunnier day without that influence. This substantial but dissociated orb of warmth provides hope in this otherwise tragic tray. The rainbow in the back of the tray also speaks of something positive, but feels far, far away right now. The other bit of goodness, Glinda the good witch, didn't make her appearance until much later in the process.

Let's look at these images of the implicit-made-tangible. It is always helpful to attend to your body's response before doing any analysis, to just sit and let the images touch you for a bit.

When I revisit this tray, I am immediately struck by a visceral sense of disconnection and things being at chaotic odds with one another, particularly in the left side of the tray (in Figure 16.3). After sitting with the tray for some time (soothing cat still in hand), Caroline spontaneously began talking about the chaotic family that had also drawn my attention. The parents are "crazy," and the child is "drowning, in great danger." The smaller boy is being pulled against his will by the taller one. This perception was particularly interesting because most people perceive this figure as comforting. The raging, misshapen figure to the left of the

Being a Brain-Wise Therapist

mother image is the embodiment of the ongoing battle at the center of this fragmented family. As she talked, my body was responding to the angle of the pieces, particularly to the way the parents don't connect with anyone, even though their arms are expressing welcome. The only connections are through violence and terror—the wolf threatening the child who is already sinking, and one boy forcing the other. Throughout this process, Caroline kept noticing that the cat was spreading warmth and calm up her arm and into her chest, regulating her nervous system, which allowed her mind to organize. We never did sort out how a "nasty cat" could do this; cognitive clarity actually doesn't matter as long as this kitty is doing its healing work. Perhaps its power goes back to her childhood, when cats were of comfort to her.

Slowly disengaging from the family, she then turned to the two large pieces closest to her. The one on the left feels like an "exploding head," with everything going to pieces. The one on the right (which can be rotated to form many different, and sometimes discordant, faces) felt to her like a swirl of emotions, with the "head and heart not matching." Everything is dangerous and out of synchrony. She briefly touched on the rainbow, but its distance makes it incapable of any influence on the scene. Then the eyeball pulled her, and she spent a long time with the vortex. Her thumb stroked the cat more rapidly. She paused in her narrative to regulate herself again. I imagined that this dance at the edge of the window of tolerance was widening that window and increasing her resources for self-regulation.

She talked of the sun's isolation, and then finally addressed the black bat huddled next to the pipe (hard to see, in the upper right corner of Figure 16.2). He is terrified and looking for a place to hide. The pipe is cold, but it's his only refuge since there is no way to escape. She told me that she felt herself gradually move out of the tray and back into her calming body as we proceeded. With this move away, she began to take in the tragic panorama, and we were able to just sit with that. I was celebrating inwardly as I felt her heart become quiet and her mind cohere around this emerging narrative—with illustrations—of her life story. We both began to wonder if there was some way to help these people. Caroline returned to the shelves, choosing Glinda, and placing her "near the sun" because she may possibly help all the others find a way to get there. Caroline said that Glinda symbolized me, and I was grateful to be a spark of hope for this aching, tormented inner community.

Whereas some people's trays show a progression, like chapters in a book, for Caroline they have served a different purpose. At the beginning of therapy, her inner world was a devastated landscape, pockmarked with pits of disorganization forged in the family chaos. Whenever life events pulled her into one of these pits, the sand provided both the medium for expressing the wordless terror and the foundation for increasing organization. Each tray was different in content, yet similar in theme. However, over time, her platform of coherence has become sturdier, as witnessed by the way she is able to handle the ongoing challenges thrown at her by this family.

Let's make a quick visit to another tray (Figure 16.4) from later in Caroline's therapy. In the final picture of the tray, a pensive gargoyle rests on the edge, carefully angled to let its warmth and goodness radiate to her and the two figures in her hands. The gargoyle is again an interesting choice of comforter, in terms of both tactile and visual characteristics, because it is made of stone and seems the antithesis of warm. Yet, Caroline sat with it in her hands for several minutes, feeling intense warmth and comfort radiating through her body while she looked at the dysregulating scene in the tray. Then she set the gargoyle down and decided to take the howling wolf, wounded and calling for help, and her lonely black bat (just his wing peeks out of her fingers) out of the tray to partake of the goodness offered by the gargoyle. She picked them up with great tenderness and surrounded them with a firm embrace. We knew that

Figure 16.4 A later tray by Caroline.

these two figures embodied parts of her younger self, and her ability to draw them into the comforting circle signaled a further move toward bringing her inner community members into connection and empathy with one another. We sat with that experience for quite awhile, the room tangibly filling with the electric sweetness that signals powerful forces of neural integration at work.

There is a lovely recursive quality to the way Caroline repeatedly gives herself to the sand and figures, then receives comfort from some of them, and then gives that back to the others—all parts of herself, all externalizations of the unspoken internal process. A profound feeling of release emerges as a result of being able to physically remove them from the abusive situation and see them elsewhere, being cared for. I imagine that this process tells even her body that the spatial and temporal distances are real. As always, she emerged from this particular experience with a sense of "connectivity that feels like the pieces coming together in my body." From that visceral sensation, she can then create another piece of coherent narrative about how living in this world had impacted her passage into adolescence, leaving her with self-hatred and a desire to harm herself in a variety of ways. Although this new awareness brought sadness, it also had the stabilizing power of truth. On such patches of quicksand made solid, a life of balance and wholeness is emerging.

Ali

In addition to regulating anxiety, sometimes sand and miniatures can help alleviate the deadness of depression. I had been working with Ali for about a year. He suffered with a persistent sense of meaninglessness and bouts of low energy, punctuated by periods of fairly active, goal-directed work. Nowhere in our discussions did he mention play, either as a child or an adult. As we made our way through his history, nothing seemed remarkable—no abuse, no social upheaval, no significant losses. This absence of trauma or difficulty made it extremely hard for him to understand why he was miserable so much of the time. I talked with him about avoidant attachment, but my left-brain explanation fell into the wide, dead zone of his own isolation from his right-brain limbic processes. So, I suggested we turn to the trays, knowing that just touching the sand might start a process of vertical integration, putting him in touch with his aliveness through body and emotions. At first, he resisted: "Toys are for children" and "Play? Why would I want to play?" Eventually, with

Figure 16.5 Parent-child
bears together.

Figure 16.6 Parent-child bears apart.

Figure 16.7 Ali's tray, with close-up of child bear figure.

Being a Brain-Wise Therapist

considerable resignation, he decided to do it anyway. For some reason he couldn't understand, he was very drawn to the wet sand. He mixed it with considerable vigor—a good sign—and then went to the shelves where he spent almost 10 minutes looking, picking up nothing. I was paying attention to my breathing to keep my anxiety in bounds. I was unclear if I was resonating with his limbic area or my own, but knew it was most important to wait with sufficient calmness to let this process unfold.

Finally, he picked up a pair of closely nestled parent–child bears; he seemed fascinated that they came apart (see Figures 16.5 and 16.6). After putting them together and separating them several times, he set the parent bear back on the shelf and brought the tiny cub to the sand (see Figure 16.7). He gently placed it in the middle of the expansive, roughed-up tray, and slowly sat down himself, engrossed in this minimal scene. I felt an intense ache that I interpreted as loneliness spread throughout my chest.

Minutes passed as the intensity of our attention created a state of full alertness in both of us. Then Ali took a deep, integrating breath, looked at me, and said, "That's it, isn't it?" I nodded "yes." It was time to end, so we spoke no more words about his profound discovery that day. However, by the following week, he was filled with new stories about the emptiness of his normal family. The back of the depression was permanently broken because he could now actively mourn rather than simply sink away into the family nothingness.

Chapter 17

Doing Art

We have just spent time understanding the integrative power of sandplay, so it may be quite natural to apply the same pictures and principles of inner community healing and brain integration to art. Building on that foundation, we can plunge into the process. None of the therapists with whom I work are credentialed in art therapy. With utmost respect for that path of training, and humility in knowing there are vast resources we have not tapped, we have, nonetheless, found great benefit in offering this experiential modality to our patients.

One young man's unfolding path looked like this. His inner world would notify him when something needed to be expressed by generating a fairly intense pressure in his chest. Using his nondominant hand (the left), he would allow drawings to emerge during our sessions, choosing large sheets of newsprint and beeswax block crayons. There is no other way to describe this process, because what came out was almost always both powerful and incomprehensible, meaning the images were not connected to language. When he finished drawing, we would do other kinds of therapeutic work, but most of the time, nothing of significance happened. Then, within hours or days, his body would bring forth the memory of abuse or neglect (he had experienced about equal portions of both) in ways that were physically unmistakable, finally giving his drawing a context. Sometimes these body memories dragged images of childhood into view, but often not. Because he had ample resources of empathy and comfort at home, he could ride this pain and fear into a new level of regulation and wholeness. Then there would be a brief period of consolidation before his chest spoke to him again. Until we began using art in therapy, the process had always stopped in his clenched chest.

No modality will work well for all people, and that has certainly proven true for making art. We always offer a choice of approaches (inner work, sand, art) when entering deep emotional waters. It is possible that our patients' earlier experiences with critical or disinterested parents and teachers may direct them away from art. That being acknowledged, it is also true that although some people get quite self-conscious about drawing anything, once that hurdle is cleared, art can be a powerful way for them to express deeper implicit processes. Just the choice of drawing materials can make a difference. Sometimes crayons evoke the child more easily than just pencil. A huge tablet, encouraging more use of large muscles, seems to stimulate greater emotion at times. However, even knowing this, we have found it is always a good idea to give our patients the choice of large or small paper as well as a variety of media.

Drawing with the Nondominant Hand

One way to surmount self-consciousness as well as evoke greater depth of experience is to ask our artists to use their nondominant hand. This request helps to remove the expectation that something aesthetically pleasing should emerge. One small caveat: Regardless of handedness, using the left hand will most often connect to the right hemisphere of the brain, to the area where hurtful and fearful relational experiences are stored. You can certainly experiment with using both hands to see which is more effective for emotional processing, given that 20% of lefties and 5% of righties connect to reversed hemispheres. The more patients begin to relax, the more the symbols and images of limbic, implicit experience may have the freedom to emerge on paper, often with surprising, sometimes frightening, results.

When patients are willing to experiment with drawing, we may start with a house–tree–person picture to help them get in touch with implicit mental models of themselves in relation with their families (internal and external). By simply saying, "Would you draw a house, a tree, and a person?" we leave the door open for patients to put all three on one page or do three separate drawings. Sometimes they ask for further clarification; we can best assist their inward journey by simply asking them to draw whatever comes into their minds. If it is difficult for them to proceed without more direction and the emotions get very intense, it can be helpful to stop and explore what comes up, maybe doing some internal work around the self-consciousness or fear or whatever has emerged. However, most people grab the crayons or markers and go to work.

When they have completed the drawing, we might ask patients to tell a story about the picture, so they have the opportunity to develop a narrative about what they have created (and, at the same time, encourage bilateral integration). They may ask us what we think, but when we keep our desire for interpretation at bay and mainly reflect what they have said, with empathy, they often feel encouraged to explore further. Sometimes it may feel right to reflect a bit of our feeling—gained through body–brain resonance with our patients—about the drawing. Maybe we could say something like, "I'm really touched by the way that child is leaning on the house."

Traditional wisdom says that the house is Mom, the tree is Dad, and the person is our patient. Windows without light and lack of chimneys may represent coldness in the household. A knothole in the tree might represent either trauma or sexual abuse, and how high the hole is from the ground may suggest the age when it happened. However, sometimes, a knothole is just a place for a squirrel to live, and a chimney is absent simply because a person's childhood home had no fireplace. Placing the drawing in the context of our patients' histories can help guide our own reflections about it. Ultimately, people's own view of their pictures always supersedes any predetermined interpretation.

We often find that the relationships between the figures, as well as where they are placed on the page, to be quite important. Is the arrangement harmonious or chaotic? Are the parts of the picture connected to each other or separate? Are the figures grounded or floating in space? Where is the person relative to the house and tree? Is there a walkway up to the house? Is the person whole or does he or she have missing parts? When you look at the picture, does your body get a feeling of wholeness, emptiness, anger, fragmentation? The answer to this last question needs to be checked (as always) for any perceptual biases the picture may have touched in us before assuming that the feelings and sensations are coming purely from the drawing. Since using the nondominant hand will encourage our patients to work from implicit processes, the art-making is probably proceeding in silence, and our own inner world will also be powerfully engaged. Although we might not choose to speak what we sense, adding it to our awareness of this person's inner community will help us gradually build a fleshed-out picture.

Thematic Possibilities

The number of thematic possibilities is as vast as the combined imagination of therapist and patient. Such themes tend to emerge organically from the evolving process. For example, one patient was particularly focused on the turmoil permeating his family when he was a child, and he found that drawing pictures of his interaction with his parents and siblings helped him get in touch with the depth of his upset then, as well as see why he needed to exert so much control in the family. It is often the case that symbolic pictures emerge, capturing some striking implicit truth about the way patients internalized patterns of relating—which now, in the form of mental models, influence current relationships.

One of my patients, who consistently shied away from peer relationships with men in ways that frustrated and confused him, had a bipolar older brother who ultimately committed suicide. When he drew pictures of the two of them, they looked like children's drawings but always included some kind of wall between them, with swirling balls of energy (reminiscent of van Gogh's later work) on his brother's side of the wall. In the drawing, my patient was always turned away from his brother, even leaning away. When he tried to draw the two of them standing side by side, the effort made his stomach lurch. Even looking at the swirling energy was physically upsetting. It became clear that he was touching the sickening fragmentation he had internalized from his brother. The pictures helped the reality of that relationship come into the room, and as we held the disruptive feelings with kindness, we felt them gradually diminish, being replaced with compassion for his brother's torment. Soon, he felt so comfortable with men that he joined an evening baseball league.

Another patient came into therapy with her husband, believing that her childhood had been perfect. She'd had a beautiful mother, a strong father, and all the hills in South Dakota to roam at will. Her tomboy spirit rejoiced. Gradually, as we talked about the actual events of childhood, she developed a beginning awareness of how rejected and neglected she had been, and that what she had called freedom was actually her parents' need to be rid of her. Even with this new awareness, she was having great difficulty getting in touch with the feelings. This was not surprising, since her father had pushed her away whenever she was sad and had never showed any emotion around her, except frequent anger. Finally, in a series of drawings using her nondominant hand, her mom transformed into a frightening Halloween mask, half skeleton and half lunatic. Only at that point was my patient able to tell me that her mother had become floridly schizophrenic at age 45 and had been institutionalized ever since. Having gotten past the shame of having a mentally ill parent, my patient was then able to get in touch with the underlying chaos and fragmentation inside her mom. She realized that this is what she had internalized as a child, and that her mother's illness had, in fact, been the determining factor in the household, even before it fully surfaced in middle age. As these drawings emerged, they frightened my patient at first, but eventually helped her trust the wisdom of her inner world. Even though neither parent had been able to summon an adequate response for her thoughts and feelings, her drawings brilliantly showed her the unspoken truth.

Sometimes, when patients are struggling spiritually, having them draw a picture of how their relationship with the divine *feels* can be helpful. Even when we have clear thoughts about the world of spirituality, our felt sense of this domain can be profoundly clouded by childhood experience. One patient, who had chosen Judaism for his path, drew a picture that looked like the Myth of Sisyphus, a man endlessly pushing a boulder up a hill, only to have it role down to be pushed again. My patient had never heard this story but felt as though God were setting him an endless, impossible task and hated him as much as his parents had. He drew more than a dozen pictures concerning his spiritual life in my presence, and we used each one to trace the feeling back to a childhood moment and then provided as much comfort as possible for the inner child. In this way, he experienced me as a caring parental presence and eventually used our relationship as a springboard to perceive God differently as well. One day, he asked if I knew of any good pictures of David, since he had grown to love the Psalms and felt particular admiration for David's ability to love God even in devastating circumstances. I offered to spend a bit of time doing a computer search of images and found about a dozen. Slowly leafing through them, trying each one on to sense the right fit, he chose one, keeping it by his bedside, to remind him of David's joy in God even in adversity. He could have found the picture himself, but the connection he felt between the picture I discovered and the experiences we had been having together seemed quite meaningful to him.

Another drawing possibility can emerge from strong feelings the patients are having in their bodies. Let's say a person is experiencing a lot of pressure in her throat. You could invite her to draw what her throat feels like, and use that image as a way to get more deeply in touch with the source of the tension. Similarly, emotions can be scrawled onto paper. This kind of nonrepresentational work sometimes serves as a powerful release. Often it will generate a momentum of its own, carrying a person through several pieces of paper almost without pause. This is body-based work, and patients often spontaneously engage in new physical movements as a result of drawing. One woman, who felt as though her body parts were connected with rubber bands that were wound too tight, drew a scrunched up figure, then spontaneously got up and stretched in a most luxurious, cat-like way. Because drawing often emerges directly from implicit, bodily-based memories, it can help reveal what needs to be released. Then, either automatically or with a little encouragement from us, the body can execute the needed movement.

After patients have some experience with drawing and have developed trust in the wisdom of their inner world, they may be able to put the crayon, pencil, or marker in their nondominant hand and let whatever happens happen. The results are always powerful and unpredictable. One patient took a large marker, started drawing circles, then began to stab the paper. By the time he was finished, the marker was destroyed and the large tablet had become a rosette of torn paper. The rage he released was life-transforming, especially because he was never allowed to be angry as a child. I felt like cheering the whole time he was attacking the paper. There is a picture of the finished product in the illustrations that follow (Figure 17.6).

Sometimes patients draw at home and bring their creations to our sessions; sometimes they draw in session. There are times when they will want us to keep the pictures, either because they are too frightening, or simply because they want to leave a piece of themselves with us. Sometimes they need to keep them for reflection or encouragement. Unlike with sand tray, I always give them the choice. Sometimes they need to destroy what they drew, a kind of emotional exorcism. Burning a drawing in the fireplace seems to work particularly well, although one patient sent his away on the ocean.

As with any kind of work, our focused presence assists the opening and then facilitates the exploration of what is emerging from the deeper places inside. Since drawing often takes place in silence, we can assist by attending closely as we allow our resonance circuits to engage fully, bringing us a sense of our patient's unfolding inner world, while offering unspoken support. Many times, patients comment, "I could feel you right with me." Sometimes, we may even show up in the picture. One young woman kept drawing a small bouquet of flowers near the center of otherwise disturbing pictures from her abusive history. At first, she was unwilling to talk about these colorful visitors but would always grin when I asked. Then one day, eyes and a smile appeared amidst the flowers, and she was ready to tell me the flowers carried the feeling of our relationship into the midst of the terrifying memories.

> If you have never done a house–tree–person drawing, you might try it with your nondominant hand. Then you could draw your family with both dominant and nondominant hands to see if there is a difference in the feeling and what you draw. Some people enjoy doing a quick drawing each day on awakening, often finding that enlightening themes emerge over a few weeks. If you do these artful exercises for yourself, you may be able to suggest them for your clients with considerable enthusiasm.

Giving Form to Disorganization

The drawings that follow may help you increase your capacity to listen with the body when in the presence of another's limbic experience. With the thought that you might enjoy allowing the pictures to have an effect on you before being tempted into analysis, they precede the brief section on each patient's history and comments about his and her pictures.

Adam's Substantiation

Figure 17.1

Doing Art   251

Figure 17.2

Being a Brain-Wise Therapist

Figure 17.3

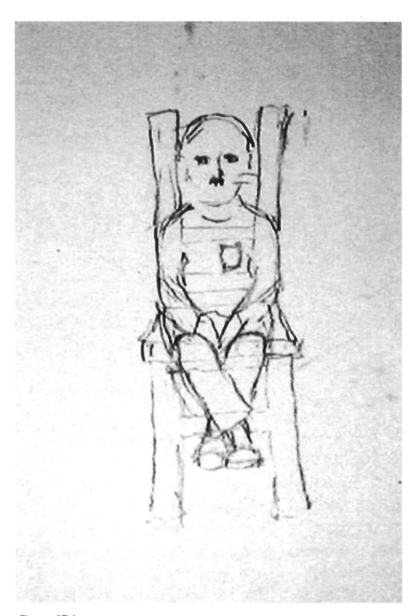

Figure 17.4

Being a Brain-Wise Therapist

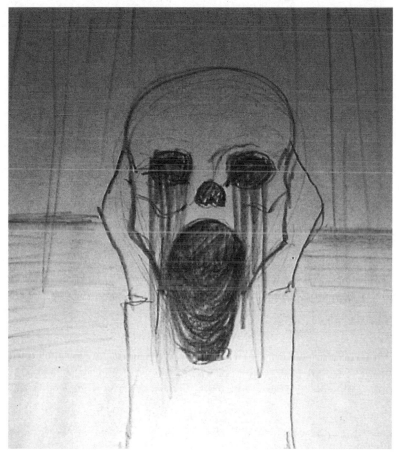

Figure 17.5

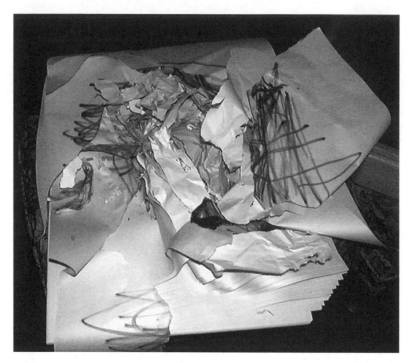

Figure 17.6

Adam is the oldest son of loving but very injured parents. He took on the role of emotional protector and guardian of them both, at great expense to his own development of selfhood. In addition, he was raised in a strict church that espoused an ideal of perfect behavior, even for children. Temperamentally, he was a wild and woolly artist with great sensitivity. His internal conflict had left him vulnerable to depressive and psychotic-seeming breakdowns whenever he left the confines of his family. Even as a child, he had night terrors so severe that he pounded 3-foot holes in the wall above his bed. It was clear to us that he would fall into substantial pockets of disorganization within enmeshed, ambivalent attachments with his mother and father.

His mother had been so criticized and shorn of selfhood as a child that she could make no decisions, and lived solely to create harmony in her household. She commanded everyone to be happy and peaceful in a gentle, insistent way, while feeling terrified inside. His father had also been criticized every day, and his own artistic aspirations crushed. This treatment had left him so frustrated that he could not hold a job for any significant or stabilizing length of time. Both parents were so emotionally

young that they depended on Adam to protect their feelings by sacrific-
ing all his normal childhood needs.

Adam came to see me because he could not practice his art. He would
see wonderful images in his head, but when he tried to put them on
paper, his hand would freeze, caught between the free movement he
wanted to make and the stroke he had learned in school. He would fall
into fragmentation and frustration, unable to finish a painting.

Paradoxically, art became one of the primary means by which Adam
recovered his emotional independence and his freedom as an artist. Once
he gave up trying to produce anything aesthetic and transferred his chalk,
crayons, and pencils to his left hand, truth began to pour out. What you
just saw is a small sample of his healing work. You may want to look at
the pictures again with these captions.

Figure 17.1. In this enormous picture that is tacked to the bookcase in
my office, Adam portrays his father's frustration and rage. The feeling of
the shaking hands and head easily permeated the room, allowing us to
hold all that dysregulation in the warm space between us.

Figure 17.2. As a child and young man, Adam would often flee to his
beloved woods, seeking solace and safety, but the emptiness and anguish
would follow him, transforming the woods into a deadened place. It is
easy to feel how his inner world overwhelmed his perception of this
lovely place.

Figure 17.3. As we began to explore the intergenerational origins of
the family pain, Adam drew this picture of his maternal grandfather, the
raging, demeaning, frightening patriarch who had terrified his mother.

Figure 17.4. This is Adam, with his mouth sewn shut, hands caught
between his legs, body feeling so transparent that we can see the chair
through his torso and legs. The pain in his parents prevented them from
providing Adam with the nourishment he needed to grow a sense of self.
However, drawing this picture and holding the bodily and emotional
experience between us helped him begin to perceive his body as having
substance.

Figure 17.5. Adam found it painful and often impossible to breathe
deeply. It was as though the tissues of his lungs were stuck together from
the shallow breathing of continual anxiety. This drawing began as a light
sketch of a pair of lungs, then became a screaming skeleton with a larger
and larger mouth. As the room resonated with the visceral experience of
his terror and anguish, this image, which calls to mind Edvard Munch's
The Scream, began to emerge from his pencil. This was a different kind

of drawing, one occurring in the moment, without any forethought about what he would draw. When he finished, he took black netting from the sand tray baskets and covered the drawing in more and more layers of darkness. We sat for a long time, both of us empathically embracing this terrified child. Afterward, Adam was able to take a deep breath. Clearly, he was beginning to break the family's history of silence and disorganizing anxiety that he carried within his own body.

Figure 17.6. Many months later, Adam was ready to look at his rage. The threat of family disintegration had been such a possibility throughout his young life that all of his emotions had been stored within his body–brain in dissociated neural nets. Pain, shame, and grief had been relatively easy to access, but rage felt too close to his father's disorganization. Still, it needed release, and when Adam was ready, we got out the largest tablet and a fat, strong marker. He began with large strokes that turned into digs and then stabs, all the way down to the cardboard backing. I felt joy welling up in my body at this magnificent integrating release—and afterward, relaxation filled the room.

Figure 17.7

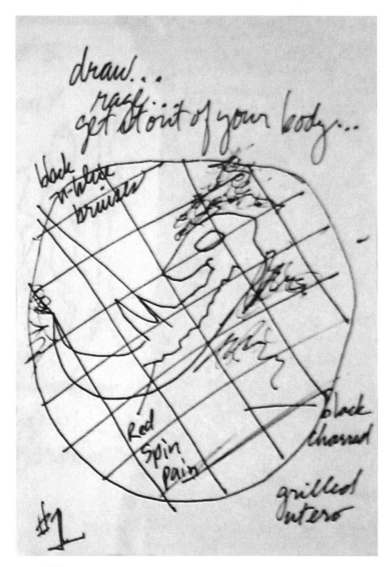

Figure 17.8

Being a Brain-Wise Therapist

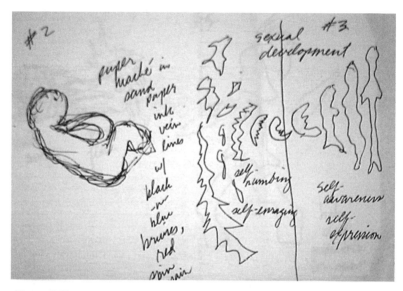

Figure 17.9

Figure 17.10

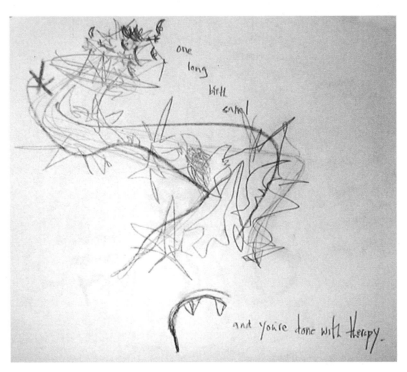
one
long
birth
canal

and you're done with therapy.

Figure 17.11

I saw Hannah for over 10 years to repair the wounds to her body, brain, mind, and relational capacity, injuries resulting from having a father whose own infant trauma locked him in a prison of hyperaroused, compulsive self-hate. The intensity of his suffering generated violent self-soothing behaviors that had a tragic impact on her young nervous system. Her mother, who had grown up in the shadow of a mentally ill parent, had learned to dissociate to survive, and, as a result, was unable to offer the slightest protection for her daughter. Hannah was the chosen child, the oldest of three children. Her father put all his hopes for normal life on her and focused all his need for containment on her as well. From birth, he poured his anxious, sexually charged energy over her being every time his need for soothing exploded in her direction. He would rub his hands and grind his mouth in an altered state of compulsion and rage, soaking Hannah in an energy that made her spine feel like it was twisting, while her nervous system was shocked as though with an electric charge. This contact with her father left her with a severe disorganized attachment, and because of her mother's dissociated emptiness— so pervasive that she had only once acknowledged her husband's

Being a Brain-Wise Therapist

behavior, while admonishing the children to never speak of it again—Hannah had nowhere to turn for security. In fact, she had never mentioned her father's behavior again until she found herself curled in a ball in my office struggling to find words to describe his violently fragmenting behavior.

When I first met her, Hannah was living two lives: as an honor student and beloved musician in public, and as a physically shattered and emotionally terrified child in private. Her health was failing and her mind was splintering. However, Hannah had the most profound call to healing. Shortly after we began therapy, my office moved from Los Angeles to Orange County. For her to continue, she had to borrow a different car each week. Once she even learned the intricacies of operating a stick shift by driving once around the block with a friend before heading onto the freeway. In the earliest days of therapy, I could see her chest silently sobbing as soon as we sat together, but there were no tears. We soon discovered that this was her daily state, so familiar to her that she was not consciously aware of her body's anguished revelation. For almost 3 years, her long trip was most often followed by sitting in disorganized silence for 90 minutes as we held the earliest implicit terror between us. Eventually, she was more able to speak, and we then began piecing together her explicit story, one fragment at a time. We imagined a large basket where each shard could find comfort and peace. These two processes formed the pattern of the first 8 years of therapy as we worked together to gradually assemble a coherent sense of self out of the shattered glass of her earliest days.

During our ninth year together, she was finally strong enough to begin dealing directly with her internal father, the part of her that bore the energy she had internalized from him as a baby. It was a very rough passage, especially because the events of 9/11 occurred just as she was beginning to experience her father's fragmentation. She was in Boston at the time. The violent and tragic fracturing of the outer world mirrored her inner world perfectly, accelerating her descent into terror. She and her husband returned home and for the next few months, she was barely able to leave her house while she worked through this debilitating energy. The beautiful, peaceful environment she had created with her husband became both protective womb and second skin while she recuperated. She kept a diary and drew pictures that externalized the terrifying, chaotic, disorganized fragmentation. In spite of—or perhaps because of—the depth of her torment, she wrote, recorded, and produced a collection of songs during that time as well. Out of the fragments, she pulled rhythm, structure, and beauty, a testimony to the symphony of integration unfolding in her brain.

Hannah drew the first picture in 1997, and the rest in 2001 during her confinement. Feeling so alien in the world, all her pictures represented her effort to be seen. She never felt that her words captured the depth of torment and fragmentation, possibly because the actual experiences that formed the foundation were prelinguistic. Adding to the fear that she would never be truly understood was the psychic isolation imposed by her father as he claimed Hannah as the receptacle of his own anguish. In truth, very few people have experienced this depth of inner destruction, and in a realistic way, this uniqueness augmented her aloneness. She believed that bringing another person into her world through her images could possibly begin to wear down this isolation. Listening to my own body as she shared the pictures did indeed give me an increasingly visceral sense of that world and allowed us both to hold that fragmented child between us. The courage to face this level of inner terror and destruction is a rare and beautiful thing, in this case, yielding nothing less than an emerging coherent mind.

You may find the description of these pictures sparse, except for the first one. As Hannah increasingly entered the fragmentation she'd internalized from her father, her pictures began to convey a visceral sense of torment and destruction that defy words.

Figure 17.7. We might call this picture "Intrusion." Something phallic (part tongue, part penis) intrudes, together with a probing eye at the upper left. This is the feeling of her father's approach, fragmenting Hannah's fractured, misshapen being. The light gray areas around the darker lines are beginning to glue the fragments together, and represent the feeling of our connection. This father feels like a monster to her. To reduce his size and impact, we were working to see her father's own destroyed child beneath his destructive, compulsive acting out. At the lower right is a drawing of maternal arms holding his destroyed child, to somehow encapsulate his power so that it would not permeate Hannah's being. This turned out to be a project that would extend over years as we worked to rewire her implicit right hemisphere, encouraging the neural integration that would allow her autonomic nervous system to regulate.

Figure 17.8. At some moments, the feelings of her father's rage would overwhelm Hannah. In an attempt to give the disorganizing energy form, pictures began to emerge in her diary, conveying images of utter destruction extending back to the womb for both her and her father.

Figure 17.9. The strong sexual flavor of her father's intrusive energy had disrupted Hannah's development of self-awareness, including her sexuality. The latter was permeated by the terror, rage, and sickness that saturated her body, brain, and mind. Because of the fear-based spiritual environment, the advent of sexual feelings in her teens contained an additional layer of terror and shame.

Figure 17.10. As Hannah contemplated her father's childhood experience, seeking to reduce the power he had inside her body–brain–mind, she drew her father in pieces that had never assembled. The very act of giving shape to the fragmentation paradoxically began to regulate the terror.

Figure 17.11. The agony of this particular spiral of healing made therapy treacherous waters, as depicted in this passage through a terrifying birth canal. The teeth awaiting her at the end of the therapeutic journey—parallel to the beginning of her life—may evoke deep grief in all who gaze on this picture, accompanied perhaps by a sense of joy or triumph that she could give her agony form.

Our capacity to hold such anguish without either withdrawing into the safety of detachment or becoming entangled in the implicit swirl is bedrock for our patients' ability to develop regulation within the therapuetic relationship. As we have moved from listening to our patients' histories to developing mindfulness, getting familiar with sharing the brain with our patients, and entering their inner worlds, we may find that we are developing our own integrative resources to create a spacious home within us for the intense disorganization wrought by living with terrified and terrifying parents. Caroline's and Ali's trays, together with Adam's and Hannah's drawings, may have given us the opportunity to observe our capacity for calm connection in the presence of dramatic internal disruption and inspired us to work to widen our windows of tolerance.

Part III

Working with Couples, Teens, and Children

Chapter 18

Preliminary Thoughts

Working with Couples, Teens, and Children— with the Brain in Mind

Now we turn to some of the people who find their way to our counseling rooms—couples, teens, and children with their parents. What follows is a series of sketches, rather than fleshed-out paintings. The complexity and variety of ways of working with any group of people appropriately fill many library shelves. The intent here is to offer some ways of thinking about the process that are infused with the awareness of inner communities and the workings of brain and mind.

In "Keeping Our Balance with Couples," we view partners as members of an interpersonal system that shares brains. We can then use this awareness to shift partners' viewpoints from mutual blame to mindful curiosity about how they got entrenched in certain hurtful relational patterns. The emergence of their new ability is grounded in our capacity to model this stance. This means doing our own work with any implicit patterns that seek to pull us into alliance with one member of the duo. As our couples follow our lead and develop this ability, they move automatically into self-responsibility and empathic concern for the other. However, sometimes, early developmental wounds make it impossible to generate the vulnerability required for such an open stance. Then what might we do—and how can neurobiological awareness help us do it?

If our work with couples requires us to embrace the dance of multiple inner worlds, working with teens present us with the challenge of holding brains that are in dramatic flux. In "Meeting Teens with Their Brains in Mind," we focus on assimilating the bounty of new discoveries about how the brain is changing during adolescence. Such a dramatic remodeling of the brain involves disorganization in the service of reorganizing at a more complex level, with all the messiness and wonder that usually define this developmental stage. This renovation particularly impacts the middle prefrontal region, seat of flexible decisions, judgment, regulation of body and emotions, empathy, and even morality. Parental support is crucial at this stage, but social norms pull against maintaining these bonds in favor of relationships with peers. Understanding these neural and cultural dynamics can help teens, parents, and therapists ease this sometimes tumultuous passage.

At the younger end of the spectrum, "Playing with Children, Supporting Their Parents" explores why nondirective play therapy makes neurobiological sense when working with children who have been traumatized or suffered attachment losses. When we are fully engaged with these children, holding their young minds in ours and responding contingently, they feel safe enough to access areas that have been too frightening or painful to visit before. Since play is their language, we can use these conversations to help them rewire their malleable brains in the direction of secure attachment. In addition, with all we know about the intergenerational transmission of neural structure, working with parents is a crucial preventive and reparative endeavor, so we weave guidance and repair for parents into our work with children. Our first focus with them seeks to bring awareness and healing to the parents' own attachment losses, because without these, new parenting techniques tend to fall apart under stress. Next, we share some attachment-repairing attitudes and processes that will help them embrace their children with empathy and understanding, even in the most trying times. Side by side with these tools, we work to ground and expand their reflective functioning through mindful awareness practices. When these three converge, parents begin to develop the capacity to make flexible choices on behalf of their children.

Chapter 19

Keeping Our Balance with Couples

When couples come to us, we meet them with a general picture of the processes we believe to be operating in all intimate relationships. Some paradigms emphasize the balance of power and control in daily life, whereas others immediately see beneath the surface to childhood patterns. Whatever the paradigm, our growing awareness of the implicit relational patterns laid down by childhood experience (Schore, 2007) and the power of resonance circuits (Siegel, 2006) now assures us that implicit mental models of attachment will come into play, and that the multiple states of mind (inner community members) we all carry will interact in increasingly intricate ways as intimacy deepens.

We know that in the normal course of relationship, more aspects of ourselves come to light over time, partly because trust deepens and partly because mental models of relationship play an increasingly pervasive role as intimacy increases. This means that old patterns engrained from living with our parents (and other people close to us) become more active and either aid or hinder closeness. Based on *implicit attachment patterns*, internal mothers or fathers may begin to direct the style of communication, or inner children may begin to supplant one or both adults as dynamics in the relationship tug on the expansive neural nets holding these patterns.

> Spending a little time thinking about the course of our own intimate relationships can illuminate this process. With some reflection, we may be able to pinpoint the interactions that began to entangle some of the

difficult aspects of our inner community. Perhaps our partner became angry, and we found our fearful, helpless child self coming forward. Or our spouse began to withdraw more and more, activating our inner needy, intrusive mother. On the helpful side, we might notice how a father skilled at negotiation regularly made his appearance when difficult interpersonal problems arose. I have found that recognizing my own inner community's daily contributions makes it much easier to support this work with couples.

Magic Radar

Most often, couples will find that their entire inner community had a voice in choosing this partner, based not only on surface compatibility but also on internal resonance between these communities. The resonating property of our minds means that we have the capacity to sense this possible partner's deeper relational intentions and patterns, even though the recognition usually remains well below the level of conscious awareness. After just a little time in therapy, many of our couples stand in awe of the "magic radar" that drew them together, for good and ill. One wife, Sandra, realized that she could unfailingly pick a verbally abusive man out of a crowd, even while he was displaying every courtesy to her and others around him. At about the same time, her husband, Jerry, discovered that he inwardly knew which women would tolerate his attacks, at least for awhile. He had no inner expectation that his partners would stay, because he had watched his mother marry and divorce five times. Sandra had tolerated his critical, angry rants for 12 years because she had no inner imagination of another relational possibility, having seen her mother berate her passive father all her life. The good news is, this story has a happy ending, which we will learn about later.

One small caveat before we leave this viewpoint. Although magic radar rules almost everyone, occasionally people will find partners whose attachment is significantly more secure than their own. Keeping this reality in mind will save us from the rigidity of making assumptions before we get to know our couples. Humility suggests that we receive our couples with completely open minds and hearts, letting them reveal their patterns without preconceptions.

The Mind of the Couple

Taking another viewpoint, we might also visualize couples as two individual minds, as well as the resonance between those minds, creating what we could call the *mind of the couple*. Most likely, all of us have experienced the difference between meeting with two people individually and then together. In fact, it is often useful to have at least one individual meeting as part of the treatment strategy early on. When we do this, it becomes immediately and viscerally obvious that the relationship is not just the sum of the two individuals. Instead, an entire self-modifying system, formed by the two of them, springs to life. As partners initially draw together, linking their two differentiated selves to form an integrating interpersonal system, they begin to develop a unique exchange of energy and information, creating a set of patterns ranging from rigid or chaotic to flexible/coherent.

After just a little work with couples, we begin to sense how these different regulatory patterns are operating in the interpersonal system. The determinedly flexible couple will usually weather enormous stress with grace and resilience, even though the partners may pass through brief periods of chaos or rigidity. Moving away from coherence toward chaos, we find that these couples are thrown into dysregulation and disarray by minor environmental shifts. We might be reminded of a stack of tissue paper disturbed by the slightest breeze. Partners can feel both fragile in coping and strong in their commitment to chaos. Rigid couples, on the other hand, try to apply old patterns to new challenges, sometimes breaking into chaos if stress overwhelms the resources of the inflexible interpersonal system, sometimes asserting the old pattern until the situation succumbs to rigidity or calms of its own accord. Initially, rigid couples can appear to be coping because of the strength of the partners' stance, but within the system, you can feel the creak and groan of metal that can't bend. We might picture how inflexible buildings in an earthquake may eventually break into pieces, if the shaking is hard and long enough. It is useful to think in terms of rigidity, chaos, and coherence when meeting with couples, because identifying their place along that continuum can be a powerful guide for how to help. Sharing our awareness with the couple, at the right empathic moment, can also assist each partner's development of a caring observer stance in regard to the relationship (more about this later).

Three-Way Partnership

As our couples come to see us, we add both our inner community and our resonating mind to the mix. Over time, this interchange becomes a fascinating three-way dance. However, at the outset of therapy, particularly with highly conflicted couples (who often come from disorganized or ambivalent attachment backgrounds), the intensity and chaos in the room can be unsettling. Maintaining our own internal mindful stance, while paying attention to the feelings flowing through our bodies, can give us a strong sense of what these people endure every day. Similarly, if we find ourselves stranded in an emotional desert with two people who are largely disconnected from themselves and each other, our inner emptiness and boredom (or anxiety because of long silences) can provide a window into the painful aloneness that has swamped the relationship. The key, as always, is maintaining our own ability to reflect from our center—from the hub of the mind.

The result of maintaining such a flexible, curious, wise, warm openness is the ability to cultivate *equal empathy for both partners*. This capacity is at the heart of successful work with couples, and it rests on our ability to compassionately hold each partner's history. Picturing the two wounded children and their inner communities can help us understand the *why* and *how* of their being together, even if one partner is acting as the perpetrator and the other as the victim. Our natural tendency to protect the victim and defend against the perpetrator can challenge our ability to remain in empathy with both partners. However, when we fall away from equal regard for any length of time, partners will sense it, often responding with feelings of unfairness and abandonment. None of us can stand in this broad empathic field all the time, so supervision or consultation can provide a haven in which we can regain balance with the help of other minds not so embroiled in this family dance.

With awareness of the inner community and the unfolding process of interpersonal integration, we can work to develop a three-way relationship based on the rapid exchange of messages below conscious awareness. Based on what we know about the nonconscious world, we are not primarily coaches for this couple, but active participants in helping implicit mental models change within a rich milieu of safety and empathy. Our inner balance is the linchpin for steadying the triad, particularly when partners are struggling to maintain even a shred of connection.

Fostering Empathic Capacity

Keeping these basic principles in mind, let's consider some practical aspects of working with couples. Because interpersonal neurobiology makes us so sensitive to the neural and relational damage done by harsh treatment, we may want to pay attention to some relational dynamics in a different way than we have before. At the beginning of therapy, it is important to assess whether the partners have the integrative capacity to *generate empathy for one another*. If they cannot be helped to get into a somewhat empathic stance fairly quickly, we might want to consider that working with them together will only exacerbate the wounds, further reinforcing those neural nets that conduce to blame and separation. Fostering such empathy then becomes the first order of business.

We have found that empathic capacity is directly related to three factors: (1) each person's age when significant, and currently unhealed, emotional wounding occurred; (2) the strength of both partners' caring adult sides, regardless of the depth and earliness of wounding; and (3) the rigidity or flexibility of the defenses they have developed in regard to each other. All of these factors are related to the degree of neural integration present in the individual minds and the couple mind. Thinking back to the nine functions of the middle prefrontal region, the integrating mind shows increasing levels of self-regulation, empathy, response flexibility, and attuned communication (among other attributes). With a little imaginative leap, we can see how these characteristics might be present or absent in the interpersonal mind of the couple.

The first factor influencing empathic capacity—*age of unhealed emotional wounding*—is perhaps most crucial because it often impacts the other two. When we are wounded severely and repeatedly in early life, we develop an enormous backlog of implicit memories that fuels a host of perceptual biases. As long as the memories remain implicit, they will be experienced as arising from current experience rather than the past. This misperception creates countless opportunities for one person to project his or her experience of relational reality onto the other person. Without the ability to say "This feeling is related to my past," this person helplessly, but with full conviction, assigns the source of the misery to the partner. This situation can be even more difficult because these engrained eyeglasses of the mind will likely already have influenced the choice of a partner, often skewing the selection toward someone who is predisposed by his or her own history to engage in this painful, self-reinforcing dance.

By the time couples with this kind of wounding are in the room, they are often in a fairly hopeless state of mind about the relationship because of the intensity and tenacity of repeating patterns based on implicit memory and reinforced by current-day actions. Relationally, they are often deeply mired in blame because that is the automatic response to their sense that the other person is repeatedly hurting them. No amount of logic from us is going to change their experience until some of the implicit wounds are healed.

To explore their capacity to move into their *caring observer states of mind*, we begin with family histories for both people. As these stories are told, we can soon see whether empathy will naturally blossom in the interpersonal system, if the focus is taken off the current relationship. Listening to one another, some partners immediately fall into empathic resonance with each other. However, even in the face of their partner's pain and fear, some people remain disengaged and dismissing; some defend with cruel, sarcastic verbal and nonverbal jabs; and some become overwhelmed by their own implicit feelings that are released by themes and emotions in their partner's story.

When the caring observer side doesn't emerge naturally, what can we do to help the misattuned person find that compassionate state of mind? From our own caring observer, we can reflect on the pain and fear in the history, bringing rich rivers of empathy into the room. There is at least some chance that our active middle prefrontal resources will energize the partner's. One usually dismissing partner said, "I was so tired of hearing his story because it always sounded like an excuse, but when I saw how it moved you, I thought maybe there was more to it." Her sad eyes helped her partner know that this change of heart and perspective was genuine.

We may also be able to cultivate the caring observer by introducing the idea of implicit memory, seeking to help these couples discover and develop the ability to be compassionately curious about the early attachment patterns encoded in one another's minds. Once they discover these patterns, it can become easier to explore the impact on them as individuals and as a couple. In addition, introducing these intellectual concepts draws on left-mode processing, which can help modulate the runaway right mode that dominates in chaotic couples. Over time, as partners are able to move into a COAL state toward one another, we all feel a visceral release into regulation. It is important to take time to consciously savor this change together because promoting awareness of

Being a Brain-Wise Therapist

this developing neural capacity adds synaptic strength, thereby increasing the likelihood of its manifestation.

Sometimes the combination of implicit pain and ongoing relational struggles prevents our combined efforts to generate empathy from bearing sustained fruit. Instead, the *rigidity of angry or aloof defenses* against further pain and fear carries the day. We can feel these defenses snap back into place at the least sign of emerging vulnerability. In therapy, partners who had been married for 18 years developed a clear conceptual understanding of why their relationship had deteriorated. Both could feel how their engrained states of mind had dominated most of the relationship, with her angry, critical side and his detached dismissing side becoming sworn, reactive enemies. After working with great determination and sincerity for months, they decided that the inner debris of their long struggle formed a hill they were not willing to climb. They saw how they remained on guard and defensive with each other and came to believe that no amount of work was going to reestablish the sense of safety they experienced in the first months of their relationship. With sadness, they parted, but did find a friendship based on the new understanding.

When people become receptive to looking at wounds in themselves or their partners, they are in an open, accepting state that can feel terrifying if they were hurt when they were in that state as a baby or young child. When they have then chosen relationships that continue the destructive interaction, sometimes there is no recovery. Generally, the earlier the unhealed wounds, the greater the perceived need for defensive strength, coupled with the greater likelihood of finding a mate who will replicate the patterns. What may have been adaptive strategies at the time they developed are now painful, self-reinforcing patterns of abandonment, isolation, and terror. If we look at the situation from the subjective viewpoint of the inner children, they are now prisoners of defensive states of mind that won't allow them to emerge and receive comfort from their partners.

Even in the grip of pain from early wounds, sparse empathic capacity for one another, and rigid defenses, some couples remain hopeful about finding a way to work toward a true partnership. If we all conclude that it doesn't make empathic sense to continue the battle in couples therapy, we may decide to do some individual work with each person, interspersed with working together. With some couples who are this injured, it is best to refer each person to his or her own therapist, with them returning to us for couples work. This is particularly true when severe personality disorders dominate the landscape. For less injured couples, doing individual work one week and couples work the next can become a supportive pattern. The greater trust and vulnerability that come with individual work may speed resolution of the implicit wounds that make joining a partner feel unsafe. Even though this is individual work, it is in the service of the couple, and that remains a stated part of the plan. We don't want to lose sight of the mind of the couple in our own minds. After the week of individual work, a session together can be a time of sharing new insights or working on emerging issues. It is also a good way to test the waters for signs of increasing empathic capacity. As soon as compassion becomes a somewhat reliable resource, there will be no more need for individual sessions.

Sharing the Brain with Couples

Fortunately, most of the time, partners are able to generate enough empathy to justify moving forward together from the beginning. After savoring histories and establishing a warm and balanced therapeutic bond with us, we might have some additional conversations that will ground us in mutually held concepts and language. Offered at the right empathic moment, these conversations support the three-way connection, while giving us additional tools for cultivating the caring observer. Near the beginning of therapy, we generally do a little sharing about the brain, the inner community, and intergenerational attachment patterns. Couples who move toward chaos under stress gain tools for using their left hemispheres to calm the arousal. Detaching couples develop the ability to at least engage in conversation about why they withdraw from each other when there are difficulties. In both cases, our couples report increased connection through this new way of understanding one another. What appears to be educational actually supports right-brain to right-brain connection.

• We might start with picturing *how individual brains develop* and how that process is similar for the mind of the couple, as partners establish the patterns unique to them. Most partners immediately elaborate on this idea, exploring how they became intertwined at the beginning in a loving way. The idea that they are continually tugging on patterns in each other's brains is often new and surprising, particularly when there has been a lot of avoidance. One quiet husband was astonished. "You mean, me just sitting in my chair reading the paper makes you anxious because that's what your father did? I thought I was staying out of your way." *Mirror neurons* and *resonance circuits* catch the imagination and can concretize the idea of mutual influence. Introducing the *hand model* helps because it offers a new language about relational processes that is not caught up in old patterns. We find that focusing on linkages between the limbic region and middle prefrontal cortex, as well as the two hemispheres, allows us to talk visually about why empathy is sometimes in short supply, or what is happening when one partner frequently becomes angry.

• Depending on the issues, it can be useful to discuss various kinds of *integration*, investigating why one person has difficulty finding words for emotions or the other struggles to contain her sadness. This focus gives partners the opportunity to become curious about what in their histories might be blocking integration. This kind of mutual investigation can draw partners closer, and, more importantly, pull them into a "we" who is discovering how each other's brains work.

• Understanding the relationship between the *limbic areas and the sympathetic nervous system* can help partners understand more clearly what happens to each person when they are triggered. Knowing that the limbic circuits operate much more quickly than our middle prefrontal region—and, in fact, can shut it down—may help alleviate guilt and shame for the times when fear or anger ran away with them. Talking about how the chemicals of stress and love impact everything from cardiac health, to immune function, to our ability to attach makes the consequences of battle or separation quite tangible.

• Many couples immediately identify with the idea of *inner communities* and how they come into play in supportive or destructive ways. A young husband described how his usually carefree and somewhat heedless wife became his steadfast caregiver for a year after an accident at work. At the time, both of them had been puzzled about why this was easy for her, then realized in therapy that her mother had cared for her this same way as she battled persistent ear infections in her early years. Another couple immediately realized that sometime in the first 5 years of their partnership, Julie's critical mother and Shawna's angry father had "stolen" the intimacy from the relationship these two compassionate, intelligent, supportive women had shared in the early years. Once these patterns become engrained, they have a self-perpetuating quality. However, awareness of the source of the patterns activates the caring observer, paving the way for doing internal work together in couples sessions to resolve the inner community pain that perpetuates the difficulty.

Creating Safe Ground

Often couples have suffered with each other's attempts to defend against relational pain. Understanding the inner community can bring compassion for even ugly defenses, which are now viewed as guardians of hurt inner children. Laying the foundation for later internal work, we stress the equation that the greater the dissociated pain, the more powerful and unrealistic (by current-day standards) the defenses tend to be. When the inner defenders are paying attention to the pain they are protecting, they have little ability to accurately assess the level of threat in the current world. The result is frequent, out-of-proportion reactions to small disturbances.

• For many couples, blame is the core communication tactic that has been practiced for years. After establishing a soothing connection between the three of us that regulates some of the arousal, talking in depth about the *amygdala* and *perceptual bias* may generate some humility about their own viewpoints and opinions. Just using the language of perception (rather than fact) begins to undermine the absoluteness of their assumptions about each other and give them room to explore why they see situations differently.

• In words that fit each couple's style, we can lay out Stephen Porges's (2001, 2007) ideas about the importance of a *neuroception of safety* for social engagement and secure attachment. We talk about how the space between them needs to become a safe haven rather than a war zone or a desert, and we promote curiosity about how that might happen. We literally sit together and picture what has gone on in that space, grieve how it has been used so far, and then begin to imagine it differently. We frequently talk about how developing a COAL state—curious, open, accepting, and loving—can be the cornerstone for the experience of interpersonal safety.

As this new knowledge becomes more deeply seated, we can begin to encourage an overall paradigm shift in the partners from an internal stance of *assigning blame* to one of *caring curiosity about how we got here*. Again, the shift from "I" to "we" immediately changes perspective. Partners can then become the caring observers of the two people struggling in the relationship. As this state of mind strengthens, response flexibility—pausing before acting—becomes a living possibility. In this new space, both partners become willing to talk about their contributions to any difficulty, rather than laying responsibility on the other. However, when there is a significant history of blaming, both in childhood and as adults, this can be a long process, requiring patience and compassion from couple and therapist alike. Initially, the new mindful state is a neural goat path and the old blaming stance a super highway of synaptic connections. Such awareness can help all of us stay realistic about the amount of neural change involved in making this new state of mind a couple's default mode.

Sandra and Jerry

How might these new capacities unfold for Sandra and Jerry, the couple we talked about at the beginning of this chapter? When they came to therapy, Sandra clearly stated that she had reached the limit of her capacity for tolerating Jerry's denigrating tirades. He, on the other hand, arrived in a condescending mood, staunchly defended against any awareness of his part in the struggle. It helped me to remember that this kind of stance usually indicates a well of shame inside. Inwardly, his mental models no doubt had him in a state of resignation about the loss of another partner. The tension between them was palpable in the room, as they turned their bodies away from each other. Listening to histories began to turn the tide. Even though they both had a surface awareness of each other's childhoods, they were each touched by listening to one another in this warm atmosphere, without distraction. Ripples of sorrow pulled Jerry's eyebrows together when Sandra shared the pain she felt every time her mother attacked her father. Sandra's hand reached for Jerry's knee before she could stop herself when he described his anguish at the loss of father after father. Each was becoming the witness of the other's childhood, and this compassion was helping the memories and the narrative become integrated. This was such a good start.

However, within a week or two, Jerry was tearing into Sandra again over minor infractions, and she was talking about divorce. My first thought was to begin doing internal work, but as I mulled the fact that Jerry's business was electrical engineering, I thought maybe some brain education would both intrigue his logical mind and help him strengthen his caring observer—a part of him that deserted ranks when he got angry. Happily, he was instantly fascinated, and began to form new mental representations of how his mind works. He then started talking to Sandra with his "hand," showing her what happens when his mind falls apart in anger. Understanding led to decreases in guilt over his present-day behavior, so he had less need for a condescending defense. As he began to talk about the many ways he'd been shamed as a child, Sandra's empathy for him flowered, and they began to work together as a team to change their communication style. While these early changes were a small beginning step, they invited hope into the relationship, as Jerry was able to hold his own mind with understanding and compassion. Then, at the right time, we did a great deal of internal work as well, relieving the implicit pain driving both of them. Within a few months, they were noticing that their whole bodies told them as soon as they were headed down the familiar, painful path, and with that awareness, they began to be able to humbly stop themselves, take responsibility for their piece of the action, and make a more flexible choice.

Exploring Attachment

In addition to the talk about brain and inner community, at some point it may be useful to explore *attachment*, particularly when those wounds are central to relationship difficulties. Some of this discussion will begin during the family history, deepening over time into a rich understanding of the meaning and impact this attachment history has had on the relationship. Often, tasting the difference between the quality of attachment available in their families and what is offered between the three of us provides a visceral awareness that words can't capture. One aspect of attachment that can help partners understand their reactivity with one another is how self-regulation is learned—or not—in our earliest relationships. So many couples are locked in a pattern of shifting into dysregulation, either toward disengagement and deadness or hyperarousal and chaos. When they see how these patterns have been engrained through lack of parental responsiveness, they can begin to develop a soothing, mindful awareness of their own state and that of their partner, immediately increasing regulation. Being able to let go of blaming the other for these disruptions makes room for mutual compassion.

The language of attachment helps us focus on the limbic longing for connection and what happens when bonding fails in various ways. On the other side, it is also about how repair is always possible. Research indicates that if a person with a disrupted attachment is in a close relationship with a partner with a secure attachment, earned security will develop in about 5 years (Schore, 2003). Two partners working together on repair can certainly move into a synergistic dance in which individual neural integration and interpersonal integration amplify each other. Knowing this, we become purveyors of hope. Deep wells of compassion have an opportunity to flower from these explorations of attachment wounds and losses.

Timing and the Triangle of Healing

Not all of these ideas need to be offered in the first few sessions. In fact, waiting for the right empathic moment is the key to these ideas becoming more than patches of soon-forgotten left-brain learning. Because this perspective is often a radically different way of understanding themselves as individuals and as humans in relationship, repetition will be an ally, particularly when delivered with patience and kindness. Also, this paradigm shift seems to happen best when it unfolds organically. If blame is center stage during one session, the door might be open to talk about defenses and perceptual bias, or perhaps about the body's sensitivity to safety. Your intuition will be the best guide about when to weave a concept into the ongoing right-to-right flow.

This point reminds us that all the work is unfolding on the foundation of micro-second, nonconscious interactions between the three of us that are already changing the implicit world and establishing a strong ground of safety. Over time, we can then add deep work with the inner communities of both partners to the therapeutic alliance and the semi-intellectual, paradigm-shifting work. The elegant flow between these three can form a triangle of healing. Including internal work is especially crucial when couples are bearing the burden of unhealed histories of pain or terror. Unless the neural nets carrying these miseries are integrated with the rest of the neural circuitry, the couple will forever be vulnerable to activating them under stress. Also, the mental models that developed from these experiences can continue to influence the moment-to-moment relational assumptions that give the mind of the couple its overall shape.

Larry and June

An example of the power of unseen implicit processes may help. Larry and June had been coming to therapy for about a year, had done the necessary internal work to resolve many of the issues that led to relationship-numbing bickering, and had renewed their sexual intimacy with vigor. They clearly had rediscovered much of their original passion, respect, and trust—the essential triumvirate of a solid relationship. However, Larry was still troubled by what he perceived to be an aloofness in June, a way that she wasn't "completely there." June had no idea what he was talking about. She felt happy, present, and engaged—although a bit busier than she'd like to be. Having gotten used to looking inward at history to solve mysteries, I asked Larry to sense what was happening in his body when he felt disconnected from June. He quickly found a sinking sensation in his stomach and stinging tears in his eyes. In his mind's eye, a 4-year-old boy appeared, attached to these bodily feelings. He was looking longingly at his mother's back as she did the dishes. He seemed to know it was useless to approach her, so he just yearned in silence. Tears welled in June's eyes as she reached for Larry's hand. She said, very quietly, "That's me. If I don't keep moving and doing, the world will fall apart." We sat in the palpable intensity in the room for quite awhile, allowing all of us to absorb the way the mind of the couple had been shaped by the mental models of these two. June then shared that when Larry was talking, she suddenly realized this was the deepest lesson she had learned from her mom, who was a single parent with four children. For her mother, the need to keep moving was an inner command related to survival itself. Although its origins were hidden far below conscious awareness, June always felt an emotional intensity related to her busyness. However, only when the meaning of this mental model became explicit did she begin to develop the capacity to shift it by doing the necessary work with the survival fears she'd internalized from her mother. Such interlocking mental models aren't obvious and conscious at the beginning of therapy, but instead gradually emerge as the more visible issues resolve.

After this landmark day, we did some more internal work with both inner children and the aspects of the parents upsetting them, easing our way toward the transformation of the mental models of relationship. When both children and inner parents could be comforted, they began to believe in their bodies, feelings, and thoughts that such profound intimacy could be possible for both of them. By the light of these gradually changing mental models, Larry and June developed an affectionate openness toward themselves and each other that they literally had not been able to picture before.

There is a lot to be said for doing individual work in the presence of the partner. Insight and empathy for each other deepen, the caring observer strengthens, humility about each person's humanness flowers, and a growing respect for each other's vulnerabilities leads to greater response flexibility, born of a wish to be gentle with the beloved. When this gentleness comes from increasing integration, it is not a codependent move, but instead blossoms from the fullness of a tender human concern for the well-being of the other, and wisdom about what will nurture the relationship.

Even calling this "individual work" is a misnomer. The apparently nonworking partner will be resonating with his or her mate, getting in touch with whatever neural nets are activated by listening. When compassion blossoms, neural integration is fostered in the individual and the couple. When old memories are triggered, the stage is set for doing internal work with the other partner. In other words, there's a lot going on for the apparent inactive person at the other end of the couch. At the same time, our conscious decision to be mindfully aware of both of them during the work will be registered as well and help the nonworking partner feel the encouragement to process whatever has been touched. Flowing organically with the unfolding experiences and staying attuned with the energy within each person and between them will guide our next moves.

Over time, we develop a rhythm with each couple that will be unique to the three of us. We may use sand tray, art, internal work, bibliotherapy with both of them reading the same book, and other inventive possibilities. After awhile, with increasing personal integration, partners will be better able to sense if the warmth of interpersonal connection is possible for them. In our experience, if there was a strong bond at the beginning of the relationship, and if the partners have not completely lost empathy for one another in spite of the interpersonal wrangling, about 90% of the time they find each other again. In the process, they often develop a deeper "us" on easy days and more ability to stay resiliently connected in stressful times.

Chapter 20

Meeting Teens
with Their Brains
in Mind

Jake slouches on the couch, staring out my window in apparent boredom. I already know that he's here under protest because his parents are worried about his slumping grades, his choice of friends (including a serious girlfriend), his preference for being away from home, his brooding silence when questioned, and one night of obvious alcohol consumption. At 16, he would rather be anywhere than in a counseling office with an aging therapist. One more adult on his case! What can we know about the teen brain, mind, and social world that could guide us toward engagement with this young man?

Challenges, Changes, and Stereotypes of Adolescence

It is possible that our adolescents are the least understood age group. Perhaps that is because they are "under construction" in so many ways that begin to pull them away from the shelter of childhood, yet they have not gained the balance they may achieve as adults. Socially, they are stepping out of the family context and into the wider world to find strong connections among their peers. Their minds are jumping into formal operations, allowing them to hold more complex—and sometimes troubling—thoughts. For many, the broader issues, such as prejudice and justice, are beginning to stir their idealism or touch them personally. Hormonally, they feel the push to connect sexually at a time that is out of sync with the demands of education and preparation for self-sufficiency, at least in Western industrialized society. As Patty Wipfler (2006h) points out, they are also leaving the familiar world of dolls and toys, and now have to find different ways to maintain the spirit of pleasure and play with newly emerging interests.

Over the course of the last decade, we have begun to discover that the brain itself is undergoing a thorough reconstruction. Changes in connectivity and myelination that pave the way for a fully mature brain leave teens with a less than consistent capacity for an integrated brain and coherent mind, just at a time when they are reaching for more independent functioning. For some teens, these new neural developments may proceed behind the scenes, for the most part, unless there is life stress. Others travel a far bumpier road, regardless of environmental circumstances. Unfortunately, we have built many forms of stress into our culture's social and relational fabric.

Part of the problem stems from stereotypes of teen behavior, no doubt reinforced by troubling experiences. In casual conversations with many other parents of teenagers, I have found that most people view adolescence as a time of suffering and irritation for parents—an expectation that makes many families warily back off from their teens, or prompts them to be so controlling that the natural adolescent push toward independence (with some missteps) is frustrated. These parental and societal beliefs then require adolscents to live down to those expectations. Frightened of their teens' errors in judgment, real or anticipated, parents often fall into their own unresolved issues—feelings of helplessness and confusion, or patterns of strict parental control from their own adolescence. They then act in ways that disconnect them from their young adult's real need for respect and a calm parental presence. Sometimes parents defend themselves from this puzzling time by simply not taking teens seriously, seeing them as going through some kind of trivial phase before they become "real" adults. Feeling demeaned in this way precipitates a disconnection that robs teens of parental input that could help steady their course. From another angle, this society also pushes for achievement in ways that may make teens feel either tormented by their workload or deficient if they can't, or don't want to, keep up. Although it is slowly improving, our educational system does not take differences in temperament, talents, or learning styles into sufficient account, especially in high school. These attitudes and experiences can chop away at one of the most crucial aspects of this developmental stage: defining a personal identity.

This process can be further impacted by attachment struggles or unresolved trauma from teens' younger years. If we think in terms of the inner community, these young people have the same range of states of mind as adults. Said another way, as they move toward independence and more complex social situations, teens will be challenged to deal with whatever implicit mental models of relationship were wired in at the beginning of life. If maltreatment is part of that picture, they are likely also bearing the burden of structural and functional deficits in their brains. These deficits can become more pronounced during the teen brain rewiring project (Lee & Hoaken, 2007; Strauch, 2003). This list of changes and challenges is certainly not exhaustive, but if we notice how our bodies feel as we imagine our way into the fluctuating world of adolescence, we may get some hint of the load some of our young people carry.

In the midst of all this transformation and stress, much also remains unchanged. As with every other stage of life, teens need affection, respect, empathy, and a listening person who understands them, especially when they are off balance. Before they can begin a process of authentic communication, they also need to feel emotionally safe enough to open their minds and hearts to an adult. To provide these qualities for our teen patients and to encourage their parents, it helps to understand both the unique developmental needs of adolescence and any personal impediments we may have to making adjustments to accommodate those needs. For many people, this may mean a major paradigm overhaul, beginning perhaps with a thorough understanding of the teen brain.

Imagining the Adolescent Brain

We can begin the story of teen brain development in the lab of Jay Giedd in 1997. Through fMRI scans of many adolescent brains, as his young people moved from the onset of puberty through late adolescence, he unexpectedly found that at the beginning of puberty (approximately 11 in girls and 12 in boys), there is a genetically triggered burst of overproduction (or "exuberance," as the scientists picturesquely call it), creating a forest of new dendrites and synapses in several regions of the brain, providing the opportunity for billions of new connections. The carefully sculpted neural pathways that developed throughout childhood now become crowded malls of possibilities. This burst of growth is followed by a dramatic decrease in the number of synaptic connections (called "pruning"), a process that proceeds until the mid-20s (Giedd et al., 1999). Sowell and colleagues (Sowell, Thompson, Holmes, Jernigan, & Toga, 1999) estimate that between the ages of 12 and 20, the teenage brain loses 7–10% of its gray matter. Such pruning gradually creates a more efficient, better integrated brain. However, it also follows that from puberty through the mid-20s, we may see some mental and emotional disorganization, followed by the gradual emergence of a more coherent mind and more regulated relationships.

It is also important to remember that when there is a burst of new growth, it may signal a period of rapid learning, of heightened neuro-plasticity (Diamond & Hopson, 1998). This growth spurt would make the quality of the environment at the onset of adolescence particularly cru-cial, since we know that what is genetically awakened is then shaped by experience. In fact, we also know that different kinds of experiences can actually influence which genes are turned on (Siegel, 1999). It is possible that the early teen brain is wide open for reshaping, not only intellectu-ally but also relationally. This period of time provides a prime opportu-nity for balanced adults to make a long-term positive difference in their teens' progress toward independent living (Neufeld & Mate, 2006).

As research proceeds, we are just beginning to discover that many structures and processes in the teen brain participate in this reconstruc-tion effort. Perhaps the most central area is the exuberance–pruning process of the middle prefrontal regions (Giedd et al., 1999). If we recall the nine functions of those circuits, it is easy to see why teens seem to sometimes lose their capacity for sound judgment, attuned communi-cation, empathy, emotional stability, and accurate perception of social cues, particularly under stress. The cerebellum is also rewiring and is the last area to complete its remodel. We now know that in addition to motor coordination, the cerebellum plays an important role in recognizing social cues (Giedd et al.). This means that early teens may be challenged when trying to sort out the meaning of social signals, sometimes reacting in what appear to be irrational and annoying ways. Parents who suddenly find that their very presence is acutely embarrassing to their 13-year old can now picture some disruption that may be occurring between limbic, prefrontal, and cerebellar circuits. Most important, we can take a step toward understanding the teen viewpoint by accepting that adolescents perceive the world somewhat differently than we adults.

There is also evidence suggesting that during this period, teen pre-frontal regions have to work much harder than the adult brain solving a similar problem. As a result, they can become overtaxed and simply shut down when faced with complicated tasks or an intense stressor (Sabbagh, 2006). This piece of physiology may be one factor in the frequent fender benders that are part of adolescent life. This gridlock appears to occur partly because pruning has not proceeded sufficiently to facilitate efficient communication of signals within the prefrontal region. Additionally, the various structures of the brain aren't communicating well over longer distances yet. As a result the brain regions that could generate rapid, accurate judgments aren't well connected to the areas making unconsidered snap judgments.

We can think of this period of growth as a time of increased differentiation, in preparation for integration at a higher level of complexity. This exuberance brings the onset of formal operations thinking; that is, the ability to think at higher levels of abstraction about a broader range of issues. However, at the same time, the coordination between different brain regions is temporarily limited because neural integration of the new structures is just beginning, and the map of connectivity is confused by the abundance of pathways. For example, scans reveal that when teens are shown the face of a person who is afraid, their amygdalae light up, triggering a full-body response of fear. When adults are shown the same picture, their middle prefrontal region immediately comes online to help them evaluate the actual level of threat (Baird et al., 1999). We can imagine that when the idea to jump off the roof into the swimming pool makes itself known in working memory, the motor strip has the young person hurtling into space before the dorsolateral prefrontal cortex can receive the middle prefrontal's suggestion that this might not be such a good idea after all. Or when a middle school teacher gives the students homework, the explicit memory of this assignment, encoded in the hippocampus, may not be retrieved and come into working memory until long after the due date has passed. It is a little like a group of creative ballet dancers coming on stage with limited choreography to tell them how to dance in synchrony. However, research also suggests that these difficulties are most noticeable under stressful conditions, so it is not accurate to imagine that all teenagers will respond in these ways.

As pruning proceeds, it follows an interesting pattern that may help to account for increases in balance as our teens move toward their 20s. Not only are there fewer synapses to snarl communication, but more excitatory than inhibitory synapses are dying away. Some estimate that the ratio goes from 7 to 1 in favor of excitement to 4 to 1 over the course of adolescence (Strauch, 2003). The brain is literally calming itself. At the same time, the dorsolateral prefrontal cortex is improving its ability to hold information in the presence of competing information, while increasing integration with the middle prefrontal cortex gradually brings

Being a Brain-Wise Therapist

the capacity for well-considered, flexible decision-making. Much of this kind of consolidation happens near the end of adolescence and into the 20s, leaving teens more vulnerable through most of junior high and high school. It helps us understand why a teenager, who holds the rational view that drug use is not a good idea, may lose that thought entirely when presented with a peer-generated opportunity to try something new.

Teen brains also go through a burst of myelination. In this process, tendrils from certain kinds of glial cells wrap themselves around axons, creating a myelin sheath that allows neurons to communicate with one another 100 times faster, while also giving strength to the synaptic connections. Although research on this topic is in its infancy, we do know that certain areas increase myelination by up to 100%—a huge and unexpected leap (Benes, Turtle, Yusuf, & Farol, 1994). One relay station of the brain that receives a myelin boost is the loop linking the posterior part of the cingulate with the limbic regions. These circuits give us an awareness of our gut reactions and place them in the context of a thought (Benes, 1989). However, initially this new speedy highway is not well connected with the calm judgment of the middle prefrontal regions (an area that myelinates later). As a result of increasing awareness of the gut, any initial fear response gives the sympathetic nervous system a jolt, such that sweaty palms and racing heart may define the truth about the current encounter. The good news is that by the end of adolescence, myelination finally creates support for faster connection between the middle prefrontal and limbic regions, allowing for a notable modulation in emotion.

Another region of the brain also benefits from the increase in speed. The corpus callosum, the band of connecting axons responsible for linking the hemispheres, improves communication between right and left halves of Wernicke's area, gradually helping teens find words for their emotions (Thompson et al., 2000). This is a good thing because young teens, in the grip of exuberance, lose about 20% of their ability to name—and, therefore, modulate—their feelings (Strauch, 2003). In addition, the areas of the parietal cortex that support complex logical functions are also being made more efficient by the myelinating corpus callosum, particularly in the earliest days of adolescence. Teens then have a better chance at algebra and may find themselves unexpectedly moved by Emily Dickinson.

Some other useful research tidbits:

1. One reason teenagers go to bed later and rise later is because, at the onset of puberty, melatonin, a sleep-encouraging brain chemical, enters

their system about 2 hours later and lingers longer in the morning (Wolfson & Carskadon, 1998). There is also good evidence that teens need about 9 hours sleep rather than the 7½ or 8 required by adults.

2. The propensity for risky behaviors may involve a combination of dysregulated dopamine levels and disrupted connections with the prefrontal cortex (Bardo et al., 1993). Although the research is far from clear at this point, we do know that dopamine circuits, which mediate pleasure and direct us toward the new, are frequently running high or low during this period. Whether they are responding to high levels or seeking to raise low levels, teens can feel the pull to try something new and exciting, whether that is driving too fast or responding to the push of hormones. Because the prefrontal cortex isn't always on call to keep consequences in mind, the act may be committed before reflection can moderate the outcome.

3. Recent research by George Bartzokis (2005), a professor of neurology at UCLA's David Geffen School of Medicine, suggests that extensive drug and alcohol use in the teen years may disrupt myelination, leaving the brain vulnerable to impulsivity, while aggravating autism, attention-deficit/hyperactivity disorder, and schizophrenia. Since the brain's excitatory circuits myelinate first, followed by inhibitory circuits (a process not complete until age 25), the push toward taking a drug is happening 100 times faster than the message to stop. In other words, the adolescent pattern of myelination may contribute to addictive behaviors. Since myelination is a genetically driven aspect of brain development, it is not clear whether myelination can resume, if drug and alcohol usage stop, once the critical period has passed.

All of these findings have emerged in the last 15 years, so the information can give us only suggestions about some challenges some teenagers face. However, even with just these discoveries, we have enough information to encourage cautious consideration of some ways we might (1) support adolescents involved in delinquent behavior, (2) modify advice to parents, and (3) impact the way we do therapy with hurting teens.

Finding Jake, Part I

How can we imagine becoming an ally of the disenchanted Jake? As with any person, respect requires me to believe that there is a good reason for his behavior at home and his attitude in my office. Asking him if he wants to be here, I get an emphatic, "NO!" Relishing this burst of aliveness, I can easily say, "I don't blame you." In my office, no one is required to stay if they don't wish to be there, so I tell him he is free to leave and that I would respect that decision. He looks at me for the first time and perhaps sees someone other than the understandably anxious and controlling parents who brought him here. Now there's room for him to express all the ways he feels oppressed by his closest adults. I have absolutely no trouble seeing his point—and he knows it. At no time in this initial session do we talk about his behavior. He talks. I listen. If the topic turns to music, I am just as interested as if he's talking about what I might judge to be more emotionally meaningful topics. I throw in the occasional question, but just to further the conversation, not to direct it the way I want it to go—because I truly don't want it to go any particular way. I just want to connect. His resonance circuits can pick up my internal state of curiosity and acceptance, and it doesn't feel anything like being with Mom and Dad. He agrees to return for another session.

Balancing Respect and Influence through Attachment

Why might this work? As at every stage of life, teens need to attach, and the vehicle for that attachment is contingent communication. However, what is contingent changes across the lifespan. Instead of wanting guidance, adolescents respond to receiving respect for their ability to find solutions. They blossom when their unique opinions are taken seriously. Instead of remaining sheltered, they need to face the world's inconsistencies and injustices, bringing that conversation to us. Just as when they were younger, their emotional wounds need to be met with listening and understanding, even when their concerns sometimes look out of proportion to our adult minds.

Finding the balance between respect and influence through attachment is the art of it. Peter Jensen, director of the Center for the Advancement of Children's Mental Health, suggests that we might do well to "function like a surrogate set of frontal lobes" at times (Strauch, 2003, p. 35). What do frontal lobes do? One function is to provide the capacity for flexible thinking, choosing the wisest alternative. This involves bringing all possibilities into awareness (dorsolateral prefrontal cortex), holding them there long enough to contemplate the consequences of each, and then making a decision. This brain sketch suggests that we might say something like "What do you think might happen if you . . . ?" If our teens are confident that we won't just dismiss their answers, giving our own "correct" version, they will often play with various ideas while we listen.

Patty Wipfler (2006a–i), founder of Hand in Hand, a parent–child organization in Palo Alto, California, is a most powerful advocate for adolescents. Her approach to parenting, through all the developmental stages, is based on connection—interpersonal linking leading to development of neural pathways that embody secure attachment. For teens, this approach continues to make excellent neurobiological sense. Since these young people sometimes struggle as their middle prefrontal cortices attempt to link into the rest of their brains, it seems wise to foster those neural connections rather than adopt either a rigid or hands-off approach that would further discombobulate what may already be challenged. We know that when people feel felt, limbic and prefrontal circuits are pulled together. Wipfler (2006h) suggests that becoming an ally may be the most effective stance to promote this joining as these young people prepare for adult life. For many parents, the ally viewpoint is a radical shift, especially as their first child exits childhood for the teen years. Even for we therapists, the challenge may be to calm our anxiety as these young adults come to us with their struggles. Wipfler bases her approach on a *radical trust in adolescents' ability to find their feet when supported by people who have resolved enough of their own issues to be truly present and confident of the teens' emerging abilities.* Imagine how such a state of mind in us would resonate within the adolescents who come to us.

Neurobiological realities also hint at the importance of nurturing adult contact during adolescence. During this period of exuberance and pruning, teen brains are being dramatically rewired. We know that the teen's ongoing experience will (1) shape these new neural connections as well as tell some genes whether to express or not; (2) reinforce certain kinds of synaptic links; and (3) create, as well as reshape, representations and implicit assumptions about the relational world. It is certainly not ideal for teens to find their main or only companions among their peers. One unfinished teen brain serving as the major force shaping another is not the ideal situation. Instead, teens need to "put down roots" with people who are not in this same transition, with well-enough integrated brains to help them wire their new neural territory in ways that will support a coherent life.

For the most part, the necessity for ongoing adult support is not the picture held by our industrialized society. An international study headed by child psychiatrist Sir Michael Rutter and criminologist David Smith suggests that peer culture first emerged in the wake of World War II (Rutter & Smith, 1995). Since the ship did not right itself after the trauma of war receded, industrialized countries now hold the view that it is natural for teens to leave the family and look to their peers for their primary attachment (Neufeld & Mate, 2006). In autonomy-driven America, we don't even question this assumption. As with all expectations, social norms now reinforce this separation. This view is so much part of the mainstream that peer orientation now begins at a very early age. Many children are in child care within weeks or months of birth, as both parents work to maintain the cultural standard. In general, we have developed into a society that does not view early secure attachment as central to a healthy life, so there is insufficient public focus on how to create a daycare system that can promote secure bonds. Vertical linkages between generations have broken down, for the most part, as mobility seems more important than continuity. Divorce offers many children competing attachments that may be confusing, especially when stepparents enter the picture. For an increasing number of children, the relationships needed for secure attachment are not available. In just the last 10 years, the percentage of securely attached children has declined from 65 to 55% (Sroufe et al., 2005). As a result, our implicit mental models often work against maintaining attachment bonds, especially with our teens.

The alarming result of such disruption was revealed in the international study cited above. Participating scholars from 16 countries linked increases in youth crime, violence, bullying, and delinquency to the breakdown in the intergenerational transmission of mainstream culture (Rutter & Smith, 1995). Another reflection of this change in attachment orientation emerged when Gordon Neufeld, Canadian child development specialist and attachment advocate, sought the reason for the fourfold increase in suicide rates among children between 10 and 14 in the last 50 years. He expected to find that problems with parents were at the root, but instead discovered that "the key trigger for the great majority was how they were being treated by their peers, not their parents" (Neufeld & Mate, 2006, p. 11). When children are not securely attached to their adults, they are likely in emotional pain, which can easily turn into mutual cruelty and bullying as they seek some kind of contact. At this time of heightened neuroplasticity, abnormally high stress can cause cell death or reduced activation in the anterior cingulate, possibly causing long-term deficits in empathy and attentional capacity (Singer et al., 1994).

A constantly disrupted stress system can become permanently dysregulated, and the corpus callosum can experience excessive pruning, reducing communication between the hemispheres (Teicher et al., 2003). When the right and left prefrontal regions have difficulty communicating, upsetting wordless experiences on the right struggle to find the words that can calm them.

These realities call for a cultural paradigm shift, so we may feel we are swimming upstream, even within our own minds, when we advocate for the primacy of adult attachments. However, a consilience between sociology, attachment theory, and neurobiology certainly emerges as we think through the gradually emerging evidence. When we can commit to these realities, we are in a much better position not only to understand our teen patients, but also to better embody a different set of norms. Neufeld (2006) points out that while attachment remains an inborn drive throughout life, the target of attachment can be anyone who is available. Any inadequate port in the storm is better than feeling lost, and that need for tethering is often the prime motivator for peer orientation. The good news is that a shift in consciousness can lead to refocusing attachment around healthy adults until the child's developing brain is ready to go it alone.

Finding Jake, Part II

Having built a beginning bond on the foundation of these beliefs, Jake and I were able to do some good work around his mom's absence when he was a child. As in so many families, she had gone back to work soon after his birth to maintain the established lifestyle. When he was 5, his sister was born, the family was on better financial footing, and Mom stayed home. However, the pain of the early loss still lived inside him in nonconscious implicit processes and was made vivid when he stepped out into the peer world. Because his parents had no way to understand his emotional needs, the family was resigned to losing him to his friends. In our work, Jake, like many teens, really took to sand tray and art, facilitating our conversation about the roots of his disconnection. As trust between us deepened, he was able to move from anger to grief. Before too long, he recognized that he missed being close to his parents but hated their anxious, overmanaging ways. So he was caught in no-man's land between his need for attachment with adults and the unsatisfying bonds with his friends.

The Parent Component

Meanwhile, Jake's parents had agreed to meet with our parenting specialist. Whenever possible, part of working with teens is supporting their parents as they undertake three projects: (1) understanding and resolving issues that may be getting in the way of their becoming their child's allies; (2) becoming familiar with the teen brain; and (3) developing a set of skills for meeting their young adults where they are. Proceeding roughly in this order seems to offer a successful path, because without awareness and some resolution of the parents' issues, new strategies will likely fall apart under stress. Spending time with childhood attachment experiences and the parents' adolescence often illuminates the reasons they are so frightened by, or frustrated with, their children. Almost immediately, Jake's mom shared that her parents had reprimanded and grounded her if she broke any of their stringent rules. Spending some time with that inner teenager, she began to collapse with shame, feeling how she lost trust in her own judgment. No wonder she couldn't trust Jake now! She even began to hear how some of the words in her lectures came straight from her parents' mouths. Dad, on the other hand, remembered that no one had bothered to keep track of his whereabouts (because he was the boy and free to roam), until one terrifying night, he got drunk and plunged his car over a cliff. When Jake came home drunk, anxiety tore through his father and came out as the burst of rage that landed Jake in my office.

Over several weeks, these parents worked toward a coherent narrative that helped them become open to different ways of responding to their son. Clearly, some of their limbic circuits were connecting with their middle prefrontal cortices. In this state of greater openness, talking about the changes going on in Jake's brain became fertile ground for developing new strategies. Soon, the parents were hanging out with Jake, creating a safe space in which he could gradually air the things that troubled him. As they took his ideas and emotional struggles seriously, he began to enjoy his time with them again. Along the way, they discovered that he had a passion for helping end hunger and some ideas about how that might be accomplished. When he occasionally made questionable decisions, they helped him think through other options that might have brought a better result, supported him as he found ways to clean up the mess, and let him know they continued to love and respect him. At their final session with their parenting person, Dad said reflectively, "I was after that kid with a cattle prod. No wonder he didn't want to be with me!"

Sadly, not all parents are this willing. Sometimes we will have to be the lone voice of confidence and respect entering this young person's world. Because the prefrontal region is in such an open and developing stage, we may have quite an ability to influence what information those new synapses will carry as we become a member of the inner community. When parents are willing, it is so helpful to have another therapist who is familiar with the developing teen brain work with them. Teens are justifiably sensitive about their confidentiality, and providing this boundary reinforces their safety.

Even with all this brain knowledge, it isn't helpful to say, "Teenagers are this way because X is happening in the brain." That is a distancing statement that lacks respect for individuality and doesn't give due weight to the fact that research is still in a very early stage. Instead, we are on firmer ground if we understand the tendencies engendered by this big surge in brain development, while becoming aware of how relationships can help teens make the most of this neural growth spurt. Interpersonal neurobiology encourages us to take the power of relationship, for good or ill, seriously. We also know that expectations play an enormous part in determining what happens next, because they bias our perceptions and behaviors, limiting the range of what we can imagine. A good example of this point comes from societies that are embedded in more structured and concrete expectations for how children pass from childhood into adulthood. Unchallenged by the need to become fully independent adults, and often not burdened by the array of stressors present in our society, these young ones often slip seamlessly from one stage to the next, with barely a hint of adolescent turmoil (Sabbagh, 2006). Cushioned by continuing primary relationships with adults, their maturing brains are not left to fend for themselves. Perhaps this can be our challenge: to create attachment richness within a culture that pushes the other way. With warm support at each stage of life, coupled with a thorough understanding of the brain–body and mind to guide us, we might be able to assist the next generation in finding a balance between the push toward individuality and the lifelong need for empathic connection.

Chapter 21

Playing with Children, Supporting Their Parents

Jenna's mom stood at the playroom door, her 4-year-old daughter peeking out from behind her hip. Our play specialist smiled her greeting to Jenna and leaned in just a little to catch a better glimpse. She stepped aside so Jenna could see what was waiting in the room. Jenna's eyes lit up, she let go of Mom's coat, and set out on a marvelous journey of recovery. When our internal arms are wide open to receive each new child into the playroom, they feel our welcoming presence, and their senses immediately encounter a feast of opportunities for expression. We meet them where they live, encouraging connection and helping them express their joys and struggles. Here, almost all experiences are child-guided, as we support their unfolding stories. We can help prepare this nourishing "meal" by first meeting with the parents with three objectives in mind: (1) to gain a sense of what this particular child may have experienced, (2) to understand what the parents' attachment struggles might be, and (3) to form a bond that will embrace the whole family. One goal for this meeting is to enter this family's world sufficiently to begin to hold this child's mind, since that will be one of the most important aspects of this play relationship.

As we listen to the difficulty that prompted the visit, our minds might begin to fill with hypothetical pictures of the possible patterns engrained in the body, brain, and mind of this child. Which neurochemicals may be flowing? Which regions may need help with integration? What might relationships be like in the child's inner community? Then, as we explore the family history of both parents, we can step the whole picture back one generation to imagine the relational legacies that have shaped the way they parent. As they are helped to catch sight of these patterns, sometimes shame and defensiveness can give way to honesty and sorrow. When this shift happens, the parents are often open to receiving ongoing help with their own losses and attachment struggles. This is the best of all worlds—working with both children and parents—because through this process, the family will flow together into healthy relating.

Not all parents are open to this much involvement, believing that if the child's offensive behavior would just change, all would be well. Even in these circumstances, it is important to do everything possible to change their perception and make it clear that this kind of therapy does not focus primarily on behavior, but on connection and repair. Sometimes the tide changes when we share the abundant research findings confirming that children who are grounded in security, with daily doses of compassion and support, will become family members who can cooperate and students who can learn. The particularly good news of neuroplasticity gives parents hope that their family dynamics can change, if they gain the personal awareness and tools to parent differently. With the prospect of relief for their feelings of helplessness and frustration, they often become collaborators. Even with initial resistance, we may enlist the cooperation of these important allies over time if we are creative and tenacious in this effort.

Nondirective Play Therapy and Brain Development

Nondirective or child-centered play therapy, inspired by the original work of Garry Landreth (1991), seems an excellent match for what we are learning from neuroscientists about how children's brains and minds get hurt and heal. Thinking back to the sections on attachment and diagnosis, we might recall that when children have not been helped with their overwhelming feelings, the neural pathways from limbic circuits to middle prefrontal regions may be insubstantial and fragile, leaving them vulnerable to limbic surges, particularly under duress. Over time, their stress system can become hyperreactive, further pulling children away from developing self-regulation. With the neurochemicals of stress rather than connection often flowing in their systems, children are disconnected from inner wellsprings of good feelings and balance. In addition, their inner community members may be a constant source of criticism, shame, and fear, or of emptiness and loss.

With a caring and balanced play therapist, all of these experiences can be reversed over time. Being able to hold a clear picture of these children's pains, fears, and strengths in our minds provides the soil and sunshine in which these children can develop. The warmth of this contingent contact, communicated through the resonance circuits, quickly or gradually settles them into enough security to move into play. From the beginning, the playroom provides a novel situation, and the therapist gives ample permission for the child to explore freely. Often, this open environment activates what neuroscientist Jaak Panksepp (1998) calls the *seeking circuits*—one of seven genetically based motivational circuits residing in our limbic regions. Three of them—rage, fear, and separation distress—become activated when children are out of connection with adults. The other four—caring, social bonding, playfulness, and seeking—arise under conditions of warm, contingent connection (Sunderland, 2006). Once it has been activated by novelty, the seeking system supports the release of dopamine (among other brain chemicals), which cascades through the frontal lobes, providing the sense of enjoyment, focus, and purpose to see something through. We can imagine that children in the playroom with a safe adult might find speedy access to the seeking system.

Whether these little ones embark on a mastery task or the expression of some frightening or maddening experience, the energy in the room becomes heightened and concentrated as this system comes online. Sensing the invitation, our own energy level might elevate, while we maintain contact with the calm core of our internal caring observer. As the play untolds, we can sense whether children need support for difficult and overwhelming feelings, or an energized collaborator who amplifies their joy. The contingency of our response has a good chance of activating the *systems for bonding and care* (Sunderland, 2006). Leaning against us for support or seeing compassion in our eyes, their brains may release oxytocin and GABA, calming their fear or anger (Sunderland, 2006). As we are empathically present with them, new neural pathways are already in the making, establishing stronger connections between the raw emotions of the limbic system and the balancing circuits of the middle prefrontal area, linkages that will eventually give them the capacity for self-regulation and well-being. Deep inside, their resonance circuits are beginning to form a representation of a responsive presence as they internalize our interaction. Over time, all these new synaptic connections will strengthen, and myelination will speed their signals while helping the new connections stay in place.

When children lead the play and we follow well, they feel valued and powerful, and their brains respond by releasing opioids, which are neurochemicals supporting well-being and connection. When these cascade through the brain, stress chemicals return to normal levels, any tendency toward aggression recedes, and children are free to fully engage (Sunderland, 2006). On the other hand, if we take the lead, children may be thwarted as they seek to open the neural nets that need attention. If we are completely off target or insistent, we might even activate the *rage system* as their natural flow is interrupted. Should that happen, we can easily repair if we remember that rage is a bid for soothing connection. It helps to keep in mind that when children come to our playroom, we invite their whole being to emerge because we have radical trust in their inborn capacity for healing. We agree to rely on their signals and to respond to them with actions that foster the integration of their brains. Things go best when we remain committed to this process, to the best of our ability. Sometimes, under the pressure of parents' need for rapid behavioral change, we may feel strongly pulled toward "making something happen." That almost never goes well, and we soon find ourselves returning to our faith in the power of the relationship and an organic pace that can't be rushed or manipulated.

As the play unfolds, we can provide words for what we are seeing—descriptions of the action or brief comments about what the children seem to be feeling. Sometimes, just our body language or a murmured recognition cements the connection—"uh-huh" or "um." Sometimes we may even tell collaborative stories that help children make sense of some difficult experiences. Part of recovery is building the interhemispheric highway of the corpus callosum, linking the verbal left to the feeling right, so that strong emotions find words—an activity that immediately calms the limbic regions (Hariri et al., 2000). While all this is going on, it helps for us to sustain an image of the child as safe, secure, and centered in our care. This is good nutrition for the child's mind via the resonance circuits that link us to one another.

In all of these processes, the way in which we embody warmth and awareness helps children integrate their brain circuitry—literally. Fresh relational experiences build new neural circuits, creating pathways for helpful neurochemicals that will balance their systems. In the process, their inner communities also gain a new supportive member. If we can get the parents fully on board, even more change is possible. With these basic principles under our belts, let's now look at specifics of the playroom environment and the experiences that may emerge there. I provide a fair amount of detail because therapists who have worked primarily with

Being a Brain-Wise Therapist

adults have told us that the transition to play therapy was a bit nerve-wracking initially.

The Physical Space

To start, let me describe our play area for you. There is no waiting room. Parents pass the time in the office upstairs, the park behind our building, or the local Starbucks. Before, when our playroom was situated next to the regular counseling offices, we observed all the ways anxious, concerned parents could find to eavesdrop on what was happening with their children. And the kids definitely knew this. Therefore, when the opportunity arose, we created a separate, protected play space. Coming in the front door, the first thing you see is a sandplay area with over a thousand carefully chosen unbreakable objects, as well as wet and dry trays. Sometimes the little ones don't make it beyond this room for awhile. We decided to set sandplay apart as something special and different, a place to reveal deep implicit processes. Since we think of it this way, that's how the children tend to use it. Stepping into the other part of the play area, the center is wide open to make room for every kind of project or drama. There are many stuffed animals and puppets, a doll house with every imaginable figure, a hospital tucked under the couch, a rocking chair and blanket, instruments and games, dress-up clothes, handcuffs and other police and fire gear, games, all kinds of art and craft supplies, a tape player for soothing music, a few books on issues of special concern for children, brains of various sizes and textures, a very large, solid-cloth dummy who can really take a beating—and the therapist. The environment is dead without him or her. Over time, the children have taught us what they need, so our room is both full (in the sense of having everything that's needed) and spare (not crowded with useless items).

The Emotional Atmosphere

When children are in the company of someone who genuinely cares about them, they become imaginative and resilient, making use of whatever is offered, regardless of how elaborate or simple the environment. Since more than one therapist might be seeing a child at the same time, we have three large, sturdy play bags upstairs that hold smaller versions of the key toys, along with a box of games, a bag of Legos, art and craft supplies, and sandplay in every room.

When children come into this warm environment (comprised of both toys and therapist), they begin to sense the possibility of expressing what is troubling in their lives. If we are doing a good job of holding their inner world in our minds, there is a constant invitation for this experience to be different from playing at home. Over the years, even before we knew about resonance circuits, we could clearly see these young ones respond to our *kind awareness* of them. During the first few weeks, we get to know one another. In a COAL atmosphere, we begin to internally sense these children—and they us. This reciprocity begins to create a neuroception of safety, the foundation for a trusting relationship. At some point, children will signal the success of bonding by playing on a deeper level, drawing us into their worlds. They may also give more overt indications of the increasing closeness by putting a figure who represents us in a sand tray or drawing, standing closer, making more eye contact, or giving us a spontaneous hug. This early process is unique for each child, depending on attachment style, temperament, and injury. Consequently, it is helpful if we can leave any preconceived notions about the speed and manner of bonding outside the door. Instead, we can watch for the palpable change in the atmosphere as the interpersonal system strengthens.

Being the Caring Observer of Children's Play

What might we look for as our children play? As stated above, the children direct the therapy. We always trust them to gradually reveal their inner worlds, given that we observe without guiding the play. More important than specific actions are *patterns* that repeat from week to week or in a single session. One little boy came to therapy struggling with his adoption proceedings. He had been chosen, and then been returned, twice by parents while in foster care. Now, it was taking over a year for his third set of foster parents to finalize the adoption. This little boy had been waiting for 7 years for a family. For months in therapy, this little guy repeatedly found homes for everything. The birds had nests, squirrels had trees, Santa Claus had the North Pole. This went on week after week while he played through the trauma of never having a secure home.

Another event to watch for is *firsts* in a session. These always indicate change. An overly dependent child might make the first attempt at self-direction, or an avoidant child might invite us to join the play for the first time. We can also look for *sudden breaks* in children's play, as they abruptly shift from one activity to another. This abruptness often indicates that the play is too intense or hurtful for them. Our play specialist worked with a child who had been molested in his grandparents' home by an uncle. Week after week, he avoided the playhouse until one day, he approached and started to open the door. Suddenly and abruptly, he turned and crossed to the other side of the playroom to the games, not able to continue playing beyond the door of the house. Just tracking these shifts internally is often sufficient because we are closely linked, via resonance circuits, and our children's bodies–brains will pick up our attention and understanding. However, at certain moments, saying a few words such as "You are going to the playhouse," or "Now, you are at the games" can be helpful as well. Some children need the verbal connection, while for others talking is a disruption. We gradually learn how to dance uniquely with each child's shifting needs over time.

The overall *theme* or *meaning* of the play carries important information as well. Over the weeks, issues of anger, control, fear, rejection, powerlessness, or hurt may linger. It can be very helpful to label these feelings and needs in words in order to help the child's right and left brains become integrated, thereby calming the right limbic circuits. No longer enacting a theme may indicate that children have been able to move on, emotionally, to something else. For example, many children going through a family divorce or separation feel like their lives are out of control. We have observed that these children will repeatedly use handcuffs, police badges, and radios, creating situations in which they have some control or power over who leaves and who stays. Other children act out roles as teachers, movie directors, and superheroes to experience empowerment. With this kind of play, we will often be invited to participate, most often being cast in the children's role as the victim of adults—powerless, shamed, or criticized. Simple reflective statements about both partners in the play may help children make meaning. We might say, "You want me to stand still so you can handcuff me to the filing cabinet," or "You want me to sit down right now." As we do this, the child feels seen and understood, a subjective experience that helps form connections between the middle prefrontal and limbic areas.

Through this kind of play in which they make these events happen to us, children are often able to create a *healing distance* from disturbing or traumatic experiences. At the same time, because these traumatic events are repeated within the warmth of our relationship, there is the opportunity, often through several reenactments, to relieve and repair the painful and frightening feelings at a deeper level. This repeated repair experience builds neural connections that may help related experiences become more emotionally manageable, even if children's day-to-day worlds aren't changing much. If we remember that contingent communication—meeting children where they are and conveying understanding—builds secure attachment, then it is easy to see how interacting with a safe, accepting person will begin to change brain structure in a way that provides more internal resources for children under stress. For example, when a child becomes very anxious in our presence and is able to use us to regulate toward greater calm, that regulatory effort means that a new neural net is being formed. When this is repeated again and again, that neural net becomes stronger until it is a reliable internal resource when we aren't there. Just our mindful awareness of the child, in his or her presence, makes this kind of neural integration possible. Explaining this process clearly to parents can help them understand that by focusing on relationship rather than only on behavior, play therapy builds a permanent foundation for their child's relational and intellectual success.

Meeting with Parents

While the child's play therapy is unfolding, we will also be meeting with the parents regularly to help them with whatever issues stand in the way of holding their child with empathy and understanding. It is helpful if these parenting sessions are more frequent at the beginning, then taper off to once every 6 or 8 weeks as parents demonstrate the ability to hold onto new ways of being with themselves and their child, even under stress. When the parents' emotional difficulties are more than can be handled in these sessions, we do everything possible to get them involved in their own therapy, as individuals or as a couple. We can provide the most help if sessions with parents are more focused on their own attachment and parenting issues than on telling them what is happening with their child in play therapy, although these issues will be the background for what we are offering. Balancing the child's need for confidentiality with parents' legal right for information can help us walk a path that is respectful of all family members. Often, sharing broad outlines of children's issues provides sufficient information for parents while keeping the parent–child relationship safe for the young ones. Injured parents may take certain kinds of specific information back to their children in critical ways that stop the therapy in its tracks. As you decide what to share with parents, it is helpful to imagine how your words would sound if they were uttered by the parent to the child.

Any of us who are parents can easily step into the shoes of moms or dads who are afraid that their children's play will reveal them (the parents) to be cruel, critical, or distant. Remembering this will help us hold the whole family in empathy. If we inwardly align with the child in a way that leaves us angry or denigrating toward the parents, we will lose traction with the parents almost immediately, even if we give no outer indication of these attitudes. This nonjudgmental stance can be one of the most inwardly challenging skills to master when our hearts go out to these young ones who have been so injured. Reminding ourselves that parents are doing the best they can, given their own internal world, can help. If sustaining a sense of compassion and equal regard for the parents remains difficult, it can be helpful to form a listening partnership with another therapist who works with families. Adding this person to the interpersonal system can restore balance. When parents are in the presence of a therapist who can consistently offer nonjudgmental understanding, neural circuits that support self-regulation can take root, allowing the new parenting patterns to hold up, even under stress.

Resources for Brain-Wise Parenting

As far as the practicalities of parenting are concerned, long bookshelves of wisdom contain helpful advice. In general, we do want to talk about the characteristics of developmental stages, about temperament fit, and any other specific issues the parents present. In this short chapter, let's talk about several resources that are particularly compatible with what neuroscience teaches us and that have proven useful under almost all circumstances: two books (*Parenting from the Inside Out*, and *The Science of Parenting*), and two skills (Playlistening/Staylistening, and mindful awareness).

Daniel Siegel and Mary Hartzell (2003) wrote *Parenting from the Inside Out* to help parents understand their crucial role in shaping their child's developing brain. The authors also often encourage parents to look deeply at their own childhood attachment struggles. These ideas are offered in such a kind way that parents often begin to feel compassion for their mistakes with their children, rather than falling into a pit of shame. This single change in the way they relate to themselves opens the door to internalizing new parenting methods. When parents are willing to read at home and do the exercises, parenting sessions become rich with the personal healing that underlies parenting for secure attachment. We also offer a second book, *The Science of Parenting*, by Margot Sunderland (2006). In clear language, accompanied by right-brain-activating illustrations, she offers extensive research evidence for methods of creating secure attachment. With an ever-compassionate sense of the demands of parenting, she embraces parents and children.

Side by side with these two books, Patty Wipfler's pamphlets (2006a–g, 1) give superb, neurobiologically sound, specific guidance for many difficult situations—tantrums, crying, anger, and setting limits. Her primary purpose is to teach parents how to listen—to their children and to each other—in ways that establish emotional contact. When connection is broken, what she calls "offline" behavior sprouts (in parents and children); when it is restored, the family can regather itself in a more harmonious way. Interpersonal joining leads to brain integration, which leads to empathic relating—a familiar triangle. Based on her work, in parenting sessions we model and teach Playlistening and Staylistening (Wipfler, 2006f) as ways to remain engaged with children, even under trying circumstances. When we can help parents understand that their relationship with their children is the most crucial factor in structuring a brain that can support self-regulation, warm relationships, and optimal learning, we have receptive ears.

Playlistening involves setting aside a time when the child directs the play, and the parent just follows. A specific amount of time is scheduled, without interruptions from phone or visitors. When the parent takes the less competent, less powerful role, the child has the opportunity to explore all kinds of feelings in safety. Most often, the hardest part for parents is truly following the child, not offering their own ideas, not suggesting a better way, not taking the power back. However, as this shift is mastered, the child's emotional world gradually blooms. By listening for what brings the most laughter, parents can sense when the child is fully engaged. This is a signal for the parent to amplify those good feelings.

Often after a rousing session of play, there is enough safety for other feelings to easily emerge, so bouts of tears over seemingly small occurrences are common. When children don't feel emotionally safe because

Being a Brain-Wise Therapist

parents are busy or internally preoccupied, feelings stockpile. As soon as they trust that their parents are fully present, big old emotions can be processed through small current disruptions. Trusting that children know what they are doing leads to the best empathic response, even if the child's current state makes no rational sense to the parent. Staylistening describes precisely this ability to stay connected during upset. The parent restrains the natural impulse to fix the situation and instead just stays in connection with the child, listening to feelings and providing comfort until the channels of emotional joining reopen. This last part is the heart of it: being with any upset until it runs its course and homeostasis returns.

Diane, one of our parents, latched onto this bit of wisdom and proceeded to hold her sobbing 1-year-old daughter, Rosie, every day for 8 months. At dusk, Rosie would start to cry hard, with no apparent provocation. After about 15 minutes of rocking, soothing, and holding, she would be restored—until the next day at dusk. As she was able to talk, she began to say, "Mommy gone! Mommy gone!" After a few days of this, Diane remembered that when Rosie was 6 months old, Diane had gone away for a week to take care of her terminally ill father. Rosie stayed with a loving, but largely unfamiliar, neighbor, and had no doubt experienced deep pain in her mother's absence. We know that separation distress uses the same circuits in the brain as physical pain (Field, 1994), so this prolonged time apart must have been excruciating for her, particularly because Rosie's father had died before she was born. Diane never knew what caused this old pain to resurface when it did, or why dusk provided the cue each day. However, her loving tenacity paid off when Rosie stopped sobbing 8 months later. The child who gradually emerged from this round of deep grieving was curious, joyous, and cooperative (for a 2-year-old). In retrospect, Diane realized that what she had believed was due to Rosie's "touchy temperament" had perhaps been depression and lack of regulation because of the big pool of unprocessed pain.

While many parents can easily learn to comfort sadness, the idea of Staylistening in response to an angry child runs against everything wired into some parents' brains about parenting. They may have the sensation of losing control of their child, or be afraid of condoning misbehavior. If we can help them understand that anger is the outward manifestation of a brain and body that have become dysregulated, we can help them distinguish between *soothing anger* and *allowing misbehavior*.

If we have visceral responses to providing kindness when a child is raging, it can be a difficult area to teach. If we are going to offer these principles, we need to be aware of how our own inner world responds to them first. Often, parental presences inside us provide a visceral jolt as we move away from the idea of punishing anger. Once we have resolved our own issue and are clear about how it is possible to be calm, connected, and filled with empathy while setting firm boundaries at the same time, we will be in the best shape to work with parents around this issue.

From our own resolved state, we can talk about the neurobiological benefits of Staylistening with angry children, and then encourage parents to listen to their bodies for signs of rebellion against what we are suggesting. Because we are calm with the idea, they will feel our support as they explore the roots of their own bodily responses. If we don't address their visceral reactions, the likelihood that parents will be able to draw on these new behaviors under stress is just about zero. However, as our parents are able to tolerate and comfort their children's strong emotions, while setting sensible boundaries, they will find that their children need to send fewer feelings underground, only to resurface another day. Through Playlistening and Staylistening, parents are literally taking the shutters off the family window of tolerance, creating a spacious home for all emotions.

Teaching Mindful Awareness to Parents

Lastly, we help parents develop *mindful awareness*. As we work together, parents often express a strong desire to be able to pause before reacting to what their children have done; they want to have a more flexible, modulated response. Some already have a well-developed reflective capacity and just need to feel secure enough in parenting principles to exercise it. Many others are more entangled with their limbic upset and consequently are out of touch with the prefrontal resources that would slow their reactivity. We offer techniques for ordinary mindfulness and encourage parents to develop awareness of their inner experience by asking themselves questions such as "What am I feeling?" and "What is occurring at this moment?" We can also present the more formal practices of mindfulness, usually beginning with a meditation that focuses on the breath, or share some resourcing techniques for calming the body in stressful circumstances (Ogden et al., 2006). One of our young fathers worked hard to develop these practices in his parenting sessions. He found that talking to himself out loud about what he was doing to ground himself helped enormously by giving words to his experience. Soon, his 8-year-old son, who was in play therapy, was talking to himself during some very upsetting play—"Now, just get your feet on the ground and take a few deep breaths. You'll feel better!" We can't help but smile as these waves of regulation and transformation wash through families.

As we share these resources, we do everything we can to model them through how we sit with our parents, since we know that much will be learned via direct experience. In order to give their bodies a visceral sense of the concepts, we encourage laughter, comfort pain and fear, maintain mindful awareness, and meet anger with an understanding of its deeper roots. As parents have some positive experiences with these new patterns at home, they become self-reinforcing, initiating a lovely spiral of brain-shaping connection. In this way, intergenerational cycles of disruption and misery can be changed permanently.

Back in the Playroom

While parents are learning all this, what's going on in the playroom? The deepening of the relationship between child and therapist brings new opportunities for more emotional upset to surface. As a result, circumstances may arise that require limit setting—a sign that the child trusts the therapist. When overly compliant children begin to push the limits, we take it as a happy sign that they feel safe enough to allow the full range of their emotions to emerge. When limit setting is necessary (if a child is deliberately destructive with toys or wants to hit us), it is best done very minimally, recognizing the feelings presented by the child. The principles of Staylistening apply. It often works well to state the limit clearly and specifically regarding a particular action, then suggest alternate ways that feelings and thoughts can be expressed. "I'm not for hitting, but you may hit that cloth person as much as you want." It is helpful to move a bit closer to the child and gently support this young one in facing how awful the limit feels. Listening involves helping the child have permission to cry or vent all feelings while we stay close, comforting with our listening presence. If the limit continues to be challenged, we can remove the toy for the rest of the session or end the session in the case of aggression toward us. All of this is done without losing our intention to maintain kind connection, to understand the source of the feelings, and to keep the future open for a more connected relationship.

In the playroom there is also ample space for experiences of success and mastery, which lead to an increasingly positive self-image. One of our little children had failed a spelling test at school and came to the session slumped over with disappointment and shame. She chose to devote the whole session that day to playing the keyboard and teaching herself a new song. For the entire 45 minutes that child practiced over and over, until she got it just right. She left the session walking strong, with her head held up and a big smile. Another child was having trouble at school with some much older kids who pushed him in the lunch line. He came into the play session very discouraged because this happened every day, and he couldn't figure out what to do about it. We pulled out the puppets, acting out numerous possibilities with the big kids. After much repetition and playacting, he felt like he could now talk to the kids with more confidence.

To give our children tools for self-regulation, even our youngest ones get some mindfulness training. Drawing on wonderful suggestions from Sumi Loudon (2004), a meditation teacher who specializes in helping children learn mindfulness, our children do fun exercises such as putting a cloth monkey on their tummies and rocking it to sleep with their breathing, and savoring the taste of a raisin for 2 minutes. They also learn to use their breath to slow their minds. One 7-year-old was having trouble with his teacher at school. She seemed to find everything he did to be a problem and criticized him in front of his class daily. After several weeks of this treatment, he started to get angry and could not seem to regulate his emotions. After a few sessions of breathing practice in the playroom, he went to school and was able to breathe through his teacher's comments, not acting out his anger and not just internalizing the bad feelings either. While their son was practicing so successfully, his parents contacted his teacher, but found they could do little to shift her attitude. However, thanks to their new learning about Staylistening, his parents made sure their son had plenty of room to process all his reactions to this tough year at school.

With each visit, the session must draw to a close. Most children get very involved in what they are doing, so we may need to remind them when the session is coming to an end in sufficient time for them to make a satisfying finish. The amount of time needed is different for each child, and even different for the same child over time. During peaks in attachment repair, some children may have great difficulty separating from us, so it will be important to allow enough time to listen to the painful or angry feelings that emerge. After our play specialist told one 6-year-old that she would be gone the next week, he glared at her, told her he didn't want to come to play anymore, and marched out of the playroom. After acknowledging his feelings, she explained to him that she would be back the next week, and would be thinking about him while she was gone. The little one kept glaring and told his mother he didn't want to come anymore. On her return, the two of them rode out this storm together, working through some big anger during the weeks following her absence. By her next vacation, he was able to let his therapist go without upset.

By the time the play is over, children's internal worlds are spread on the floor and in the sand. Just as we wouldn't ask adults to tidy up their words before leaving, we choose not to have children pick up their play world. To avoid conflict with parents, we do let our children know that this rule only applies in the playroom and not in their homes. After taking pictures of sand trays and other scenes, all objects are returned to their accustomed place on the shelf (as much as possible), because these little people do expect that their world will be intact for them on their return. As they go back into their parents' care, they may choose to share their therapy day by bringing Mom or Dad in to see what they have created. This is sometimes a warm way to conclude and also gives us the opportunity to observe the child and parent together. In general, it is helpful to keep conversation with the parents to a minimum when their children are present, so the young ones continue to sense the specialness of their relationship with us. However, we can always be available for parenting sessions or by phone to meet parents' legitimate needs for support.

Attachment-Aware Resources for Families

Play therapy is certainly not the only way to help children and their parents. In fact, in the last few years, quite a few attachment-aware processes for working with families have emerged. All promise excellent help. One wonderful example is the Circle of Security Early Intervention Program for Parents and Children (Cooper, Hoffman, Powell, & Marvin, 2005; Marvin et al., 2002). The assumptions of this program recognize that all change must be grounded in a secure relationship between parents and those providing the help; that a child's life path will be strongly impacted by the attachment relationship with his or her parents; that interventions must rest on a scientific foundation; and that change comes from parents developing their relational capacities, rather than learning specific techniques to modify behavior (*Circle of Security Early Intervention Program for Parents and Children*, 2007). They identify these relational capacities as the ability to *observe* the child based on an understanding of *developmental needs*; the capacity for *reflective functioning* that is then translated into *reflective dialogue*; the ability to engage with the child in a way that *regulates emotion*; and the capacity for *empathy*. Based on the same brain-wise, attachment-savvy roots as the model offered in this chapter, Circle of Security seeks similar outcomes for parents and their children, but through somewhat different processes. When we weave these basic principles into the way each of us does therapy with families, we can help fashion a safety net for future generations—and, step by step, possibly for society as well.

To conclude this chapter on working with children, we would like to share one healing relationship that traces the marvelous process of a child who untangled herself from the inner models created by a traumatic birth. Her family was fully involved at every step, assisting this brave child in walking toward health with speed and grace.

Rachel Rewired

At the beginning of life—as our undifferentiated brains are seeking to form patterns of warmth and goodness through connection—tragic conditions can sometimes set patterns for physical, perceptual, and emotional disturbances that threaten to wreck a young life. We met Rachel when she was 7 years old and suffering every day with debilitating symptoms. Her lovely family—comprised of Mom, Dad, older sister, and two younger brothers—was becoming chaotic, partly from fear, partly from hopelessness, partly from exhaustion. Her mom, Sarah, had left no stone unturned in finding help, but because those she talked with saw only a loving family, she had been advised that Rachel would simply grow out of her difficulties. It seems that none of the people she consulted could get a hold on what was making Rachel so vulnerable to upset, because they couldn't even imagine what questions to ask. So far, Sarah had found no one with neural nets that could guide them in picturing what might be happening in this child's brain–mind–body. This is not a criticism. We all have these neural blind spots when we haven't been exposed to particular ways of thinking. However, it was increasingly discouraging for Sarah because she could see her daughter's symptoms gradually worsening in what appeared to be a self-reinforcing cycle.

At this juncture, Sarah met with Cindy, our child development specialist, in a last-ditch effort to find someone who could make sense of Rachel's story. She told Cindy that since very early in life, Rachel had experienced night terrors, often several times a night. She woke up screaming with signs of profound fear, but no recall of a nightmare. The sound of flying insects sent her into a panic. She "saw" swarms of colored specks that scared her. During many meals, she choked, making it difficult for her to eat. Most puzzling, she became terrified when her name was spoken by anyone not in her line of sight. She would also sometimes panic when she had to separate from her mom. Between bouts of fear, Rachel's life was pleasant—she was a playful, happy, creative, and very bright child with no sign of severe emotional disturbance.

Based on our understanding of how brain structure develops, we always begin with the belief that a person's symptoms make sense, and that they are an adaptation to something real. Because brain structure is most impacted early in life, Cindy asked for a detailed narrative of Rachel's beginnings. Sarah shared that when Rachel was born, the baby was gravely ill, and her doctors didn't believe that she would survive. She was placed in neonatal ICU, on a ventilator, with her eyes blindfolded, engulfed in the staff's sense of emergency for about 2 weeks, as she hovered between life and death. Sarah spent most of the 2 weeks in the hospital chapel, praying for Rachel's survival and developing a profound love for this child. Although it was almost 3 months before they could take their little one home, after the initial 2 weeks, Mom and Dad were at least able to spend some time with her.

How can we picture what happened in Rachel's brain at this most vulnerable time? Like every other child, her attachment system came into full bloom as soon as she emerged into the world, seeking closeness and safe haven. What met her? The noise of machines and anxious voices instead of calm reassurance. Invasion of her body, instead of a sense of safety. Blindfolded eyes, cutting off one of the main channels of attachment. Many people coming and going with a sense of urgency, instead of the two predictable caregivers she was "expecting." At birth, the limbic and cortical areas of our brains are largely undifferentiated, awaiting our initial experiences to begin to connect neurons and form patterns of expectation about the world. So with these as the initial firings and wirings, mostly in the right-hemisphere limbic areas, Rachel's brain encoded profound and terrifying loss. When someone is traumatized, we also know that the neural circuits containing that experience are often prevented from integrating with the rest of the brain, so they lie in wait like a time bomb, only to be triggered by reminders in the external world at a later date. This is particularly true with early trauma because the brain is working on differentiating many of its systems in isolation from each other, to be linked with other systems later. This means that all of Rachel's disastrous experiences were encoded in implicit memory, the only kind available to an infant. When implicit neural nets are activated, the information they contain is experienced as being caused by something in the present. All of these factors combined to make Rachel so vulnerable to terror when these neural nets were activated.

Armed with this knowledge, Cindy immediately began to form a working hypothesis about Rachel's symptoms, in the form of picturing what was patterned in her brain during these traumatic events. This allowed her to begin to hold Rachel's mind in her own. Perhaps sleep plunged her into the initial nameless terror as she moved from conscious awareness into the deeper structures of her brain. Could bugs remind her of the sound of the machines that kept her alive? Would the pressure on her eyes as she was blindfolded cause these flecks of light? When she would choke, was she feeling the ventilator tube in her throat? The most perplexing symptom was the terror she would feel when her name was spoken by someone she couldn't see, but Cindy began to wonder if she might have heard her name spoken many times by disconnected voices in the NICU as she lay blindfolded, wiring this experience in with her initial terror. It was highly plausible that her panic when separating from her mom came from the initial broken attachment, when she was without her parents at this most crucial time.

As we may remember, Hebb's axiom says that whatever fires together wires together (and now we can add, survives together), so Rachel's initial experiences were like a tangled ball of string, and stimulating one part of the neural net had some probability of drawing in the rest. Consequently, whenever Rachel's sensory cortex passed a signal to her limbic areas that resembled her hospital experience—a bug flying near her ear, her name spoken by someone out of her line of sight—it could generate a resonance with the whole of her hospital experience, catapulting her into a swirl of disorienting and disorganizing symptoms as the wired-together neural circuits of the trauma were activated. Because of the disconnection from other parts of the brain, through both the trauma and her brain's immaturity in infancy, Rachel would be trapped there for a while with a set of terrifying feelings she couldn't understand.

By picturing Rachel's developing brain in this way, Cindy was already beginning to hold Rachel's mind in her own mind, creating the matrix in which play therapy could unfold along the empathic super highway of two interwoven minds. Through resonance circuits, Rachel could begin to sense Cindy's intention to be with her in this frightening world, as well as the warmth of her empathy. Cindy, in turn, could continue to deepen her connection to Rachel's earlier experience in the same fashion. In this way, we can picture the two of them spiraling ever deeper into the heart of the original wound.

On the foundation of this joining, from her first day in the playroom, Rachel used the sand tray to play out scenes of children being lost without help. Repeatedly, Parrot was caught under the webbing of an overturned container, perhaps reminiscent of her incubator prison. After watching this pattern for many sessions and sensing that Rachel was having difficulty imagining a way out, Cindy began to encourage Rachel to find helpers for Parrot. Interestingly enough, it was mostly birds who came to rescue Parrot—creatures free to fly, perhaps the antithesis of her earliest experience. After much practice, one day, the helpers were able to do more than listen to Parrot in her trap, releasing her at last from her prison.

It seemed clear that, catalyzed by her relationship with Cindy and coupled with her own hard rescue work, Rachel's mind began to make the natural move toward integration as the neural networks formed by the trauma were modified by the new energy and information of help, safety, and comfort. Research suggests that GABA-bearing fibers—literally fibers of comfort—were growing from the orbitofrontal cortex into the terror-filled amygdala. This kind of vertical integration began to bring the neural network containing the representations of the trauma into the embrace of interpersonal care. This work was bearing fruit rapidly as Rachel's night terrors began to subside. Over almost a year, as Cindy and Rachel played out scenes of rescue, the rest of her symptoms began to slowly decrease as well.

Cindy was also helping Rachel learn to pay attention to her breathing when her symptoms would overtake her. Watching her breath come and go helped her move toward the calm space in her mind where she could see her fears rather than be swallowed by them. At 7, she was proving to be very capable of getting into a caring observer state of mind, at least part of the time. In this way, Rachel was gradually being able to manage her often overwhelming feelings.

At this point, Cindy sensed something else was needed, some dimension of horizontal integration of the original trauma. Rachel had no story, no coherent narrative, to go with her feelings. Sarah had taken pictures of her time in NICU, but had never shown these scary images to her daughter. After much careful discussion, Cindy and Sarah decided to share the pictures with Rachel and talk together about her birth. The science tells us that one of the most powerful ways our brains integrate isolated neural networks is when we work to generate coherent stories about our lives. This makes sense, given that putting words to feelings calms the amygdala. So Cindy and Sarah sat together with an alert Rachel, surrounding her with care, and shared the pictures while her mom told her the story of those first 3 months. They were careful to not overwhelm her and respected her pace. But she was ready and very attentive while she took in the whole story in one sitting. Afterward she was very calm and with a smile simply said, "Oh!" Then she bounced off the couch to go play with her close friends, the stuffed animals in Cindy's playroom.

This narrative experience was close to the final step in her healing. She continued to play out scenes that now always included help, and Cindy continued to teach her how to breathe through her fear. In her daily life, she became the outgoing, talented child she was always meant to be. The night terrors were a thing of the past, and she had a new story to tell herself about the bugs when they scared her. The specks mostly went away except when she was frightened for good reason, and then she knew why they were there, so they didn't upset her. She was now able to eat and soon achieved a normal weight, because when she would feel her throat begin to constrict, she would breathe herself into relaxation and say to herself, "That's just from the ventilator." Best of all, she was able to be away from her mom at night, and so could go on sleepovers for the first time.

We still hear from this family, almost all of whom have been in therapy with us over the years to work through their own portion of the family trauma. At this point, the family is resilient, taking new stressors in stride and exhibiting the humor and joy that are hallmarks of well-grounded mental health.

Being a Brain-Wise Therapist

Summing Up

Rachel's story is a heartening place to end this journey. When we are able to help young, malleable minds mend their torn attachments, we know that solid ground has been put beneath their feet. Their lives have the possibility of unfolding in fulfilling ways. Rachel's children will no doubt have a good chance of being securely attached. The part of this family's story we didn't share includes the years Rachel's mom spent in therapy, dealing with the pain of ongoing rejection she'd suffered as a child. She volunteered for this journey so that her children would not be wounded in the same way. If we foster enough repair with people of all ages (beginning with ourselves), the firm foundation for personal well-being and compassionate relationships will be wider in the next generation, so that society can begin to be shaped by greater integration rather than increasing fragmentation. In this way, the current pattern of insecure attachments outpacing secure ones can be reversed. An ounce of prevention will indeed be worth a pound—or possibly a ton—of cure.

Our scientifically grounded awareness of the brain's processes, the mind's capacity to change the brain, and the power of empathic relationships can make us ambassadors of neuroplasticity, beating the drum of hope for real change. This kind of thinking may sound grandiose. How can we imagine that our very small efforts will steer the currents of societal rigidity and chaos into the path of coherence? Everyone from the editors of *Time* magazine to 30,000 neuroscientists in Washington, DC to preschool teachers with their mindful 3-year-olds are picking up the rhythm. Articles are appearing about how public policy must take the science into account—everything from the criminal justice system to how we treat our soldiers returning from war. This is a time when our society's reliance on the objective findings of science is an ally of positive change.

On a smaller scale, my patients share the hand model with their friends, starting conversations that ripple outward in unexpected ways. A young man called to say he knew his life was screwed up from having two alcoholic parents, but had no idea anything could really change for him—until his classmate talked about the way her brain was rewiring in therapy. He explained in detail how she showed him her runaway limbic circuits (pointing to her thumb), telling him that they had been ruining her relationships, and going on to say that now that her prefrontal area was getting connected (wrapping her fingers around her thumb), she wasn't so angry anymore. He told me he had thought about counseling before but couldn't quite get a focus on how it could work for him. Once the science helped him create the imagination of real, tangible change in his brain, he made the call. Shortly after that, his professor e-mailed to ask if someone could speak to his sociology class about the brain. I get giddy when I feel hearts and minds perk up at glimpses of the underpinnings of mental health and joyous life.

Our responsibility in all this—both as clinicians and human beings—is to keep feeding our own wellsprings of hope and wisdom. What do we have to lose? The more we are attentive to our inner worlds, building empathic communities inside and integrating neural circuits that have never been on speaking terms, the more joyous and harmonious our lives will become. Then, as we see faces light up in the embrace of our empathy, in therapy and daily life, we can know that our small contribution to goodness is gaining the strength of a thousand voices.

References

Abercrombie, H. C., Schaefer, S. M., Larson, C. L., Oakes, T. R., Lindgren, K. A., Holden, J. E., et al. (1998). Metabolic rate in the right amygdala predicts negative affect in depressed patients. *Neuroreport, 9,* 3301–3307.

Ainsworth, M. D. S., Blchar, J. C., Waters, E., & Wall, S. (1978). *Patterns of attachment: A psychological study of the strange situation.* Hillsdale, NJ: Erlbaum.

Allen, G., Buxton, R. B., Wong, E. C., & Courchesne, E. (1997). Attentional activation of the cerebellum independent of motor involvement. *Science, 275,* 1940–1943.

American Psychiatric Association. (2000). *Diagnostic and statistical manual of mental disorders* (4th ed., text rev.). Washington, DC: Author.

Armory, J. L., Corbo, V., Clement, M. H., & Brunet, A. (2005). Amygdala response in patients with acute PTSD to masked and unmasked emotional facial expressions. *American Journal of Psychiatry, 162,* 1960–1963.

Armour, J. A., & Ardell, J. L. (2004). *Basic and clinical neurocardiology.* Cambridge, UK: Oxford University Press.

Badenoch, B. (1991a, April). *Demythologyzing MPD: A continuum approach to treatment.* Paper presented at a meeting of the International Society for the Study of Multiple Personalities and Dissociation, San Francisco, CA.

Badenoch, B. (1991b, November). *A developmental perspective on the client–therapist relationship in the treatment of MPD.* Paper presented at the 8th international conference of the International Society for the Study of Multiple Personality and Dissociation, Chicago, IL.

Baer, R. A., Smith, G. T., Hopkins, J., Krietemeyer, J., & Toney, L. (2006). Using self-report assessment methods to explore facets of mindfulness. *Assessment, 13*(1), 27–45.

Baird A. A., Gruber, S. A., Fein, D. A., Steingard, R. J., Renshaw, P. F. & Yurgelun-Todd, D. A. (1999). Functional magnetic resonance imaging of facial affect recognition in children. *Journal of the American Academy of Child and Adolescent Psychiatry, 38*(2), 195–199.

Bardo, M. T., Bowling, S. L., Robinet, P. M., Rowlett, J. K., Lacy, M., & Mattingly, B. A. (1993). Role of dopamine D1 and D2 receptors in novelty-maintained place preference. *Experimental and Clinical Psychopharmacology, 1*(1–4), 101–109.

Bartzokis, G. (2005). Brain myelination in prevalent neuropsychiatric developmental disorders: Primary and comorbid addiction. *Adolescent Psychiatry, 29,* 55–96.

Bateman, A., & Fonagy, P. (2001). Treatment of borderline personality disorder with psychoanalytically oriented partial hospitalization: An 18-month follow-up. *American Journal of Psychiatry, 156*(10), 1563–1569.

Begley, S. (2007). *Train your mind, change your brain: How a new science reveals our extraordinary potential to transform ourselves.* New York: Ballantine.

Benes, F. M. (1989). Myelination of cortical–hippocampal relays during late adolescence: Anatomical correlates to the onset of schizophrenia. *Schizophrenia Bulletin, 15,* 585–594.

Benes, F. M., Turtle, M., Yusuf, K., & Farol, P. (1994). Myelination of a key relay zone in the hippocampal formation occurs in the human brain during childhood, adolescence and adulthood. *Archives of General Psychiatry, 51*(6), 477–484.

Bowen, M. (1994). *Family therapy in clinical practice.* New York: Jason Aronson.

Bowlby, J. (1983). *Attachment.* New York: Basic Books. (Original work published 1969).

Bowlby, J. (1991). *Loss: Sadness and depression.* New York: Penguin. (Original work published 1980).

Bowlby, J. (2000). *Separation: Anxiety and anger.* New York: Basic Books. (Original work published 1973).

Bowlby, J. (2005). *A secure base: Parent–child attachment and healthy human development.* London: Routledge. (Original work published 1988).

Brach, T. (2007, October). *Mindfulness and psychotherapy.* Paper presented at Lifespan Learning Institute, UCLA, Los Angeles, CA.

Bradway, K., Signell, K., Spare, G., Stewart, C., Stewart, L., & Thompson, C. (1990). *Sandplay studies: Origins, theories and practice.* Boston: Sigo Press.

Bremner, J. D., Narayan, M., Anderson, E. R., Staib, L. H., Miller, H. L., & Charney, D. S. (2000). Hippocampal volume reduction in major depression. *American Journal of Psychiatry, 157*(1), 115–118.

Bremner, J. D., Randall, R., Scott, T., Bronen, R., Seibyl, J., Southwick, S., et al. (1995). MRI-based measurement of hippocampal volume in patients with combat-related posttraumatic stress disorder. *American Journal of Psychiatry, 152,* 973–981.

Bremner, J. D., Randall, P., Vermetten, E., Staib, L., Bronen, R., Mazure, C., et al. (1997). Magnetic resonance imaging-based measurement of hippocampal volume in posttraumatic stress disorder related to childhood physical and sexual abuse: A preliminary report. *Biological Psychiatry, 41,* 23–32.

Bremner, J. D., Vythilingam, M., Vermetten, E., Nazeer, A., Adil, J., Khan, S., et al. (2002). Reduced volume of orbitofrontal cortex in major depression. *Biological Psychiatry, 51,* 273–279.

Bugental, J. F. T. (1992). *The art of the psychotherapist.* New York: Norton.

Carlson, V., Cicchetti, D., Barnett, D., & Braunwald, K. (1989). Finding order in disorganization: Lessons from research on maltreated infants' attachments to their caregivers. In D. Cicchetti & V. Carlson (Eds.), *Child maltreatment: Theory and research* on *the causes and consequences of child abuse and neglect* (pp. 494–528). New York: Cambridge University Press.

Carr, L., Iacoboni, M., Dubeau, M., Mazzlotta, J., & Lenzi, G. (2003). Neural mechanisms of empathy in humans: A relay from neural systems for imitation to limbic areas. *Proceedings of the National Academy of Sciences of the United States of America, 100,* 5497–5502.

Caspi, A., Sugden, K., Moffitt, T. E., Taylor, A., Craig, I. W., Harrington, H., et al. (2003). Influence of life stress on depression: Moderation by a polymorphism in the 5-HTT gene. *Science, 301,* 386–389.

Chambers, R. A., Bremner, J. D., Moghaddam, B., Southwick, S. M., Charney, D. S., & Krystal, J. H. (1999). Glutamate and post-traumatic stress disorder: Toward a psychobiology of dissociation. *Seminars in Clinical Neuropsychiatry, 4,* 274–281.

Chang, A., Hawley, H. B., Kalumuck, K. E., Katz, L. M., Piotrowski, N. A., & Rizzo, C. (Eds.). (2004). *Magill's medical guide (3rd ed.).* Pasadena, CA: Salem Press.

Cicchetti, D., & Rogosch, F. A. (Eds.). (1997). Self-organization [Special issue]. *Development and Psychopathology, 9*(1).

Circle of Security early intervention program for parents and children. (2007). Retrieved August 8, 2007, from *http://www.circleofsecurity.org/treatmentassumptions.html.*

Cooper, G., Hoffman, K., Powell, B., & Marvin, R. (2005). The Circle of Security intervention: Differential diagnosis and differential treatment. In L. Berlin, Y. Ziv, & M. Greenberg (Eds.), *Enhancing early attachments* (127–151). New York: Guilford Press.

Courchesne, E., & Allen, G. (1997). Prediction and preparation: Fundamental functions of the cerebellum. *Learning and Memory, 4,* 1–35.

Cozolino, L. (2006). *The neuroscience of human relationships: Attachment and the developing brain.* New York: Norton.

Craig, A. D. (2002). How do you feel? Interoception: The sense of the physiological condition of the body. *Nature Neuroscience, 3,* 655–666.

Creswell, D. J., Way, B. M., Eisenberger, N. I., & Lieberman, M. D. (2007). Neural correlates of dispositional mindfulness during affect labeling. *Psychosomatic Medicine, 69,* 560–565.

Damasio, A. (1994). *Descartes' error: Emotion, reason, and the human brain.* New York: Penguin.

Damasio, A. (1999). *The feeling of what happens: Body and emotion in the making of consciousness.* New York: Harcourt Brace.

Davidson, R. J., Jackson, D. C., & Kalin, N. H. (2000). Emotion, plasticity, context, and regulation: Perspectives from affective neuroscience. *Psychological Bulletin, 126,* 890–909.

Davidson, R. J., Kabat-Zinn, J., Schumacher, J., Rosenkranz, M., Muller, D., Santorelli, S. F., et al. (2003). Alterations in brain and immune function produced by mindfulness meditation. *Psychosomatic Medicine, 65*(4), 564–570.

Demos, V. (1991). Resiliency in infancy. In T. F. Dugan & R. Coles (Eds.), *The child in our times: Studies in the development of resiliency* (pp. 3–17). New York: Brunner/ Mazel.

Dennett, D. C. (1993). *Consciousness explained.* New York: Penguin.

Diamond, A., & Hopson, J. (1998). *Magic trees of the mind*. New York: Dutton.

Dobbs, D. (2006, April/May). Human see, human do. *Scientific American Mind*, 22–27.

Dowling, A. L. S., Martz, G. U., Leonard, J. L., & Zoeller, R. T. (2000). Acute changes in maternal thyroid hormone induce rapid and transient changes in gene expression in fetal rat. *Journal of Neuroscience, 20*, 2255–2265.

Drevets, W. C. (1999). Prefrontal cortical–amygdalar metabolism in major depression. *Annals of the New York Academy of Sciences, 877*, 614–637.

Drevets, W. C. (2003). Neuroimaging abnormalities in the amygdala in mood disorders. *Annals of New York Academy of Sciences, 985*, 420–444.

Drevets, W. C., Price, J. L., Simpson, J. R., Jr., Todd, R. D., Reich, T., Vannier, M., et al. (1997). Subgenual prefrontal cortex abnormalities in mood disorders. *Nature, 386*, 824–827.

Einstein, A. E. (1957). Retrieved May 6, 2007, from *http://www.spaceandmotion.com/ Albert-Einstein-Quotes.htm.*

Eisenberger, N. I., Lieberman, M. D., & Williams, K. D. (2003). Does rejection hurt? An fMRI study of social exclusion. *Science, 10*, 302, 290–292.

Erikson, E. (1989). *Insight and responsibility*. New York: Norton.

Farb, N. A. S., Segal, Z. V., Mayberg, H., Bean, J., McKeon, D., & Fatima, Z. (2007). Attending to the present: Mindfulness meditation reveals distinct neural modes of self-reference. *Social Cognitive and Affective Neuroscience, 2*, 313–322.

ffrench-Constant, C., Colognato, H., & Franklin, R. J. (2004). The mysteries of myelin unwrapped. *Science, 238*, 688–689.

Field, T. (1994). The effects of Mother's physical and emotional unavailability on emotion regulation. *Monographs of the Society for Research in Child Development, 59*(2–3), 208–217.

Field, T. (2001). Withdrawn and intrusive depressed mothers. *Developmental Psychologist*, 1–6.

Field, T., Diego, M., & Hernandez-Reif, M. (2006). Prenatal depression effects on the fetus and newborn: A review. *Infant Behavior and Development, 29*(3), 445–455.

Field, T., Diego, M., Hernandez-Reif, M., Schanberg, S., & Kuhn C. (2004). Massage therapy effects on depressed pregnant women. *Journal of Psychosomatic Obstetrics and Gynecology, 25*(2), 115–122.

Field, T., Healy, B., Goldstein, S., Perry, S., Bendell, D., Schanberg, S., et al. (1988). Infants of depressed mothers show "depressed" behavior even with nondepressed adults. *Child Development, 59*(6), 1569–1579.

Field, T., Hernandez-Reif, M., Hart, S., Theakston, H., Schanberg, S., Kuhn, C., et al. (1999). Pregnant women benefit from massage therapy. *Journal of Psychosomatic Obstetrics and Gynecology, 19*, 31–38.

Fields, R. D. (2006). Beyond the neuron doctrine. *Scientific American Mind*, 21–27.

Fischer, H., Andersson, J. L. R., Furmark, T., & Fredrickson, M. (1998). Brain correlates of an unexpected panic attack: A human positron emission tomographic study. *Neuroscience Letters, 251*(2), 137–140.

Forrest, K. A. (2001). Toward an etiology of dissociative identity disorder: A neurodevelopmental approach. *Consciousness and Cognition, 10*, 259–293.

Franklin, T. R., Acton, P. D., Maldjian, J. A., Gray, J. D., Croft, J. R., Dackis, C. A., et al. (2002). Decreased gray matter concentration in the insular, orbitofrontal, cingulate, and temporal cortices of cocaine patients. *Biological Psychiatry, 51*(2), 134–142.

Frewen, P. A., & Lanius, R. A. (2006a). Alexithymia and PTSD: Psychometric and fMRI studies. *Annals of the New York Academy of Sciences, 1071,* 110–124.

Frewen, P. A., & Lanius, R. A. (2006b). Toward a psychobiology of posttraumatic self-dysregulation: Reexperiencing, hyperarousal, dissociation, and emotional numbing. *Annals of the New York Academy of Sciences, 1071,* 110–124.

Frodl, T., Meisenzahl, E., Zetzsche, T., Bottlender, R., Born, C., Groll, C., et al. (2002). Enlargement of the amygdala in patients with a first episode of major depression. *Biological Psychology, 51*(9), 708–714.

Fuster, J. M. (1997). *The prefrontal cortex: Anatomy, physiology, and neuropsychology of the frontal lobe (3rd ed.).* Philadelphia: Lippincott-Raven.

Giedd, J. N., Blumenthal J., Jeffries, N. O., Castellanos, F. X., Liu, H., Zijdenbos, A., et al (1999). Brain development during childhood and adolescence: A longitudinal MRI study. *Nature Neuroscience, 2*(10), 861–863.

Glassman, A. H., & Shapiro, P. A. (1998). Depression and the course of coronary artery disease. *American Journal of Psychiatry, 155,* 4–111.

Goleman, D. (2006). *Social intelligence: The new science of human relationships.* New York: Bantam.

Goodman, M., Mitropoulou, V., New, A. S., Sprung, L., & Siever, L. J. (2000). Pathological dissociation in borderline personality disorder: The role of childhood trauma and serotonergic genes. *Biological Psychiatry, 17,* 138–134S.

Gould, E., McEwen, B. S., Tanapat, P., Galea, L. A., & Fuchs, E. (1997). Neurogenesis in the dentate gyrus of the adult tree shrew is regulated by psychosocial stress and NMDA receptor activation. *Journal of Neuroscience, 17*(7), 2492–2498.

Gurvits, T., Shenton, M., Hokama, H., Ohta, H., Lasko, N., Gilbertson, M., et al. (1996). Magnetic resonance imaging study of hippocampal volume in chronic, combat-related posttraumatic stress disorder. *Biological Psychiatry, 40,* 1091–1099.

Gusnard, D. A., Akbudak, E., Shulman, G. L, & Raichle, M. E. (2001). Medial prefrontal cortex and self referential mental activity: Relation to a default mode of brain function. *Proceedings of the National Academy of Sciences, 98*(2), 676–682.

Hariri, A. R., Bookheimer, S. Y., & Maziotta, J. C. (2000). Modulating emotional responses: Effects of a neocortical network on the limbic system. *Neuroreport, 11*(1), 43–48.

Hawkins, J., & Blakeslee, S. (2004). *On intelligence: How a new understanding of the brain will lead to the creation of truly intelligent machines.* New York: Times Books.

Hazlett, E. A., Speiser, L. J., Goodman, M., Roy, M., Carrizal, M., Wynn, J. K., et al. (2006). Exaggerated affect-modulated startle during unpleasant stimuli in borderline personality disorder. *Biological Psychiatry, 62*(3), 250–255.

Hebb, D. O. (1949). *The organization of behavior: A neuropsychological theory.* New York: Wiley.

Henriques, J. B., & Davidson, R. J. (1990). Regional brain electrical asymmetries discriminate between previously depressed and healthy control subjects. *Journal of Abnormal Psychology, 99,* 22–31.

Herman, J., Perry, J., & van der Kolk, B. A. (1989). Childhood trauma in borderline personality disorder. *American Journal of Psychiatry, 146*, 490–495.

Hernandez-Reif, M., Field, T., Diego, M., & Ruddock, M. (2006). Greater arousal and less attentiveness to face/voice stimuli by neonates of depressed mothers on the Brazelton Neonatal Behavioral Assessment Scale. *Infant Behavior and Development, 29*(4), 594–598.

Herpetz, S., Dietrich, T. M., Wenning, B., Krings, T., Erberich, S. G., Wilmes, K., et al. (2001). Evidence of abnormal amygdala functioning in borderline personality disorder: A functional MRI study. *Biological Psychiatry, 50*, 292–298.

Hesse, E. (1996). Discourse, memory and the Adult Attachment Interview: A note with emphasis on the emerging cannot classify category. *Infant Mental Health Journal, 17*, 4–11.

Hesse, E. (1999). The Adult Attachment Interview: Historical and current perspectives. In J. Cassidy & P. R. Shaver (Eds.), *Handbook of attachment* (pp. 395–433). New York: Guilford Press.

Hesse, E., & Main, M. (1999). Unresolved/disorganized responses to trauma in nonmaltreating parents: Previously unexamined risk factor for offspring. *Psychoanalytic Inquiry, 19*, 4–11.

Hilyard, K. L., & Wolfe, D. A. (2002). Child neglect: Developmental issues and outcomes. *Child Abuse and Neglect, 26*, 679–695.

Hilgard, E. R. (1977). *Divided consciousness: Multiple controls in human thought and action.* New York: Wiley.

Hoefgen, B., Schulze, T. G., Ohlraun, S., von Widdern, O., Hofels, S., Gross, M., et al. (2005). The power of sample size and homogenous sampling: Association between the 5-HTTLPR serotonin transporter polymorphism and major depressive disorder. *Biological Psychiatry, 57*, 247–251.

Huttenlocher, P. R. (2002). *Neural plasticity: The effects of environment on the development of the cerebral cortex.* Cambridge, MA: Harvard University Press.

Hutterer, J., & Liss, M. (2006). Cognitive development, memory, trauma, treatment: An integration of psychoanalytic and behavioral concepts in light of current neuroscience research. *Journal of the American Academy of Psychoanalysis and Dynamic Psychiatry, 34*, 287–302.

Iacoboni, M. (2007). Face to face: The neural basis of social mirroring and empathy. *Psychiatric Annals, 374*, 236–241.

Janet, P. (1889). *L'automatisme psychlogique [Psychological automatisms].* Paris: Felix Alcan.

Johnstone, T., van Reekum, C. J., Urry, H. L., Kalin, N. H., & Davidson, R. J. (2007). Failure to regulate: Counterproductive recruitment of top-down prefrontal–subcortical circuitry in major depression. *Journal of Neuroscience, 27*(33), 8877–8884.

Kabat-Zinn, J. (1990). *Full catastrophe living: Using the wisdom of your body and mind to face stress, pain, and illness.* New York: Dell.

Kabat-Zinn, J. (2003). *Coming to our senses: Healing ourselves and the world through mindfulness.* New York: Hyperion Press.

Kabat-Zinn, J. (2005). *Wherever you go, there you are: Mindfulness meditation in everyday life.* New York: Hyperion.

Kagan, J. (1994). *Galen's prophecy: Temperament in human nature.* Boulder, CO: Westview Press.

Kalff, D. (1980). *Sandplay.* Boston: Sigo.

Kalsched, D. (1996). *The inner world of trauma: Archetypal defenses of the personal spirit.* New York: Routledge.

Kaufman, J., Yang, B., Douglas-Palumberi, H., Grasso, D., Lipschitz, D., Houshyar, S., et al. (2006). Brain-derived neurotrophic factor: 5HTTLPR gene interactions and environmental modifiers of depression in children. *Biological Psychiatry, 59*(8), 673–680.

Kelley, A. E., & Berridge, K. C. (2002). The neuroscience of natural rewards: Relevance to addictive drugs. *Journal of Neuroscience, 22,* 3306–3311.

Kendler, K. S., Kuhn, J. W., Vittum, J., Prescott, C. A., & Riley, B. (2005). The interaction of stressful life events and a serotonin transporter polymorphism in the prediction of episodes of major depression: A replication. *Archives of General Psychiatry, 62,* 529–535.

Kessler, R. C. (2006). *National Comorbidity Survey: Baseline (NCS-1).* Retrieved August 20, 2007, from *http://webapp.icpsr.umich.edu/cgi-bin/bob/newark?study=6693&path= ICPSR.*

Kisilevsky, B., Hains, S. M. J., Lee, K., Xie, X., Huang, H., Ye, H. H., et al. (2003). Effects of experience on fetal voice recognition. *Psychological Science, 14,* 220–224.

Kohut, H. (1976). *The restoration of the self.* London: International Universities Press.

Kohut, H. (1982). Introspection, empathy, and the semi-circle of mental health. *International Journal of Psychoanalysis, 63,* 395–407.

Koob, G. F., & LeMoal, M. (2006). *Neurobiology of addiction.* London: Academic Press.

Kornfield, J. (2007a, June). *The wise heart and the mindful brain.* Paper presented at R. Cassidy Seminars, San Francisco, CA.

Kornfield, J. (2007b, October). *Mindfulness and psychotherapy.* Paper presented at Lifespan Learning Institute UCLA, Los Angeles, CA.

Kurtz, R. (1997). *Body-centered psychotherapy: The Hakomi Method: The integrated use of mindfulness, nonviolence and the body.* Mendocino, CA: LifeRhythm.

Landreth, G. (1991). *Play therapy: The art of the relationship.* PA: Accelerated Development.

Lanius, R. A., Williamson, P. C., Bluhm, R. L., Densmore, M., Boksman, K., Neufeld, R. W. J., et al. (2005). Functional connectivity of dissociative responses in post-traumatic stress disorder: A functional magnetic resonance imaging investigation. *Biological Psychology, 57*(8), 873–884.

Lanius, R. A., Williamson, P. C., Boksman, K., Densmore, M., Gupta, M., Neufeld,R.W. J., et al. (2002). Brain activation during script-driven imagery induced dissociative responses in PTSD: A functional magnetic resonance imaging investigation. *Biological Psychology, 52*(4), 305–311.

Lanius, R. A., Williamson, P. C., Densmore, M., Boksman, K., Neufeld, R. W., Gati, J. S., et al. (2005). The nature of traumatic memories: A 4-T fMRI functional connectivity analysis. *American Journal of Psychiatry, 161,* 36–44.

Lazar, S. W. (2007, October). *Mindfulness and psychotherapy.* Paper presented at Lifespan Learning Institute UCLA, Los Angeles, CA.

Lazar, S. W., Kerr, C. E., Wasserman, R. H., Gray, J. R., Greve, D. N., Treadway, M. T., et al. (2005). Meditation experience is associated with increased cortical thickness. *Neuroreport, 16*(17), 1893–1897.

LeDoux, J. E. (1994). Emotion, memory and the brain. *Scientific American, 270*(6), 50–57.

Lee, V., & Hoaken, P. N. S. (2007). Cognition, emotion, and neurobiological development: Mediating the relation between maltreatment and aggression. *Child Maltreatment, 12*(3), 281–298.

Lesch, K., Bengal, D., Heils, A., Sabol, S. A., Greenberg, B. D., Petri, S., et al. (1996). Association of anxiety-related traits with polymorphism in the serotonin transporter gene regulatory region. *Science, 274*, 1527–1531.

Levine, P. (1997). *Waking the tiger: Healing trauma.* Berkeley, CA: North Atlantic Books.

Levine, P. (2005). *Healing trauma: A pioneering program for restoring the wisdom of your body.* Boulder, CO: Sounds True.

Linehan, M. M. (1993). *Cognitive–behavioral treatment of borderline personality disorder.* New York: Guilford Press.

London, S. (2004). Teaching meditation to children and beginners. *Insight Journal, 22*, 24–29.

Lowen, A. (1994). *Bioenergetics.* New York: Penguin.

Lowenfeld, M. (1979). *The world technique.* London: Allen & Unwin.

Main, M. (1996). Introduction to the special section on attachment and psychopathology: 2. Overview of the field of attchment. *Journal of Consulting and Clinical Psychology, 64*, 237–243.

Main, M. (2000). The Adult Attachment Interview: Fear, attention, safety, and discourse processes. *Journal of the American Psychoanalytic Association, 48*, 1055–1096.

Main, M., & Hesse, E. (1999). Second-generation effects of unresolved trauma in non-maltreating parents: Dissociated, frightened, and threatening parental behavior. *Psychoanalytic Inquiry, 19*, 481–540.

Main, M., & Solomon, J. (1986). Discovery of an insecure-disorganized/disoriented attachment pattern. In T. B. Brazelton & M. Yogaman (Eds.), *Affective development in infancy* (pp. 95–124). Norwood, NJ: Ablex.

Main, M., & Solomon, J. (1990). Procedures for identifying infants as disorganized/disoriented during the Ainsworth Strange Situation. In M. T. Greenberg, D. Cicchetti, & E. M. Cummings (Eds.), *Attachment in the preschool years: Theory, research, and intervention* (pp. 121–160). Chicago: University of Chicago Press.

Mann, J. J., Malone, K. M., Diehl, D. J., Perel, J., Cooper, T. B., & Mintun, J. A. (1996). Demonstration in vivo of reduced serotonin responsivity in the brain of untreated depressed patients. *American Journal of Psychiatry, 153*(2), 174–182.

Marvin, R., Cooper, G., Hoffman, K., & Powell, B. (2002). The Circle of Security project: Attachment-based intervention with caregiver–pre-school child dyads. *Attachment and Human Development (4)*1, 107–124.

Mayberg, H. S., Branna, S. K., Mahurin, R. K., Jerabek, P. A., Brickman, J. S., Tekell, J. L., et al. (1997). Cingulate function in depression: A potential predictor of treatment response. *Neuroreport, 8*, 1057–1061.

McCauley, K. T. (2003). *Is addiction really a "disease"?* Retrieved August 1, 2006, from *http://addictiondoctor.com.*

Milham, M. P., Nugent, A. C., Drevets, W. C., Dickstein, D. P., Leibenluft, E., Ernst, M., et al. (2005). Selective reduction in amygdala volume in pediatric anxiety disorders: A voxel-based morphometry investigation. *Biological Psychiatry, 57*, 961–966.

Morris, J. S., Ohman, A., & Dolan, R. J. (1999). A subcortical pathway to the right amygdala mediating "unseen" fear. *Proceedings of the National Academy of Science, USA, 96*, 1680–1685.

Murata A., Fadiga L., Fogassi L., Gallese V., Raos V., & Rizzolatti G. (1997). Object representation in the ventral premotor cortex (area F5) of the monkey. *Journal of Neurophysiology, 78*, 2226–2230.

Nemeroff, C. B. (1998). The neurobiology of depression. *Scientific American, 278*(6), 42–49.

Neufeld, G., & Mate, G. (2006). *Hold on to your kids.* New York: Ballantine.

——. (2002, April 15). *Neural stem cells can develop into functional neurons.* Retrieved May 6, 2007, from *http://www.sciencedaily.com/releases/2002/04/020415073115.htm.*

Nilsson, K. W., Sjoberg, R. L., Dambert, M., Alm, P. O., Ohrvile, J., Leppert, J., et al. (2005). Role of the serotonin transporter gene and family function in adolescent alcohol consumption. *Alcoholism: Clinical and Experimental Research, 29*, 564–570.

Ochsner, K. N., Bunge, S. A., Gross, J. J., & Gabrieli, J. D. E. (2002). Rethinking feelings: An fMRI study of the cognitive regulation of emotion. *Journal of Cognitive Neuroscience, 14*, 1215–1229.

Ogden, P., Minton, K., & Pain, C. (2006). *Trauma and the body: A sensorimotor approach to psychotherapy.* New York: Norton.

Palacios, R., & Sugawara I. (1982). Hydrocortisone abrogates proliferation of T cells in autologous mixed lymphocyte reaction by rendering the interleukin-2 producer T cells unresponsive to interleukin 1 and unable to synthesize the T-cell growth factor. *Scandanavian Journal of Immunology 15*(1), 25–31.

Panksepp, J. (1998). *Affective neuroscience: The foundations of human and animal emotions.* New York: Oxford University Press.

Panksepp, J. (2003). Feeling the pain of social loss. *Science, 302*(5643), 237–239.

Panksepp, J. (2005). Beyond a joke: From animal laughter to human joy? *Science, 300*, 62–63.

Paus, T., Zijdenbos, A., Worsley, K., Collins, D. L., Blumenthal, J., Giedd, J. N., et al. (1999). Structural maturation of neural pathways in children and adolescents: In vivo study. *Science, 283*, 1908–1911.

Perry, B. D. (1998). Neurophysiological aspects of anxiety disorders in children. Downloaded at *http://www.childtrauma.org/CTAMATERIALS/anxiety_disorder.asp* on July 1, 2006.

Phan, K. L., Fitzgerald, D. A., Nathan, P. J., Moore, G. J., Uhde, T. W., & Tancer, M. E. (2005). Neural substrates for voluntary suppression of negative affect: A functional magnetic resonance imaging study. *Biological Psychology, 57*(3), 210–219.

Porges, S. W. (2001). The polyvagal theory: Phylogenetic substrates of a social nervous system. *International Journal of Psychophysiology, 42*, 123–146.

Porges, S. W. (2007). The polyvagal perspective. *Biological Psychology, 74*, 116–143.

Post, R. M., Weiss, S. R. B., Li, H., Smith, M. A., Zhang, L. X., Xing, G., et al. (1998). Neural plasticity and emotional memory. *Development and Psychopathology, 10,* 829–856.

Putnam, F. W. (1989). *Diagnosis and treatment of multiple personality disorder.* New York: Guilford Press.

Putnam, F. W. (1997). *Dissociation in children and adolescents: A developmental approach.* New York: Guilford Press.

Rauch, S. L., Shin, L. M., & Phelps, E. A. (2006). Neurocircuitry models of posttraumatic stress disorder and extinction: Human neuroimaging research—past, present and future. *Biological Psychology, 60*(4), 376–382.

Rauch, S. L., Shin, L. M., & Wright, C. I. (2003). Neuroimaging studies of amygdala function in anxiety disorders. *Annals of the New York Academy of Sciences, 985,* 389–410.

Rechlin, T. (1994). Are affective disorders associated with alterations in heart rate variability? *Journal of Affective Disoders, 32,* 271–275.

Reinders, A. A. T. S., Nijenhuis, E. R. S., Paans, A. M. J., Korf, J., Willemsen, A. T. M., & den Boer, J. A. (2003). One brain, two selves. *Neuroimage, 20,* 2119–2125.

Rizzolatti, G., Fogassi, L., & Gallese, V. (2001). Neurophysiological mechanisms underlying the understanding and the imitation of action. *Nature Review Neuroscience, 2,* 660–670.

Rutter, M., & Smith, D. J. (Eds.). (1995). *Psychosocial disorders in young people: Time trends and their causes.* New York: Wiley.

Sabbagh, L. (2006). The teen brain, hard at work. *Scientific American Mind,* 20–25.

Santarelli, L., Saxe, M., Gross, C., Surget, A., Basttaglia, F., Dulawa, S., et al. (2003). Requirement of hippocampal neurogenesis for the behavioral effects of antidepressants. *Science, 301,* 805–809.

Sapolsky, R. M. (2000). Is impaired neurogenesis relevant to the affective symptoms of depression? *Biological Psychiatry, 56,* 137–139.

Sapolsky, R. M. (2001). Depression, antidepressants, and the shrinking hippocampus. *Proceedings of the National Academy of Sciences, USA, 98*(22), 12320–12322.

Scaer, R. (2001). The neurophysiology of dissociation and chronic disease. *Applied Psychophysiology and Biofeedback, 26*(1), 73–91.

Schore, A. N. (1994). *Affect regulation and the origin of the self: The neurobiology of emotional development.* New York: Erlbaum.

Schore, A. N. (1996). The experience-dependent maturation of a regulatory system in the orbital prefrontal cortex and the origin of developmental psychopathology. *Development and Psychopathology, 8,* 59–87.

Schore, A. N. (2003a). *Affect dysregulation and disorders of the self.* New York: Norton.

Schore, A. N. (2003b). *Affect regulation and the repair of the self.* New York: Norton.

Schore, A. N. (2003c, March). *New developments in attachment theory: Application to clinical practice,* Lifespan Learning Institute UCLA, Attachment Conference, Los Angeles, CA.

Schore, A. N. (2005). Back to basics: Attachment, affect regulation, and the right brain: Linking developmental neuroscience to pediatrics. *Pediatrics in Review, 26*(6), 204–217.

Schore, A. N. (2007). *The science of the art of psychotherapy.* Paper presented at conference. Los Angeles, CA.

Schwartz, J. M. (1997). *Brain lock: Free yourself from obsessive–compulsive behavior.* New York: Harper Perennial.

Schwartz, J. M., & Begley, S. (2002). *The mind and the brain: Neuroplasticity and the power of mental force.* New York: HarperCollins.

Schwartz, R. C. (1997). *Internal family systems therapy.* New York: Guilford Press.

Schwartz, R. C. (2007). *The internal family systems model outline.* Retrieved September 16, 2007, from *http://www.selfleadership.org/ifsmodel.asp.*

Sedlak, A. J., & Broadhurst, D. D. (1996). *The third national incidence study of child abuse and neglect.* Washington, DC: U.S. Department of Health and Human Services.

Sheline, Y. I., Barch, D.M., Donnelly, J.M., Ollinger, J.M., Snyder, A.Z., & Mintun, M.A. (2001). Increased amygdala response to masked emotional faces in depressed subjects resolves with antidepressant treatment: An fMRI study. *Biological Psychiatry, 50*(9), 651–658.

Sheline, Y. I., Gado, M.H., & Price, J. L. (1998). Amygdala core nuclei volumes are decreased in recurrent major depression. *Neuroreport, 9*(9), 2023–2028.

Sheline, Y. I., Wang, P. W., Gado, M. H., Csernansky, J. G., & Vannier, M. W. (1996). Hippocampal atrophy in recurrent major depression. *Proceedings of National Academy of Science, USA, 93*(9), 3908–4013.

Shin, L. M., Shin, P. S., Heckers, S., Krangel, T., Macklin, M. L., Orr, S. P., et al. (2004). Explicit memory and hippocampal function in posttraumatic stress disorder. *Hippocampus, 14,* 292–300.

Shin, L. M., Whalen, P. J., Pitman, R. K., Bush, G., Macklin, M. L., Lasko, N. B., et al. (2001). An fMRI study of anterior cingulate function in posttraumatic stress disorder. *Biological Psychiatry, 50*(12), 932–942.

Shook, L. (2001). *Changing history, one baby at a time.* Retrieved May 12, 2007, from *http://circleofsecurity.org.*

Siegel, D. J. (1999). *The developing mind: How relationship and the brain interact to shape who we are.* New York: Guilford Press.

Siegel, D. J. (2001). Toward an interpersonal neurobiology of the developing mind: Attachment relationships, "mindsight," and neural integration. *Infant Mental Health Journal, (22),* 1–2, 67–94.

Siegel, D. J. (2006). An interpersonal neurobiology approach to psychotherapy: Awareness, mirror neurons, and neural plasticity in the development of well-being. *Psychiatric Annals, 36*(4), 247–258.

Siegel, D. J. (2007). *The mindful brain: Reflection and attunement in the cultivation of well-being.* New York: Norton.

Siegel, D. J. (2007). Mindfulness training and neural integration: Differentiation of distinct streams of awareness and the cultivation of well-being. *Social, Cognitive, and Affective Neuroscience, 2,* 259–263.

Siegel, D. J., & Hartzell, M. (2003). *Parenting from the inside out: How a deeper self-understanding can help you raise children who thrive.* New York: Tarcher/Putnam.

Siegle, G. J., Konecky, R. O., Thase, M. E., & Carter, C. S. (2003). Relationship between amygdala volume and activity during emotional information processing tasks in depressed and never-depressed individuals: An fMRI investigation. *Annals of the New York Academy of Sciences, 985*, 481–484.

Singer, T., Seymour, B., O'Doherty, J., Kaube, H., Dolan, R. J., & Frith, C. D. (1994). Empathy for pain involves the affective but not sensory components of pain. *Science, 303*, 1157–1162.

Song, H., Stevens, C. F., & Gage, F. H. (2002). Neural stem cells from adult hippocampus develop essential properties of functional CNS neurons. *Nature Neuroscience, 5*, 438–445.

Sowell, E. R., Thompson, P. M., Holmes, C. J., Jernigan, T. I., & Toga, A. W. (1999). In vivo evidence for post-adolescent brain maturation in frontal and striatal regions. *Nature Neuroscience, 2*(10), 859–861.

Sroufe, L. A., Egland, B., Carlson, E. A., & Collins W. A. (2005). *The development of the person: The Minnesota study of risk and adaptation from birth to adulthood.* New York: Guilford Press.

Stratowski, S. M. (1999). Brain magnetic resonance imaging of structural abnormalities in bipolar disorder. *Archives of General Psychiatry, 56*, 254–260.

Strauch, B. (2003). *The primal teen: What the new discoveries about the teenage brain tell us about our kids.* New York: Anchor Books.

Stein, M. B. (1998). Neurobiological perspectives on social phobia: From affiliation to zoology. *Biological Psychiatry, 44*, 1277–1285.

Sunderland, M. (2006). *The science of parenting: How today's brain research can help you raise happy, emotionally balanced children.* New York: DK Publishing.

Teicher, M. H., Andersen, S. L., Polcari, A., Anderson, C. M., Navalta, C. P., & Kim, D. M. (2003). The neurobiological consequences of early stress and childhood maltreatment. *Neuroscience and Biobehavioral Reviews, 27*(1), 33–44.

Thompson, P. M., Giedd, J. N., Woods, R. P., MacDonald, D., Evans, A.C., & Toga, A. W. (2000). Growth patterns in the developing brain detected by using continuum mechanical tensor maps. *Nature, 404*, 190–193.

Tronick, E. Z. (1989). Emotions and emotional communication in infants. *American Psychologist, 44*, 112–119.

Tronick, E. Z. (2003, March). Of course all relationships are unique: How co-creative processes generate unique mother–infant and patient–therapist relationships and change other relationships. Lifespan Learning Institute, UCLA, Los Angeles, CA.

Trudeau, G. B. (2006). *Heckuva job, Bushie!* Kansas City, MO: Andrews McMeel.

Urry, H. L., Nitschke, J. B., Dolski, I., Jackson, D. C., Dalton, K. M., Mueller, C. J. et al. (2004). Making a life worth living: Neural correlates of well-being. *Psychological Science, 15*(6), 367–372.

Veith, R. C., Lewis, N., Linares, O. A., Barnes, R. F., Raskind, M. A., Villacres, E. C., et al. (1994). Sympathetic nervous system activity in major depression. *Archives of General Psychiatry, 51*, 411–422.

Vermetten, E., Schmahl, C., Lindner, S., Lowenstein, R. J., & Bremner, J. D. (2006). Hippocampal and amygdalar volumes in dissociative identity disorder. *American Journal of Psychiatry, 163*, 630–636.

Volkow, N. D., & Fowler, J. S. (2000). Addiction, a disease of compulsion and drive: Involvement of the orbitofrontal cortex. *Cerebral Cortex, 10*(3), 318–325.

References

Warneken, F., & Tomasello, M. (2006). Altruistic helping in human infants and young chimpanzees. *Science, 311*, 1301–1302.

Watkins, J. G. (1997). *Ego states: Theory and therapy.* New York: Norton.

Wilson, E. O. (1998). *Consilience: The unity of knowledge.* New York: Knopf.

Wipfler, P. (2006a). *A tool for caring parents.* Palo Alto, CA: Hand in Hand.

Wipfler, P. (2006b). *Crying.* Palo Alto, CA: Hand in Hand.

Wipfler, P. (2006c). *Healing children's fears.* Palo Alto, CA: Hand in Hand.

Wipfler, P. (2006d). *How children's emotions work.* Palo Alto, CA: Hand in Hand.

Wipfler, P. (2006e). *Reaching for your angry child.* Palo Alto, CA: Hand in Hand.

Wipfler, P. (2006f). *Parenting by connection.* Palo Alto, CA: Hand in Hand.

Wipfler, P. (2006g). *Setting limits with children.* Palo Alto, CA: Hand in Hand.

Wipfler, P. (2006h). *Supporting adolescents.* Palo Alto, CA: Hand in Hand.

Wipfler, P. (2006i). *Tantrums and indignation.* Palo Alto, CA: Hand in Hand.

Wolfson, A. R., & Carskadon, M. A. (1998). Sleep schedules and daytime functioning in adolescents. *Child Development, 69*(4), 875–887.

Zanarini, M. C., Williams, A. A., Lewis, R. E., Reich, R. B., Vera, S. C., Marino, M. F., et al. (2000). Reported pathological childhood experiences associated with the development of borderline personality disorder. *American Journal of Psychiatry, 154*, 1101–1106.

Zohar, D. (1991). *The quantum self.* New York: Harper Perennial.

Index

abuse
  borderline personality disorder and, 142
  brain structure/function and, 137–39
  effects of, 136–40
acceptance, 175
acts of triumph, 99, 213–14, 234
addiction
  brain structure/function and, 149–51
  coping through, 149, 150
  craving and, 149, 150
  teens and, 292
adolescents. *See* teens
adrenocorticotropic hormone
    (ACTH), 127
Adult Attachment Interview, 58
adults
  attachment of, 54–58
  sandplay with, 228–33
affection, 169–70
age, of unhealed emotional wounding,
    275–76
Ainsworth, Mary, 58
alcohol use, teen, 292
ambivalent attachment, 68–71
amygdala
  abuse/neglect and, 137
  addiction and, 149–50
  anxiety and, 126–28
  attachment and, 52, 55
  borderline personality disorder
    and, 140
  brain-wise narratives and, 202, 203
  compassion and, 204
  defined, 16
  depression and, 123–24
  dissociation and, 147
  emotions and, 120–21, 125
  implicit memories and, 24

information reception of, 126–27
judgment and, 178
meaning-making centered in, 24
PTSD and, 125
safety assessment in, 60
therapeutic relationship and, 156
anger
  brain structure/function and, 194, 279
  parenting guidance for, 309–10
  shame as source of, 105–6
anterior cingulate
  addiction and, 150
  defined, 16, 23
  depression and, 122
  dissociation and, 128
  emotions and, 120–21, 125
  meditation and, 175
  neglect and, 138
  obsessive-compulsive disorder and,
    43
anticipation, 179
anxiety, 124–28
  brain structure/function and, 125–28
  depression comorbid with, 124
  family history questions on, 170
  fear as origin of, 125
  generalized anxiety disorder in chil-
    dren, 128
  physiological response to, 127
  social, 128
approach emotions, 20, 121
art, 244–65. *See also* images
  body and, 248–49
  case studies in, 250–65
  directions for, 245
  disposition of, 249
  interpretation of, 246
  materials for, 245

art (*continued*)
   narratives about, 246
   nondominant hand in, 245–46
   relationships of figures in, 246
   spirituality and, 248
   thematic possibilities for, 247–50
attachment, 52–75
   adult processes of, 54–58
   ambivalent, 68–71
   avoidant, 63–68
   at birth, 52
   brain development and, 15, 23–24,
      52–53
   childrearing and, 295–96
   communication and, 57
   couples and, 282–83
   disorganized, 71–74
   early processes of, 52–54, 59, 74–75
   earned secure, 57
   in family histories, 166
   family history questions on,
      168–70
   family therapy based on, 313–14
   indirect revelation of early, 75
   mother-child relations and, 34,
      52, 62
   narrative and, 166
   patterns of, 57–75
   safe/dangerous circumstances and,
      59–61
   secure, 61–63
   self-regulation and, 59
   teens and, 293–96
   in therapy, 54–57
attention
   brain and, 16
   as change agent, 45–46
   consciousness of, 48
   executive, 37
   exogenous, 37
   focused, 43–44
   mind and, 48
   mindfulness and, 174, 175, 179
   obsessive-compulsive disorder and,
      43–44
   quantum physics and, 44–45
   therapeutic role of, 45–46
attribution, 31, 55
attunement, 29–30. *See also* empathic
      attunement
autobiographical memory, 28
autonomic nervous system (ANS),
      20–21. *See also* parasympathetic
      nervous system; sympathetic
      nervous system
   body regulation and, 29
   depression and, 124–25
avoidance/withdrawal emotions, 20
avoidant attachment, 63–68
axons, 8

Baer, Ruth, 182–84
baking in new knowledge, xxiii–xxiv
Bartzokis, George, 292
Begley, S., 45
being, continuity of, 40, 55, 96
birth, 52
blame
   couples and, 280–81
   self-, 184
body
   art and, 248–49
   avoidant attachment and, 65
   awareness of, 182–83
   embracing the whole person and,
      96–100
   empathy as experienced by, 39
   intuition and, 31
   mindfulness and, 182–83
   outer-inner focus shift and, 206
   patient awareness of, 98
   regulation of, 29, 99–100
   sandplay and, 221, 222, 228, 233
   as starting point for therapy, 208–9
   therapeutic work using, 96–100
   therapist awareness of, 34
   traumatic effects on, 97–99
   vertical integration and, 33–34
   wisdom of, 98
borderline personality disorder
   characteristics of, 140–41
   formation of, 140–42
   PTSD comorbid with, 142
bottom-up processing, 180
Bowen, Murray, 77
Bowlby, John, 58
Brach, Tara, 181
Bradway, Kay, 229
brain. *See also* left hemisphere of brain;
      right hemisphere of brain
   abuse/neglect and, 137–39
   activity of, 7
   addiction and, 149–51
   adolescent, 287–94
   ambivalent attachment and, 69–70
   anxiety and, 125–28
   attachment and, 52–53
   avoidant attachment and, 64–66
   basic principles of, 7–12
   as complex system, 4–5, 193–95
   depression and, 122–24, 151
   development and change in, 10–12
   disorders and, 119–21
   disorganized attachment and, 71–72
   dissociation and, 128–29, 147
   emotional regulation and, 120–21, 125
   experiential role in, 9, 49
   fear and, 125
   genetic role in, 9, 49
   hand model of, 13–14, 13*f*, 199–200,
      279, 319

injury to, 131
internalization and, 78
interpersonal interaction and, 21
meaning of term, xxvi
meditation's effect on, 43–44, 175,
   187–88
mind in relation to, xii, xxi–xxii, 9,
   42–51
mindfulness and, 179–80
mind's effect on, 43–45
mother-child relations and, 114–15
parenting guidance based on, 307–10
play therapy and, 300–303
prenatal experience and, 134
pruning of cells in, 8, 288–90, 296
sandplay and, 221
self-organizing capacity of, 5, 193
shame and, 106–9
structures and regions of, 12–18
therapeutic use of information about,
   21–22, 117, 191–204, 278–80
triune, 12–14
brain injury, 131
brain-wise therapy
benefits of, 192, 195–98
narratives from, 200–203
patient responses to, 198–200
brainstem, 14
Buddhism, 176

caring observer
couples and, 276–77, 281
dissociation and, 129
self-awareness and, 188
watchers compared to, 85
Caspi, A., 130
cerebellum, 14, 289
cerebral cortex (neocortex), 17f
components of, 17–18
emergence and recursion in, 194
meditation and, 179–80, 187
chaos
ambivalent attachment and, 68–70
couples and, 273
emergent properties and, 194
integration process and, 50–51
origins of, 194
patient awareness of, 192
child-centered play therapy. See play
   therapy
children
inner, therapeutic role of, 214–15
mindfulness for, 312
overview of therapy with, 270
parents of, therapeutic work with, 270,
   299–300, 306–7
play therapy with, 270, 299–318
sandplay with, 225–26
choices. See decision making
cingulate gyrus, 16

Circle of Security Early Intervention
   Program for Parents and
   Children, 64, 313–14
clinical practice. See therapy
COAL state of mind
in couples, 276, 280
mindfulness and, 178, 180–81, 184, 192
in play therapy, 304
cognitive-behavioral therapy, 3
coherence. See also integration
in narratives, 195–96, 200–201, 318
patient awareness of, 192
therapeutic work on, 194–95
comfort, providing, 92, 210–13
commissures, 19, 20
communication
attuned, 29–30
contingent, 57, 306
family history questions on, 169
nonverbal, 33, 34, 57
in therapy, 33
unconscious, 33, 91
compassion. See also empathy
brain structure/function and, 203–4
intergenerational, 164–65, 203, 217–18
mindfulness and, 185
self-, 184–85
complexity theory, 4–5, 192–95
conscious awareness. See mindful
   awareness
consciousness, 37
consilience, 47
contingent communication, 57, 306
continuity of being, 40, 55, 96
Cooper, G., 64
corpus callosum
in adolescent brain, 291, 296
in child's brain, 302
interhemispheric communication
   through, 19, 20, 291, 296, 302
corticotropin-releasing factor (CRF), 127
cortisol
anxiety and, 127
depression and, 124
therapeutic relationship and, 156
countertransference, 56
couples, 271–85
attachment and, 282–83
brain structure/function information
   for, 278–80
chaotic, 273
defenses of, 277
empathic capacity in, 275–78, 285
empathy in therapy with, 274–78
individual meetings with members of,
   273, 277–78
individual work during therapy
   with, 285
inner community and, 272, 279–80
internal work for, 283–85

couples (*continued*)
    language used in therapy for, 280
    mind of the couple, 273
    overview of therapy with, 269
    partner choice of, 272
    perspective-taking by, 280
    relational experience of, 271–72
    rigid, 273, 277
    safety and, 280–82
    sandplay with, 226–28
    therapist's relationship with, 274
    timing in therapy for, 283
craving, 149, 150
Creswell, D. J., 184

daily life, nature of, 189
daily mindfulness, 182
danger, 60, 68
Davidson, Richard, 43–44, 135
death, 40
decision making
    brain and, 16, 293
    illogical, 59
defenses
    in couples, 277
    exploration of, 216–17
    strength of, 280
dendrites, 8
depression
    anxiety comorbid with, 124
    brain structure/function and, 122–24,
        151
    family history questions on, 170
    infants and, 135
    maternal, 78, 133–36
    prenatal experience and, 78, 133–34
    sandplay involving, 241–43
diagnosis, 113–15
dialectical behavior therapy, 141, 176
differentiation, in brain, 193
disappointment, 170
discipline, 169
dismissing-type personalities
    avoidant attachment and, 63–67
    narratives of, 65–66
disorders. *See also* anxiety; borderline
        personality disorder; depression;
        dissociation; dissociative identity
        disorder
    brain development and, 119–21
    brain injury and, 131
    genetic role in, 130–31
    meaning of term, 119
    prenatal experiences and, 132–36
    temperament and, 131–32
disorganized attachment, 71–74, 235–41
dissociation. *See also* dissociative
        identity disorder
    brain structure/function and, 24,
        128–29, 147

defined, 128, 205
    in infants, 139
    of neural nets, 206–19
    of states of mind, 36
    subjective experience of, 145
    therapeutic work on, 148, 205–19
dissociative identity disorder
    formation of, 142–48
    parents and, 144
    structural separation of
        identities in, 146
    subjective experience of, 145
    therapeutic treatment of, 216–17
    watchers and, 84
Doonesbury (Trudeau), 143–44
dopamine
    addiction and, 149–50
    child development and, 301
    mother-child relations and, 135
    social anxiety and, 128
    teens and, 292
dorsal vagus
    dissociation and, 128
    freeze response and, 60, 128
dorsolateral prefrontal cortex
    in adolescent brain, 290
    decision making and, 293
    defined, 18
    depression and, 122
    emotions and, 120–21
drug use, teen, 292
dyadic dances, 144
dyadic regulation, 59

earned secure attachment, 57
Einstein, A. E., 40
emergence, in body-brain-mind system,
    194
emotions
    adolescent, 291
    brain structure/function and, 20,
        120–21, 125
    genetic role in, 130–31
    layers of, 211–12
    mindfulness and, 178, 182–84
    perceptual biases and, 30
    regulation of, 30
    staying with, 213–14
empathic attunement
    autobiographical memory and, 28
    nonverbal communication and, 33
    therapeutic significance of, 5–6, 28
    unconscious communication and, 33
empathy. *See also* compassion; empathic
        attunement
    avoidant attachment and, 65–66
    bodily perception of, 39
    brain and, 30–31, 37–40
    capacity for, in couples, 275–78, 285
    in couples therapy, 274–78

mother-child, 34
process of, 31, 54–55
rupture and repair in, 100–101
shame as obstacle to, 105–6
therapeutic role of, xxiii, 54–57, 90–91,
    116, 213, 274–78
empathy of identification, 206, 210
endogenous attention. *See* executive
    attention
energy, 9, 48
environment. *See* experience
Erikson, Erik, 77
ET (film), 209
eudaimonia, 107
executive attention, 37
exogenous attention, 37
experience
adolescent, 289, 292
brain organization and, 9, 49
G x E research and, 130
genes in relation to, 47, 130, 289
invariant representations and,
    179–80, 189
mind development and, 47, 49
new, 180, 189, 292
sandplay and, 221–23
explicit memories, 16, 28
external constraints, on brain/mind
    development, 193
eyes, closing of, 209

FACES of mental health, xiii, 50, 192
factual memory, 28
families. *See also* parents
attachment-based resources for, 313–14
sandplay with, 226–28
family histories, 163–73. *See also*
    intergenerational issues
affection in, 169–70
anxiety/depression in, 170
approaches to, 167–68
attachment in, 166, 168–70
communication in, 169
in course of therapy, 172–73
disappointment in, 170
discipline in, 169
family tree and, 173
guidelines for, 168–73
illness in, 171
importance of, 116–17
influential people in, 171–72
listening to, 163
note-taking during, 164
people in, 166–67, 171–72
questions for, 168–73
school in, 170–71
spirituality in, 171
what to listen for in, 166
whole-person to whole-person joining
    in, 166–68

family trees, 173
Farb, N. A. S., 188
fear
brain and, 125
disorganized attachment and,
    71–74
extinction of, 31
forms of, 212
feelings. *See* emotions
Field, T., 78, 133, 135
fight-flight response
danger and, 60
dissociation and, 128
trauma and, 98
"fires together-wires together" principle,
    9, 140, 316
5-HTT, 130
focused attention, 43–44. *See also*
    mindfulness
Fogassi, L., 197
fornix, 16
Forrest, Kelly, 147
free will, 42, 44–45
freedom, 51, 61
freeze response, 60, 128
Freud, Sigmund, 3
frontal cortex, 10
frontal lobes, 293
functional magnetic resonance imaging
    (fMRI), 11
Fuster, J. M., 147
future, orientation of daily life
    toward, 189

G x E research, 130
GABA. *See* gamma-aminobutyric acid
Gage, Fred H., 12
Gallese, V., 197
gamma-aminobutyric acid (GABA)
addiction and, 149–50
brain-wise narratives and, 202, 203
comfort and, 31, 109, 317
therapeutic relationship and, 156
generalized anxiety disorder
in children, 128
genes
brain organization and, 9, 49
emotions and, 130–31
experience in relation to, 47,
    130, 289
G x E research and, 130
internalization and, 78
mind development and, 47, 49
genograms, 164
Giedd, Jay, 288
glia, 7–8
Gone with the Wind (film), 201
grandparents, internalization of, 83–84.
    See also intergenerational issues
guided imagery, 84

hand model of brain, 13–14, 13*f*,
    199–200, 279, 319
hands. *See* non-dominant hand
Hartzell, Mary, 307–8
Hawkins, Jeff, 179
healing distance, 305
Hebb's axiom, 9, 316
hedonia, 187
helplessness, 129, 134, 141, 146, 150
Henriques, J. B., 135
Hesse, Erik, 58
hippocampus
    anxiety and, 127
    defined, 16
    depression and, 122–23, 151
    dissociation and, 147
    memory and, 18, 28
    PTSD and, 126
    sandplay and, 221
history taking. *See* family histories
Hoffman, K., 64
hope, 90
house-tree-person pictures, 245–46
HPA axis. *See* hypothalamic-pituitary-
    adreno (HPA) axis
hypnosis, 84
hypothalamic-pituitary-adreno
        (HPA) axis
    abuse/neglect and, 137
    addiction and, 149
    anxiety and, 127
hypothalamus, 16

Iacoboni, Marco, 53
illness, 171
images. *See also* art
    in internal work, 214
    in sandplay, 227
implicit memories
    brain and, 16, 24
    contents of, 24
    function of, 24–25
    power of, 26
    prenatal experiences and, 79–80
    therapeutic integration of, 26–28
    time and, 25
implicit processes, 198
infants
    attachment of, 52–54, 59
    case study in trauma of, 314–18
    crying, parent response to, 63
    depressed mothers and, 135
    dissociation in, 139
    inner community of, 53
    LMP in, 23
    neglected, 138–39
    relational expectations of, 135
    RMP in, 23, 59, 132
    self of, 53
    shame in, 106

inferior frontal area, 38
information
    brain and, 16, 17, 126–27
    defined, 9, 48
inner community, 76–89
    couples and, 272, 279–80
    defined, xxiv, 4
    disorganized attachment and, 71–72
    example of, 87*f*
    integrated, 142–43
    internal work on, 209–10
    internalization and, 78–82
    interpersonal neurobiology and,
        101–4
    members of, 82–84, 217–18
    mindfulness of, 177
    mother-child relations as
        origin of, 77
    narrative related to, 88–89*f*
    origins of, 53
    pairs in, 84, 144, 217
    parent-child relationship and devel-
        opment of, 144
    protectors in, 85–86
    respect for members of, 217–18
    schema of, 82–84, 83*f*
    states of mind and, 36, 102
    therapist's holding of patient's, 93
    therapists in, 212–13
    tracking of, 93–94, 211
    watchers in, 84–85
inner focus, 206
inner sanctuary, 93
InnerKids, 176
insight, 31
insular cortex (insula)
    function of, 17, 38
    meditation and, 43, 175, 187
    sandplay and, 221
integration. *See also* coherence; neural
        integration
    bilateral, 35
    chaos versus, xiii, 50–51
    of consciousness, 37
    couples therapy and, 279
    freedom and, 51
    horizontal. *See* bilateral integration
    interpersonal, 37–40
    narrative-memory-state, 35–37
    rigidity versus, xiii, 50–51
    temporal, 40
    therapeutic approach to, 51
    transpirational, 40–41, 96
    vertical, 33–34, 155
intentions
    mirroring of, 38
    toddler's reading of, 28
intergenerational issues. *See also* family
        histories; grandparents; parents
    avoidant attachment and, 64

brain structure/function information
 and, 192
childrearing and, 295–96, 298
compassion and, 164–65, 203,
 217–18
internalization of parents and, 83–84
pain and, 217–18
secure attachment and, 63
teens and, 295–96
tragedy of, 165, 192, 201
internal constraints, on brain/mind
 development, 193
Internal Family Systems, 76
internal state of the other (ISO), 54
internal time travel, 206
internal work, 205–19
 body as starting point for, 208–9
 child in, 214–15
 closed eyes for, 209
 in couples therapy, 283–85
 defenses in, 216–17
 guidelines for, 208–19
 images in, 214
 inner community and, 209–10
 layers in, 211–12
 present as starting point for, 208
 resistance in, 216–17
 respect for internalized others in,
  217–18
 staying with emotions in, 213–14
 tracking in, 211
internalization
 brain and, 78
 genetic role in, 78
 lifelong, 81
 of parents/grandparents, 83–84, 218
 during pregnancy, 78–80
 process of, 78–82
 of whole person, 82–83
interoception, 31, 54
interpersonal integration, 37–40, 53
interpersonal interaction. See also
  relationships; therapeutic
  relationship
 brain and, 21, 37–40
 defined, 48
 mind's emergence linked to, 47, 48
interpersonal neurobiology (IPNB). See
  also brain; brain-wise therapy
 inner community therapy integrated
  with, 101–4
 therapeutic applications of, xxii–xxvii,
  3–6
interpretation, 31, 54
intrusive mothers, 135
intuition, 31
invariant representations, 179–80, 189
IPNB. See interpersonal neurobiology
Iraq war veterans, 143–44
ISO. See internal state of the other

Janet, Pierre, 96
Jensen, Peter, 293
judgment
 mindfulness and, 178, 184
 of teens, 289
Jung, C. G., 3
Jungian tradition, 220–21, 223

Kabat-Zinn, John, 176
Kagan, Jerome, 131
Kaiser-Greenland, Susan, 176
Kalff, Dora, 220–21
Kaufman, Joan, 130
Kisilevsky, Barbara, 78
Kohut, Heinz, 77, 165
Kornfield, Jack, 178, 181
Kurtz, Ron, 96

Landreth, Garry, 300
language
 brain hemispheres and, 19
 mindfulness and, 177, 182–84
laughter, 99
Lazar, Sara, 43
left hemisphere of brain. See also
  left-mode processing (LMP)
 integration of, with right, 35
 narrative process of, 195
 right versus, 19–20
 sandplay and, 224–25
left-mode processing (LMP)
 characteristics of, 19–20
 emotions and, 20
 in infancy, 23
Lesch, K., 130
Levine, Peter, 97–98
life-threatening circumstances, 60
limbic region, 15f
 ambivalent attachment and, 69
 attachment and, 52, 55
 avoidant attachment and, 65
 child development and, 300, 301
 components of, 15–17
 in infants, 316
 location of, 14
 middle prefrontal region and, 23–33,
  279
 self-regulation and, 109
 sympathetic nervous system and, 279
Linehan, Marsha, 176
LMP. See left-mode processing
Loudon, Sumi, 312
Lowen, Alexander, 96
Lowenfeld, Margaret, 220

macaque monkeys, 197
Main, Mary, 53, 58, 73, 132
Marvin, R., 64
meaning, death and, 40
meaning-making processes, 16

medial orbitofrontal cortex, 122
medial prefrontal cortex
    defined, 16, 23
    depression and, 122
    dissociation and, 128
    emotions and, 120–21, 125
medication, 151–52
meditation. *See also* mindfulness
    brain changes through, 43–44, 175,
        187–88
    timers for, 189–90
melatonin, 291–92
memory and memories
    autobiographical memory, 28
    brain structure/function information
        and, 192
    defined, 9
    explicit memories, 16, 28
    extraordinary instances of, 103–4
    factual memory, 28
    implicit memories, 16, 24–28, 79–80
    integration involving, 35–37
    internal work on, 210
    strength of, 10
    therapeutic value of, 9, 206
    working memory, 18
middle prefrontal region, 15*f*
    in adolescent brain, 289–90, 294
    attuned communication and, 29–30
    body regulation and, 29
    compassion and, 204
    components of, 14–15, 16, 23
    emotional regulation and, 30
    fear extinction and, 31
    insight and, 31
    integrative functions of, 28–33,
        121, 176
    interpersonal integration and, 39
    intuition and, 31
    limbic region and, 23–33, 279
    location of, 14
    meditation and, 43, 175–76
    morality and, 32
    response flexibility and, 30
    sandplay and, 221
    self-regulation and, 109
    in teens, 270
    therapeutic relationship and, 108
    in toddlers, 28
    vertical integration and, 33–34
mind
    attentional processes as, 48
    brain changed through, 43–45
    brain in relation to, xii, xxi–xxii, 9,
        42–51
    chaos in, 50–51
    defined, 48
    dynamic nature of, 47
    experience's role in, 47, 49
    genetic role in, 47, 49

interpersonal interaction and
        emergence of, 47, 48
    rigidity of, 50–51
    wheel metaphor of, 174–75
mind of the couple, 273
Mindful Awareness Research Center, 176
The Mindful Brain (Siegel), 176
mindfulness, 174–90. *See also* focused
        attention
    of activities, 183
    aspects of, 117
    attention and, 174, 175, 179
    benefits of, 175
    body awareness and, 182–83
    bottom-up processing and, 180
    brain changed through, 43–44
    for children, 312
    compassion and, 185
    daily, 182
    defined, 37, 175, 178–79
    emotions and, 178, 182–84
    formal practices of, 186–90
    of inner community, 177
    judgment and, 178, 184
    language used in, 177, 182–84
    mainstream practices of, 176
    neural underpinnings of, 179–80
    ordinary, 180–81
    for parents, 310–11
    perspective in, 177, 182
    practice of, 37, 186–90
    principles of, 182–86
    RAIN process in, 181
    as relationship, 176–78
    research on, 175–76
    state of mind in, 177–78
    therapeutic relationship and, 181,
        186–90
    therapeutic use of, 46, 174–75,
        180–90
mindfulness-based stress reduction
        (MBSR), 176
mindsight, 56
mirror neurons
    couples therapy and, 279
    empathy and, 30–31, 37–39
    patients' understanding of, 197
Moffitt, T. E., 130
morality
    brain and, 32
    free will and, 42
mother-child relations. *See also* parents;
        prenatal experiences
    ambivalent attachment and, 68–69
    attachment in, 34, 52, 62
    at birth, 52
    brain development and, 114–15
    depression and, 135
    inner community originating in, 77
    intrusive, 135

right-brain to right-brain connection in, 157
secure attachment and, 62
social circuits and, 138
withdrawn, 135, 136 (*see also* neglect)
multiple personalities, 71–72. *See also* dissociative identity disorder
mutuality, foundations of, 91–94
myelin, 7
myelination, 10, 291, 292

narrative of the other (NOTO), 55
narratives. *See also* family histories
art and, 246
attachment and, 166
brain-wise, 200–203
coherent, 195–96, 200–201, 318
cohesive, 195–96
of dismissing-type personalities, 65–66
of disorganized-type personalities, 73
integration involving, 35–37
of preoccupied-type personalities, 70
sandplay and, 226, 231
nature versus nurture. *See* experience; genes
neglect
borderline personality disorder and, 142
brain structure/function and, 137–39
effects of, 136–40
neocortex. *See* cerebral cortex
nervous system. *See* autonomic nervous system
Neufeld, Gordon, 295, 298
neural integration. *See also* integration
in adolescent brain, 289–91, 294
middle prefrontal region and, 16, 28–33, 121, 176, 289
patients' understanding of, 197
process of, 4–5, 50, 193
states of mind as, 36
as therapeutic principle, xxiii
therapeutic promotion of, 32
neural nets
dissociation of, 206–19
formation of, 9
strength of, 10
neurobiological processes
defined, 48
of disorders, 119–51
neuroception, 60, 280
neurochemicals
abuse/neglect and, 137–38
anxiety and, 126–27
neurogenesis, 12
neuroimaging, 146
neurons, 7–8
neuroplasticity, 10–12
neurotransmitters, 7–8, 149

new experiences, 180, 189, 292
nondirective play therapy. *See* play therapy
nondominant hand
in art, 245–46
in sandplay, 229
nonlinearity, of complex systems, 193
nonverbal communication
of intergenerational empathy, 165–66
in therapy, 33, 34, 57, 156
note-taking, 164, 230
NOTO. *See* narrative of the other
novel experiences, 180, 189, 292
nurture. *See* experience

object constancy, 213
objective countertransference, 56
objects in sandplay
children and, 225
couples/families and, 227
placement of, 223, 229
selection of, 222, 229
therapist's collection of, 220
obsessive-compulsive disorder (OCD), 43–44
occipital lobe, 17, 221
OCD. *See* obsessive-compulsive disorder
Ogden, Pat, 97–99, 183, 234
opioids
abuse/neglect and, 137–38
addiction and, 149–50
child development and, 301–2
therapeutic relationship and, 156
orbitofrontal cortex
addiction and, 150
defined, 16, 23
depression and, 122
emotions and, 120–21, 125
obsessive-compulsive disorder and, 43
state-of-mind integration and, 142, 145, 147–48
therapeutic relationship and, 156
ordinary mindfulness, 180–81
outer focus, 206
oxytocin, 137, 156

pain
forms of, 212
intergenerational, 217–18
mindfulness and, 176
pairs, in inner community, 84, 144, 217
panic, 126–27
Panksepp, Jaak, 99, 301
paranoia, 141
parasympathetic nervous system
dissociation and, 128, 139
function of, 20–21
shame and, 106–7

Parenting from the Inside Out (Siegel and Hartzell), 307–8
parents. *See also* intergenerational issues; mother-child relations
    with avoidant attachment, 63–64, 66–67
    brain development dependent on relationships with, 15
    brain-wise guidance for, 307–10
    of children in therapy, 270, 299–300, 306–7
    with disorganized attachment, 71–72
    in inner community, 218
    internalization of, 83–84, 218
    mindfulness for, 310–11
    outer versus inner, 218
    with secure attachment, 62–63
    of teens, 287, 293–98
    understanding pain of, 218
parietal cortex, 291
parietal lobe, 17–18, 221
patients. *See also* therapeutic relationship; therapy
    with ambivalent attachment, 70–71
    with avoidant attachment, 65–68
    bodily awareness of, 98
    brain-wise therapy benefits for, 192, 195–98
    brain-wise therapy responses of, 198–200
    change in, 59, 77, 81, 109–10
    defenses of, 216–17
    with disorganized attachment, 72–74
    embracing whole, 94–100
    family histories of, 163–73
    following the lead of, 168, 208, 216
    inner focus of, 206
    internal work of, 208–19
    learning from, 219
    outer focus of, 206
    resistance of, 216–17
    responsibility of, 74
    with secure attachment, 61–63
    therapeutic experience of, 172
    therapeutic work of, 206–7
    as vocabulary term, xxvi
peer relationships, 294–95
perceptual biases
    emotions and, 30
    empathy and, 31, 38–39
    in infants, 135
    modulation of, 32
    source of, 25–26
    therapeutic relationship and, 55–56
personality. *See* temperament
play therapy
    brain development and, 300–303
    child- versus adult-led, 301–2, 304
    cleanup after, 313
    emotional atmosphere of, 303–4

firsts in, 304
    limit setting in, 311–12
    objects for, 303
    observation of, 304–6
    parent meetings about, 306–7
    parents barred from, 303
    patterns in, 304
    physical setting for, 303
    session endings in, 312–13
    success and mastery in, 312
    sudden breaks in, 305
    themes/meanings of, 305
    value of, 270, 300–301
Playlistening, 308
Porges, Stephen, 59, 61, 133, 280
posterior parietal area, 38
posttraumatic stress disorder (PTSD)
    borderline personality disorder comorbid with, 142
    brain structure and, 125–26
    physiological response to, 127
    subjective experience of, 126
Powell, B., 64
prebirth experiences. *See* prenatal experiences
prefrontal cortex
    adolescent, 292
    components of, 16
    meditation and, 187
pregnancy. *See* prenatal experiences
prenatal experiences
    brain development and, 134
    depression and, 78, 133–34
    disorders and, 132–36
    implicit memories and, 79–80
    internalization and, 78–81
    relational experience in, 79
preoccupied-type personalities, 68–71
priming, 38
prolactin, 137
protectors
    emotions as, 211
    forms of, 85–86
    role of, 85–86
pruning, 8, 288–90, 296
psychodynamic therapy
    basis of, 3
    borderline personality disorder and, 141
PTSD. *See* posttraumatic stress disorder
Putnam, F. W., 147

quantum physics, 44–45

rage. *See* anger
RAIN process, 181
reattribution, 46
recursion, in body-brain-mind system, 194

reflection exercises
  anxiety/fear responses, 61
  art, 250
  brain complexity, 9
  chaos, 50–51
  explanation of, xxiii
  family histories, 165, 172
  implicit memories, 26
  inner community, 78, 88
  journal for personal healing, 93
  middle prefrontal region, 32
  mind development, 49
  mindfulness, 177, 185
  neural integration, 41
  parenting, 310
  relationships, 271–72
  responsibility, 74
  rigidity, 50–51
  sandplay, 233
  therapist's early relationships, 63
  value of, 4
refocusing, 46
regulation. See also self-regulation
  bodily, 29, 99–100
  dyadic, 59
  emotional, 30, 120–21, 125
  sandplay and, 233
  therapeutic relationship and,
    59, 265
relabeling, 46
relationship(s). See also couples;
    interpersonal interaction;
    therapeutic relationship
  in art, 246
  centrality of, 77
  external, as mirror of internal, 81, 89
  of infants, 135
  intimate, and depth of past, 89
  mindfulness as, 176–78
releasing factors, 127
repair, in therapy, 100–101
resilience, 121
resistance, 216–17
resonance circuits
  avoidant attachment and, 65
  couples therapy and, 279
  empathy and, 31
  in infants, 53
  mechanism of, 39–40
  patients' understanding of, 197
  therapeutic relationship and, 54–57
  therapeutic significance of, 39–40
resourcing, 99–100
respect, teens and, 293
response flexibility, 30
responsibility
  free will and, 42
  of patients, 74, 191
revaluing, 46
reward system, 149

right-brain to right-brain connection
  importance of, 116
  mindfulness and, 181
  in mother-child relations, 157
  neural change and, 91
  in parent-child relations, 59
  as therapeutic principle, xxiii
  in therapy, 94, 156–62
right hemisphere of brain, 17f. See also
    right-mode processing (RMP)
  attachment experiences and, 23–24
  flow in, 23–33
  images and, 214
  integration of, with left, 35
  left-handedness and, 245
  left versus, 19–20
  sandplay and, 222–23, 227
  trauma and, 23–24
  vertical integration of, 33–34
right-mode processing (RMP)
  characteristics of, 19–20
  emotions and, 20
  in infancy, 23, 59, 132
  therapeutic significance of, 20, 23
  in toddlers, 59, 132
rigidity
  couples and, 273, 277
  integration process and, 50–51
  origins of, 194
  patient awareness of, 192
  recursive properties and, 194
Rizzolatti, G., 197
RMP. See right-mode processing
rupture, in therapy, 100–101
Rutter, Michael, 294

safety
  as central concern, 59–61
  couples and, 280–82
  response to, 60
  therapeutic establishment of, 93
sandplay, 220–43. See also objects in
    sandplay
  adults and, 228–33
  benefits of, 220
  body and, 221, 222, 228, 233
  brain processes activated by, 221
  case studies in, 233–43
  children and, 225–26
  couples and, 226–28
  course of, 222
  depression and, 241–43
  directions for, 222, 223, 225, 227,
    228–29
  discussion of, 224–25
  dismantling of, 225, 232
  disorganized attachment and, 235–41
  experiential processes activated by,
    221–23
  families and, 226–28

sandplay (*continued*)
  interpretation of, 231–32
  left hemisphere and, 224–25
  narratives about, 226, 231
  note-taking during, 230
  photographing, 224, 226, 232
  in play therapy, 303
  process of, 222–23
  questions about, 231
  regulation in, 233
  right hemisphere and, 222–23, 227
school, 170–71
Schore, Allan N., xxii, 59, 147
Schwartz, Jeffrey, 43, 45–46, 176
Schwartz, Richard, 76
The Science of Parenting
    (Sunderland), 308
secure attachment, 61–63
seeking circuits, 301
self. *See also* inner community; states
    of mind
  defined, 35–36
  infants and, 53
  multiplicity in, 77, 81–82, 148
self-awareness, 188
self-blame, 184
self-compassion. *See* compassion.
self-esteem, 137
self-organization, of brain, 5, 193
self-regulation
  attachment and, 59
  brain and, 109
  child development and, 300
  couples and, 282
  mindfulness and, 175
serotonin
  addiction and, 149–50
  depression and, 124
shame
  brain and, 106–9
  brain structure/function information
      and relief from, 191, 192
  characteristics of, 105–6
  disorganized attachment and, 74
  empathy blocked by, 105–6
  nervous system and, 21
  origins of, 106–7
  therapy for, 108–10
short-term therapies, xxiv–xxv
Siegel, Daniel J., xxii, 4, 13, 29, 33, 35, 39,
    40, 47, 48, 50, 56, 102, 174, 176,
    177, 192, 199, 307–8
SIFTing the mind, 192
Skinner, B. F., 3
Smith, David, 294
SNAGing the mind, 192
social anxiety, 128
social brain, 15
social circuits, in brain, 138
Solomon, J., 73

Sowell, E. R., 288
spinal cord, 14
spirituality
  art and, 248
  conceptual versus emotional aspects
      of, 96
  embracing the whole person and,
      95–96
  family history questions on, 171
  implicit models and, 95–96
states of mind
  COAL, 178, 180–81, 184, 192,
      276, 280, 304
  description of, 183–84
  inner community and, 36, 102
  integration-dissociation of, 35–37,
      142–45
  mindfulness and, 177–78
  multiplicity in, 77
  pairs of, 36
  therapeutic work on, 36
  transformation of, into stable
      traits, 196
  variety of, 36
Staylistening, 309–12
stem cells, 12
storytelling. *See* narratives
Strange Situation, 58, 62, 67, 68–69,
    72, 139
stress system. *See* hypothalamic-
    pituitary-adreno (HPA) axis
subjective countertransference, 56
Sunderland, Margot, 138, 308
superior temporal cortex, 38
superior temporal gyrus, 175
sympathetic nervous system
  anxiety and, 127
  borderline personality
      disorder and, 141
  brain-wise narratives and, 202
  dissociation and, 128, 139
  function of, 20–21
  limbic region and, 279
  shame and, 106–7
synapse, 7
synaptic cleft, 7
synaptogenesis, 11

teens, 286–98
  adult support for, 294–98
  attachment and, 293–96
  brain development of, 287–94
  brain structure/function of, 270
  challenges facing, 286–88
  development of, 286–88
  overview of therapy with, 269–70
  parenting, 287, 293–98
  peer relationships for, 294–95
  respect sought by, 293
  therapeutic relationship with, 292–94

temperament, 131–32
temporal lobes, 18
thalamus, 221
theory, 154
therapeutic relationship. *See also*
  empathic attunement
  avoidant attachment and, 67–68
  body awareness and, 34
  character of, 93
  with couples, 274
  disorganized attachment and, 74
  dyadic regulation in, 59
  embracing the whole person in, 94–100
  foundations of, 91–94
  hand model of brain and, 199–200
  importance of, 5–6, 60–61, 77,
    90–91, 210
  individuality of, 103
  inner community as site for, 212–13
  memory modification and, 9–10, 18
  mindfulness and, 181, 186–90
  mutuality of, 90–104
  neuroplasticity and, 11, 12
  patients' previous experiences of, 172
  regulation and, 59, 265
  resonance circuits and, 39–40, 54–57
  right-brain to right-brain connection
    in, 94, 156–62
  shame and, 108–10
  with teens, 292–94
therapist health, as therapeutic
    principle, xxiii
therapists. *See also* right-brain to right-
    brain connection; therapeutic
    relationship; therapy
  awareness of own pain, 91–92, 211
  body awareness of, 34
  brain structure/function knowledge
    possessed by, 191
  comforting role of, 92, 210–13
  as companions, 93
  early relationships of, 63
  learning from patients, 219
  left-hemisphere thinking of, 153–54
  mental health of, xxiii, 155–58
  neural integration of, 33
  in patient's inner community,
    212–13
  perceptual biases of, 55–56
  response of, to severe disorders, 140
  responsibility of, 91
  and sandplay, 222, 230
  spirituality of, 96
therapy. *See also* art; internal work; play
    therapy; sandplay; therapeutic
    relationship; therapists
  agenda for, 32, 51
  attachment in, 54–57
  attention's role in, 45–46
  body as focus of, 96–100

brain structure/function information
    used in, 21–22, 117, 191–204,
    278–80
  complexity theory and, 192–95
  for dissociation, 148, 216–17
  empathy in, 54–57, 90–91, 116, 213,
    274–78
  family histories in, 163
  IPNB and, xxii–xxvii, 3–6
  memory central to, 206
  mindfulness in, 174–75, 180–90
  nest of processes in, 115
  nonverbal communication in, 33, 34,
    57, 156
  note-taking during, 164
  principles of, xxii–xxiii, 4
  process of, 115, 205–6
  right-brain grounding of, 156–62
  right-mode processing and, 20
  rupture and repair in, 100–101
  sequence of processes in, 115
  as tracking, 93–94
  types of, 3
  unconscious communication in, 33,
    91
  watchers in, 84–85
threat to life, 60
time
  ambivalent attachment and, 70
  implicit memories and, 25
  integration of, 40
toddlers
  attachment of, 59
  brain of, 28
  explicit memories of, 20
  intentions understood by, 28
  RMP in, 59, 132
  shame in, 106–7
Tomasello, Michael, 28
top-down processing, 179
tracking, of inner community,
    93–94, 211
tragedy, intergenerational, 165,
    192, 201
transpirational integration, 40–41, 96
trauma. *See also* posttraumatic stress
    disorder
  bodily effects of, 97–99
  borderline personality disorder and,
    140
  brain development in response to,
    23–24
  case study in infant, 314–18
  disorganized attachment and, 71
  dissociation and, 128–29
  dissociative identity disorder and, 140
  fight-flight response and, 98
Tronick, E. Z., 34, 100
Trudeau, G. B., 143–44
two-slit experiment, 45

unconscious communication,
33, 91

vagal tone, 133–34
ventral prefrontal cortex
    defined, 16, 23
    emotions and, 120–21, 125
ventral vagus
    attachment and, 60, 133–34
    dissociation and, 128

Warneken, Felix, 28
watchers
    forms of, 85
    role of, 84–85
well-being
    FACES model of, xiii, 50
    triangle of, xii, 102*f*
Wernicke's area, 291
Westwood Institute for Anxiety
        Disorders, 176
"what if" statements, 216
wheel metaphor of mind, 174–75

whole person, embracing of, 94–100
    family histories and, 166–68
    somatic aspects of, 96–100
    spiritual aspects of,
        95–96
Wilson, E. O., 47
window of tolerance
    breaching of, 209
    integration process and, 51
    maintenance of, 207
    medication and, 151
    rupture-repair process and, 107
    sympathetic-parasympathetic
        nervous systems and, 21
    therapist's, 155
Wipfler, Patty, 286, 294, 308
withdrawn mothers, 135, 136. *See also*
        neglect
working memory, 18

Yankelovich, Daniel, 63

Zen meditation timers, 189–90